WANDERER

WANDERER

STERLING HAYDEN

NEW YORK

ALFRED·A·KNOPF   1963

L. C. catalog card number: 63–20142

THIS IS A BORZOI BOOK,
PUBLISHED BY ALFRED A. KNOPF, INC.

FIRST EDITION

The poetry on page 37 is quoted from "Sea Fever" in Collected Poems *by John Masefield. The Macmillan Company, New York, and William Heinemann, Ltd., London. The passage from* N by E *by Rockwell Kent is reprinted by permission of the author. Copyright 1930 by Rockwell Kent.*

To C. D. H.
Who had the heart
To join with me
And plunge
Into the abyss
Where books like this are written

And to
Warwick M. Tompkins and Rockwell Kent
SAILORMEN   ARTISTS   RADICALS
Who chose Cape Horn
This work is dedicated
By one who chose Tahiti

CONTENTS

BOOK I

———

MAN AT BAY

CHAPTER 1

The black pit of oblivion opens like a giant clamshell. I feel myself released, then shot toward the surface. My body is long and cold as it streaks upward, torpedolike, trailing the bubbles of a dream. The pit below grows dim. Light spreads all around.

Suddenly I breach the surface of consciousness, hang for a moment—erect and terrified—before falling back on the old familiar bunk, with the light of dawn seen overhead through a prism set in the deck.

The prism winks with a lusterless eye. A bead of condensation grows at its conical tip, pauses, shudders, then drops toward a pool of wet.

I cradle my head and close my eyes—groping for the severed thread of the dream. No good. Too late. I feel exhausted. Without thinking I know it's six o'clock. From the main cabin comes the chime of a bell.

Out on the bay the foghorns chant: growl from Alcatraz, grunt from Mile Rock, and a blast from Lime Point. Distant strident tones all mixed and lost in the thick damp wool of the fog.

From far aloft in the rigging a drop of moisture falls. Through bar-taut cordage it slips—past tarred shroud and cunning marline seizing—down and down until it plops on the pale blue eye of the prism, forcing it to blink.

Six o'clock of a morning. Eight hours more to wait for the verdict of the court. I fumble for the piece of yellow paper:

STERLING HAYDEN—CARE SCHOONER WANDERER—SAUSALITO/CAL. JUDGE WILL RECEIVE ALL COUNSEL HIS CHAMBERS TWO PM TOMORROW THURSDAY JANUARY 15/59 AND RENDER DECISION THEN WILL PHONE AT ONCE—CONFIDENTLY—GRANT

Throughout the cold cavity of the ship silence absolute. Twenty bodies lost in sleep. Adults sprawled with mouths agape. Children curled round wooly animals. All mute this time of precious predawn rest.

I mount the ladder and ease myself on deck. Thickafog. Horns louder all around. Gray-green morning world with topmasts indistinct and the long proud sweep of the maindeck jutting east. I draw the sheepskin coat around me—two buttons missing—and burrow my chin in the matted warmth of the collar. My back aches; sign of tension. Gulls stand inert atop stumps of wooden piling.

The five-foot iron wheel bucks gently, softly. I lean wearily against the cockpit's rim, then run a hand through the dew on the ovaled teak. Rustlings from below: Mate and his wife astir. Plumed woodsmoke curls from the fo'c'sle stove, and a rattle of pots and pans.

The twin doors part. A tattooed hand gropes as the mate ascends the steps. "Good morning," he says.

"Morning, Spike."

He plants himself with a small shiver and closes the halibut shirt. His face is hard, with a whiskered jaw, lean and leathered, and a ravaged look in the eyes and a scar across one cheek. We stand apart to stare out with the mainsail furled overhead.

"This is the big day," I observe, offhand.

"High time, at that."

"What's your guess? Will the man say yes or no?"

He leans and spits in an offshore arc. "I'm past guessing, I'm all guessed out. But I think he'll let us go."

I take a cigarette.

A rap on the doors and we open up. His wife stands down on

the ladder with a tray at half-arm's length. He takes his mug of coffee. I reach for a pot of tea, and there's a slice of lime in the saucer's mouth. She has a shock of red hair drawn back from a fresh strong face, and it's tied with a small green bow. The tea burns down.

"Can I offer you something to go with that?" she asks. I look at the mate, who pretends he doesn't hear, but one eyebrow lifts as he looks away.

"Why not?" I say. "Can't do us any harm."

"Not after last night," she laughs.

A bottle of aquavit: I pour till the mugs are full. Our eyes meet and the mugs touch. "To the goddamed judge," he says.

"Never mind the judge. To the voyage no matter what."

We drink.

A splash of blue sky from the paling east with the sun below, burning at the fog. Inshore the whine of a Greyhound bus. Action on the foredeck as Kit Africa, aged eight, pops from hatch to rail to rigging overhead, with Matt Hayden, not quite eight, in hot pursuit. They clutch bananas in dirty paws and shirttails flap astern of small dungarees.

Refill the mug—half and half—then over the side and shoreward along the old dock, with happy playtime yachts to the right and left. The fog thins out and some hillside homes come clear. A window flames when struck by the sun. The ancient harbormaster pedals past on a beat-up bike.

"How are you, Sid?"

"Good morning, Cap—sailing soon, do you think?"

"I think."

He waves and the bike commences a pirouette till his free hand grips the bars. His face looks puffed, as though he'd been in a fight.

The bank building by the village square all brown and squat and neat. I peer in. Very orderly here. Rows of windows that front on boxlike stalls; a swinging excuse of a plywood gate leads to the executive branch. Let into one wall is the steel-clad safety vault; cold and hostile glass; behind, a wondrous mechanism showing forth, proud at the thought of all that green stacked safely out of reach.

My inner man awakes:

You could do with some money like that. Here you are like an arrow in a drawn bow.

That's right.

You're insane. You haven't the ways and means. How much are you worth this day, a thousand dollars perhaps?

Perhaps.

And you're six thousand in debt?

That's right.

And you owe your lawyers ten thousand more for their services to date?

I do.

Plus five thousand to your ex-wife's counsel for the same action?

Oh yes.

Yet if the judge says it's all right you'll take your ship and let her ride for Copenhagen.

You're goddam right.

Nonsense! You're in a financial abyss.

Maybe not.

A bus comes snarling in, blue-gas banners high, windows veiled in steam, faces blurred behind cleared moist circles as they gaze at the bay.

Incongruous sight, I bet: this tall lone man in a sheepskin, arms crossed on a parking meter, wool socks that rise from leather boots, his hand holding a mug of tea. Hair tousled and damp above a four-day growth of beard.

The bus halts by the coffee shop. A man with a hat peers from his private circle. Relaxed he is, with his collar white and neat. My arm goes up in a gesture of mute salute.

The ship at rest in the crooked left arm of the dock. A driven row of piling protects her from the bay. Some old fallen spars are linked in series to ride always with the tide. I stand beneath her taffrail looking out. The copper-painted hull bursts from the water's edge. The white sweep of her topsides comes running aft to blend with a broad transom, where a gilt eagle with outspread wings looks hard to starboard with an angry eye. He is pinned between two names: one steeped in mystery, *Wanderer*; one crowned with majesty, *San Francisco*.

Breakfast time and an empty deck. I go on board just long enough to freshen up the tea. Then down and out along the line of wet and heaving logs to a vantage point some hundred feet beyond the bows of the ship. A gull leans out, shoves free, and sweeps skyward with a lorn and raucous cry. Ebb tide.

Free water. Free to pour seaward through the Gate. Beholden
to no man. Free to link up with the California Current beyond
the Farallones and head for the Bering Sea. To curve west and
roam for months toward Asiatic shores. To slip southward into
the blue arms of tropic seas roiled by the northeast trade, then
to range on and on, not far above the Line.

Where from, you growling water? How old are you? Did you
come in from the sea with the midnight flood? Were you sired
by an iceberg out of the South Polar Cap, or was your dam a
cloud knocked up by the High Sierra? Were you falling rain
short months ago? What's the news from Donner Pass and
Emigrant Gap, and how are those new motels? You look a little
wan, as though you're tired of the land. Tried to trap you, did
they—up Sacramento way? Piped you through a tunnel, dumped
chlorine in your face, spun you through a toilet bowl—small
wonder you're brown as a sportsman's chest. Don't quit now;
two hours will see you through the Gate, and once you're clear
keep rolling on. I'll join you one day soon. Maybe.

The fog recoils from the sun's grasp. I shuck the coat and
turn to look at the ship. Well now you great old bastard! Today
we'll know. Harsh names they've been calling you in Department 34 (in the Superior Court of and for the people and the
County of Los Angeles): "Antique." "Decrepit." "Obsolete."
"Dangerously small." Seems we might have grounds for a little
libel action.

"Antique," is it! Who cares that you were built in 1893 just
across the bay? What matters is your strength, the strength of
oak and fir and teak, of hackmatack knees and locust treenails
that alternate with bronze.

"Decrepit," they say—too old to keep the sea. Well, you served
the pilots for fifty-two years just beyond the Bar. Winter and
summer, blow high blow low, you lived out there with the sea
all wild when the gales came roaring in. Nothing could put you
down. Save progress: diesel power and wireless sets and fancy
cabins with steam heat—all alien to you. So when the war died
down and the surplus sales began, they dumped you and I
snatched you up for a song.

"Obsolete," her lawyers claimed. I laugh, for the winds and
the seas don't change. Has the circular storm grown obsolete?
Or the heave of a long ground swell? Are they planning a new
model of a doldrums calm? Is there a stench of decay on the
warm breath of the smiling southeast trade? You were made to

spread your canvas and find your way with the elements, and you'll be obsolete when the oceans drain and the winds no longer blow.

"Dangerously small!" As though your size were a factor. The lifeboat swims when the liner drowns. You're 98 feet on deck my friend and you gross one hundred tons. You've spent a solid twenty-six years at sea. What do they think you were doing there? You've had sails blown out and spars splintered and you've crippled some men at their job. Remember Nels Rasmussen? (He was boatkeeper in you before the First World War.) Ten days ago—after I showed him around—he placed one hand on a spoke of your wheel and he gazed aloft and he stomped on your cockpit's floor. "You know, Cap," he said to me, "she's the best vessel the pilots ever had." Then, under his breath: "You must have spent a power of money bringing her back, no?"

I agreed I had.

"You've given her new wire an' chain an' rope and blocks and spars?"

"Yes."

"You've had her canvas cut in Gloucester. You've painted her out—you've even changed her name?"

"*Gracie S.* meant nothing to me," I said. "Daughter of a sugar merchant, so they say, and I never cared for tycoons."

Then he hefted the wheel and looked beyond your bows and his eyes seemed blurred as he said: "Any judge that holds you now is nothing but a fool."

With that he was over the side and gone, and he never looked back. Two days ago he died.

We look at each other. Tall ship and tallish man. The tar on the shrouds begins to shine and I hear the soft moan of a breeze from the north. I raise my mug; the ship nods ever so slightly. To Rasmussen, I think. To you, too, you proud old wagon, and to all those men—wherever they are—who framed you out and planked you up and rattled you down with hemp. To the ones, also, who made you go, who clung to that wheel with boot heels grinding your deck. To those who worked by your lee rail up to their waists in water, or who—while fisting the inner jib—would plunge out of sight when you pitched.

I throw back my head and drain the mug and tonight I'll drink to the judge. Maybe.

CHAPTER 2

Measured in terms of enchantment, is there anything can compare with a chartroom? And should this castle belong to a schooner, then you've kingdom enough. Unless you're preoccupied with wealth, prestige, success—or other shallow pursuits.

Carefully I close the teakwood door; the lock clicks. Silence, silence so deep the ears ring, as they did in that first-discovered childhood thrill: alone in a living room with the seashell to one ear—and from the chambered nave the sullen wondrous sound—and the eyes pressed shut with a vision of lost and lonely seas running to curl and break up and down some unknown shore.

Silence broken only by the rhythmic heartbeat of the chronometer where it nests in a padded case. The varnished hardwood table reaches outboard to the skin of the hull. Floor space minimal. Headroom five foot ten below the beams. Oil lamps gimbaled on both bulkheads.

Prominent between lamp and the barometer's face a photograph is tacked to the wall, telling a grisly tale of a winter's gale in the far-off North Atlantic, with a Gloucester schooner hove on shore, her hull split like an eggshell and her masts gone by the board. High and dry she lies, with the rockweed matted under the hull and a man standing disconsolately looking on. Icicles trail from the vessel's bows. Reminders from long ago and far away of what the sea can do.

Around me the tools of the navigator's trade: sextant, dividers, and parallel rules; azimuth tables and Bowditch and H.O. 214; pilot books and sailing directions from French Frigate Shoal to the Outer Hebrides, from the Gulf of Finland to the Pass of Balmaha. Light lists and current tables; Norrie, Dutton, Mixter. Most cherished of all, a thick blue tome with a gilt anchor embossed beneath the words: *Ocean Passages for the World.*

Spread out under my arms a pilot chart of the North Pacific —month of January—any year since time began. Divided graphlike into oceanic squares, blue arrows that fly with the wind, dotted serpentine lines where trade winds roam, stubbed black

arrows indicating drift, data on ice and fog, and red thin lines
to trace the track of storms.

I glance at the chronometer: twenty-three hundred hours on
the meridian of Greenwich, not far from London town. Two
p.m. California time. I stare at the thin red lines . . . if only the
shore world were regulated by a force as logical—as honest—
as the Law of Storms.

I open and close my hands; the chronometric pulse gives way
and the lines on the chart grow dim. I hear the belching roar
of city traffic beyond an interchange. I see the multimillion-
dollar majesty of a courthouse set in the smoggy din of the
idiot city Los Angeles. Up the stairs and through some swinging
doors. Armed bailiffs with soft bellies lounge around. Escalators
purr in futile, endless circles and there's tension everywhere,
in faces and voices and on the very gilt upon the doors.

Three men converge between the sands of twin chromium
cuspidors. My attorney: fifty-three or four, stylish, lean, bristling
iron-gray hair; an old pro; scarred like the harem bull of a seal
rookery in cold subtropic seas.

The other two are younger—come this day to hear a ruling
of the court, to learn just how well they have done their job.
This means a lot to them—this first excursion into the rarefied
realm of the big time with names in headlines and pictures
sprawled about. Ask them how it feels to be badgered by the
press: "Not bad," says one, "not bad at all, off the record, that
is." His pal in the baggy suit keeps smiling quietly.

Greetings all around: "Hello, Marv. Chester, how are you?"

"Tired, Grant. God I'm tired. This case is getting me down;
can't sleep nights, overworked; cramps here—my bowels, you
know. Thank God it's almost done."

Three wrists bared for the time. They vanish through some
doors. Somewhere a siren wails. Wreaths of smoke rise from
cuspidors.

I stare at the phone. Everything is ready: the cord is clear,
cigarettes just so, pencils sharp in hand. Down comes the numb-
ness, the glazed sensation that always comes when you're truly
impotent—the same feeling first felt at the age of eight—when
the batted ball ran arrow-true for a vast expanse of glass. Nothing to do but wait; impossible to look ahead, futile to turn
around.

The year just past, one soaring headlong drive toward escape

from the captive life—and here you sit all buttoned down—
proposed voyage stymied in a mass of litigation. Not so much a
voyage as a gesture of defiance—known only to those who
stand on their own two feet; who stand with legs widespread
to flail at windmills (so some say) but answerable nevertheless
to no man, no combination of men, no force save that intangible
malignancy the conscience.

Two-twenty. Overhead the cr-rump cr-r-ump of the mate's
boots as he paces, staring off, shifting his quid from side to
side—waiting.

High aloft, big Nyborg tarring down, watching the traffic
ashore, daubing the black salve from Stockholm into recessed
marline corners.

Stretched prone beside his diesel, Don Bahl, with a full black
beard, hammering doggedly with an eye on the bulkhead clock.

How goes it with the kids, I wonder. Do they know what
hangs on this hour? Of course not—how do you explain some
things? I see them ranged on the fo'c'sle settees in afternoon
studyhall. Pencils poised—an eye for the teacher, an eye for
the ship, and sunlight streaming down.

A preliminary click from the phone and I spear it before it
rings.

Long distance calling—

"Yes, Ma'am, this is he—yes, that's right—yes, operator, I
will accept the charges, thank you very much—"

"Sterling, this is Grant—look fellow, I'm calling from a booth
in the courthouse, that's why it's collect—now listen, fellow, I
have some bad news—"

"Don't tell me I lost custody of the kids?"

"No, God no, nothing like that. But the voyage is off—did
you hear me?—the court rules the voyage is off—"

"Yeah, I heard you—you're not kidding, are you?"

"Sterling. I wouldn't kid about this—why, I've never been
more stunned or disappointed in all my life—"

"I'm a little surprised myself."

"I know that, fellow. But the judge said some great things
about you as a father—"

"Well what do you know." Bitterly.

"I have a copy of his ruling—here, let me read it to you—"

"No. Just send it along in the mail. I'll get it first thing in the
morning. I'll be goddamned that's all I can say just yet."

"Don't be upset. Let me tell you something'll make you feel

better. There's every reason to believe that if we wait nine or ten months, then go back to the court, they'll give us—"

"The hell you say. I've been in that court fourteen times in the past eight months—that's enough—"

"Look, fellow, don't get carried away. I'm trying to help you. Within a year, I promise you, we'll go back and get permission to take the children out of the country—you can sail the schooner and they can fly from port to port to greet you as you come in—I know that's not what you want but we have to be practical sometimes—"

"Yeah! Sounds great. Just what they need. Only maybe I can find them work in a movie and let them travel at some studio's expense and go to a nice school in the basement of a sound stage next to the make-up hall. The court ought to go for that."

"Easy now—I know you're upset and I've got to run along. Come down the first of the week and we can talk things out, okay?"

"Sure, why not."

Phone rammed on the hook. Cigarette. A yellow taste of sulphur where the first drag hits.

Again the chronometer's pulse; the fine-etched face serene 'neath a glass-roofed padded box. Freedom lost. "To what avail the plough or sail, or love, or life—if freedom fail?"

Freedom. Freedom to what? Escape, run, wander turning your back on a cowed society that stutters, staggers, and stagnates every man for himself and fuck you Jack I've got mine. Freedom to leave all this—is that what I really want? Better by far stay home and slug it out with the monster twin heads of greed and glut. Well, why not do it then? Because I'm not well enough strong enough hard enough just yet that's why. Maybe a year from now I could do it. The thing I need now is change. Change and a chance and a passage of time in which to reflect and tool up for a future.

Beat-beat, beat-beat, beat-beat: fine old chronometer all rated and oiled and wound with no damn place to go. Maybe it's all the chronometer's fault. Maybe if I hadn't been such a stubborn bastard the court might have ruled in favor of the voyage. My mind snakes back to a day in court.

To a smog-stuffed sweltering day ten shopping days till Christmas with the county courthouse rearing dismayed from the roar and welter of the City of the Angles. The judge on his bench in a flowing black robe; four lawyers at the bar; one clerk of the court, one massive Negro bailiff with sad kind eyes and hands like hymnals—a man and a woman no longer married yet wed by bonds of savage contempt. (A calendar lifts its topmost page as a fan trains its breath down the wall. When the page settles back, what I see is fair—the Grand Teton Range, and wild flowers leading to a distant sky-blue lake.)

Enters now one expert yachting witness who swears to tell nothing but the truth so help him God if you will. Chester my foe leads him by the nose through a brief recital of his credentials: very impressive, here a yacht there a yacht yachts all over the lot; long voyages down to Mexico mostly. A nice enough man, you might say—but five hundred miles to the north rests a gnarled vessel about to be libeled.

For the truth as this witness sees it is that the schooner *Wanderer* is a romantic old ship no doubt, and the man who commands her is skilled, but, he sadly relates, he was onceuponatime called in to survey said ship and found her wasting away in her rivets:

Rivets! My chair comes down with a crash and I lean to my counsel and whisper: "Rivets for Jesus Christ's sake, there's not a single rivet in all the hull of the schooner. Put me up on the stand and I'll destroy this sonofabitch. Break in and—"

He waves me away with a smile. The witness goes on: speaking of the perils of the sea, of the infinite frailty of children, and how—of a dark night—they well might slip and vanish forever into the trackless waste. Yes, he tells the court, he too has tender-aged children, and were the decision in his hands he would have to rule—reluctantly of course—that the schooner concerned is suitable for coastwise journeys only. As he moves toward the hall, he favors me with a shrug and a cheerless smile.

They call me to the stand. Under direct examination I explain with some emotion that a wooden ship knows no rivets. Maybe our expert had some other craft in mind, but his being a yachtsman calls for some compassion: yachtsmen are consumed with the notion that their boats must be one hundred per cent sound. They are oblivious to the fact that the majority of the world's working vessels are plagued with rot. Yet these are the ships that do the work, year after year, no holds barred when it comes to weather.

Under cross-examination the talk veers to radios. The man in

the baggy suit wants to know why I have no radio, not even the
simplest receiving set.

I tell him my creed with pleasure. Why go to sea under sail
at all if you're so concerned with security? Why not go as a
tourist, as a kind of frozen vegetable buying your way across
the world surrounded by hot running water, epicurean cuisine,
swimming pools, and tiny-tot programs, teen-age programs,
mommy and daddy programs—designed for your delectation,
and designed too to quarantine you from the contagion of elemental wonder and awe known only to simple living? For navigation I rely on simple tools: sextant and chronometer, charts
and parallel rules, and a precious selection of passage-worn
triangles made of celluloid gone yellow over the years.

Three p.m. Pacific standard time. The mate now—motionless
in the doorway, felt hat askew in a Napoleonic twist. "You can
pass the word: I say 'the voyage is dead and done, as of now—
they can have the afternoon off' and we'll talk at eight tonight."
He starts to speak, shakes his head, goes forward in disbelief.

Cable address GRIPPO, BEVERLY HILLS.

A Mercury two-tone two-door pulls up and parks—yellow
trimmed with black. The spare tire stuck on like an afterthought, like the tail on the donkey forgotten years ago.

This one's a hustler. Not tall, but solid gristle and grit with
cuff links as big as his watch. He's an agent—hard as nails
when it comes to making deals.

An office flooded with light. A ravished blonde in the ante-
room. Dress adjusted just so. Legs crossed delectably. Calves
eager and alert. The hustler gives her a glance—made possible
by an adjustment of the collar with an urgent sideways
twist.

He scans his messages. "Get me Mr. Daves at Warners." He
retires to an inner chamber. The girl recrosses her legs—patiently. After all, it's early yet—not quite six o'clock.

"Hello, Del? Joe Grippo. What's on your mind?"

"Yeah, Del, I know, I heard it on the radio coming through
the Pass. No, I haven't talked with him yet. I'd say your chances
were great—he's played his string out and now he's got to get
to work—and I'll tell you something else, just between the two
of us and a blonde in the outer room, he needs the loot. Yeah,
you bet—"

"I'll call him right away. Right. Six weeks. Forty thousand cash. Co-star billing. Picture starts February 10—"

"You're kidding—the whole picture'll be shot around Monterey and the Big Sur? Wait till he hears that. By the way, Del, who's the girl? Oh. Oh great. Del, I'll call you back."

The hustler renews his cigarette, speaking offhand to an unseen assistant. "Hank, get me Hayden up on the boat—no crap this time—get through no matter what—"

The hairy voice of the hustler: "Sterling? It's your old friend Joe. It's no use to say I'm sorry—about the trip, that is—"

"I gather you heard the news."

"Sure, it's all over town—must've been an awful jolt—what do you figure on now?"

"I don't know just yet."

"Well, don't think I'm a scavenger, but—how would you like to make some big dough?"

"I could use it."

"Del Daves called a while ago. He thinks you're a hell of a guy—and he'd like to put you to work."

"Go on."

"It seems there's forty thousand dollars over at Warners with Hayden written all over it—"

"Yeah."

"Picture called *A Summer Place*—you've heard of it—"

"No, I haven't."

"Well then listen to this: they're shooting on location—at Monterey and along the Big Sur Coast—"

"Really, the Big Sur?"

"Aha! I thought you'd react to that. Co-star billing. Just six weeks' work. Del's a talented man, as you know."

"When do they want an answer?"

"Sooner the better, I'd say. Peck's just dying to do the role."

"Don't give me that Peck crap."

"Not so fast—he's dying to do it, but he don't come cheap."

"All right, it's a deal."

"Serious? You serious you'll do it?"

"Yes goddam it I'll do it—what else do you want to know?"

"Sure, sure—funny thing you know—I had a hunch you'd go for this."

"You did, eh."

"Sure. Old Joe has to come up winners once in a while, my friend."

The voice seems hairless now: "They'll be giving this to the papers, you know—sure you don't want to think it over?"

"I know when I'm licked I guess."

"Must be a hell of a disappointment—"

"Yeah."

"We were all on your side, you know."

"I know."

The phone put down with a tender plunk. Muscles that ache and groan. A tentative rap on the cabin door. "Open up," I call.

A small head not five feet off the floor—freckled face and a broad smile, revealing a mouthful of braces. "Father? Since we're not going on the trip, do we get to keep the dogs?"

"Sure, Son, I guess you do. Remind me the first of the week."

The hollow man rolls into the bunk. Gimbaled lamp turned low. Somewhere the wail of a steamer's horn—outward bound on the ebb.

≥

CHAPTER 3

Midnight: moving aft through the chambered hull of the ship. In the utmost bow, which seamen call the peak, crammed with deck and bosun stores—red lead, litharge, and tins of linseed oil; turps and paints and solvents and a drum of pine-tar oil; the squared balk of the kingpost rammed upward through the deck. A water closet with sea water gurgling at the bottom of the bowl.

The forecastle: in time gone by, a home away from home (or the only home on earth) to unsung sailormen. Wedge-shaped and flaring out with a steep wooden ladder that climbs to the cowl of the hatch. The huge round bole of the foremast painted white beneath a collar of concave wedges—backbone of a schooner's rig—granitic—monument to fir. A central table with wings that fold from sight. Rows of lockers holding food, and troughs for the anchor chain. Against the bulkhead aft an iron-bellied stove, piles of sawn driftwood, and racks of children's books.

Turn up the lamp and look around: seven bunks quarried into the ship, yellow curtains slung on wire. Drawings tacked to the walls—incomplete to the jaundiced eyes of adults, yet full of life to a child. Above one head the legend: "Bunk Sweet Bunk."

Three little girls and four small boys. Dolls and post cards and a rosary, bits of wood and twine—and a rare collection of old tin cans. Seven children under twelve: far gone just now, hopeful, trusting, innocent—needing nothing but love and the chance to find their way.

Aft of this the galley: rows of china mugs nodding overhead, stacks of dishes in deep, barred racks, a shallow sink and a white enameled stove—its oven door held in place with wire. Non-skid strips on the floor, a broad ladder and a fire extinguisher. To port a double cabin, claimed for the voyage by Nyborg and Bahl—bosun and engineer.

Next in line the engine space, three times as big as the galley, where a hundred and sixty-five horses slumber, compressed in a block of iron and steel. Generators, pumps and valves and tanks and tools, and a bank of batteries salvaged from the wreck of a cable car.

Across from this a narrow alleyway with a refrigerator on the outboard side, and an excuse of a cabin with a sliding door and two long slits for bunks. A lanky figure lost in sleep—Jerry Burns, late of UCLA, trained in the arts of cinematography, too aware of the wide world to settle in Hollywood.

A half-step up, with the massive break-timber overhead, and into the ship's main cabin. Eight more bunks ranged around. Ten tons of fresh water tanked beneath the floor. Books and books and books—some five hundred volumes in all. Books of the sea and books of the land, some of them streaked with salt, collected with love and care over more than twenty-five years.

Melville, Conrad, London, Stevenson; Gauguin and Loti and Rupert Brooke; Lubbock, Masefield, De Hartog—Slocum and Rockwell Kent; Trelawny and Cook and Bligh; Chapelle and Underhill—Nansen, Frobisher, Villiers and Scott and Louis Becke. Homer, Gerbault, and Tompkins. Hundreds more: all cast in a common mold—blessed with the genius that makes men feel, and dream, and go.

And a special section of books that deal with the greatest frontier of all—the relationship between men: Marx and Whitman, Thoreau and Henry George, Victor Hugo, Thomas Paine and Jefferson. Lincoln and Emerson, Rousseau, Voltaire and Upton Sinclair, Shaw. Byron, Mark Twain, Roosevelt, Garrison, Jack London again and Shakespeare.

Five hundred books, distillate of distant seas, of a hundred thousand night watches. Of despair and agonies and conviction. Standing by this night, peering out from recessed shelves onto the inert and blanketed forms of seven young men and women come together—haphazardly perhaps—yet drawn as though by magic to the soft and urgent promise of the windship's lonely world.

Two more cabins now, across the narrow passage, facing each other with the averted eyes of closed doors. Master's cabin to starboard (traditional at sea), the mate and his wife to port.

A few more steps and there is the lazarette, indisputably (along with the chartroom) the most integral part of the ship's accommodations. A sprawling cave that reaches out of sight far aft beneath the quarter-deck—a treasure house of gear that enables the ship to keep the sea for months on end with no recourse to the land. A dozen coils of rope (manila, cotton, and hemp), reels of wire and lengths of chain, spare blocks and sheaves and pins. Shackles, thimbles, cringles; sail twine, needles, and wax; sewing palms and flares, canvas in bolts, oddments of ironwork by the keg.

Storm sails and trade-wind sails; mooring lines; hardwood, softwood, brass and galvanized rod. A bale of tarred oakum at rest by a barrel of pitch, and the tanned hide of a cow. All sorted and lashed in place. The rudderpost encased in a brute of a boxlike shaft.

Poised this night: seven children and thirteen adults; ten tons of water, six tons of fuel; a four-month supply of food; three hundred charts—within the trussed shell of the last merchant-built windjammer to fly the American flag (museum ships excepted). Primed and able to go.

So near, yet so far—three miles to the Golden Gate; fifteen miles to the inshore boundary of the high seas; six hundred miles to the realm of the northeast trade; four hundred and eighty miles to the rancid Mecca corner of Hollywood and Vine.

The stilled form of a wanderer, somewhat asleep in his bunk. Pillow swept in a locked embrace—lamp turned low on the wall—empty sheepskin coat above dank and hollow boots. Over his head a telltale compass peering down with dry card inverted—older than the ship, brassbound, incorruptible, absolute. How does she head this night? North by east it is. What is her port of hail? San Francisco. And where is she bound? Nowhere. So they say.

CHAPTER 4

A mind full of fear. Thoughts that steal up, whisper something ugly, then dart away with a laugh. Crackling phantom thoughts rising like bubbles through a pot of steaming mush.

Curious. How a man can fool the world—almost, at least— by a lifetime of pretense. Hayden pacing restlessly in other men's offices, pacing and smoking, laughing with arms out-swept and lost in the telling of some recent adventure. ". . . Then we swung her off onto north northwest, let her go for Cape Farewell . . . hove her to off Bounty Bay in half a gale of wind . . . coming up with the southwest monsoon. . . ."

Incredible, really—how I got away with it; parlaying nine years at sea into two decades of posturing. Poor wanderer: trapped in the greenbacked cradle of Outer Hollywood; laced in the strait jacket of the big time—big houses big salaries big fuss when you walk down a street big fuss as you check into hotels—big big big.

Tonight. Facing anew the old threat that gorges the mind— knowing the problem to be simply this: *How to break the endless chain?* But a chain like this is strong, each link a memory of something tried—and given up at the last minute.

As it was in the old days with a girl from time to time. Not all the time, but enough—enough to breed the foulest kind of fear. Like that night in Havana.

You were nineteen, working as fireman in a P & O liner, and you had to laugh because you'd always dreamed of sailing in past Morro Castle. And there you were, scaling rust inside the funnel in a hundred and fifty degrees of heat, with sweat clouts above the eye and under the jaw, and you felt pretty tough and away far overhead was the tiniest patch of pale blue sky. And all the while you kept thinking how it would be that night: going ashore with Mario who was waiter in the firemen's mess, Mario who knew the ropes, whose brother ran "the hottest place in town an' jus' you wait, Yank, you come wit' me an' we'll fix you up wit' the works."

Exciting enough when you thought about it through the long watches, standing under a ventilator to cool off, with the tourists from back home escorted through the boiler room by ruddy-faced officers—fine long-legged girls all clean and fresh with their skirts billowing out and the engine room gang maneuvering under the pitched steel ladders to get a better look.

Then up to the jammed and filthy fo'c'sle, with the old-timer in the bunk over yours leaning out to hock great green-yellow gobs into a Chase and Sanborn can below your pillow. And out through the port you could see the Pan American Airways seaplane dock, and the tourists milling around in the sun, and some palms by the driveway to the city. You were making forty-two dollars a month and were given a ten-dollar advance, which you creased in your money belt. Mario came bounding in with a broad smile, and you had on the white shirt you'd pressed yourself.

Down on the dock the first thing hit you was the noise—and the dirt—and everywhere wild-eyed Cuban kids trying to scrounge a dime: "Good place, Boss. Clean young girls, Boss. Come, Yank, we show you—ten cents we take you quick."

A melodious burst from Mario, and they slink away—dark eyes flashing hate—barefooted and scrawny—torn patches on torn clothes—spitting through clenched and perfect teeth. Then began the fight with the fears shadowboxing through you as you strode along jammed and narrow streets. The swarthy people stepped aside as you charged along and you tried to tell yourself this was the man's way—no more frustration, no more non-sensical necking in rumble seats with a girl who parried your awkward boyish body all taut and aching from hours of tentative play. This would be the real thing. Action pure and straight —with a flourish.

A narrow alley leading to a big brown door. A secret signal, and some words flung through the thick wood. Then the door wideswung and I step inside. At the end of a hall a parlor. Three girls run squealing at Mario; one leaps onto his waist, locking her legs behind him; the other two try to climb on his back. Where moments before he seemed small, now he's nothing but strength. He jogs back and forth in the hall, then throws himself on a couch, his hands playing fast and easily beneath loose folds of cheap gowns that fall open and are snatched together with squeals of mock dismay.

I look back toward the entrance. The door is chained and barred. Mario leaps up and a girl starts combing his hair. I feel ridiculously tall and cold and small. What I want is time now. Nothing else matters—just time to catch my balance and get in the swing of things. I feel a deep disgust—not with the girls, not with the place—but with myself. What's wrong with me? This is what I've been thinking about for years. This is the end of the masculine trail—the single subject of fo'c'sle conversation in a dozen bygone ships. I wish I were back on the esplanade, where I'd be free—free to roam, free to find a quiet lonesome girl, my counterpart, and we could walk down toward the harbor and look at the sea, or at the ships coming in, with the ramparts of Morro Castle outlined against the stars.

Mario hands me a drink. I gulp it down and pretend to size up the girls. They look away shyly. He leads me down a dark hall and into a bathroom with thick red carpet: the tub is full and smoke curls from an incense burner beneath a huge mirror. A bathrobe hangs over a chair.

"Big Yank, how you feel?"

"Oh great. I feel just fine."

"Okay okay okay, you take bath, then we have something to eat." He fixes one eye in a slow wink. When he has gone, I lock the door and stand looking down. I want to stay and I know I can't. I want to go but I don't dare. What would happen when they heard about it back on the ship? I can see the men now—looking away as I turn around, laughing, saying something among themselves in words I can't comprehend. At least I can have a bath. The water is deep and hot as I soak—the money belt wrapped in a towel.

The door opens and shuts; and Mario stands inside. I look at the lock in surprise. He is dressed as a waiter now, with a napkin over one arm. There's something wrong with this guy, I think. He bows stiffly. "Mister Big Yank, you would like the two-course dinner or the three-course dinner, please?"

I sit up in the tub. "Mario—Jesus—all I got is ten dollars." He shakes his head with his eyes closed. "No matter. You my guest tonight."

"Well, I guess the two-course will do okay."

"Yes sir. Ten minutes?"

"Sure, Mario, that's great." As he leaves, he takes my clothes. The robe is too small. I brush my hair and my hands tremble. Why don't I speak up? Put an end to this nonsense. If I want to get out, then say so. To hell with the crew of the ship. But—there's nothing to be scared of—this must go on all the time. The girls looked harmless enough—not pretty, but—I move quietly to the door and try the lock; it simply goes round and round. I look in the mirror and try a hearty smile. The door opens.

"We have—what you say?—the old custom here." It is Mario with his napkin drawn tight between the spread of his arms. "You wear this over the eyes, please."

I recoil and stand like a stiff-legged colt at the end of a rope. "Where'd you go with my pants?"

"My friend, she pressing them."

"Oh."

He places the cloth over my eyes as I stand with thumbs hooked in the money belt under the robe. I know I should call it off right now. But what for? They can't do anything to me.

We walk down a hall and up some stairs. It is very quiet. Twice I sense someone standing aside. A door opens and I make a move toward my blindfold. Something inside me takes control. I plant myself and refuse to move. He tries to urge me along.

"No goddamit, Mario, this is enough."

"Just a few more steps, then you sit."

"No." I shake my head.

There's a rustling, and the incense smell again. I want to tear off the napkin but my thumbs stay hooked in the belt. I feel Mario fumbling with the knot. The bandage drops and I'm in a small room. A chandelier hangs over a long, narrow table that stands on a pedestal. An armchair is drawn up with its back to me and a naked girl reclines on the white tablecloth with one foot on each of the arms. A second girl kneels in front of the chair, gazing at me through savage half-closed eyes.

Mario bows and indicates the chair. I slack off the money belt and fumble with the zipper until I come up with the ten-dollar bill. The girl on the table has her head turned to watch. The kneeling girl keeps her head bowed and her hands press down on her knees.

I try to behave with aplomb. "Mario, just get me my clothes." He starts to speak but a wave of anger sweeps over me. I say a lot of things and before I know it he's gone. The girl on the table sits up, says something to her companion, then crosses unlovely legs and lets them dangle to and fro while she lights a cigarette.

Mario comes in with my clothes. He rips out some words toward the girls. I dress. The ten dollars I press toward the girls. They look at Mario, then shake their heads, so I throw the bill on the table.

Once free of the alley, I look upward for the stars but there's only the murk overhead reflecting the city's light. I feel free. Alone and free. The humiliation will have to wait. Right now all I care about is the knowledge of independence, the warm, flowing thought that I can find a skiff if I please and row it clean out of the harbor and past the Morro and on to the west or north, the thought that I can jump ship and walk toward the eastern end of the island and splash in rivers or maybe find a little island close inshore that belongs to nobody and build a camp of sorts.

Some raindrops fall. As I find the promenade, the sky lets go, but I turn to the right, where instinctively I know the sea lies. The rain pours down; people scurry for doorways on either side. It is an elevated walk reserved for people on foot and the benches and fountains are shining white. I feel so good I break into a shambling jog, taking care not to slip. The pillared lights end up ahead so I slow down, and it comes to me I'm hungry.

A lighthouse looms in the night. The rain slacks off. I come to the sea wall and lean on the cold cement. A buoy blinks offshore, and stars stand low over the western horizon.

The memory fades. No more than a link it was—a link in the endless chain.

The hollow man outstretched, more or less asleep. Inside, nothing but callow fear.

CHAPTER 5

To be truly challenging, a voyage, like a life, must rest on a firm foundation of financial unrest. Otherwise you are doomed to a routine traverse, the kind known to yachtsmen, who play

with their boats at sea—"cruising," it is called. Voyaging belongs
to seamen, and to the wanderers of the world who cannot, or
will not, fit in. If you are contemplating a voyage and you have
the means, abandon the venture until your fortunes change.
Only then will you know what the sea is all about.

Little has been said or written about the ways a man may
blast himself free. Why? I don't know, unless the answer lies in
our diseased values. A man seldom hesitates to describe his
work; he gladly divulges the privacies of alleged sexual
conquests. But ask him how much he has in the bank and he
recoils into a shocked and stubborn silence.

"I've always wanted to sail to the South Seas, but I can't
afford it." What these men can't afford is *not* to go. They are
enmeshed in the cancerous discipline of "security." And in the
worship of security we fling our lives beneath the wheels of
routine—and before we know it our lives are gone.

What does a man need—really need? A few pounds of food
each day, heat and shelter, six feet to lie down in—and some
form of working activity that will yield a sense of accomplish-
ment. That's all—in the material sense. And we know it. But
we are brainwashed by our economic system until we end up
in a tomb beneath a pyramid of time payments, mortgages,
preposterous gadgetry, playthings that divert our attention from
the sheer idiocy of the charade.

The years thunder by. The dreams of youth grow dim where
they lie caked in dust on the shelves of patience. Before we
know it, the tomb is sealed.

Where, then, lies the answer? In choice. Which shall it be:
bankruptcy of purse or bankruptcy of life? What follows is not a
blueprint for the man entombed; not many people find themselves in a situation paying a hundred and fifty thousand
dollars a year (as if any man is worth that much). But the
struggle is relative: it's a lot harder to walk away from an
income like that than from a fraction thereof.

There's nothing wrong with being an actor, if that's what a
man wants. But there's everything wrong with achieving an
exalted status simply because one photographs well and is able
to handle dialogue put in one's mouth by others. In 1956 and
1957 I earned an average of $160,000 gross. I was divorced and
had the custody of four children from five to nine. I lived in a
leased house that cost $600 a month; I employed a proxy-mother

and a cook, which cost an additional $500; I owned two Volkswagens and not much else. I paid an agent ten per cent, and a business manager and an attorney each received five per cent. A smart man would have invested wisely and become rich, I suppose. I have yet to invest the first dime because I don't believe in unearned income.

The question is inevitable: If you don't believe in taking what you don't earn, then how could you be reconciled to the astronomical figures just mentioned? I never was. Furthermore, I couldn't stand the work.

Why get into such a situation in the first place, then? And why not get out? Simple. The same deficiencies of character that led me into Hollywood prevented my escape.

We are a systematic people. We have a systematic approach to almost everything—from raising children to getting buried. Somehow it is the male's duty to put the best years of his life into work he doesn't like in order that he may "retire" and enjoy himself as soon as he is too old to do so. This is more than just the system—it is the credo. It is the same thing that prompted Thoreau to say, in 1839: "The majority of men lead lives of quiet desperation."

This was the procedure my advisors urged on me in the spring of 1958. For one reason or another I had very little money— maybe three thousand dollars cash—not much when you're thinking of taking a hundred-ton schooner halfway around the world. Numerous plans were presented to me, but there was a flaw in each—my services as an actor would be required in a continuing series of films. The time involved was from four to seven years. I was forty-two, and five years seemed precious.

Around March I determined to get out, no matter what. The rest was simple.

The first thing to do was to get the ship safely away from the gaseous Basin of the Angels and up to San Francisco. This was done over a long weekend. I returned to collect the bills and close out the house. The children held still for a haircut, then I photographed them in approved passport fashion and turned them over to their mother for a month. In mid-June the mate showed up with his bag and a brass cuspidor which he kept between his feet all the way to the Gate.

That was a memorable day. We pulled up the grade leading north from Necropolis and crested a barren hill, then we stopped long enough to get out and turn around. To the south lay the

land of the Big Sink. A crust of yellow air hung over endless
square miles of housing tracts, resembling an acute case of
acne on the ruddy cheeks of the valley. Somewhere ahead of
that lay the ship. We exhaled mightily, not wanting to carry
away with us any more air than was necessary—then a silent
glance and the journey continued. The mate, too, had been
entombed, under the sponsorship of a tug and salvage company
with headquarters in Long Beach. Long Beach is on the water
—and that's the sum of its virtues.

Certain facts were obvious. If there was going to be any
voyaging, I would have to come up with some capital. For two
years I had tried to get enough backing to recruit an amateur
crew of young people who shared some of my feelings about
life and liberty. We would move from California to Scandinavia
by way of Peru, Panama, the Indies, and the old highroad—
windswept and unimproved—of the malevolent North Atlantic.
We would try to capture on sound film the essence of the
journey. This could be cut into segments of suitable length and
shared with those back home by means of television. It seemed
a reasonable idea. Indeed, it appealed enormously to many
people I knew—educators, writers, documentary-film workers,
and any number of citizens whose sensitivity had not been
scorched by the inexorable logic of the big sell.

Investors, of course, would have none of it. Why risk capital
in such a venture when the sponsor and the network cried for
blood and guts and sex? What could you show when all you had
to work with were an old schooner and the ocean or a distant
port, along with some children and starry-eyed pseudo-adults?
I prepared a prospectus and wormed my way into the busy
schedules of at least eighty potential investors. There was no
interest—beyond a minimal politeness calculated to ensnare
me at some later date on a more solid commercial basis.

I was stumped. But I recalled a discovery made long ago
as a kid. I began to work in the depth of the Depression, in 1933,
when I was sixteen. Jobs weren't hard to get—there simply
were no jobs. But I soon learned that if in some way you could
catapult yourself into waters well over your head, then one
way or another you'd survive.

Late in June of '59 I placed identical announcements in the
personals column of five papers: *The New York Times, San Fran-*

cisco *Chronicle, Territorial Enterprise* (for some obscure reason), *Saturday Review,* and *Christian Science Monitor.*

VOYAGE UNDER SAIL

100-ton ex-Pilot schooner sailing from San Francisco August 15 for Copenhagen Sept. 15, 1959. Need six active intelligent young men and women. Send details to Sterling Hayden, Box 655—Sausalito, California.

That was all. Sixty dollars' worth of advertising. Nothing to sell but escape—from security, from oblivion. Two thousand replies came in within a month—telegrams, letters, phone calls. People showed up night and day: some of them bag in hand, others—more tactful—with luggage stashed out of sight while they pleaded for a chance to turn to and show just how much they could contribute.

It was a fine and hectic time. Some of the letters I shall always treasure, for they spoke in eloquent terms of the vision of youth, of the unrest and the incredible capacity of people to feel and dream.

This letter is the result of two things; first, the announcement of your voyage and second, the talk you gave a few months ago to the Cinema Dept. at USC.

I, as a student, was listening. Your words meant a great deal to me; they moved me but I couldn't speak to you at the time since you had touched on so many things that paralleled my own interests and I didn't know where to begin.

The topics you brought up: Time and the sea and sailors, tramps and lost men with little homes and the decadence of our everyday life. It reminded me of something Norman Cousins said, "In three hundred years the American soul has not found a home."

It is fitting (your dedication to the sea), for the sea is the symbol of migration and movement and wandering. It is a barbaric place and it stands opposed to society and it is a constant symbol too in all of literature.

As Thomas Wolfe said, "It is that state of barbaric disorder out of which civilization has emerged and into which it is liable to return."

You will excuse me, I have rambled on too long. I can't

go with you but feel better for knowing such a voyage is in progress.

From a newlywed couple in Arlington, Virginia:

We are not too happy with the way the world goes . . . this business of working at humdrum jobs all day, then coming home so tired all we can do is get some sleep to get back to work, doesn't seem to be enough. It is not what we had in mind a few years ago when we were in college together. We were on our way to Israel some months ago but my father talked us out of it on the ground that we would have to sell everything we owned. Unfortunately we took that advice, but perhaps—

Other people just couldn't get the point:

From the co-owner of a Health Club. "I have a completely equipped gym in storage; am glad to offer this to you as it will help while away the idle hours between ports."

From Clayton, Missouri. "May I include my wife? We are both professional dancers. This should prove invaluable as we can instruct your crew during the dull days at sea."

And if I thought my problems were acute I could always refer to the words of a woman in Connecticut:

I have been married. Our honeymoon was spent in Jamaica and Haiti where a friend introduced me to skin-diving. I had never been sailing but this was the next best thing; as a result I spent my entire honeymoon underwater! This may have had something to do with my husband's trading me in on a member in good standing of the Scarsdale Ladies Garden Club.

Those were extremes. The average applicant was neither profoundly imaginative nor ridiculous. He was disturbed to find himself—for most were in their mid-twenties—standing suddenly at a fork in the path of life. Then the magical announcement in the personals column and instant wild enthusiasm, for here was a chance to become aligned with a caravan of sorts that would go down the lonely road of independence.

Also, and unfortunately, such a proclamation inevitably stirs up the lees of things. And so it was that the mother of my four children, my ex-wife, upon learning of the undertaking, had her lawyers petition the court for an order restraining the voyage, or my taking the children with me—which amounted to the same thing.

I was aloft when the deputy sheriff showed up. From where I worked on the foremasthead he looked like an immigration or quarantine inspector, in search perhaps of the Mexican black beetle or a covey of wetbacks who had tired of picking lettuce at ninety cents an hour in the Promised Land.

I climbed down and with distaste noticed the insignia on his arm. The children hovered nearby, in secret delight at the prospect of seeing the old man carted away to the bastille. A glance at the documents told me all I needed to know. Suddenly the question of finance paled. There was no longer a voyage to finance. He had some coffee and told me I had picked the wrong state to get divorced in. I grinned and shook my head in sympathy as he unfolded a tale of woe regarding his ex-wife. As soon as he left, I called my attorneys. I had to laugh: I had been naïve enough to think I was free of Necropolis for good. As it turned out, I made sixteen trips to the Big Sink in connection with a piece of paper no bigger than a second mortgage.

CHAPTER 6

I used to think the businessman was bright. Not so. He's dedicated, that's all—dedicated and ruthless. He's the vulture of a cannibalistic society. But in the tactical sense we can profit by his example. There's nothing wrong with ruthless dedication—it depends on the end in view. I emerged from my cocoon that summer of '58. Without even knowing it, I began to operate in approved business fashion. And my goal was anything but profit. It was pride and self-respect. I had known success on these terms a long time ago—but that was before I gave up the sea to come on shore, where I tried to keep step with the vulture.

The problem was how to survive, at any cost—save that of self-respect. I threw a fifteen-thousand-dollar mortgage on the ship when she wasn't looking. (What vessel worth a damn hasn't been mortgaged half her life?) Then I found that rarest of gems—an honest shipyard run by able and hard-boiled men.

Anderson & Cristofani's it was called, and for two sweltering months the vessel lay under the lee of a south San Francisco ghetto, where ribbons of houses clung to parched hills and Negroes in thousands laughed and raged and loved. Hunters Point Naval Dockyard lay to the south, and Butchertown to the north.

A hundred jobs were done by crew and yard, always under the corrosive eye of the mate. Dollars poured through my hands that summer like hot sand through a child's toy sieve. And day and night the eager would-be crew came, some to work, others to stand around in awkward earnest: wanting desperately to insinuate themselves into the alien world of the tall old ship—before it was too late—but not knowing how to begin.

By the first of August she was ready to go, with new canvas stopped to her spars and tanks full up and a nest of dories lashed in the starboard waterway across from the small whaleboat. True, there were plenty of things missing, but the bulk of the work had been done and what we didn't have we could do without. And if it hadn't been for the law I would have slammed her offshore and worried about finance later. If it hadn't been for the law—there's a phrase to remember.

As it was, I holed up in a tiny office made from the salvaged wheelhouse of a wrecked corvette. I hung on the phone, chain-smoking and tense, trying to get financial support for the venture. Trying to understand every time my lawyers phoned: "Sterling? Don't be upset now, but the hearing has been delayed for another ten days or two weeks."

The weeks would pass, and I'd fly south with a brief case jammed with papers—only to have the trial postponed because of pretexts presented by my ex-wife's attorneys; for they sensed that enough of a delay would call an end to the venture.

The date of departure was put back to September 15, then to November 1 and November 15 and December 1—and finally till after Christmas. We went to trial on the fourth of December. In the meantime I'd gotten my money.

In early November it happened—all fifty thousand dollars' worth of it. Not because the corporation really believed in what I was trying to do, but because I was desperate enough by this time to make any deal, regardless of potential disaster. So willing that I leapt at a chance to give away forty per cent of my ownership in the film to be shot, along with multiple other concessions. Such is the call toward freedom—freedom to make a start—at least to get clear away from the land and the law.

My lawyer (I had two sets of them at the time) erupted in anguish when I told him the terms of the deal. "Suicide," he said, "you'll regret it as long as you live."

"Draw up the papers," I said.

"You'll be in so deep you'll never get out—unless you go for a bankruptcy bath—"

"Just fix us up with the papers."

"If you had any judgment, you could make yourself rich, you know."

"Sure, I know."

"The Ziv people are still interested—dying to get you, in fact. Remember their offer last spring? Do a series for them in Europe —set up a Swiss company on a tax-free basis—put your family in a fine school—and bank a hundred and forty thousand a year. . . ."

"I remember all about it—and I wouldn't be caught dead in the act."

"Three years—five at the most—you'd be fixed for life."

"I sure as hell would. Now let's get to work on the papers."

And he turned away with a shrug, looking off toward the phony fireplace. The air conditioning purred overhead, and the smoke from his big cigar hung suspended before a solid wall of law books.

A few weeks later I signed the papers—not without a nagging doubt—for there was a clause I knew might give me trouble. If the film idea failed, I'd owe the corporation fifty thousand dollars. And to secure this loan they had tied me up in a fashion that could force me to perform in from four to six feature pictures—paying them fifty per cent of my gross—until they'd recouperated their loss. This was the last thing I wanted from life. . . . To hell with it. I'd worry about it later. The only thing to do was battle it out for the court's permission—then get to Scandinavia as planned and come through with the film en route.

I paid off the mortgage and freed the ship. Simultaneously I cleared up most of my marine indebtedness and laid in a four-month supply of food. With time hanging heavily on their hands, the crew performed a miracle of patience; not one of them quit or grew lame. But they also found things in need of replacement and modification—by Christmas time I had a thousand dollars left in the bank.

But the driving force within held firm. Like a gale of wind it held—like a winter's gale in the high latitudes—blowing day after day in a roaring headlong drive, with the sprays slicing masthead high and the vessel rolling down to her sheer poles, yet all the time shouldering the hungry seas to one side and making you smile and to hell with the wind and the sea—to hell with everything. You're on your way.

CHAPTER 7

The sun rose that Friday in a pale and hostile sky and with it came the wind—from somewhere east of north—to set up a deep moan in the rigging while the blue smoke broke fast for the Gate in kind of a running crouch. It was cold back aft, and the oil stove from a junk shop pouted like a black stump on the cabin floor.

The mate was on the phone: "It's Healey from United Press—wants to know what your plans are for the future."

I was hard at work in the chartroom—trying to extract a second shave from a much-advertised blade: "Tell him we're sailing for Santa Barbara—all the way nonstop."

"He wants to know when."

"Sunday morning ten-thirty sharp—ask him to come along."

"He says is it true you're going to make this movie for Warner Brothers."

"Tell him yes. Tell him I'm looking forward to it because I've got grease paint in my blood."

I looked in the mirror. A shudder went through me at the thought of make-up, the cheap jokes, the gossip, and the high-priced executives who fawned over female stars with lonely frigid eyes.

The mate shoved his head in the door. "Healey said he'll be down to see us off. He also said: 'Tell Hayden I think he's full of shit.' "

There was work to do that day. I needed money and needed it fast—before the banks closed and the business world wrapped up for the weekend.

It was one thing to contemplate going to sea stone broke— quite another to do it with a court injunction hanging round one's neck. If I could muster nerve to go on with the voyage, I'd need cash wherever I went, particularly with the legal fireworks that were bound to occur. For if I found myself tied up in some foreign port I'd have to repatriate the crew. And if things went smoothly I'd need time—time to adjust to the disciplines of freedom.

I thought of my debts too. Never had I been in this deep. If I could raise ten thousand that day, and squared my accounts, I'd be broke all over again. Well, they'd have to stand in line; I'd write from the South Seas begging their indulgence. For years I'd spent money with practiced nonchalance; this was all to the good from the merchant's point of view—maybe now he'd ride along with me for a time.

Go and go and go! But where? American ports were out, for "the law follows the flag"—that much I had learned long before. Panama was out—Samoa, Hawaii. Just as well, I thought. Panama was only a ditch, and Samoa had no appeal. Hawaii—most of it—was nothing more than one of the Acapulco–Miami Chamber of Commerce Axis.

Aloft a halyard flogged a tattoo on a spar. My two oldest boys came shuffling aft with tears in their eyes. Christian's chin quivered as he shook his head in distress.

"Daddy, where are the dogs?" Dana blurted out.

"I sent them away last night. They have a good home, and they'll be together. I thought it best if you didn't have to tell them goodbye."

"But why, Daddy, if we're only going to Santa Barbara?"

"Because—look, boys, there's always the chance we might keep going. I told you that before. Now try to understand. If we go to Santa Barbara, we get them back—okay?"

The boys went forward. I arranged the papers on the cabin table and went to work on the phone.

Ten thousand dollars is a lot of money. Few people have it. Those who do can't risk losing it. This is a common complaint—particularly among the rich. There was one hope: of my fifty-thousand loan, ten thousand remained on deposit, to be drawn —so the papers said—when I had legal permission to sail.

I looked at the clock overhead—five past nine. Someone on deck went aft dragging a shot of chain. My call went through.

"Hell, Jack—Hayden."

"Oh yes, Sterling, I was about to call you. We're in plenty of trouble, from what I read in the press."

"Jack, I need that ten thousand up here today—before six this afternoon."

"You what? What are you talking about? The whole deal is off—we're concerned about getting back the forty we've already advanced."

"Look, Jack, just send me the ten, and I give you my word everything will turn out fine in the long run."

"How come?"

"I can't talk on the phone. You've gone along this far, and I'm asking you to go a little further—what the hell is ten thousand dollars when you get right down to it?"

Silence. Spike drops out of the hatch and slams his hands together. "Cold as a bastard on deck," he says.

Life in the phone again. "I think I follow you, Hayden; you're planning to sail without the kids, is that it?"

My mind swarms—why the devil hadn't I thought of that—sure, perfect out. Now go ahead and lie—follow up before it's too late.

"Yeah, yeah, Jack, sure, that's it."

"Well, in that case, I don't see why. . . . All right, I'll start things moving—take a few days, of course."

"I need it today."

"This I can't understand. Why the big rush?"

Go ahead and tell him—tell him if you don't get out over the weekend they might tie us up with further court orders—all kinds of things might go wrong—sheriffs and marshals and—

"Jack, I need it, that's all. Things are pretty complicated around here."

"All right. And you'll sign a document to the effect that the children stay home—correct?"

"That is right."

"I hope you know what you're doing. If you want my opinion, I think you should reconsider. You live in a vortex up there."

"Thanks, Jack."

I call a cab, jam a chart catalogue in the brief case, and bolt for the deck. The bay is furrowed with white-plumed waves. Riding over the gaunt bridge, I turn and look to the west. There it is—the thin gray line where the sky comes flush with the sea —stretched far and wide—no shipping in sight and the Farallones lost in the murk.

The taxi driver speaks. "Sold your little car, eh?"
"Sure did."
"And now you gotta buy another one. Tough break—a man
ain't got a chance in this state."

The Branch Hydrographic Office lies lost on the eighth
floor. It is immaculate: rows of cabinets and racks under rows
of neon tubes. Rows of Venetian slats at half hoist reveal an
air shaft, and through the windows beyond lie rows on rows of
desks with rows of people at work, heads bent forward in mute
submission, typewriters spaced between.

The clerk of the charts appears; cardboard gauntlets encase
his sleeves and they're held in place with doubled rubber hands.
I hand in my list:

#3002   Eastern Archipelago. Moluccas Passage to Timor.

#4514   Tawitawi.

#3412   Bangkok Harbor.

#3003   Halmahera to Gulf of Carpenteria.

#2123   Tanjong Baram to Tanjong Nosong.

#3332   East portion of Java incl. Madura, Bali & Lombok.

So it begins—to run for three pages and more—with pilot books
and current tables and light lists. Some two hundred dollars'
worth.

"Captain, do you want these delivered?" he asks.

I play it with dignity. "No, thanks, I'll take them along." "Captain," the man said. Captain? I should apologize and set him
straight; I'm no captain, mister, just an actor fighting to become an ex-actor, but thanks—thank you very much.

Across town to the French consul. Visas for Tahiti just in
case. Passports stamped and validated—bearing the names
Africa, Weston, Bentzen, Garvey, Powers, Saindon, Aune, Burns,
Nyborg, and Bahl. And Hayden—one Hayden—while not far
from Market Street, in another government office with rows on
rows of desks, lie four more Hayden passports safely locked
away, per order of the court. Worry about it later.

Some business at the Custom House regarding a bill of health,
issued in less than a minute, and a strange and curious look on
the face of the man as he hands me the paper. What was your
thought that day, my unknown friend?

Now a cautious inquiry made of the consul for Indonesia.

"You will have to write Jakarta, sir."

Thank you, ma'am, and it's twelve o'clock, with no time for lunch.

The check list grows longer as thoughts come crowding in: confirm chronometer's rate; fresh meat, vegetables, and milk; power of attorney to Walker; names of next of kin; letters (to be mailed in a week) to friends and foes, agents and lawyers and creditors perhaps. A girl in New York City. Cancel the ship's insurance.

And an urge to call the ship. Good thing. The voice of Red. ". . . Just came in—call Mr. Davis of Loeb and Loeb—urgent."

Big electronic logjam in the coin box with dimes that won't come back. Put in a quarter and call collect: "Hello, Roger? Hayden. Hell of a note to be calling collect, but—"

"Mr. Hayden, I hate to tell you this, but as counsel for the corporation I can't approve of this thing you've asked them to do."

"Oh? Didn't Jack explain what I had in mind?"

"Yes, he did. But it's not as simple as you seem to think. I have a copy of the court's order. It states very clearly, page 6, line 26, and I quote: 'The proposed ocean voyage is enjoined' unquote."

"That's a lousy word, 'enjoined.' "

"Well, that's no affair of ours. You'd better come see us the first thing next week. There will be no further monies advanced."

"Roger, look, have you got kids?"

"Yes. A boy sixteen and a girl fourteen."

"Can you put yourself in my position and—"

"Actually I can't, and if I could it would have nothing to do with the problem."

Across the bridge once more, and don't bother looking west. Forget the sea, forget the winds and the clouds. Give up and get back on the track. Find a house—maybe in a nice little tract, exclusive and antiseptic in a luxurious way: Royal Oaks Estates, 4 bedrooms 3½ baths and rumpus room. Terms, 6 blocks to the new shopping center; put the kids in Little League, Brownies, and Scouts; turn them to racing karts round and round miniature tracks across from the bowling alley, with helmets pulled low and safety belts cinched tight . . . Paper a room with charts—#2025 should fit—"Papeete Pass to Papenu Pass—N. coast of Tahiti"—

And all I ask is a tall ship
And a star to steer her by . . .
Tall ship—tall in the saddle. What the hell's the difference.

The crew glance at me as I come over the rail, their plates of stew held up to the sun, the dories making a lee. It is close to high water and the mooring warps are taut. I pause by the wheel and the bow rises gently with the surge, the jibboom tracing a line on the Belvedere shore—coupon country over there. Red and Spike are alone in the cabin as I dump the charts in a corner.

"Going somewhere?" There's a challenge in her eye.

"We were—for about three hours."

I pour a mug of tea.

"What's your problem?" she asks.

"Money."

Spike rakes his throat with a rasp, then leans and spits toward the weathered cuspidor. "Who needs it," he says as he goes for the galley.

Good point. I'm the one who for years has been talking about blasting free. Get up and go. Let her roll for Tahiti; write some articles on the way; make a real documentary instead of the series—if you can't make it, then peddle the film and the lights but keep going. Write that book you've had in mind for so long.

I glance toward Red. She is buried in her accounts. I come up with some paper and pretend to work on a letter, but the pen is stilled. I watch her as she works. Last chance, this; where would I find another pair like this? A man who was raised in boxcars and windjammers, hobo jungles and canneries, shipyards and rigging lofts. Where's the wife to throw in with three small kids of her own and become mother, overnight almost, to four small Haydens, give them love and a sense of values while running the domestic end of the ship, keeping the books, mending britches and heads with equal dexterity? And if I did find such people, what are the odds they'd chuck everything—dump the house, hock the furniture, sell the car, and quit the jobs—then stand firm through nine months, all for no salary? Where would I find this again?

It was past two when the phone rang. "Sterling? Don't ask me any questions, but you're going to get your money. It's on the way, should be in Sausalito by five-thirty. Bank closes at six. That's all. Have a good trip."

I realized suddenly I hadn't said a word. In a way I felt let down; my dislike and distrust of businessmen was suddenly knocked to hell. The corporation was controlled by one man— he turned loose the money, in spite of his lawyers and, I am sure, his better business judgment.

The bank clock says five to six. A girl in a plaid skirt pulls some shades, and the terraced steel of the vault's door glints hard in what's left of the light. I feel tired. The man in the cage counts from one to ten—bills that look like singles, with some added zeros. I earmark two thousand for checks. An ad card leers up from the counter: "Never carry more cash than you can afford to lose." This makes me pause—but how do you bribe a man on an isolated atoll—assuming that you must— with a traveler's check? The eight thousand goes into a small white sack—twice the size of a Bull Durham packet and half the size of a sewing kit given me years ago, made by my mother my first year at sea.

A bus goes past in the twilight. I walk slowly down the dock.

CHAPTER 8

Look to the west. Now form a circle with arms outstretched and fists clenched—this is the shape of the bay—between your knuckles a narrow thread known as the Golden Gate. The city flows all gray and cool round the curve of your left forearm. Your body is the mainland. A hundred miles to the east, paralleling the line of your ribs, stands the High Sierra, known to wilderness lovers as "The Range of Light." Snug within your right hand's heel and beneath the mound of your thumb lies the village of Sausalito: hillside homes alight, rotting old wharves that rest on wasted pilings to which starfish cling in the shadows, and a schooner readied for sea.

It was quiet that Saturday night. Most of the crew were on shore, engaged in the ritual of farewell—not that they had much idea of what lay ahead. They knew we'd sail in the morn- ing, with the question of destination to be announced once we'd entered the sea's domain. I was playing for time. And a sailing ship is no democracy; you don't caucus a crew as to where you'll go any more than you inquire when they'd like to shorten sail.

It's strange, I thought—the way a man can react; when a goal is out of reach, he's on fire to drive to a finish. Then, when the pieces fall in place and he has what he needs, the fire within starts to flicker and gasp.

I finished a batch of letters and took a look at the kids. Like flowers they slept, all limp and closed—still warm from the heat of the day. I boiled some tea and went aft to stand in the hatch. So peaceful and safe it seemed with the ship in the arms of the basin. Straight up she stood—no pressure on halyard or sheet, no growl in the throat of the wire. Not like it would be if we got clear of the land. Not like I'd known it in times gone by. I thought of the past and the failures I'd never forget . . . of the times I'd quit and run for cover when I knew I could have gone on.

I thought of a night southeast of Cape Hatteras back in '39— Christmas Eve—with a great steel sliver of a schooner called *Aldebaran* (named for a star I could see even now—above San Francisco), with a Gulf Stream sea gone mad in a northerly gale. With some sails blown out and her deck awash and five feet of water in the bilge. Oh, it was a mess all right, and I was justified in quitting—perhaps. But as I ran for Charleston I knew I should have gone on, and I soon found out I was right; for the cost of repairs proved the end of a dream and she never got free of the port—they towed her north and broke her in bits for scrap.

The tea felt good and I tried to kill off such thoughts but it wasn't any use. Small wonder, what with the goading of conscience and the harsh truth that the ship had a prior place in the record. I stood there encased in my vessel—up to the shoulders in her, you might say—and it seemed I could hear her thinking:

Do you suppose you can make it this time? Do you remember '48? When you came galloping out from the land and bought me up and talked and talked about the voyaging we'd know before we were through—"before it's too late," you said. And you hauled me out and you spread some paint and some tar. . . . And three months later you quit. You claimed I was rotten and you bored me with holes to prove it. But I wasn't rotten then any more than I'm rotten now, and you knew it at the time. You

were the one full of rot. You fooled the others perhaps, but you
never fooled me and you never fooled yourself. Three years ago
you bought me back—was it your conscience? But we haven't
been anywhere, except on paper, and maybe we never will—
unless you've changed. Tell me, you wandering clown, have you
changed—do you think—perhaps?

It was midnight before I knew it. The crew came drifting
back and I roused myself and went on shore for a walk. Something typical about that—the patterned escape of the loner. Let
a group gather on deck and I generally drift below. Let a crowd
convene in the cabin—I soon find work on deck. Even in time
of war I played it that way; ninety-nine per cent of the Marines
did their bloody work in the Pacific, while I did what I could in
the Balkans. A peculiar sort of a talent—guaranteed to attract
attention—and loneliness.

Halfway up the dock were two craft. One of them a glass-
faced yacht with no canvas to cause a man any trouble. A party
was under way in the deckhouse—maybe twenty people, including some of my crew, laughter and drinking and shouting out,
and a guitar holding court in a corner. I stood in a shadow
and watched, wondering if after all they hadn't the right idea—
wondering about a lot of things. Then I turned to look at a
ship, or what was left of one, for that night she was only a
hulk.

I knew her well; her name was *Wander Bird*. Twenty-seven
years before, I had tried to join her in Boston. How proud she
had looked that day—and here she was, with her masts chopped
off ten feet above the deck and her keel at home in the mud. A
far cry from her youth and her glory. As I looked, I saw again
a shy and lanky kid—standing enraptured, with the roar of the
city around him, and then he started forward, touching a belay-
ing pin here and a halyard there, as though he knew about such
things. Then he moved toward the bow and cradled his arms on
the bulwarks and gazed down where the stem bit the waters—
fascinated, rigid inside, telling himself: "One day I'll be going
to sea."

I walked for a time on the offshore side of the street, with
the sound of life in the bars and couples darting arm in arm
toward their private worlds. Then back on board.

The barometer stood at 30.14. I called the district forecaster:

nothing to worry about; moderate westerly winds with a threatened disturbance that apparently had curved to the north.

As I undressed, I flipped my wallet onto the shelf beyond the bunk. It felt plump. Then I remembered the money. I reached far into a locker and came up with the small white sack. It was almost like holding a world in your hand—or the promise of one. Eight thousand dollars. I had to laugh, for at times I had made as much in a week—not that it meant much, except distaste.

The typewriter looked up from its corner under the prism. Now I thought of the girl. I wanted to write—more than anything in the world I did, but something held me back—and besides, it was cold. I carried the phone in from the outer cabin and laid it to rest by the bunk. My watch showed one o'clock— four where she lived, in New York; not the ideal hour to call, not under certain conditions, at least, not when you hadn't talked or written in months.

I turned in. Where had the tiredness gone? I tossed around, then rolled out and came back with pencil and paper. I turned up the lamp and pressed myself deep in the sleeping bag's cowl.

"Dear Lorna"—no. "Lorna Dear" . . . "Dearest One". . . . I toyed with the pen, then shoved it aside and turned down the lamp and rolled up with my back to the world.

I see again the living room in the big old house, with a log fire and books all around and paneled walls, and a picture above the hearth—of a black schooner reaching toward home in the soft light of some forgotten afternoon. I see the half-empty glasses; and throughout the beamed room the wail of a trumpet enveloping two people as they dance for the first time. The wondrous sensation that floods through from another body— a body so superb, yet almost that of a child. The proud thought that this at last is someone to cherish, as one would a wildflower, so gentle yet firm, so trusting and wise, accepting whatever one might be able to offer, no questions asked or promises made, only acceptance and yielding and giving—and understanding. Perhaps that was the core of it all—the finding at last, at long long bitter last, of someone who understood and cared, not simply projected the emotion of caring.

Oh, the wonder of that night. The laughter when the needle stuck in its groove, causing the trumpet to bay in its echo. The scent of her hair. The gentlest trembling running the length of her body under just a suggestion of pressure. The arrogant denial of common sense as the clock hands sped circling through the night. And the awareness growing that while no girl had seemed so desirable, this time you would gladly wait until you knew what you felt was shared.

Now the angered blast of a steamer's horn mixed with the need to hear again the vanished sound of her voice. The voice that never once was raised, that over three years spoke in terms of love and hope for the outcome of things. Except for the time in Seattle . . . when bewilderment took over, bewilderment born of hurt and the knowledge that this was the end—no matter how hard two people might try, no matter how desperate their desire to erase and forget. All because in one savage senseless outburst a man had taken the flower in his tortured grasp and raked it into pulp.

It was June in Seattle. Traditional month of fruition. Fertility of spring giving way to summer. Two-fisted young Seattle, with maritime roots dug deep in Alaskan seas. Four people having an early dinner—a baggy-eyed producer and the writer who was as fine a friend as any man could have, who startled strangers, as the time came to leave, when he hove the bulk of his bearlike body upright with the help of aluminum sticks—resonant-voiced, forced from time to time to pause on steelclad legs and knead the circulation back into heavily muscled hands.

Two others at the table—an incredibly beautiful girl and the tall hulk of a man—holding hands, tasting the joy of lovers engaged to be married, cherishing every second, laughing and drinking and joking with an inner eye on the clock.

And the sudden crazy idea—go down and visit the ship where she lay prone in the shipyard. The producer excused himself: "Business first thing in the morning; have to get my sleep." The fresh bottles of iced aquavit, and the writer hoisted on board by a gantline led to the winch.

And now the maggots start to crawl. (Did the aquavit bring them to life?) The first rumblings of savage unrest. Three people alone in the cabin. One of them a wanderer, seeing them both together for the first time: ship and girl.

The measured clink of bottle meeting glass. The deceptive— oh so deceptive—sensation of unleashed power. And then the deck reeling (as though in a breeze of wind), and a feeling of pride as the gantline is sweated, then eased.

The friend seen safely framed in his hotel door. It's late now, well past three—time for just one good-night drink, straight Scotch with no ice and a layer of water on top (no thicker than a leaf). And the drink drained, and the bore of the anger comes down.

Vicious unreasoning criticism of the imagined defect. Tearing and ripping through any attempt at defense. And yet not un-aware—sensing that this is the beginning of the end. Which only serves to multiply the venom. Tears; so move in and finish her off—speaking softly, through clenched teeth, from vast reserves of bitter swollen hate.

Exit now. Skip the elevator and up two flights of steps. Through the door, with eyes drenched—then a sprawling plunge into space.

I rise within myself. The prism's eye shows signs of life—just the palest trace of blue. And the first full thought—"It's half past eight in New York."

There's wind aloft, and I know the voyage is done and gone, but we'll go through the motions anyway—what else is there to do?

🦶

CHAPTER 9

There was no sun. A chill wind out of the north northeast came slicing down the bay and an overcast lay on the headlands. Up on the hill a church bell tolled while old Sid went zigzag along the dock in quest of his Sunday paper.

Now, as a rule in this wheel-sick society, when a big sailing ship is outward bound on a long haul, you'll be sure to attract a crowd. But ours was no resounding departure. We tiptoed out of port like a thief. Perhaps thirty people assembled on the wharf —relatives mostly, and a couple of newsmen, more discerning than most.

The engine had been idling for an hour or more; I gunned it a couple of times and watched little clouds of exhaust belch from the mainmasthead. The mate took a fresh chaw of Copenhagen, replaced the lid of the small round can, wiped a

finger on his pants, and never took his eyes off me in the process.
I gave him a nod and he put the gang to work on the headlines.
The engineer shot a glance toward his father on the dock and
dropped from sight down the hatch.

We held one line aft. I rang two bells and the line crackled
a bit as her bow eased out from the land. One bell now and a
moment's pause with the engine free of the load. Hard astar-
board with the big iron wheel. A single bell and the heavy
clunk as the clutch engaged, while under the counter I could
hear the rippling sucking noise of roiled waters just above the
propeller.

I glanced at the clock—ten thirty-five on the nose; I felt taut
and irritable and my hands shook a little with a match cupped
in between. Not a boat was in sight on the bay so I opened her
up and she swung in a wide curve toward the mouth of the
Golden Gate. I spun the wheel and she settled down. Inshore a
couple of cars moved slowly down the main street. The folks on
the dock were quiet. A man stood in a picture window wearing
a robe, with a paper under one arm.

On deck, the children seemed less than elated. They hunched
taut against the cold and kept their hands out of sight, and
little Dana Africa—not quite six—said to her mother: "Br-r-r-r,
Mommy, it's f-f-freezing out here."

We picked up the ebb and scurried beneath the bridge. With
the span overhead, Red took a mighty drag on her cigarette,
covered both eyes with one arm, then snapped the maggot over
the rail in a vow of abstinence.

A long swell came heaving in from the west and the land
breeze died as we gave her the foresail and staysail, followed by
the inner jib and the main and at last the outer jib. One of the
girls brought me a mug of tea. By way of thanks I put her behind the wheel and told her to steer west by south. She re-
sponded with a vague expression, then peered into the binnacle.
I wasn't much in the mood, but it had to be done, so I gave her
a lesson in steering: "West by south is the first little triangle to
the left of west."

She had sailed with a yachtsman a few times, which prompted
her to say: "Oh, that looks like 260 degrees."

"Forget the degrees," I said. "We steer by points. See that
black line on the compass bowl? That represents the bow of
the ship—when you see it go off the point, you have to bring it
back—whatever you do, don't try to bring the point back to the

line, or we'll just keep making circles. It's like a car—if you want to go left, turn the wheel to the left, and vice versa."

"I wish I was back in my little MG."

The mate saunters aft, so I go below. The logbook is an informal affair bound in black with red triangular corners. I rule some lines and print at the top of the page: SCHOONER WANDERER—FROM SAN FRANCISCO TOWARD ————. Below this I put a heading for each of several columns: HOUR, COURSE, LOG, WIND, BAROMETER, REMARKS. No need for explanation—even to the greenest of hands. The hour is the hour and the course is the course and the wind is the wind. The barometer stands fixed to the wall above an empty space that once contained something known to the maritime world as a Notice of Mortgage. The "Remarks" space is available to one and all for ad-lib comment on anything under the sun. "Log" means distance run each hour—determined by estimate, by gauging the speed of the lee wake flowing by, a very accurate system—in fact, quite as accurate as the tally rendered by a fancy brass gadget full of dials.

Territorial waters are, like rates of exchange and stock-market trends, subject to change without notice—or reason. Some say there is a three-mile limit, others favor the figure twelve, while still others claim you have to be eighteen miles offshore before you're officially free. It mattered not at all. From time to time I glanced astern; no sheriff or U.S. marshal in hot pursuit, so I called all hands aft and passed the word.

"We're bound for Tahiti, by way of Nuku Hiva in the Marquesas Islands and one or two atolls in the Tuamotu group."

Dramatic pause. Red and Spike and one or two others do an off-balance jig on the deck. Others are glum. Already certain faces have assumed the mustard look with the waxen finish that heralds seasickness.

"I appreciate your standing by in recent months. It was a tough go at times, but these first eight hundred miles are apt to be a lot worse. You can't saunter through town any more with a sheath knife on your belt and a rolling gait. If we catch a breeze of wind before you've had time to adjust, I assure you that you'll wish you were back in neon country where the land stands still and the girls come down to ooh and ahh at the ship."

Then a few words to the kids, telling them to stay away from the rails and always fight for balance. Three of them are old enough to wonder about legal ramifications. True, they're hard-

ened somewhat through exposure to the pistol whippings and
the applied butchery of television, but this is the first direct
contact with lawbreaking, however modest—oh, we can talk
about that later. They scamper forward.

A westerly breeze. We slacked some sheet and hooked up the
boom tackles, and I noted with relief that the land was out of
sight. "Now," I said, "the key to this operation lies in vigilance.
Always regard the elements out here as an opponent—cunning,
implacable, and able to knock you down and stomp you before
you know it. Keep a sharp eye out at all times—you can tell an
experienced seaman in many ways, one of them his habit of
sweeping the horizon constantly. For all we know, there may be
some poor devil adrift in a boat or a raft, so forget what they
practice on shore and remember the golden rule.

"When you steer, goddam it you steer. Stand up to the
wheel, don't smoke and don't discuss the Big Ten and rock 'n
roll. The brighter the man, the poorer the helmsman—that's an
old adage in sailing—just in case you were feeling discour-
aged.

"When you work, try to protect your hands. Cuts don't heal
in the tropics and if you sprain something it's that much harder
for everyone else.

"If you don't understand an order, say so—don't just sashay
around pulling on any old line till you come to the right one—
because you can maim somebody that way.

"When you're awakened to go on watch, roll out and think
it over afterwards. If you need an hour to get dressed, we can
call you an hour early—otherwise you have twenty minutes . . .
And if you hear the call 'All hands on deck!' that means to come
as you are as fast as you can—don't reach for a cigarette or
mess around with your clothes, just come on up and dive into
the work. . . What's more, if you're off watch and you hear hell
break loose on deck, there's no law against your coming up
uninvited to lend a hand—this has obvious advantages: first,
you have time to get the feel of things, and second, you might
learn something—but I won't hold my breath until you do it,
either.

"This is 1959 and the chances are there's no other sailing
vessel at large in this portion of the Pacific—steamers know this
and behave accordingly; steamer mates are fine guys, but they
don't strain themselves looking out for windjammers at night.
And never mind the nonsense about a sailing ship having the

right of way—right of way is purely a matter of tonnage. If a steamer busts out of the murk and it's obvious he doesn't see us, then the best thing to do is take the signal gun and put a flare right in front of his wheelhouse windows—the ones with the windshield wipers.

"One final word—and this is the most critical of all. This ship lives off the wind—wind is to us what money is to life on shore. Always scan the windward horizon. Always keep in tune with the feel and heft of the wind . . . and don't forget that a sudden squall could lay this wagon down so she'd never get up, no matter how hard you prayed."

I set the watches—four hours on, four hours off—then climbed out of the deep cockpit and took a look about the deck. There was some weight in the wind. We killed the engine and swayed up on the gear all around. I let her go southwest and she lay over a bit, her white stem slashing its way through the long blue hills where they came shouldering in for the shore. Something told me it was going to blow, so I had a look at the glass. Sure enough, it had fallen, and we passed extra lashings about the dories and flaked down all the gear.

The mate had the deck from eight till twelve, but I stayed too for a time. What a glorious feeling—the vessel sailing hard, the moonlight seen through the rigging. From time to time, the sea slapped against the starboard bows and the spray flew wide. The stars were so much brighter than they'd been a week ago—and the sea glowed red in her lee when she pitched.

It breezed some and I knew that wind—real wind—was on the way. "See if you can't harden down that outer jib sheet," I said to the mate. The minutes passed, with a figure or two silhouetted against the glow of the running lights. Suddenly a thundering roar split the night—awkward hands fumbling with wet rope had lost control and the sail had taken charge. Far aloft it flogged, like a giant gone berserk—his head in the stars and his feet all wet from the sea. Sparks flew as wire sheets snagged on the stays. Hard on the gear, I thought; one minute of this is more damaging than hours in a living gale . . . "lee jib sheet out of hand by mistake" . . . that's what the log would read. We should keep a separate log in which to record mistakes —make a fascinating book—humorous, too.

Mistakes made at sea are, on the surface, cause for annoyance. But to the men in charge they're more disturbing than that; they're outrageous and inexcusable and they tell you just how vulnerable you are. Suddenly your vessel looms in a new and anxious light—the light that comes in the pitch-black windswept midnight hours. Gone is her aura of romance, her colorful water-front image—massive old bastard of a windship full of grace. Instead, she is nothing but a collection of timbers and planks joined together some seventy years ago—made to be shoved through the water by means of scraps of canvas hoisted to interrupt the wind, thus causing the whole contrivance to inch along at less than five miles to the hour.

And the control of this apparatus lies in a dozen pair of hands (one reserved to photograph the tangle)—hands that short months ago were shuffling invoices, holding textbooks, hoisting highball glasses—even those of the leader were flitting sense-lessly from make-believe weapons to phony saloon doors. By god, Mister Judge, perhaps you were right all along.

With the sail gone mad, I put up the helm and ran the vessel off. As the wind came aft, the canvas subsided. I jumped forward and said, with due deliberation: "Now haul the bastard down." Then I threw off the turns and let the halyard fly.

"What happened to the wind?" A puzzled voice in the night.

"Shut up and get to work," I rumbled. "You'll soon enough find out."

CHAPTER 10

I didn't lie down that night. The ship plowed on, just a little more vexed with the passing of each hour. The malignancy of transformation was now at work within. Where was the old sea-lust? Was I too far gone to know again the old delight? Braced against the chart table, I tried to call up my lost enthusiasm, that wild exultant response to challenge I had known in the old days at sea—clinging alone in the night a hundred feet up from some deck, the mastheads scribing frenzied arcs against the limitless reach of the sky—or out on the bowsprit's end, with the ship charging down, her bow wave aflame as it went boiling aft with a roar. All of this was gone —gone in the wake of the years.

I felt detached—suspended—elbows dug under my ribs, staring with glazed eyes at the promised land of the chart. So it was all over. Simple, really—with no conscious effort a decision had been reached—we'd alter course in the morning and run her in for the land. I dozed.

A rap of a hand on my shoulder—"Jesus," I said, "don't jab me, just speak to me." I turned and saw the mate.

"Sorry," he said. "You'd better have a look on deck—she's blowing now—like a whore at a Legion convention."

The ship rolled down to leeward, scooped up a ton or two from the sea, then forced herself back on her feet, the water cascading riotously over the deck. I swung into the night and and looked at the compass. "Where in hell are you taking her?" I inquired of the man at the wheel.

He leaned forward. "What did you say?"

"I said, what are you steering?"

"She's right on, sir."

"Never mind that 'sir' crap; what's the course?"

"Uh, southwest by south?"

"You're not on southwest by south."

"I'm not?"

"Hell no. You're on south by west—let her come up two points." Awkward silence while he ponders how. I jump him. "What did I tell you people yesterday—when you're given a course—repeat it—don't puzzle over it—just repeat it—so we know you heard correctly—then go ahead and figure it out—understand?"

"Yes."

"All right. Steer southwest by south."

"Oh, steer—southwest—by—south."

Up she drives with a rush. I reach back and steady her down. Now the whine of the wind with a vengeance, and the sprays volleying aft. For a time she drags her rail. Figures spraddled about. "Where's the girl who belongs to this watch?" I ask.

"She's below," yells Spike. "Wasn't feelin' too good, so I told her to sleep it off—no use, anyway."

"Well"—I wipe the spray from my face—"I bought three thousand dollars' worth of food not long back—and I wonder if I could please have a pot of tea."

A light flares up from the galley. It shines on the foresail, killing one's sense of the sea, distorting the feel of the ship.

"Pull the lid," I bark, "or tell him to cook with a lamp."

Eight bells now, and the old watch dives below in time to catch the fading of the chime. Pretty damn blasé, as though they were born out here and had been at sea all their lives.

The next watch comes aft—lurching blindly and half awake —foul-breathed—bewildered by the shrouded alien deck.

Doc Garvey takes the wheel. He wears a queer hat and there's a trace of laughter in his wiry bloodshot eyes. I knock her off a point and he handles the change with ease. Thank God, I tell myself, there's a helmsman among us. A natural, rarest of finds in this high-compression age. We share a cigarette while I give her a touch of mainsheet, then work my way up to the bows. It's here that the wind can howl. I squat to my work at the cleat. Under my boots lie the children. I crack the sheet with one fist, and it surges a bit, the water squishing through my hands.

Now up to the weather rail, where I crouch with an arm hooked on a halyard—feeling the weight of the wind and watching her go . . . time for a reef . . . best wait till it's light, then haul the mains'l in altogether . . . no telling what might happen if we tried to reef her down with a crowd like this . . . run her off before it—Santa Barbara bound. I go aft and take the wheel, telling Doc to get his coffee. As she rolls, I pivot to leeward of the wheel, block off the binnacle, and steer by the feel of the wind. She runs in a groove, balanced and true. Nine and a half she's doing—maybe ten in the puffs.

My spirits lift. I look to the east and I laugh, for I think of those who said it shouldn't—or couldn't—be done. All snug now in oversized beds they'd be; bellies full of pills and minds at work, figuring, straining, balancing profit and loss, wracked and laboring in the cross sea of commercial endeavor. Maybe we'll keep on going. We're free now. Free of the crawling and petty life; free to go west or south for weeks and months on end. I feel refreshed and strong, and I spit in my hands and work the wheel with a sweeping surge of affection, come mysteriously alive.

From aloft the report like a cannon—of wood burst wide under too much compression—foretopmast—or could it be the main? "Call all hands!" I bellow down the deck.

But the topmasts stand—it's the fore gaff that's gone instead. They horse the crippled sail down on deck, and Spike comes aft with the torch. She rolls more wildly now.

"Rotten," he says. "Busted spang in two, midway between the

bands." He fingers some black and spongy wood. I smell the stuff and he flings it over the rail. "Lousy goddam rot."

A schooner without a foresail is like a man without pants—there's a limit to what he can do.

The brush of dawn sweeps low in the eastern skies, leaving a pale green band all shot with copper strands.

Along with the dawn came more wind, to set up a mournful howling moan in the rigging, driving the seas before it into steep blue-surfaced hills—not very high just then—but with an ugly promise. It was ten past six when we went to work on the mains'l. The crowd showed up in brittle yellow oilers, some in parkas, like the dummies you see in the ads—motivated by the landsman's urge to keep dry.

I staked them about the deck—one to a halyard and one to clear the coil, three on the vang and two on the throat downhaul. Broad off the wind she ran. But the slides jammed, and there was nothing to do but bring her back and let her shake the bastard down. A wild sight it was, looking forward: Dennis the fullback on all fours, puking through a wispy stubble of beard.

The sky to windward was barren of cloud and cold. A pair of marauding seas came jumbling down. The first threw the ship back on her heels, with her nose hooked out free of the surge; then down she plunged with a shivering smash, and she buckled a little as she hit the trough. The second thundered waist-high over the rail, and the headgear dove out of sight, then rose with a marvelous effort, the water streaming off like a cloud. From below, the crash of crockery and the cry of a girl. "There goes breakfast," I yelled at Russ as he worked.

But the sail came down—inch by inch at first, then foot by foot as she spilled her wind, until we dumped the boom in the gallows' notch and took up the slack on the sheet. Now up with the helm and jibe the jumbo across and let her run—southeast toward the Big Sink—southeast toward No Man's Land. Hail the death of a dream.

One more failure. Again I knew the wretched taste of defeat. What quirk of fate was this—greeting us at the outset of the voyage with a slashing gale, laying naked the frailty of man and ship? Suppose instead the wind had been fair off the land—enabling us to run for a week till it was too late to come back, till I had grown accustomed to this fabulous frightening mood of newborn defiance? What a different tale there might have been to tell. Never mind all that—what matters is the present.

Under normal circumstances the weather could go to hell, but with the Law riding my back, everything seemed hazardous. Suppose we were stove by a drifting redwood log? Suppose a fitting let go and we crippled one of the kids? What then? Why ask for trouble? Why risk having the kids taken from me once we limped back to port? Let her run on in, try again some other time.

She rolled so hard she rang her bell, which rested on the fife rail by the open main deck. I let her go, leaning over the slide of the hatch, smoking, hollow and numb. I glanced from time to time off to the far southwest. There lay the true highroad—to freedom and challenge, to a whole new way of life.

The starboard door swung back and Red came out on deck, and handed me my mug and a pot of tea, a lime in the pocket of her shirt. Her hair flew up and around and she grabbed ahold of a cleat. I jammed the pot in a corner and our eyes met, till I turned away.

"How about a shot to go with that?" she called.

"No, thanks."

"Why not? Might help. Might give you a push."

I said nothing, just leaned down and took a sip.

She kept boring in. "I hear tell we're homeward bound."

"Looks that way."

"Why?"

"Maybe because I've seen how weak we are. Maybe because I'm reminded now of what can happen with a bunch of clowns who can't even slack a sheet."

"Baloney."

"Like hell it is. I guess I know too well what can happen. None of the rest of you do—except Spike." I relieve the man at the wheel. He ducks below for a smoke.

"Didn't you take a ship out of Gloucester one winter with a completely green crew?"

"Sure I did."

"And you took her through to Tahiti."

"Just like that." I snap my fingers and look away.

"And you were all of twenty-two."

"Knock it off, Red. I didn't have seven kids with me. I didn't have four girls sliding around in the galley. And I didn't have lawyers and courts on my tail either."

I hand her a cigarette. She puts it in her mouth and it comes to me this is the first time I've seen her eyes full of pure, livid

anger. When I cup my match, she snaps her cigarette downwind
—it goes quite a distance. She freshens my mug and starts below. "If you want that shot, just say so and I'll send a runner—
might even bring it myself."

The door slams shut and I watch the seas race by. The mate
comes aft, moving in spurts timed to the roll. I give him the
wheel and the course.

"Southeast by east it is," he repeats.

The brim of his hat slaps up and down as he works with the
wheel.

"Spike, if you were me, what in hell would you do?"

There's a roar astern. A wall of water hangs high above our
heads, hiding the horizon, poised as though gauging the set of
the ship. The vessel waits and Spike wrestles the wheel a bit.

Then forward the vessel leaps, lunging up and over and out.
The sea thunders past. And the carved eagle with the angry
weather eye stares defiantly into the wind. The mate pats a spoke
with the coarse inside of his hand. "You're running this show,
Ishmael. I'm just taking orders."

🖃

CHAPTER 11

For a day and a night we staggered along to the east. The wind
came out of the northwest with relentless energy, and always
the sky was clear. It was a small dry gale, but the seas were
bald blue promontories that moved with majestic savage grace.

Except for three of us, the galley was so much useless space.
Now and then someone would tackle a bowl of mush or crack
a can of juice. Even the kids were sick. They would work their
way up to stand in the hatch once in a while, and gaze in awe
at the face of the sea or fix me with a baleful stare.

I moved through the ship like a stranger, feeling alone and
split within myself. From time to time I broke out the sextant
and ran a series of sights with my boots rammed home in a
corner. There was a certain assurance in this ritual, reminding
me of bygone days when I had a grip on the world.

The sun's image would weave and swing like the ball of a

pendulum atop the steel gray rim of the sea. And as it swung I followed suit—at one watch I was almost ready to make the break, then within the space of hours I wavered and change my mind. I thought of the recent years, of the films I'd made since the war, stretching off into oblivion under a crust of wasted time, four or five each year. Bastards most of them, conceived in contempt of life and spewn out onto screens across the world with noxious ballyhoo; saying nothing, contemptuous of truth, sullen and lecherous.

Arrow in the Dust, Flaming Feather and *Fort Defiance, Manhandled* and *Kerry Drake; Take Me to Town* and *Variety Girl* and *Golden Hawk*. . . . Maybe two dozen others, names forgotten now. Small wonder I dumped the money they paid me. Money earned like that doesn't deserve to be saved. It's as bad—very nearly—as outright inherited wealth, which is saying a great deal.

The night came down and the moon rose; the constellations wheeled by in somber solitude, looking precisely as they had half my life ago when I was just a sea-struck kid out to conquer the world.

The wind took off at last—around midnight, I think it was. One more gale, I thought, for the faithful vessel to chalk up. I wondered what her total count would show. Fifty years off the Bar, half that time at sea—twenty-five years, with maybe eight hard gales in each. Two hundred storms in all—a lot of wind— a lot of sea—too bad she couldn't speak. And here I was, holding her by the hand, taking her down the road to oblivion.

It was a long night. I dozed, standing, with the teak of the hatch locked in a cold embrace. I saw myself tackling live television for the first time—back to the wall and scared— knowing that in less than three weeks I'd be completely on my own, with five or six million people to witness the wreck.

"A Sound of Different Drummers" the show was called. Produced through Playhouse 90. Directed by John Frankenheimer. It was the fourth day of rehearsal in a barren great hall that was part of Television City—not far from the Mecca corner. The place was full of New York actors—real actors.

And I knew I was in trouble. The ogre of impending memory failure rode me. I tensed up, my mind roamed; when I tried to work or move, I seemed to be half embalmed. And the New York people looked on, and I wondered what was in their minds. They sat in little groups, talking softly, studying the script—yet always alert, it seemed, to my stumbling efforts.

All right, I had decided, I'm licked and that's all there is to it. Best to bow out now instead of on the air. Lunchtime came at last and Frankenheimer drew me to one side.

"What's up, kid?"

"John, I can't go through with this thing."

"That's crap." He spat the words, but there was warmth in his face.

"I'm telling you I'm finished."

"Look. This is nothing unusual, see? Look around. Everyone here has been through the same thing. They survived."

"It's not the same."

"Why not?" He stood in front of me, blocking my view of the doors, one hand hooked in his belt while the other endlessly flicked ash from a cigarette.

"I don't know why—exactly. Maybe because I did a radio show once; it was live, with two thousand people in the audience, back in 1940; and even then, with a script to read, I blew. The goddam paper went blank; not a word on it all of a sudden, and a girl reached over and put her finger on the place—I can see her red nail now—but there wasn't a word in sight—"

"Not a word?"

"No."

"What happened?"

"They cut to a commercial. And afterwards we finished, and it has haunted me ever since. The press had a lot of fun with it, I tell you."

"I still say you can do it. You're made for the part. But you've got to make your fear work for—not against—you."

I shook my head. "No use. You can still replace me, I know that, so that's what you'd better do, because I won't be here after lunch."

Hours later I lay in the back yard under a tree, with the script burning low in the incinerator while the sun beat down and some jazz came over the fence from the house next door. The agent called and the producer called but I held firm, feeling relieved and tortured at the same time. Then Frankenheimer phoned, and when he was through I'd agreed to a meeting later on that night.

Four men now in a doctor's office, somewhere in Beverly Hills: Bob Aurthur, who had written the script; Frankenheimer; Hayden; and Wexler, a psychiatrist and friend. The comfortable room dim-lit, charged with smoke. Quiet and serious talk, punctuated once by a phone call to Van Heflin, who two weeks previously had gone on a live show for the first time.

The voice of the doctor. ". . . I'd like to know how you felt during rehearsal, Van." He waves me toward a second phone—

Heflin speaking. "Terrible. You know I had done thirty or forty shows on Broadway so I was familiar with opening nights —but this was something special. I had to have three martinis at lunch and even then I was so nervous I threw up every day."

Seventy minutes of talk. And somewhere along the way I realized I had to go ahead and give it a try.

After that—freedom. Fourteen hours of work seven days a week. And never any doubt as to the outcome—even toward the end.

The day of the show: a mammoth sound stage hushed; eighty or ninety people standing by while ninety minutes of air time barrel down remorselessly.

An assistant speaks into a mike: "Four minutes until air . . . three minutes . . . places please and stand by—"

From nowhere the coiled gaunt form of Frankenheimer—tie askew, sleeves rolled up, eyes ablaze—a thousand problems shoved aside for what might well be the biggest one of all.

Our eyes meet and he snaps his cigarette, rocking to and fro. "Screw 'em all," he says. Then he turns and jumps for the booth.

The lifting sound of music from far far off—and, incredibly, a feeling of relaxed confidence as I spread my hands and note how steady they are.

Ninety minutes that pass as ten. A hundred and thirty pages of dialogue and never a hitch—until the final speech, when I find myself at a moment of execution—back now to a wall, literally —and suddenly my mind goes blank. "Good God I'm up," I say to myself, "what a hell of a time to blow." And then, to my amazement, the words come slashing out and the executioner pulls the trigger and I pitch sideways into the dirt. And I'm breathing hard as the music swells and the twin red eyes blink off—music to remember, almost a funeral dirge, commemorating the burial of a man's implacable foe, the enemy within.

Tuesday, January 20, 1959. Ten o'clock in the morning. Schooner *Wanderer*—from San Francisco toward ————. Course, SE; Log, 320; Wind, NW (4); Barometer 30.01. Remarks: Moderating all around. Warmer now.

I work a series of sights and make a cross on a chart. Then

I take the brass dividers and step off the miles from the vessel to various ports of call:

Ship to San Francisco Light Vessel 309
Ship to Mecca corner—Hollywood & Vine 169
Ship to Nuku Hiva, Marquesas Islands 3004

A final look and the gathering trace of a smile.

I make my way on deck. "You can set the main," I tell the mate. He throws the coils on deck and spits his quid over the side.

With the big sail set, she shows some sign of life.

"Now run up both your jibs. Then we'll give her the balloon maintopmast stays'l."

Hand over hand, the halyards come home from aloft. The jibs dump barrels of water back where it belongs. Sway up and make fast and coil down.

The foresail is drying amidships, spread around, full of canvas caves, each cave holding a child—hiding from a teacher, with recess about to end.

She moves ahead and settles down, and I go to the wheel. Her head is on southeast by east—Catalina dead ahead.

"Now we'll jibe her around," I say.

Up with the helm, and five men heave away on the mainsheet while Spike holds a turn on the capstan. On south southeast the boom lifts, then leaps to port with a crash.

"Hook up the boom tackle and let her run to the knot."

She gathers her way again and comes to rest, with the compass showing a course of south southwest. Quietly she slides— and fast—as though aware that she's bound for the northeast trade.

Spike straightens up and looks toward the far sea-rim. He stretches and strips to the waist, pressing thick grimed fingers deep in the small of his back. "What'll I put in the log?" he asks.

I think for a moment and then I give him the word. "Just put down: 'Your Honor, sir, the proposed ocean voyage is no longer enjoined—for the record, that is.'"

BOOK II

OUTWARD BOUND

CHAPTER 12

The ship runs free.

Oh the magic of those words! Free as a cloud she goes, with the sun in the east a brass balloon and the shadows adrift in her lee, undulating shadows that swell and collapse in convoluted patterns. Beneath her bows play the porpoise—rending the sea, trailing scarves of stillborn bubbles, lunging sideways in ecstasy, breaching at intervals the blue sea dome of their dark subsurface world; then, grown impatient with the plodding of the ship, they turn and stampede toward the east—hurdlers of hollows and crests.

Now imagine yourself at large on the plains of the broad Pacific eight hundred miles off the coast of Mexico. The Tropic of Cancer lies just ahead, and with it the northeast trades. It is a mellow winter's day, with a vagrant wind that is lost and wandering too.

No need to exert yourself. Just narrow the eyes on the everyday world and loose the imagination . . .

. . . Let the hoarse-voiced traffic fade into the silence of the sea. Silence everywhere, broken now and again when a wave top tumbles forward with the sound of crumpling paper. Your ears are bathed with wind and the sun comes pouring down. Face south and fill your soul with the far horizon's rapture. Now pivot clockwise slowly and rest for a time, looking west. What do you see? Nothing. Nothing but sea and sky. Turn quietly north, with the line of the sea and the low-hung spread of cloud, the shimmer of light and shade, and the spell of loneliness mixed with the call of the sea—the beckoning, bursting, smiling call with a wild promise of worlds unknown and dreams undreamed and a life to live. A wondrous world—undiscovered as yet—a world of challenge and beauty, and peace.

Pivot now toward the east. But wait! Look back. There's a speck on the northern horizon, just a splinter at first; but it grows as it comes, grows to a tower of canvas, leaning away from the wind, rolling lazily—a tall two-masted schooner painted white, her mastheads etching crude legends on the scroll of the sky. An hour and more goes by.

You tread the water now directly under her bows. She stomps on the hills of the sea and buries her stem as she pitches with a flurry of spray and foam. You thrust with your legs as you climb and grasp her bobstay's chain. It is hard and cold in your hands. You're buried clear to the shoulders, with the chain clutched next to your neck. You set your body; her bow soars up, jerking you free of the slope of a watery hill. You twist and you kick and thrash about till you find yourself on her deck, and you're short of breath to be sure, and the sky is full of sails.

Two men at work nearby: stripped to the waist, barefoot; they work in silence, pausing from time to time to glance aloft or scan the sea. Seven youngsters sit cross-legged in the sun by the galley hatch. They're in school, with a teacher young and lean, her black hair cropped short and her eyes a firm brown flecked with green. A clothes line is stretched between the rigging and you hear the crackle of shirts. Pause now and look around—

You are part of an orderly world, the world of a windship's deck. A maze of yellowed cordage leads down from aloft. Each line is belayed to lignum-vitae pins jammed through teak pin-rails. Whaleboat and dories are crammed with oars and gear. Abaft the mainmast stand wooden water casks white of belly and belted with black iron hoops, and they're trimmed with ornamental stars picked out in black and red. Squat iron capstans rise from the quarterdeck. About the ship lie coils of gear, and tackles are hung in the rigging along with odd bits of line and marline strops and a cluster of spare snatch blocks. A workbench straddles the engine-room hatch, with a blacksmith's vise to starboard and a carpenter's vise to port. Beneath the bench stands a sixty-pound anvil on a stump of blackened timber. Next to this is a forge with a bellows that pumps off a treadle.

You, stranger, coming to this deck for the first time would naturally feel ill at ease. Surely, you think, there must be something here to remind a man of the land. There is. Far aft it stands, on legs widespread, to windward of the helm—a Morris chair—fashioned of bastard mahogany, with low-slung lines; a great old hulk of a thing with boards where springs once lay, with six turned stanchionettes beneath each arm and cushions of blood-red canvas long since faded the color of claret (when held to a noonday sun). And, best of all, a pair of cherubs carved at each arm's end, positioned so that a man with a fair-sized hand can cup their heads in his palms as he braces himself against the scend and roll of the ship. When the wind is fair these nymphets smile and when it is foul they frown . . . and sometimes—in the depth of the graveyard watch—they can be heard whispering in a gentle and alien tongue known only to children and wandering homeless men.

Armchair. Midnight: thoughts and stars. Stars and thoughts. The heavens ablaze with a billion distant worlds. The mind ablaze, too, in its own fashion. Something's wrong—with this whirl of emotion and struggle. What in the hell for? The point—what is it? Why take life so seriously, for Jesus Christ's sake? Why not, instead, do as the majority do? Barge along down the road of least resistance, asking no questions, dreaming no dreams save those you hold within grasp.

Six feet ahead of me the helmsman stands, transfixed by a compass rose. I hunch down into the sheepskin coat, my cloth-visored cap pulled low; its flaps encase my ears to their lobes. Stars glow everywhere—ice-cold sparks held by infinity.

Midnight. Tomorrow becomes today. Resolution time—New Day's Resolutions—what will they be? STOP SMOKING! The words flash in my mind: insistent, infuriating, and devoid of conviction. How many times have I danced to this siren song? Twenty-five years of smoking, with the swearing-off vows ever present—ten thousand private treaties to go with ten thousand dawns, to be broken an hour later.

I grope for the cigarettes.

What power is this? This crawling malevolent need to indulge a habit that cakes the throat and dulls the brain? I shake my head with a muttered oath as I rake the match and inhale. When will some fellow slave write the truth of this matter? Forgetting the cancer quotient, which isn't the point at all. Forgetting the perversion of truth in the advertisements; bad as that is, the tobacco merchant is only playing the game. Sell Sell Sell. And the public be damned. Which it is.

A deep drag and the cloudlet of smoke feels good as it pounces on the lungs. A miracle, this. What other resolution can be sworn to and raped in a breath?

Then why the lure of abstinence? Perhaps the answer is simple, for the reward is readily seen. Stop smoking for only a few hours and a feeling of sharpness grows; irritability too, but with it a drive and precision and a need to go and do.

I flick the ash and ram the butt in my mouth. The cheeks contract as I suck, and the peak of my cap looms close, with the void of the night beyond. The man at the wheel looks aft. This I pretend to ignore. He turns up his collar and thrashes his arms.

"What are you steering?" I growl, by way of being cordial.

"South southwest," he says, full of confidence.

"Oh, so it's you, Doc—I thought you were Dennis—"

"I wish I was." He stifles a yawn. "I'm a little behind on my sleep." Then, an afterthought: "I borrowed Dennis's jacket."

I ditch the cigarette, get to my feet, and clump toward the break of the poop. The stars play peekaboo between a patchwork of cloud, and the tendons of halyard are rigid as bone, and moist. The ladderlike ratlines between the shrouds comb up and down against Orion's massive belt. I drop down the galley steps and go for a mug of tea.

Armchair. Four bells in the graveyard watch:

My legs crossed at the ankles, with a heel on the quarter bitt, and I'm neither asleep nor awake. Two sides of the mind at war—beyond my conscious control. It's as though I were banished to some outermost seat in a gigantic amphitheater with a prize fight in progress below. I follow the action as best I can with a powerful telescope. The only trouble is, I'm holding it wrong end to . . .

So the feeling of triumph is gone—

And why not?

Too bad. That was a brave big start you made—

I'm fresh out of guts, so it seems.

Who says?

I do. How do I know? Simple. We're running for cover already. Hand over hand for Tahiti, where the girls and the living are soft.

Change course, then. Indonesia lies west by south, six thousand miles away. Screw Tahiti, go west before it's too late—

But it's friendly and safe in Tahiti.

Quiet! Span the Pacific in one flamboyant passage, leave New Guinea under your lee and prowl for a time in the labyrinthine Celebes—

Easier said than done. Let's quit while we're still ahead. Let's just barrel down through the trades and reap the rewards of Defiance.

What defiance?

Why, don't you know? Of the California courts, what else?

That's a joke, isn't it? Defiance for Christ's sake. So what if you thumbed your nose at a legal paper, does this entitle you to pose as a hero of sorts? Is this your claim to membership in the brigade of embattled men?

It's better than being an actor.

Damn near anything is! Very well, then, why not go east instead, to a place like Cuba perhaps—

Cuba?

Yes Cuba, C-U-B-A. You're immersed (so you say) in the cult of revolt. Put up or shut up. Go where the fighting is rough; go anywhere in Central or South America since you're frightened of going to Asia—

Not frightened—sensible, that's all. There's a hell of a difference, you know.

Sure I know; but we digress. Stop kidding yourself. Your mind was made up two weeks ago, on the day you bought those charts. There's something intriguing in this—you bought the charts, then ten minutes later you covered yourself with visas, French visas, to be used in French Oceania. What a character. Quite the Actor really. All you've managed to do is trade in the spotlight of Hollywood for the glow (you trust) of public acclaim—

Not so!

Can't wait, can you, till you get to Tahiti and pick up the mail and bask in your headlined reviews. Big deal. HAYDEN THE WANDERER—Hayden the Hero, fresh from the barricades and the no-man's-land of Department 34. Great. Great title for a story, wouldn't you say?

Perhaps.

Not by a goddamned sight!

Armchair. Daybreak.

The morning star lies low in the east like the masthead light of a liner. Behind it the pitch-black wall of sky dissolves, struggling in vain to stem the advance of the fog-gray dawn.

I awake with a start, a bitter taste in the mouth. What's this, I think, as I sense the force of the wind. You, stranger! Do you hear that moan in the rigging? Do you hear that roar overside? She's rolling now, logging a good nine knots, I'd guess, to the tune of each passing hour. The tousled heads of the nymphets lie patient and hard in my palms.

The mate, with a hold on the wheel, his halibut shirt turned up.

"How does she feel?" I ask as I search for the cigarettes.

"Great." He gives her a couple of spokes. "Steers like she's charmed."

"Maybe she is." I smile as she wets her rail.

"Plenty of wind in them clouds." He thrusts his jaw to the east.

"You bet your life there is." I chew on the filter tip and lurch to leeward of the thickset binnacle housing. "Something tells me, friend, that we've got us the northeast trade." I get rid of my flannel cap, then line up the rose of the compass with the place where the wind comes from.

Some ash blows into my eyes. I spit the butt toward the rail.

I stiffen one hand and chop it at arm's length above the bowl of the compass. My eyes water as I vane the wind with a measured shake of the head. When the draft feels even on both my ears I chop once more with the hand and read the compass bearing. "Northeast by north it is, by God."

The east banked high with a glacial predawn light. I stand to the wheel. "Go get your coffee." He climbs from the cockpit with a hand on the brim of his hat. "And while you're passing by, give her three fathom of main sheet—"

I steady her down and look about for the watch. No one in sight, but the folds of a sail in the dory reveal a couple of bodies

—dead to the world in quest of rest or escape. Let them sleep. I prefer to be by myself.

Night thoughts race in review. I try to hold them and sort them out, but they vanish like smoke, and I'm left with the wheel in my hands and a vessel that thunders downwind.

The sense of disturbance prevails—deep-set, its roots in self-contempt. This is the feeling that gnaws at a man whether he wants to admit it or not. I've lived with such torment for years and maybe I always will.

But—I can't help asking myself—was it really always this way? Weren't there years when I thought of my life with pride? Yes, there were. Those were the seafaring years, with my eyes on the goal of command, with each new ship and each new job a challenge, when I hurled myself at the work with good strong hands and never a thought of failure—so it seemed at the time.

Now the eastern sky erupts: the cloud wrack aflame in scarlet and gold, with a backdrop of ivory and jade. Spike comes up on deck and prods the forms in the canvas. He leans on the workbench with folded arms and gazes at the dawn.

And I follow his gaze—to an eastward sky—to a long-gone world of childhood—far oh far to the east. The core and the key to it all.

🖎

CHAPTER 13

The world was like this.

Ours was a nice house in a nice part of a nice town. Everything was nice—neighborhood, flower beds, cars, schools, clubs, churches—nice and pleasant, nice and neat and law-abiding and clean.

The parents were nice, too.

At the foot of the hill was Grove Street, and on the far side it wasn't so nice; it was full of wops and crude farmers with rickety houses and children that played in junked cars where the front lawn was supposed to be.

New Jersey was proud of Upper Montclair, an island five

miles in diameter surrounded by a sea of coarse common people, surrounded by tough towns, dismal towns—like Newark, Passaic, Patterson, and Boonton.

This is what they taught me. Nonsense. They didn't have to teach me. I simply knew it was true. All of us knew it. There were no two ways about it.

America, "My America," was the greatest place in the world. Ours were the proudest heritage and the highest standard of living the world had ever known—or ever would know. I was one lucky lad to be born an American. The American Revolution was the greatest event since the birth of Christ. Europe was made up mostly of ignorant peasants who loved to war with one another, which was no affair of ours (until the dirty Hun sank the *Lusitania,* then we jumped a patriotic jump into the air and came down with both fists flying and knocked out the Hun and that was the end of that). But, sad to relate, our allies were too stupid to appreciate this and admit we won their war.

Oh they taught me—I mean I knew—a lot of things.

Asia was full of yellow people. The "Chinks," good for running laundries and making lanterns and firecrackers but not to be trusted at all. The "Japs" of course were not to be trusted either. But we had to admit they were capable, capable of copying the U.S.A. (except for the time their spies stole our battleship blueprints and built themselves a copy that turned upside down when launched—served them right, too).

The rest of the world was made up of "natives"—shiftless natives miles behind the times who would always be vastly inferior no matter how hard we tried to help. They weren't so bad really, provided they stayed at home. But they took advantage of our hospitality. As soon as they came in past the Statue of Liberty, they began to stir up trouble; they clung together in tenements and robbed and went on strikes and gnawed away at the strong clean roots of the American Way of Life. Yes sir.

The world was round. We all knew that. It was round and big, and right spang in the center was the United States of America. We were mighty proud of our doughboys, who had just won the war for the snobs in England, who couldn't get over the Revolution and the War of 1812, and the same went for the Frogs in France, who drank wine all the time and didn't have any morals.

Eddie Rickenbacker and his buddies of the "Hat in the Ring

Squadron" pretty nearly won the war singlehandedly. But some of the Huns who flew in the air were good eggs too. It didn't matter much which side you were on if you were a flier because they did not use poison gas or sink women and children with U-boats. All fliers wore scarves of pure white silk that trailed in the wind, and they waved with gauntleted hands and smiled broad smiles through great big goggles.

And there was never going to be another war. America had seen to that. You bet.

You could tell what your neighbors were like by the size house they had, the kind of car they drove, and the way they dressed. Also by the part of town they lived in. Upper Montclair was of course the best place in the U.S.A., and the best part of it was along the hills on Upper Mountain Avenue where the biggest houses were. (Some of these houses had three and four cars and a wing full of maids.)

The next nicest part of town was the flatland between our house and where the rich folks lived. Mostly these were two-car houses and the men wore knickers weekends, but it was seldom you saw them washing their cars or mowing their lawns. Some of them had servants, too, but not the kind that lived in.

Where we lived wasn't quite so nice, but it was all right, you understand. The trouble was the houses were close together and most of them were ugly. We were different, though. Our house was on a corner, which gave us a certain distinction and more lawn space and almost twice as many trees. We had four climbing trees and several big bushes and four separate flower beds, not counting the rhubarb patch in the shade of the garage. Also we had flower boxes around the sunporch and a driveway made of gravel.

The Lucases lived next door. Virginia was my age, with straight hair and thick ankles, and our bedroom windows faced each other, which was good when she didn't get the shade all the way down. But they didn't have a garage. Or even a driveway.

Next to them lived the Lords. I called him Uncle Jack. His wife had cancer and her bedroom smelled a horrible smell and once I saw the tube. He drove an Essex sedan and the garage was lined with different-colored license plates. In fact, he had the biggest collection of license plates anywhere around. We knew who made these plates all right. The prisoners did—

maybe up at Sing Sing, which was an important institution because it helped to purify the country.

Beyond the Lords's house was a partially thicketed field. This
was handy for hiding in, if there was trouble at home. It had
furrows and goldenrod. The goldenrod was okay but the furrows
weren't, not for baseball. The field also had mounds of dirt
overgrown with bushes and grass. For a time we thought Indians
were buried underneath, but as we grew up we had to admit
that the place was a dumping ground. These mounds were good
for storming. We pretended there were trenches in between
and we'd choose sides and play "Yankees and Huns." It was
tough being a Hun because you had to get bayoneted no matter
how hard you fought.

Two doors away, on the other side, lived Colonel MacNair.
He was our hero. In addition to being an ex-warrior, he towered
six foot four, was built in proportion, and had a bristling red
mustache. Always he walked to and from the railroad depot a
mile and a half away. When he came to the corners, he didn't
turn like most commutermen did. Instead he performed a
ninety-degree maneuver and banged one foot on the walk as he
took off in the new direction. He taught us to drill with wooden
rifles and to sneak up on the enemy's position. Weekends his
yard was full of kids crawling across the grass on elbows and
bellies, with bullets flying over their heads. He also had a bad-
minton game set up next to his garage. This was a sissy thing
for a colonel to have, but we did not let on.

My father was six foot three, which was plenty tall, and he
looked even taller because he was skinny. He had hunched-up
narrow shoulders, delicate hands, huge brown eyes, and he
dressed like the men in the ads. But what I wanted was a father
like my Uncle Mont Sterling. They had named me after him,
and also he was my godfather, whatever that meant—I didn't
see him often. But I knew he was six foot two and he weighed
more than two hundred pounds and his shoulders were mighty
broad. He lived in an apartment in New York and he boxed and
taught revolver shooting in his spare time to the state police.
He was president of a business corporation, which was natural
and fine—except it was a perfume company. He had a tanned
face and he parted his hair in the middle. People said I looked
just like him, or would when I grew up. He gave me a real
bayonet. It had dried blood near the handle—German blood, I
could tell; but it turned out later on to be nothing but rust.

My father's name was George and there was something wrong with his health. He would never play with me and when he came home from work in the evening he went to bed right away. I felt a little sorry for him. He never talked to me either, except to bawl me out. He sold advertising for the *World*, a New York newspaper. I was glad that he worked on a paper but sorry he wasn't a reporter. But he was paid more than a hundred a week, which made up for some of the other things. He had been born in upstate New York and orphaned before he was eight. Relatives raised him, but they were mean, so he ran away to Manhattan at sixteen or so.

My mother was something special. She was big and strong and weighed twenty pounds more than my father. She loved me very much. Next to me, what she loved most was her Steinway grand piano. She played beautifully, and no wonder: until she met my father she practiced eight hours a day, and was said to be a genius of sorts.

We lived a peaceful life, so peaceful, in fact, that it made me restless. My father went to the city six days a week, fifty weeks a year. In he would go on the seven eighteen and back he would come on the train that arrived at six fifty-three. He couldn't walk the way Colonel MacNair and some of the other men did, so my mother took him back and forth from the depot. Each morning he picked a sweet william from the flower bed that was too wide to jump across unless you backed off and came on with a run.

We owned a Willys Knight sedan. It was blue and black, and its wheels had big wooden spokes. There was an odd-looking vase between the doors, and the radiator cap was crowned with a round thermometer that looked back at you whenever you went for a drive.

Saturday afternoons my father washed and polished the car, and that night was the time for playing bridge or mahjong, or sometimes a movie. Sundays were worst of all, not because of church so much, though that was bad enough, but because we always went for long long drives in the country. Everyone else was driving too, and there was always traffic in long black lines no matter which way we went. When we got some place, we had to get out and picnic and collect a vine called bittersweet. It always grew in the brambles or in old dead trees, and the fields were blazing hot. I came to hate those orange-red berries.

On the return trip the air would be full of exhaust smoke and people would peer at one another and little squirts would make faces at you with ice cream running down and mustard under their noses. The turnpikes were lined with hot-dog stands and balloon stands, and I would be in the back seat, up to my neck in bittersweet, with nothing better to do than count cars and telephone poles and stare at the red mark as it rose in the temperature gauge. Our two-week vacation was always spent at Lake Minnewaska, at a huge frame hotel in the Catskills—the only good thing about it was the lake, which had no bottom. The women wore bloomers and the men wore knickers and ties, except in the evening, when they changed to white flannel pants and coats and two-toned shoes that were pointed and dotted with holes.

The water on the lake plop-plopped on the floats and the people looked strange in canoes. I saw my father in a bathing suit only once. He looked like a baby giraffe without spots. He taught me to swim by throwing me off the dock with a rope made fast to my middle. He and mother had an argument about that.

That was our life, and the years rolled by.

I could tell from the start that the main thing in life was to make a success of yourself. Success meant money. If you behaved at home and got good marks in school, you might go to college, and with college you had a running start up the hill that led to success. But also you had to be clever and full of steam and determination to work your way to the top. And if you were all these things, there was a chance you would grow up to be a millionaire, or even President.

Money of course was for grown-ups. Kids had to be honest and decent and clean. I did not do very well in school so I decided to make it up by being pure. I was about the purest boy in the neighborhood and the closer I got to the house the purer I became.

There was no drinking at home. Except for the time I awakened one night to the sound of a row in the street. I peered from my window and saw three men with their arms around one another. They were doing a kind of foxtrot in the street which went all right till they veered off into the gutter. Then one fellow threw a rock at the street light overhead and he spun around and fell on his face in our tulips.

First thing next morning I checked the tulip bed, but he was gone. We sat down to breakfast, my father all buttoned up in his severe suit, with a stiff collar and a stickpin, and as he sipped his coffee his little finger stuck straight out.

"Mother, did you see those men last night?"

"What men, son?"

"The ones in the street who were singing."

She looked toward my father, who was all wrapped up in his paper. Then she tried a smile and looked down until at last she said: "Yes son, I'm sorry to say I did."

"They were dizzy, weren't they, Mother? Maybe they were sick or something."

Father took out his watch, looked at his nails, then got up and went toward the kitchen.

"No, son, they weren't sick, not really." She leaned forward. "Son, I'm going to tell you something. Those boys were DRUNK. Terrible! Just think, son, how their mothers would feel if they'd seen their boys last night."

I thought about it as I stood by the tulip bed and the sedan went by with Mother driving and Father erect, his eyes on the temperature gauge.

᠀

CHAPTER 14

He might have been five years old that night.

His pajamas were woolly and warm and all in one piece, with built-in feet and a trap in the back. He waited in taut-stretched silence for his parents to disappear. (They would be gone all evening, that much he knew.)

The door closed with a click and moments later the ceiling was scoured by the light of the green-lidded headlamps, and at last they were alone. Her name was Margaret. She lived beyond the foot of the hill. She had a sister who was also a baby sitter but Margaret was prettier, and the boy was secretly in love with her.

She had beautiful legs that pulled at the boy like a magnet. His heart began to pound, and he watched with the sides of his eyes as she settled herself in the big chair with the deep cushion not far from the fireplace. From his place on the floor by the bookcase he could see what she did with her legs. (He

paged through a volume of *The Book of Knowledge*—the one
with pictures of armor.)

You could hear the shouts of the coasters when their sleds
ran down the hill. He still had an hour before he must go to
bed. (Even the horses had armor, with slits for their eyes.)

"Margaret, will you tuck me into bed?"

"Yes, of course. Be quiet now and let me read."

She kicked off her shoes and rubbed the calf of a leg with
the arch of her other foot. He climbed to his feet and found
the footstool ("toadstool," he called it) and dragged it up to
her feet. "Thank you," she said without looking up from her
book; then she snuggled in the chair and crossed her legs with
one foot at rest on his toadstool.

It was time now. Time to start on his journey. All through the
day he had relished the thought of this moment. His heart was
pounding faster and his chest felt tight when he breathed. He
closed the big book and lay on the floor and began to pretend
he was swimming. Each time he turned up his head for a
breath, he could see her under the light. Her skirt hung loose
from above her knees, and across from her was the couch.

He rolled on his back, which moved him toward her a little.
Now he spread wide his arms and tried to look as if he were
floating on top of the lake that didn't have any bottom. He
breathed deep to keep from sinking. After a time he turned to
the right and saw that she hadn't moved. She was lost in her
book, and the line of her skirt was the same. He began to swim
toward the porch, and he puffed out a noise like that of a small
steam launch—just enough steam to be heard.

His path lay close to her legs. He got up steam, his eyes
staring up at the ceiling, but he rolled in her direction as he
brushed past the stool; and he looked a quick look and he could
see where her thighs disappeared. He felt all choked up. It was
dark and astounding above the roll of her stockings.

Much too dark. Yet his head was bursting, like the times he'd
stood on it with his feet against a tree, so he turned on the
steam and rolled back on his belly and swam like a streak
toward the porch.

He sat right side up for a bit next to the fireplace tongs. She
picked at her teeth. He measured the angle from the light by
the couch to the place where her legs were resting. Just like my
father, he thought—turning off all the lights except one. He
took himself out to the porch. The clock struck seven-thirty.

Two sleds zipped like rockets through the band of light in front of the telephone pole. "Gangway!" cried the coaster as sparks shot out from the runners.

She nodded a little. The book slipped from her thigh toward her lap, pulling the skirt up with it. He wished he had the nerve to take up his book and plunk himself down on the couch across from her and turn on the light by his shoulder. Nothing doing. What if she woke up and discovered what he was doing? What if she told his parents? Or the folks in the neighborhood—

Nothing to do but crawl on all fours behind the back of the couch. Softly. When he came to the place where he wanted to be, he placed his cheek to the floor and peered underneath toward her chair. Just as he figured—the base of the couch was too low, and all he could see were the edge of the rug and some cobwebs.

Back to the bookcase, back to the armor on the page. (What on earth did a knight do if he was all armored up and wanted to pee or something?)

The girl comes awake with a shudder. She leans past the wing of the chair and looks at the clock and glances at him, then she takes up her book once more. She recrosses her legs, this time wide apart with one ankle at rest on a knee.

He feels he's about to be swallowed. He looks away and his eyes roam the room till they rest on an unused door. It leads to the kitchen—right at the foot of the stairs—directly across from her chair.

Like a flash he bounds through the darkened dining room. He butts through the swinging door and punches the pearl-tipped button that triggers the kitchen light. The big bulb lights up. He takes a banana and peels it down as he slides the side door open and enters the living room.

She hasn't changed position. The shaft of the kitchen light lies up and down her body, and her face is in the shade of the book. He puts down the banana, then drops flat out on the rug. No time for a backstroke now. Full ahead he goes, arms aflail.

What if she finds him out? Never mind that, never mind a thing in the world, her legs are right and the light is right and he scrunches along, and just as he starts to look up, her legs snap shut and her book snaps shut and she leans right down toward his face. She laughs and tosses her head. "For heaven's sake, you silly thing, whatever on earth are you doing?"

Straight for the porch he goes: "Look, Margaret, I'm swimming, I'm doing the Australian crawl. . . ."

The sill of the sun porch door hurts as he crosses.

Then he stands by himself in the sun porch. At least his body
does (all done up in the woolly pajamas with the built-in feet
and the trap door in back with the buttons). But his mind is
lost and gone, swept out of reach in a thundering wave of
humiliation.

And up in the sky there are stars, but the street light steals
them away and all you can see are some branches, naked and
cold and gaunt.

He must have been seven that summer, or eight at the most.
The table was set, the candles were lit, and in one corner stood a
tall parcel wrapped in thick brown paper. His father came into
the room, fresh from his after-work nap, wearing a long narrow
robe with a fancy silk kerchief splayed flat between the lapels.

The boy remained standing until both his parents were seated.
His eyes were fixed on the parcel. "Please, Father, can't I open
it now, while you're carving?"

"*Mayn't* not *can't* I open it; no, you *may* not, but you *may*
open it after we've finished our supper—"

He knew well enough what was in the parcel. A telescope. A
gift from his Uncle Mont—a brand-new instrument to observe
the heavens with. It took the astronomical bodies and turned
them upside down, which meant it wasn't an ordinary 'scope at
all. He had been studying for months to be an astronomer (or
at least a surveyor or a civil engineer with high boots and a hat
like Teddy Roosevelt's). One thing sure—nothing was more
worthwhile for a boy than to be an astronomer. His father didn't
agree.

The parents ate with infinite care, chewing and chewing and
chewing. The boy felt he would jump out of his skin if they
didn't excuse him. He had a secret load of lima beans in one
side of his mouth; he would spit it in the sink when he carried
the first dishes to the kitchen—but when would that be? He
fidgeted and fixed his eyes on the bowl of moss and sprigs and
things with the Japanese bridge in the middle; he wished he
lived under the bridge or in one of the tiny trees along with
his telescope and his collie dog; and after a long while his father
cleared his throat and that meant you could clear the table.

The tube of the telescope was three feet long and slender and painted with gray enamel, and there were brass pinions and knobs to manipulate, and a tripod with sliding legs. He took it outside and walked across the yard and the road and set it up on the sidewalk in front of a vacant lot. The moon was rising over Passaic, but where he was there were branches overhead.

He cradled the gift and trudged out into the field. Mosquitoes swarmed round his face and clung to his neck and hands, and he stood there staring back at his house across the street. It looked just like his father, tall and narrow and white all over, with two big bedroom windows upstairs staring coldly into the night.

The boy came on tiptoes into the living room. His mother was knitting some socks, and his father lay prone on the couch with his hair slicked back, reading the evening paper.

"Father?"

"What is it?"

"Can—may I build an observatory on top of the garage?"

"On top of the what? Of course not—split the shingles and start leaks all over the place—or fall off and kill yourself."

"But, Father, it's only ten feet high—"

"No."

"But if I'm going to be an astronomer I need a place to study."

"You have windows in your room. Use them. Now don't bother me any more."

He kissed his mother good-night and slipped up to bed in his attic room. When the town clock struck ten, he eased out of bed and put on his sneakers. The heat of the day lay trapped in the room. He peered down the slab of the house front to be sure their lights were out; then he picked up the magical gift and moved down the hall and climbed through the dormer window onto the porch roof. Virginia's window was just a few yards away. It was black as coal between the houses and the ground seemed a long way off and he didn't dare look down. (She and her folks were away on their summer vacation on Long Island Sound, so they wouldn't discover him and give the alarm.)

Overhead was the moon in a whole great world full of stars. The air smelled fresh and cool, and the fireflies were busy signaling one another with their orange lanterns. The shingles made crackling sounds and the roof seemed to rise like the steeple of the Congregational Church. He clung to the ridge of the dormer and hauled himself to the top and rested there with his telescope held as if it were an infant. And his heart was jumping.

Virginia's window stared up with a sullen look—strange, he thought, that they don't divide all windows into panes like those on old New England farmhouses. What could be less attractive than a big window divided in two down the middle—suddenly he thought of what they used to do when both of them were small. (How long ago it seemed, and the longer the better too— he was glad to have outgrown that kind of thing before it got him in trouble.)

Every so often their parents would go out for the evening together, and since they lived next door he'd stay at the Lucases' house. He would have on his robe and slippers and he'd fill a little black satchel with make-believe instruments and this would make him a doctor—scissors and a bandage and shoe-horns and a flashlight and even a buttonhook (with a pearl handle). Then he would go to the other room to wait for the emergency call—

"Ding a ling a ling a ling," she would say.

"Hello there," he replied.

"Oh, Doctor, it's me, could you please come over right now because there is something wrong with my health."

"Yes yes, I'll be right over."

He'd make an automobile sound and slam on the brakes and bang the door; then he'd vault up the steps and knock on her door. Her voice would say "Come in" and he would find her cross-legged on her big white bed, with her pillow clutched to her tummy. Back and forth she would rock and you could tell right away she was in agonizing pain. He would make her lie down and drink some water while he commenced the examination. First the ears and the nose and the mouth, with the flash-light held in one hand and the shoehorn to hold down the tongue. "Well," he exclaimed, "nothing wrong up here," and he'd shake his head. "Can you tell me just where it hurts?"

"Somewheres—right—down here." Her voice was faint as she placed one little hand near her belly.

"Oh ho, that's different." He would thump and probe from her shoulders to her waist, careful not to hurry or let on that his fingers were nervous.

Then he'd switch to her feet and work slowly up toward the pillow, and about this time she would take the pillow and bury her face under it. The rest wasn't quite so clear; all he remembered was the way her body looked and it would jump a little from time to time and once she cried out, which frightened him. And he promised he wouldn't do that again; to prove how sorry he was he took sick himself and let her be the doctor for once. Girls were a nuisance most of the time, but not if a fellow was sick.

The memory drifted away, and he spraddled the roof and pointed his telescope toward a big yellow planet above the Westendorfs' house. Once or twice he saw it streaking past but he could not make it come to rest in the tube. The moon was too high to look at, and he felt tired and shivered a little. Dew formed on the tube so he tucked it under one arm and climbed back down and through the window. He wiped off the telescope with a towel and flopped into bed, but he didn't fall asleep until after the clock struck two.

There was something mysterious about certain things—vague thoughts, sometimes veiled so much you felt they maybe didn't exist, though something told you they did.

What bothered you most was that you had no way of knowing if these things bothered your friends too. It didn't seem they did: you could easily picture the rest of the gang worrying about home runs and homework and report cards and lima beans, but you couldn't even dream they'd do things with button-hooks or spend an evening doing the Australian crawl up and down the living-room floor.

My father taught me one thing and my mother taught me something else, and their teachings were somehow related to the veiled part but not the way I had hoped.

He was shaving one morning when I had a hurry call so I bounded through the bathroom door and put up the seat with a crash. Then I stood there trying to drill clear through the water in the bowl before my pressure gave out. The window was open enough so you could see the trees in the brilliant sunshine, but there wasn't much wind.

He slapped his razor back and forth on the brown side of the strop. His hair was combed to perfection as if he hadn't even slept. "Boy, why do you make all that noise?"

This didn't seem like much of a question and I didn't know how to answer. "A gentleman," he went on, "always hits the back or the sides of the bowl, never the water itself."

I mulled this over and lifted my sights and tried to erase the little oval trademark without spilling a drop or even spraying over the rim toward where the Dutch girl on the can was scuttling along in pursuit of old devil dirt.

"Also, young fellow, if you would pull the chain before you begin, it would deaden the sound altogether." He turned away and bent down and went on with his shaving.

Some time after that—or it might have been before—I was taking a bath when my mother came into the room. I had a homemade heavy cruiser the size of a watermelon with me in the tub, as well as a submarine that wouldn't sink unless you kept one foot on it. I had been preparing to ambush the cruiser, but I could tell right away my mother was bothered by something.

She kept fussing around with the towels, and once I caught her looking at me over her shoulder in the mirror. Finally she cleared her throat and turned around and took a deep breath and her voice had a different tone. "Buzz, you're going to grow up to be a very fine man and some day you will marry a lovely girl."

"Like you, Mother?" This slowed her down, and the sides of her mouth seemed to quiver, but she managed to keep going. "And of course after you're married you'll want to have babies just like everyone else—"

I allowed the submarine to float up and I gave her my strict attention. "Now son," she said, "perhaps you've heard your friends making jokes about things—" She stopped.

I said nothing.

"Have you?" Hopefully.

"What kind of jokes?"

"About boys and girls. About men and women. About their being different and about their doing things together?"

"No, Mother."

"Well, son, just remember that having babies is the most beautiful thing in the world, and if you ever hear anything nasty or dirty—if you ever hear any bad stories and jokes about this—then your father and I want you to close your ears, and you must always feel free to come to us with your questions."

I nodded my head and wondered what she had in mind.

"They may make fun of you for this, but if you just walk away, why some day when you're a big man and you've found the right girl you'll be proud of what you did. Do you understand?"

I understood nothing. So I sank the sub by the drain and opened up with my best smile and said: "Yes, Mother, I understand."

She drew a deep breath.

"Thank you, son. Oh Buzzy, you have such a wonderful smile, you should try to use it more often."

I smiled all the harder. "Yes, I will."

She glanced at my battleship and dabbed at her eyes as she swept toward the doorway, and I heard her stumble when she came to the rug in the hall.

CHAPTER 15

The door was of varnished oak, and it might have been twenty feet tall, with a huge brass knob and gilt lettering (edged with black)—PRINCIPAL. My hands felt perishing small.

"Sit down, Sterling." Indicating a chair, like a king crab, with a back rest of blackened leather. He was tall and had a beaked nose; his spectacles were secured by a black ribbon draped over one ear; and his teeth were perfect. The flag stood in a corner, with a golden fringe.

The shades were lowered and green, with a border of sunlight that spoke of the outer world. He leaned back in his swivel chair, made a tepee out of his hands, then placed the tips of his index fingers flush against his mouth. I thought for a second he was going to try to whistle, but he just tapped the tips together, lifted his eyebrows twice, and looked with distaste at a report beyond his wrist. The desk was enormous—good for courts-martial and turning down pardons.

"Young man, what are we going to do about Sterling Relyea Walter?"

"I don't know, sir."

"He's a nice young fellow, wouldn't you say?"

"I don't know, sir."

"But he won't study, will he. He's repeating third grade, and he may not pass this time either, since he's failing four out of five subjects."

I take deep breaths one on top of the other because that, according to Strongfort the muscle-builder, is the way to remain calm.

"And this morning he brought a pea-shooter to class instead of a written assignment and at lunch time he fought in the hall with Eleanor Finley and now, not more than two hours ago, he threw a rock—" He exhibits a stone, medium-sized and veined, suitable for throwing. "He threw this, this boulder at Miss Finley in the cafeteria. . . . Had you heard about this episode?"

"Yes sir, I had, sir."

"The window was halfway open, but he smashed it, and that window, by the way, is one of the most expensive in the school. . . . Quite a chap, wouldn't you have to agree—this Sterling Relyea Walter?"

I tried to look him in the eye. He filled his pipe, inspected it, packed it, and finally put a match to it. "I don't like to expel any student, provided he tries. But when a student refuses to co-operate, my hands are tied and there is nothing for me to do but send that boy away. You are expelled, young man. I will call your mother now and tell her you're coming home."

"Yes, sir."

The door looks not so huge and the knob feels cold. I close it with care as I leave.

My mother said nothing. When she tried to smile, her mouth quivered and she sobbed. I could see the tears as I started for my room in the attic. It was hot under the eaves and I lay on the bed thinking—about nothing in particular and about everything. I thought of running away. But where? I didn't want to run away. I wanted another chance to make good at school so they could all be proud of me and then I'd grow up to be proper and a big success and maybe even a millionaire. But a gentleman for sure.

The car ground up the hill to the station in second gear, and twenty minutes later it came back down. I couldn't see my father, but I heard him climb to the floor below, and I knew he was taking his rest before dealing out punishment.

What wind there had been went down with the sun. It was doubly hot now. He came up the steps slowly, pausing at the landing with both hands on the rail. I was puzzled to see him, for as a rule when things went wrong he called me down to the basement, where he sat on the fireless cooker holding the thin piece of wood with the special hole in the far end. Sometimes he dipped it in water he'd drawn in the laundry tub, and then it hurt even more.

Now he sat on my bed and I stood in the corner. He looked out the window for a long time, saying nothing. His face seemed soft and gentle. I could hear Mother at the foot of my stairs. I thought of the way I treated him, not with open defiance so much as with silent contempt, with sly remarks about other fathers who did this and that. The crickets were busy out in the field, and so was the frog by the gutter.

"Son"—his voice had a sorrowful tone—"I don't know what to do with you."

"Why don't you go ahead and wallop me?"

He shook his head with his jaws thrown out of line, which gave him a puzzled look. "No. You're too old for spanking. I'm going to try something different this time. There's a man I know who has a son who has been a good deal of trouble."

I tried to look contrite and eager to understand.

"When this man's son was your age, he was expelled from school, too. And do you know where he is today?"

"No, Father, where is he?"

"He is in prison. In Sing Sing."

I felt an aching down inside.

"So I'm going to take you with me tomorrow into the city. And when Mr. Wexon has the time, I want him to talk with you. And after that, maybe we can go for a visit to a place where they keep boys who have been in trouble. Do you know, son, what they call places like that?"

"Yes, Father."

"What?"

"Reformatories?"

"How would you like to live in a place like that?"

I wanted to cry but I couldn't. I wanted to cry for the effect it would make, not because I was scared. I knew he would never send me away, and if he tried, Mother would come to my rescue. I managed to sob but my eyes stayed dry so I dabbed at them anyhow. He rose to his feet slowly; his head touched the ceiling and he had to duck.

That night I dreamed of a huge brick building set on the side of a hill, with a tall wire fence all around. I knew well enough what was in the wires: electricity. And there was concrete instead of grass and bars in the windows and the toughest gang of boys you could imagine in long ragged pants with big arms and bad teeth who fought all the time.

When I awakened at dawn, I slid out of bed and came back with a leap and *The Wonder Book of Ships.* My troubles seemed unimportant. The one thing that mattered was the trip to Manhattan.

I hustled through dressing and took care not to make noise in the toilet; in fact, I sat down, though I didn't need to, but it was safest that way. He was dressed like Wilson was in the picture in the *National Geographic,* and I wore my church suit with long trousers.

We waited at the east end of the station platform so as to avoid the smoking cars. The place was lined with men all dressed alike, with papers folded just so. When I tried to fold my paper the way they did, the whole thing fell apart. As soon as Mother was out of sight, I began really to feel free. What if he did try to put me away somewhere—I'd make an escape and go out West and join the Forest Rangers.

He sat by the window, and I dangled out on the aisle. This was a setback; part of the fun was watching the world go by, even if it was mostly dump heaps and the backs of houses.

I began to count the advertisements that ranged the length of the coach. They had to do with tooth decay and bad breath and saving your money. It was much more fun to look at the little stained-glass windows across from the fans. A friend of my father's showed up, and my father gave me a nudge: "Run along, son, and mind you stay out of trouble."

I moved to the rear and found the paper cups but the water wouldn't work so I braced myself like a man of the world and peered through the rear-door window. The stations were close together, and each stop let in a stream of men with satchels and papers. Finally I hauled open the door and stepped to the side of the platform.

This was the way to do it! The wind rushed by full of cinders. The clouds were right overhead, and I staked a claim on one that had a dent on top, where you could lie down and observe the earth. I waved happily to people standing by the crossing gates with the bells ringing, particularly to the old codgers with vests who held a sign saying "STOP."

It seemed to me these men had the right idea. Each had his guardhouse with a stovepipe sticking up and geranium beds all around, and once I saw a cat sitting in a window as we blasted past in a swirl of dirt. They did not wear ties and they smoked pipes. What more did anybody want? No one bossed them around, and if they wanted to, they could sit in the sun or work on the flowers. Maybe if my father did something like this he wouldn't be so tired all the time.

We started to cross a wide belt of swampland called the Meadows. It stretched for miles, and I pretended it was the prairie out West. Huge smouldering dumps appeared, and nests of broken-down shanties clustered together like savage villages, but made of rusted sheet iron, with splintered doors, and great big packing crates. There had to be something wrong with a man who would live that way. And some of the shanties had women in them, which was worse. I thought one of the men on the train should get off and tell these shanty fellows that there was a lot of pretty country just a little farther west.

After a time we came to the tidal channels. The water was low, and all you could see was black mud and tires and bottles and cans, and a horrible stench came up onto the platform.

The conductor came by, full of laughter, with egg on his thin blue vest. He gave me the time and said good and loud: "Hang on, son, hang on for your life." But as soon as he slammed through the door I let go and practiced balancing the way the shipmasters did.

Beyond the Meadows lay the long low hill that led to Jersey City. It looked like the veterans' cemetery, but with houses in place of crosses and without flags—row after row of three-story houses up and down the hills. Overhead, the clouds were like sails without ships. I searched for my private cloud—it was gone, so I claimed another.

Into a tunnel now, with each man in the coach staring at the man ahead, or dozing, or still reading the paper, and the wan yellow light streaking down. I leaned against the locked door to the men's room. Next to it was an advertising poster of two dwarfs in caps with long red tassels. One had a shiny saw in his hand, and he was being chased by his friend, who carried a shiny hammer, and they were both laughing as they winked from above the faucet.

After the tunnel, we crawled through miles of back yards piled high with fenders; the houses had outside stairs and lines of wash. But I felt a new excitement, for the river lay ahead.

The engine was panting, now the train had stopped, so I kept an eye on it till we passed the cowcatcher, for fear the boiler might burst. The engineer waved to me; he leaned on one elbow, wearing a bandanna and gloves and a cap just as in the picture books. I studied it all, though my father was walking fast.

The commuters looked broken down as they shuffled along. Motes of dust swirled in the sunlight, and the horses went by, snorting and arching their tails.

A cold, clean wave of salt air broke like magic over my head. It curled through the terminal, wiping the land away. Challenging, changing, rioting up and down the wharves with a crying of gulls, while out in the river the sunlight sparkled on the windy green water.

I felt so excited I laughed and I turned to my father, for I thought he might feel the same. No sign that he did. All the men looked straight ahead as they marched with pressed faces above pressed pants.

Chains clanged and an iron wheel spun as we passed down the ramp to the ferry. The upper deck was empty: nothing but blue overhead. We filed into a long room; in it were benches that faced both ways, and life preservers along the walls, and here and there a red-pointed ax. I hoped we would continue through to the outside river deck, but instead he sighed and sat in a middle row.

Bells jingled. Engine-room bells, muffled and throttled below. The boat shivered, and ever so slowly the pilings began to move toward the shore—and the whistle blew. Father's paper had a big headline about the New York Yankees.

"Father, can I go to the bathroom, please?"

"*May* I go to the bathroom."

"MAY I please?"

"Yes. Don't get lost and hurry back."

The aisles are choked with grown-ups who gaze off with unseeing eyes or read the papers. I take the stairs two at a time— then around and up some more stairs and out to a world without people, a world with a sky full of birds, presided over by smiling clouds. Down on my level the black funnel looms and the great diamond-shaped walking beam's web rears back with a sucking sound and plunges down through the hiss of steam. The air is pungent now as it slants upriver; I face the wind and chew off chunks and swallow them alive.

The skyscrapers of Lower Manhattan loom toward us, but I

wish they were far away. I wish I could ride back and forth for days and months and live in a lifeboat or up in the pilothouse.

I move to the rail and stare far off down the river. Tugboats and barges and other ferries cross each other: first you see a spurt of steam and then you hear a whistle.

Right over my head was the pilothouse, its windows open wide. Over them a gilt eagle with outstretched wings as if it had trouble holding its balance. A man appeared in the window chewing a cigar. His face looked rough, and his cap was tipped to one side, with *Captain* sewn on it. He spoke to someone I couldn't see, and there came a jingling of bells. The shivering stopped; we coasted crabwise toward the big green building. I could see the elevated trains running beneath the skyscrapers.

At a level with my feet, the commuters crowded behind the gate. I looked at the captain. He didn't look like a captain. I wished he had big shoulders and a square jaw and a look in the eye that said: "Don't Tread on Me." That was my motto.

And I ran toward the head of the stairs.

CHAPTER 16

My father was dead before I knew he was dying.

It was a Friday morning in February, and I was nine years old. I came downstairs to find the house full of people. I thought a celebration was going on because Uncle Mont was there, and my grandmother, who looked like a pussycat with one shoulder lower than the other, and all kinds of people.

My heart plunged when I saw my mother. She had been crying, and I knew my father was dead. He had been ill all winter—since around Thanksgiving. And what else could cause such a fuss? Uncle Mont and Mother took me out to the sun porch. The sun was bright and it was cozy and warm in spite of the snow outside. There was suet in the pine tree in the front yard: before I died I would have to find out what suet was made from.

I sat on my mother's lap, and she started to speak but all she could do was gasp. Uncle Mont leaned toward me with his fine tan face and said: "Son, your father went to sleep last night and he's never going to wake up again." I nodded and tried not to cry. I thought of what had happened just before Thanksgiving, and I wanted to ask if it was my fault.

When they had gone, I stood by the goldfish bowl. The fish swam in and out of the castle on the sand. It was a pretty fair castle, with levels and windows, and just because a fish went in one floor was no guarantee he wouldn't come out on another.

People were going and coming, and all I wanted was to get away so I wouldn't have to avoid looking at anybody and no one would have to avoid looking at me. I put on my galoshes and jacket and took my mittens from their place by the stove. Then I started down to the cellar, and suddenly it came to me—from now on, who would tend the furnace?

I stopped by the laundry room and turned on the light and looked in, and I could almost see him as he had been the day it happened. This frightened me so I went out the cellar entrance and slipped away without being seen and across to the field where the trouble had started. The snow was fairly deep but I could see the outline of leaves humped up where the little fort used to be.

It was the first store-bought slingshot I had had: the price had been 29 cents. My friend Bobby Gies had one, too. We built an outpost in honor of the occasion. It was just before Thanksgiving, and we had two types of ammunition, acorns and staples. Acorns were for people and staples for cars and crows.

Tires were our principal target. Mostly we missed—you could be sure of that because a staple hitting the side of a car makes quite a noise.

A Maxwell roadster with isinglass curtains cruised toward us, its windshield wipers going. Bobby took the rear wheel, and I the front. I fixed a staple in the leather sling and pulled back. But it slipped, and there came the worst scream I had ever heard and a screech of brakes. Bobby flew across the field through the dead goldenrod and over the bodies of long-gone Indians.

A tall man in a long black slicker came toward me, and I dropped the sling and sprinted for home. But he was very fast and he caught me alongside Uncle Jack's garage. He grabbed me by the ear and twisted it, and when he spoke his voice was breathless and thin. "Is this your—house?"

I shook my head.

"Is—that—your house?" indicating Virginia's house.

Again I shook my head. Then I pointed toward our back door and he half carried me by the ear to the kitchen. At that moment

my mother rounded the driveway with my father erect and sad
in the seat next to her.

The rest is vague. We returned to the scene of the trouble. I
found the slingshot and surrendered it. The wife of the man had
a gash along her cheek, and there were apologies and an exchange of names and numbers.

One naked bulb hung over the laundry tubs. He rolled up his
sleeves slowly; there was something new in his face. He took
the stick and began to soak it in one of the tubs. I started to cry.
Then he sat on the fireless cooker and I lay across his legs. I
screamed as loud as I could, but he was carried away with anger.
I remember my mother stamped on the kitchen floor; he only
yelled something. Then suddenly his body froze and the stick
slipped out of his hand.

He was fighting for breath and calling my mother's name. I
stood to one side when she rushed down; then I ran and called
some neighbors, who carried him up to his room.

That night the doctor came. And every week all winter long
he came back, but it never occurred to me that my father was
sick enough to die.

They kept me away from the funeral and afterwards it was
understood that we would never mention my father. I began to
go for long walks up and down the place where the brook ran
under its dome of ice and snow. The brook led along one side of
the cemetery, and I wondered where he was buried—and where
the rest of him had gone. I didn't believe in heaven, but now it
seemed you had to go some place.

Suddenly he seemed the most sensitive man I'd ever known,
far more so than Colonel MacNair, who was a blustery sort of
a man, when you came right down to it, or Uncle Mont, who
smiled too much and was always anxious to please.

I sat on the sun-warmed face of a boulder and held my knees
in my arms. I wondered again where in the cemetery he was
buried. I had a place picked out where great old trees stood with
arms interlocked above cool marble vaults. That was best. Next
to that I hoped he was in the rolling part, where there were
shrubs all around and the grass was pretty and green.

One day I scaled the fence and walked back and forth among
the graves searching for his tombstone. It hadn't occurred to
me that he might not have a stone, or that he might not be in
the attractive part of the cemetery. But he was: the gardener

showed me a mound with some dried-up wreaths and a jar of
dead flowers. Out on Valley Road the snout-nosed buses rattled
past and I pictured him lying beneath my feet looking up with
that wide-nostriled thoroughbred look. His life hadn't amounted
to much and this wasn't much of a place to be buried . . . Boys
don't cry very often, because it's so important to be tough. But
sometimes their heart just starts aching; then they hide somewhere and let it all pour out, which helps—unless they're really
frightened.

CHAPTER 17

Trade-wind clouds saunter across the bowl of the sky. Up
from some unknown valley they come, and over the spars they
glide and gently descend till they're lost in another valley beyond the rim of the sea. The ship follows with a crumpling of
waters under her bow—and the slat of a sail aloft—and a sound
like a sigh in her rigging.

Some day I must come back to this wilderness, with a whaleboat perhaps and very little else—oars and biscuit and water
and maybe a case full of books; and I'll rig a scrap of canvas and
drift westward . . . . here on the tenth parallel of latitude in the
equatorial precincts of the lonely North Pacific . . . a proper
place, indeed, for a man to ponder the meaning of life, and
liberty, and the question of vindication.

A proper place to be buried, too. What more could a body ask?
What could be better than to drift through six thousand miles
of benign and empty ocean? Consigned to the northeast trades.
Consigned to the trades, supported on the heaving shoulders of
the North Equatorial Current.

All this I thought as I held down the master's armchair while
the nymphs gazed the length of the deck and out across the sea.
My thoughts were drawn to the west, for there lay the final
chance to alter course and cut the cord that was gently—oh so
gently—drawing us on toward Tahiti.

I pounded my fists on the heads of the nymphs and, heaving
myself to my feet, picked up a book—broken-backed and dog-
eared and worn—published in 1939 for the British Admiralty.

EASTERN ARCHIPELAGO PILOT
Vol. IV
Comprising
THE WESTERN END OF JAVA, THE SOUTHERN AND EASTERN
COASTS OF SUMATRA, STRAAT SOENDA, STRAAT BANKA, GAS-
PAR STRAIT, STRAAT KARIMATA, THE WESTERN COAST OF
BORNEO FROM TANJONG SAMBAR TO THE ENTRANCE OF THE
KLEINE KAPOEAS RIVIER, THE RIOUW AND LONGGA ARCHIPEL,
WITH THE VARIOUS ROUTES LEADING TO SINGAPORE AND THE
CHINA SEA

A handful of words, but such magical names.

I dropped the book and paced by the rail for a time. The sun lay close to the sea, and off to the east the sky was gun-metal gray, cold, hostile; but the western horizon was a beckoning gold that led like a mountain pass to a valley laden with promise. An old trick, this habit of scanning the horizon in search of a challenging quadrant and wondering: Is this my destiny?

A childish trick, for we know if we go far enough we're bound to return full circle—to the point of departure.

An old game with its roots perhaps lost in those querulous boyhood years.

The boy in the window is nine. He kneels in a stiff-backed chair and peers down the hillside road in the glow of a late spring evening. An old lady who looks like a pussycat shuffles from kitchen to dining room. Five nights a week he plays at this game—guessing headlights, you might call it—inspecting them, counting them, the world full of headlights. His mother is due home and she's late; which lights will be hers and what if something is wrong? There! Those will be hers—they are, I know they are! No, they're not.

Dirty goddamed railroad—why can't it get her home on time? A car starts up the hill; it turns into the dirt road, then left and up the drive. The boy bursts from the house and lurks in a shadow across the street. He kicks at stones and breaks twigs and chews on a stem of grass. Five minutes go by. Now he saunters into the house and finds his mother at supper. "Oh, Mother, are you home already?" His voice is like milkweed but there's a greedy look in his eye.

Another car pulled up one day, and a bouncing man walked in. "Buzzy," his mother said, "say how do you do to Mr. Paul Pierce."

"How do you do, Mr. Pierce."

"Well, son, I do just fine, how do you do—whoo whoo whoo!"
This last with the pantomime of an Indian hitting himself in
the mouth with the palm of his hand.

"You see, Buzzy, Mr. Pierce owns a wonderful camp for boys
on a wonderful lake up in Maine. You would like to go to camp
this summer, wouldn't you, Buzz dear?"

"Well—"

The man leaned over; his breath was bad. The boy blinked
and swallowed. "Now let me tell you the name of the camp, son.
Once upon a time, you see, the woods in Maine were full of Indians, and when they met the white man the first words they
learned to speak were: 'Ha-wa-ya.' Get it? 'How are you.' So
that's the name of the camp—Camp Ha-Wa-Ya!" He threw back
his head and laughed. He danced around the room and told the
boy to speak up and look up and stand up straight. Then he
bounced down the walk.

The boy turned to his mother. "I don't think I want to go—to
camp—we can't afford it either—"

"Buzzy, Aunt Meta has offered to send you, and you're all enrolled, and I'm sure it will be just the thing for you this summer."

Morning roll call. Three hundred boys stand in formation in
itchy gray jerseys emblazoned with the camp insignia. Overhead
the flag and a family of crows, and the heat. A canoe is adrift
on the lake, and a speedboat goes by, pulling an aquaplane. Beneath the flagpole stands the director's son, P. Paul Pierce, Jr.
"Beets," for short—"They call my boy 'Beets' because of his
cheeks, you know—" Three hundred voices lifted high in the
thin Maine air, singing the camp song: "Marching Along for
Camp Ha-Wa-Ya. . . ."

One boy silent—a tall skinny towhead with a tentative chin
and freckles. Counselors walk up and down. One wears a blue
bathing suit; he singles out the towhead and places one palm to
his ear in mock dismay. The boy looks down. The counselor
signals to the ranking officer, calling a halt to the chorus, and
the towhead with the fluttery chin is led to the base of the flagpole.

Beets is a dynamo. He wears crisp white flannels and a special
jersey deep-cut under the arms, and his hair is letter perfect. He
greets the boy: "Are you well, young sir?"

"Yes, sir."

"Do you have a sore throat?"

"No, sir."

"Well then, why weren't we singing?"

"Because I—don't know—the words, sir."

"Speak up!"

The boy does not speak up. All he can do is shake his head and stare at the tip of a sneaker.

"All right," says Beets, "you and I are going to sing a duet. Are you ready, young sir? A-one, a-two. . . ." He lifts a high clear note toward the dining hall, and the boy's lips move in misery.

Suddenly the high voice stops. There is silence. All up and down the formation there isn't a sound—save that of a crow somewhere. Beets touches fingertips to ears and looks around. Now it comes, slowly at first—just a snicker that builds and curls and breaks—a roaring comber of laughter—with some whistlings and catcalls thrown in.

The boy is numb. He doesn't cry. His face feels glazed and his mouth is hot and down inside he aches.

Afterwards: a huge boulder moss-encrusted, with a cloud-like dent in the top—birch trees all around—patches of sunlight fragrant—and a boy outstretched, sobbing, deep racking sobs—temporarily out of tears—and in the distance the laughter of happy youngsters full of aggression—the clink-clunk of horse-shoes—and from out in the lake, the drone of an outboard motor.

Sometime later: the camp infirmary, a tidy building with screens, full of disinfectant and little boys who limp. The tow-head enters on crutches, left foot favored. He stretches flat. An ominous swelling distends the left thigh. "Abscessed," says the camp doctor as he thumbs it and pokes it and raps it with the edge of his hand. This hurts, but the boy is grateful, for it means he may leave camp ahead of time. He is smug, too, because he willed this infection. They asked him how he did it and he said: "I fell on a pointed stone." And they said: "Ah-h-h." And all the time he knew that the ailment had simply appeared—out of nowhere—in response to his need to break free.

September 1925: The County Hospital in downtown Newark—all grimed brick—scalded-looking nurses—windows facing rows of tenements—towhead boy in private room, thin, with caked lips moving as he sheds the skin of ether—nurse and mother pacing. The surgeon enters as the boy comes awake from his dream of the giant grizzly bear who held him down and took three great deep bites from the thigh of his left leg. "How do you feel, son?" The boy tries his winning smile, terrified lest this be the end of running and walking through silent woods and climbing the boughed ramparts of trees. "I feel fine, Doctor, thank you."

The surgeon stares through the window while feeling the pulse of the boy. "Buck up, son. One of these days you're going to grow up to be a two-hundred-pound fullback." The mother is choked with relief. And the boy smiles as he soars off into the clouds.

CHAPTER 18

Where my mother found him, I don't know. He showed up about three years after my father died. She was still working for *Good Housekeeping* magazine, and this was to be a big occasion. He was coming to the house for the first time.

Grandma was drying her hands on her apron. She wiped a bead of sweat; I peeked through the curtains till the last minute, then jumped back. Mother wore a fixed smile as she came through the front door, tripping slightly on the sill. "Buzzy, this is Mr. Hayden," her voice trilled; she was nervous. Then she waved toward my grandmother. "Jim, this is Buzzy and this is my mother and here we are. My, it's good to be home."

Everyone smiled. He stepped toward me and bowed formally with one hand behind his back like a waiter. I was nearly five feet four and he didn't seem much taller. He had a raw face, a bell-shaped nose, bushy red eyebrows, and there was a sore place on one side of his chin. His voice was deep. "How do you do, young fellow. My, Frances! This is going to be a strapping great man some day!"

I thought better of him. When he smiled his teeth were custard color, which matched the tobacco stains on his fingers, and he smelled of tobacco. I thought for a moment he was going to kiss my grandmother's hand, but he stood erect like a general reviewing his troops. His tweed suit was a rich brown color and the knickers led to muscular calves. He rocked from heel to toe; this made the muscles work. His socks were woolly and had a neat fold and a fob hanging down that made me think of Harlech Castle and all those poor bastards fighting it out in the hollow.

I took his hat. It was heavy, with a broad rim such as a plainsman might wear. The lining was red silk, and his initials were stamped on the sweatband in gold. I figured him for a Locomobile man, maybe a Pierce-Arrow man; and if not, then he must have a Packard for sure. I checked the driveway—no car. Something wrong. We had been hearing about him for months now—how he ran a boys' camp in upstate New Hampshire and was part-owner too; how he wanted to go into the resort-hotel business; how he had a tremendous deal lined up. Something told me there would be a marriage here. This was great . . . just what mother needed . . . and deserved, too, after working so hard on the magazine for thirty dollars a week.

But now that I had met him it didn't appeal so much.

Sometime later Mother let on that he was married and seeking a divorce. This upset Grandma. Her face took on color for once, and she trembled and had to sit for a time with a damp cloth on her forehead.

I found myself with a new outfit of itchy blue jerseys and a new camper's outfit, all of it blue this time. I ended up in a tent on an island in the middle of Lake Winnepesaukee, along with three hundred other children. There were horses, rowboats, tennis courts half caved-in, horseshoe areas, and a baseball field so rough that you couldn't see the outfielders unless they were six feet tall. Also there were blue canoes and rows of outhouses and a noisy Chris-Craft and a camp mother. She had a blowzy look and she smiled whenever she heard a voice and it was said she loved to darn socks and sew on buttons, but I gave her a wide berth just in case.

Mother and Grandma were going to spend August at an abandoned farmhouse on a nearby island. This was exciting. I watched him every morning at Assembly with a certain admiration. He stood at attention while the flag was raised and the bugle blew. Then he would bark: "At ease!" and he would deliver the orders of the day in a sonorous baritone. I found it hard to picture him slipping out of camp in the evening and launching a canoe surreptitiously to go courting my mother.

A number of things happened that year. He asked for a divorce and the owners of the camp asked for his resignation. The deal on the resort collapsed and he found another to talk about, but that too collapsed. I had to go through another year in Upper Montclair.

Nineteen twenty-nine was the year of the Wall Street crash, but we were busy packing.

"How would you like," he had said—seated now, because we were the same height—"how would you like to call me Dad Jim?" Mother stood with an arm on his shoulder—somewhat apprehensively, I thought, as if I held the veto power.

I took my time and looked at each of them in turn and I smiled as I said: "Really? You mean you're going to get married? When? Can I watch?" Then: "But—could I call you Daddy Jim? It sounds better."

His glasses fogged up; she wiped her eyes as she gave me a hug; he hugged us both; and I thought to myself: at least we'll get out of this place, we'll travel and maybe live in a better house, and I'll go to a different school, and I won't have to wait for Mother to come up the hill at night because she'll be home all the time and he can do the work.

We hit the road. The road to Nowhere Sure . . .

Beware the man who looks in the mirror of his name. There was nothing wrong with James Hayden, or James W. Hayden; but no sooner had the house been sold than a stranger emerged in our midst, to be known henceforth as J. Watson Hayden. And that was only a beginning. . . .

He plunged into mid-Manhattan, and remained there; when he finally returned, it was resplendent with custom suits, robes, silk shirts and ascot ties and buckskin shoes, and riding breeches and golf outfits and lined tweed caps. His luggage was made of the finest leather, with brass fittings and locks; in it was a collection of special cases—collar case, tie case, cuff-links case, jewelry case, and a toilet case that weighed ten pounds, with tortoise-shell soap cup and a leather-backed mirror.

During his spree, he had us safely out of the way, back at the farmhouse on the island in Winnepesaukee. It would not be for long, of course. "Just ten days or so," he said, "just till the papers come through and we close the deal."

It was a quiet time: hayfields everywhere, crows on patrol, hot sun, a house under a huge elm, crumbling stone walls in the distance, a barn full of bats, and a swirl of dust three times a day when a farmer went by in his truck.

Each week he sent word it wouldn't be long now: just be patient and maybe we'd go to Palm Beach for the winter. In the meantime he was awaiting delivery of a marvelous automobile we would all enjoy.

Mother went on cooking on the wood stove and washing in the stone sink and using the pitcher pump that coughed and spewed a thread of rusty water. Grandma sat on a rocking chair on the porch. I amused myself tramping all day through the woods or trying to pull old buggies out of the barn.

Our nearest neighbors were two ancient sisters who clung like shellfish within the rickety frame of a shuttered summer hotel. It had four floors and forty rooms, each with cast-iron bed, carved commode, two stiff-backed chairs, and several rusted wire hangers. They lived in the kitchen and parlor and kept the shades drawn most of the time. One of them was a hunchback and the other had a mustache; they owned more than half the island.

"When is J. Watson coming back?" Miss Alice would ask with a smile, her head inclined to one side.

"Oh, any day now."

"And the papers are sure to be signed?"

"Yes, indeed," said Mother, picking a rose from the bush by the railing.

"Oh, Frances, if you only knew what this means to us," Miss Polly chimed in. "It's like all our dreams was coming true at last."

Miss Alice nodded toward the fields and woods that rolled down toward the lake. "And to think that next year this will all be tennis courts and an eighteen-hole golf course and—" She clapped her hands like a girl. "Oh, I can hear the people now, laughing and talking. Won't it be just grand."

The telegram said that although the papers weren't signed, he had the car and we could look for him Saturday. We were all there: the sisters in their dresses that reached to the floor, Grandma with her summer shawl and the sewing basket made from a reptile with a horned back, Mother with her shoes that turned out and her smile. "Here it comes!" I cried from my place in the crown of the tree.

He came slowly up the dirt road. The top was down, and he sat straight, with the brim of his hat pulled low. "It's a Packard!" I shouted. Not an ordinary Packard, but a roadster de luxe: especially chromed wire wheels, a red underbody, and spare tires in fender wells, each with a chromed mirror slung by a chain. The interior was red leather, with rumble seat to match and a small square opening for the golf clubs under your feet. A special luggage case perched in back like the rear driver on a hook and ladder.

He made a slow circle between the barn and the well, plowing through daisies and Queen Anne's lace, till he came to rest in the shade. No one spoke. He wiped the inside of his hat, switched from goggles to glasses, and stepped down.

CHAPTER 19

It was a long summer, hot, with the days never-changing, with the blue outline of distant mountains and the drone of insects in idle fields.

A shroud enveloped the farmhouse. Grandma shuffled from room to room, her head at an angle, her skin drawn taut and her shoulder sucked down on her breast. Daddy Jim paced by the hour, his teeth clamped as he smoked in an endless chain. He picked at the spots on his chin with the nail of a finger.

The deal in New York collapsed. He spoke now of far-off places—Washington, D.C., Maryland, Florida. They argued in monotones, in their bedroom or in the Packard in the cool dark cave of the barn, where they sat by the hour—wide apart—staring out through the squared frame of the door to a shining world beyond.

One day the sisters came up the road arm in arm, moving with effort. Miss Polly's head was thrust forward with the hump on her back: she looked like a smallish camel. I hid in my room and lay on the floor with an ear to the crack.

"Jim." I could picture Miss Alice, her lips pursed as though amazed at the world. "Jim, we know this has been an awkward time for you and dear Frances and Buzzy and Mother Simonson,

but Jim—" She worked at her throat with a gurgling sound.
"We loaned you what few savings we had and—"

He got to his feet and began to pace again.

"And we just don't know what to do now, Jim, or where to
turn, and it's soon going to be winter and—well—we just don't
have any money."

I could feel my heart against the floor. After a time he spoke.
He told them how frightened all the people were in New York;
nobody knew what was going to happen. He would go to Washington, where he had influence, and next spring we'd come
back with the financial backing he needed to turn the island into
a paradise for the elite of the Western world.

"Oh," she said, "we know you will come back, we trust you,
Jim—it isn't that—but we must have our money to take us
through the winter—"

"Of course, and you shall." His voice rang through the house.
"I'll forward it the first of the week—as soon as we get to
Boston—if that will be all right—"

"Oh yes, Jim—we're sorry we have to mention this at all."

Suddenly they all began to chatter, so I slipped from the
house and scuttled up into the tree. He put them in the car and
they sat there leaning forward. Miss Alice had her lips pursed
and they were holding hands as they trundled past my tree.

My heart lunged like a walking beam the day we loaded the
car. I wanted to laugh and jump up and down; the dog ran in
wild circles with his belly low to the ground. Autumn had
burned the maples barn-red and the curled-up leaves lay scat-
tered all over the road.

We paused by the old hotel. A shutter banged on a third-floor
window, and Miss Polly gave me some apples. The motor idled
softly. He had his hat in his hand as he climbed to the porch
and he bowed to Miss Polly and Miss Alice and spoke in his
deep soft voice; then he hurried back to the car.

The sisters huddled together in the grip of a chill north wind.
"Goodbye," they called. "Goodbye Frances, goodbye Jim,
Buzzy—" They lifted their arms as the car rolled slowly away.
"Next spring then, Jim—good luck—goodbye—God Bless—"
A handkerchief fluttered. "Do please write, please do!"

He fondled the wheel between his legs, his back resting on a
special cushion. Mother sat in the center holding the map;
Grandma huddled low on the outside, with her balsam pillow

pressed to the jowl to absorb the bite of the wind. It was cold
too in the rumble seat, but I didn't care so long as we kept on
the move. They gave me a thick gray robe and I made this
into a tent for the dog and myself. Whenever we came to a
town, I emerged, for I loved to see our reflection in big store
windows.

Daddy Jim relished it, too. Mother kept one hand near the
wheel as we rumbled past plate-glass windows. And he kept
the spare-tire mirror pointed toward his face instead of where
it belonged.

We came to the suburbs of Boston. Miles on miles of yel-
lowish-brown frame dwellings crowded together, with a trace
of grass in front and ugly two-paned windows leering at one
another across the scar-tissued street. We passed by schools
with kids clawing and screaming and tearing around, with the
swart-faced buildings in the background. I knew that when the
bell for dismissal rang they'd go home to some box of a house—
and I'd be rolling along free of school, bound for God knew
where.

The Hotel Statler lay just ahead, beyond a blockful of cars.
The doorman saw us coming and gave us a royal welcome. Bell-
boys rushed our bags through the doors, and Daddy Jim let it
be known that J. Watson Hayden had arrived. I began to understand the importance of a fancy car and fine clothes and special
luggage.

We stayed in Boston for more than a month. And I realized
gradually that we didn't have any friends. Wherever we went, it
was just the four of us. I noticed people meeting people in
lobbies and joining each other for meals, but we simply filed
into the dining room and sat there. Boston was supposed to be
Daddy Jim's home town. But, except for the sisters in the
haunted hotel, I hadn't talked with anyone else for more than
seven months.

Not far from the hotel were the public gardens. These became my daytime home. They were laced with paths and flower
gardens and had a lake. And they were full of men who had
nothing to do. Even at night you could see them curled up in
brown wrapping paper or newspaper, asleep on benches or
inside the passageways that led to the comfort stations. These
men lined the benches day after day, collars turned up, hands
in pockets, and legs crossed so you could see the holes in their

shoes. They had a tough way of looking at you. Once I saw a really tough-looking fellow, so tough that I tore off across the grass and didn't stop till I reached my room.

Daddy Jim was a very busy man. Every morning after breakfast he would glance at his watch, slip a Lucky into his mouth, and with a little twitch of the head stride toward the exit like a vaudeville comedian walking off stage.

He never took a taxi. Instead, he would swing off down the block as though he were late. I leaned out of my window sometimes to watch him go; he always walked that way. But sometimes I found him at the far end of the park dozing in the sunshine with his glasses off and his shoelaces untied.

Later on, I would find both Daddy Jim and Mother in the park, and I'd go running, looking for dangerous bums. When I came back sometimes she had been crying. One day he said: "Frances, it's time to move on."

Bright and early the following day he parked the car alongside the hotel entrance and we began to load it. The side curtains were in place, for it was November and you could see your breath. Some bums were huddled in the doorways looking for a handout; Daddy Jim had on his touring outfit and knickers. I helped Laird into the rumble seat, and the doorman helped me. You could feel the dirt blowing through the air as we waved. I crawled into my fur tent and pulled the lid and settled down with the golf bags and Mother's extra hatbox.

On this trip we paid a visit to Aunt Vina and Uncle Austin Glick, who lived in Catasauqua, Pennsylvania, between Bethlehem and Mauk Chunk. Nobody told me, but I guessed the reason for this—Auntie and Uncle were rich. Small wonder: they even dated each new cereal box they opened and they kept a record of it in the ledger next to the sink.

I had visited them off and on all my life. They lived in a huge Old Nineties house painted gray with black trim. It had a slate roof with lightning rods all over, a pointed fence, an open garbage dump out back, and a Buick that lived like a hermit in what had once been a barn.

Auntie was handsome and cold. She had a thin nose and gray hair and always wore arch-preserver shoes. Uncle Austin had studied law, but he had been left a lot of money and had quit work. They had no children and they didn't know anyone who had; Catasauqua was perhaps the only place in the world where there was nothing for a kid to do. Uncle always wore a smoking jacket but he didn't smoke, and of course they didn't drink.

The car had been brightly polished. As it pulled up to the curb, Laird jumped off. Grandma grunted and tried to get out but couldn't. Mother was nervous. Daddy Jim was his most charming but Uncle looked skeptical. I gave Auntie a duty kiss; she smelled like mushrooms.

I was given the tiny room by the back stairs, from where I could hear the switching engines down by the smelting works. I went outside and gave the pump a try and checked on the garbage dump. Then there was nothing more to do.

When we left, my eyes were dry.

Our wire wheels and chromed louvers glistened as the sleek superdreadnought car glided down Pennsylvania Avenue and swung to the curb in front of the Washington Hotel (across from the U.S. Treasury Building). From my room I could see the Washington Monument and a corner of the White House lawn.

"Who is our President?" Daddy Jim asked as we stood on the balcony.

"That's easy," I replied. "President Herbert Hoover is."

"And what do you know about him?"

"Well—I know he is a great man. He used to be a great engineer and he went to Stanford College, and he is really great because he helped the people of the world." Mother smiled and he scratched his head.

Christmas was coming, so I didn't go to school right away. There was nothing to do but take the dog on long exploring trips through the parks and down by the Potomac.

One day Mother and Daddy Jim started to look for an old plantation to settle in. They found it a few weeks later. It was called "Goodwood" and it looked like a run-down military academy, with great pillars and broken windows all bearded with ivy and vines. The trees were strangled by creepers—the dreadnought looked mighty strange drawn up in front of the slaves' quarters.

I was told to pick out a room so I roamed up to my ankles in plaster and broken glass. One room looked much the same as another, but I made a choice, to show I was a good sport.

"How much is it?" I asked.

"More than a body can afford, if you ask me—" Grandma snapped from her crate in the sun by a pillar.

"Gentlemen don't ask questions like that," Mother said.

Just then Daddy Jim rounded a corner swinging his cane that converted into a seat. "Frances," he began, "I believe perhaps we should wait until spring before we close this deal."

I lit out for the car along with Laird, and we hit the rumble seat standing up.

One of the highlights of the season in Washington that year was the formal opening of the Shoreham Hotel. We were right there when it happened, having leased apartment 703-C, a three-bedroom suite that rented for seven hundred dollars a month—so I knew Daddy Jim was in touch with success.

I found myself in an international fairyland of ballrooms, aquacades, horse shows, and fashion shows. There were elevators wherever you looked, and gorgeous girls going up and down with dignified-looking men who were said to be congressmen and senators, and the garage was full of limousines and foreign cars with distinguished license plates.

At last I was sent to school—the Friends School. There were girls there, and I made friends easily, which came as a surprise. I became attached to a large girl with red hair who lived in an elegant house because her family owned a chain of bakeries. I learned to dance and hold hands, looking at the moon and wondering what came next.

Along about spring I dropped out; Daddy Jim hadn't paid the tuition. That was the week Grandma died. She was carried back to Catasauqua—this was my first funeral. When it was over, I rode the hearse back to Washington while my parents went on to New York. So I thought. They went to Upper Montclair instead; and they sold all our furniture and most of Mother's jewelry and linens, but she kept her beloved piano.

I was taking riding lessons. It was exciting to be in the middle of things, with foreigners driving up in diplomatic cars; before long, I decided to enter the Diplomatic Corps. I would travel and automatically become the most important man in any country because I represented the United States. And I would meet exciting people and beautiful women and have a special car with a native driver and Marines to guard me and police escorts all the time. And after dinner every evening I would go into the library with a trusted advisor or the head of the country, and there I would drink rare old liqueurs and play chess, with a log fire casting shadows on walls covered with books.

When Mother and Daddy Jim returned from New York, I found out about the money. I sensed there was trouble because the sores on his chin were inflamed and he was never without a cigarette; sometimes there'd be a second one burning in another room for good luck. Also he took the car and hid it in a little garage half a mile away.

I tried to go for a swim one afternoon, but I was turned away. This was embarrassing: I had a girl with me who lived in the Wardman Park Hotel and I was trying to show off. I rushed upstairs to protest; Daddy Jim peered through a crack in the door, then yanked me inside and put me to work packing.

During the night he carried the bags down the back stairs. I helped; it seemed good in a way to be on the move again. This was the first time I had actually seen Daddy Jim at work, though he was full of stories about "when I was your age I worked as a hard-rock miner out in Ouray, Colorado." I liked that name, Ouray. He had the Packard in a quiet corner behind some vegetable crates. Mother put out all the lights and left the key and I walked down the seven flights with her and we said goodbye to the Shoreham.

CHAPTER 20

1959. We change worlds.

"Do you see it, kids?"

"See what, Daddy?"

"Why, the equator of course—what are you, blind?" An arm flung back at the north. "There, see that dark blue line, running east and west? That's the—"

"Aw cut it out, you're kidding—"

"You're goddam right I am."

Across the Line and downhill now—all the way to the Pole. A different world with a different sea and a different kind of a sky.

This is the backward hemisphere. Underdeveloped. The realm

of the second-class (save for an upper crust, with their silvered spoons). This is the kingdom of poverty, of disease and the starving peasant . . . the hemisphere of silence . . . of patient resignation . . . up to a point.

I don't belong and I know it. Instead I bring a rubberneck crew down out of the north in my ship and we cross the Line like a covey of pink-cheeked fugitives. Fugitive from what? From boredom? Overindulgence? From lives without purpose? Principle?

It is just past nine of an evening. Dishes are done and prayers are said (by some); lights are dim below, while up on deck the world is blacker than doom except for millions of stars.

A soft wind blows and the ship ghosts into the night with her canvas spread. There's a gurgle of water under her stem and more where the rudderpost looms. The mate treads a lone traverse on the windward side of the deck.

"Hey Spike," comes Russ from the wheel, "I think there's a squall downwind." The mate bends low and stares past the boom at a coal-black cloud that has stolen some stars from the west. "Well I'll be a son of a bitch." He straightens himself and goes to the wheel. "Get everything ready," he says.

"Shall I call the skipper?"

"No not just yet—yeah go ahead, you might as well."

I know it's me they're calling and I sense a light somewhere so I keep my eyes shut tight and feel my way for the deck with a lurch or two as she rolls. Then I lean on the door and open my eyes and there is the squall directly under our lee. I throw back my head and note with distaste that we've everything set: outer jib, inner jib (from forward aft this is), fore stays'l, fores'l, mains'l—and far up aloft a fisherman stays'l and main gaff tops'l.

The scarred black growth of the cloud comes closer. It has feelers that writhe with delight as they glimpse a schooner. Its belly is misshapen and ready to burst with wind.

The ship lies checked. What wind there was has bowed to the wrath of the squall. "Clew up your topsail," I say, just loud enough to be heard, "and somebody grab the staysail 'cause I'm running her down right now—"

Jesus, I think, that's a mean-looking goddam squall, maybe I'd best run both jibs down and then the main, take it easy and let her blow. . . .

"That's a lousy-looking squall, if you ask me," says Spike.

I jump for the rail and let the peak of the staysail go on the run—it snakes out, its wire gnashing away aloft, and the sail begins to flog. I get to the forward pinrail and drop her down flat in the dory. A figure vanishes under the downcoming sail with a feeble cry: "Not so fast, not so fast!"

"Screw you," I think as I go for the sheet and slack the boom tackle and take up the slack on the capstan's barrel with the big main sheet, and it's in with the backstay and get your jibs across as an air wafts in from our lee.

Now the squall growth towers high above the vessel. No stars remain and some raindrops fall as I go for the wheel. "Stand by your main sheet." My throat feels tight. Spike bundles himself out of the cockpit. The air turns cold. "Slack a little," I rasp.

A throttled roar. Angry. Distant. Yet close. The growth comes toppling forward. The night explodes in the rigging and over she goes like a switch lever thrown and all too leeward the wake turns to fire and rushes aft and the rain comes next as I feed the old vessel a wheelful of spokes.

The compass is vague. (To hell with the course. When Mister Squall comes down on you, you go where he says, not anywhere else, until he's satisfied.) SE the compass says, more or less— we're bound for Cape Horn . . . screw that too.

She thunders along dragging her rail and the rain lets up and an extra-stiff puff sets up shop high aloft. A sea cascades through the lee fore rigging and sweeps over the decks. She lays down more; I think of the foretopmast by itself up there with its fibers crackling under compression. What if a shroud lets go?

The jibs protest, so I knock her off and she sifts through the baby seas. She has her stride; I take a look through the wind. There—ever so faint and blurred—lie some stars all solemn and cold (like street lights when you're driving home drunk). I smile.

Becalmed. She slats for a time. The stars much brighter now. A breath comes back from the east southeast. Maybe the trades? The boys coil down and Nyborg's face is a copperplate in the glow of the binnacle lamp. I go below.

Too hot to sleep. I turn up the light and stare at the shelves full of books. The sweat crawls down the groove of my chest and my eyes come to rest on a photograph in a dime-store frame. Snow in the foreground leading to a rock-bound shore, and off on the breast of a harbor a small island with shimmering water around it, and a lighthouse far in the distance. There are pines on this island, and I see a towheaded boy sitting there on the rocks, and once more I hear that sound.

It's a sound like no other sound in the world. If you've ever been on an island on the coast of Maine on a cold clear northwest day—then you've heard the sound I mean. I heard it first when I was just thirteen—but I've heard it since and I hear it now and I guess I always will.

CHAPTER 21

The road led down toward the sea. Through inland valleys drowned in heat, alive with the hum of insects, presided over by men in faded overalls, with pale-blue slits of eyes.

We came to a sleepy settlement spread by the side of a river, a broad river laced with mud flats and tiny islets of marsh grass that broke the flow of the current. A long low rickety bridge went clumpeting under our wheels, and a little shack marked the center where the lift span lay, under a slab of cement.

Gulls zoomed by and landed on the flats; others rode like toys out toward the channel buoys. There was a signboard at the easternmost end of the bridge. One arrow pointed straight ahead: ROCKLAND 55 MILES. Another pointed to our right and down where the river went: BOOTHBAY HARBOR 12 MILES. Daddy Jim pulled off to one side, glanced at the map, studied his chin in the mirror, and shrugged: "Which way shall we go, Frances?"

"Whatever you say, Jim."

He lit a Lucky Strike and watched some cars pass by. We turned toward the sea.

. . . For months now we had languished in the peeling clapboard arms of another resort hotel: the Lake Spofford Golf and Country Club, featuring eight holes of golf, fire escapes, shuffleboard, cupolas, and New England boiled dinners. Daddy Jim had a deal pending in Boston; as soon as the papers were signed, he would become managing owner. In the meantime, we lived in the servants' annex. But the Packard was parked out front—to impress the innocent.

Nothing happened. Bad luck, I thought. Finally they wired Aunt Vina, and the moment the money arrived we packed and got under way.

"Where to?" he had asked.

"I don't know, Jim, I just don't know. But perhaps if we try the shore this time our luck might change. . . ."

"Why not?" he had said.

A week ago that was.

I knew the sea was up ahead—you could tell that from the air. We followed the river part of the time, through fields of corn and patches wooded with pines. Not much traffic. I felt a strange sensation, a warm exciting flow kin to the feelings of years past when I had watched the clouds sail by or waved to the guards at railroad crossings. I thought now of the big river outside Manhattan, with its ferries and liners and miles on miles of wharves.

Boothbay slumbered in the sun that day, with the sea in its arms and a sky full of cloud drifting lazily overhead. We rode into town with Daddy Jim wearing goggles and perforated gloves and a vest and buckskin shoes. The brim of his hat was low; his face was tired and scared. Mother sat with her chin tucked in; now and then a smile would play round her mouth till something brushed it away.

. . . Where was the water? Where were the ships and the wharves? All I could see were back yards and piles of lumber and a small footbridge. Men with boots turned down to their knees lounged on corners. They wore checkered wool shirts and long-visored caps, and their sleeves were rolled back from forearms like hairy teak with gouged-out hollows between the ridges of muscle.

How ridiculous we seemed. What gave us the right to put on this show when we flitted from place to place with somebody else's money? A knot of fishermen followed us now with their eyes. One man laughed and slammed his thigh, and I wished I were one of them; then I could lean on the bank with a boot against the wall, and I'd joke and spit and smile at the pale-faced tourists with big cars and soft little hands like ours.

I caught a glimpse of the harbor. The glow inside me turned to a dancing flame. At the end of a sun-swept wharf lay a ship with two high masts. She was gone in a flash but I knew I'd be back, and I shivered. This was an enchanted village, compared to the places we'd been. People moved slowly through the streets and smiled, and the sea birds cried.

Beyond the center of town, on the seaward side of the road, stood a large white house with a sign that swung in the wind: TINKER TAVERN—ROOMS & MEALS. We stopped by the curb, and J. Watson Hayden strode into the office.

I wanted to vault from the car and take a look at the docks. My heart raced, but I pretended not to care. I leaned back and gazed up through an enormous elm tree. What did it matter if we didn't have money and he didn't have a job—we were here. They could leave if they wanted to, but I was staying. That much I knew.

The staircase was narrow and steep and it looked as if paint had been splattered all over the floors and everything smelled clean. My room was barely six feet square, but it had a huge window directly over the harbor. I pulled the bed across so I could look right out at night.

I rapped on the wall. "Mother?"

"Yes, son?"

"I think I'll go for a walk."

"Yes, son. Be back in time for supper."

Three hours! Three hours alone in a town by the sea. Nothing to do but explore. . . .

The road, as it passed the tavern, sloped up just enough to conceal what lay ahead. I paused, uncertain whether to look beyond the slope or head for the docks of the town.

I turned toward the sea and the hill gave way and I stepped like magic into a new and glorious world. Before me lay the vast blue outer harbor fringed with pine and spruce that rose from the granite shore.

As though in a trance, I passed the brow of the hill. A wharf leaned out on the inner harbor beyond a crude sign: BOATS TO LET. A little farther along was an old building that looked like a loft. The sign in fading gilt letters read: BILLY SAWYER—SHIP CHANDLER.

I stared at the words. Here was a new kind of sign to go with a new kind of world. Ship chandlers were people in books and museums. . . .

I could see—far in the distance—the spire of a lighthouse

against the sea and the sky. There (I told myself) is the harbor's mouth. There is where the ships go and that is where they come from. Right out there, down that shining wind-swept channel with islands on either side . . . and beyond that lighthouse a few miles you'd be out of sight of the land—and alone on the wilderness sea.

A cloud shadow swallowed me up. It was colder. I turned and my eyes fell on a forlorn sight—three sailing ships, tall wooden vessels with four masts apiece, huddled in a landlocked cove, leaning awkwardly in on one another—derelicts.

I wanted to talk to someone so I turned in a circle or two. Alone. All right. Maybe it's best this way. These things belong to me. Maybe the Maine coast people don't care. Well? I don't need them. Let them have their houses and cars and papers and fancy clothes and the rest—just give me the rockweed and the pines and the clouds, let me have the sea and the sky and the big old ships and the docks, and I'll talk to the birds and some day I'll find out where that horizon goes and—

A great black schooner was coming in from sea with her wake a widening wedge that rippled abroad toward tiny clusters of islands, plowing straight toward the head of the harbor. There came a shout, and some sails ran down. Slowly she came into the wind and the sun hit her oiled spars till they glowed orange-red; she had four masts with patched sails all grimed. I heard them flog as they spilled the wind, and I saw a splash right under her bows, and a thundering roar came in as her chain went down.

A launch appeared from beneath her stern. I moved to the dock and watched the wind ruffles go dancing across the harbor. My eyes swung restlessly from launch to islands to hilltop pines, then back to the wharves. The launch nosed up to the wharf. Two men went up the dock with never a backward glance. The man who remained behind wore leather boots. One wrist was swathed in a bandage, and he had a scar from mouth to ear. I'd have liked to ask him the name of his ship, but I didn't have the nerve.

Now the sun was low and the harbor was bathed in an amber glow and the shadows lay long and even the birds looked bronzed. The spire of the lighthouse held a ball of light at its tip, then all at once it was gone. Other lights winked on and off, all reds and greens, and a ghostlike figure out on the schooner walked toward the bow with a lantern. Somewhere a dog barked as I moved up the street toward the village. When I came to the brow of the hill I turned for a lingering look, and a shiver ran down my spine.

CHAPTER 22

It sounded like cannon fire—a sharp report that volleyed across the harbor, splitting the predawn light, invading my room, where the dog lay asleep on the bed. The window was flung wide and the morning air felt cold. I shuddered a little and pulled a blanket over my head, leaving a space to give me a view of the boats and lights as the 'fishing fleet headed for sea. I thought of dressing and rushing down to the docks, but it was warm and snug so I stayed like a gnome in a cave, with my eyes on a hilltop of pines that were coming to life in the east.

We ate breakfast in silence. "How long are we staying?" I asked.

"There's no way of telling," he said.

"Just run along, Buzzy, and have a good time. Your father is troubled this morning."

The dock next door was cluttered with anchors and chains. An old man in a black hat was working away in a shed. He looked like a sea captain, with stooped shoulders and a handlebar mustache curved beneath pale blue eyes. His hands hung like weights as he moved.

The shed was jammed with oars and sails. A workbench ran under the windows and there were cobwebs overhead. He pumped on a treadle that turned a huge grindstone. "What is it, boy?" he asked.

"I would like to rent some kind of a rowing boat."

"Fer how long?"

"All day—if it doesn't cost too much."

"Is fifty cents too much?" He led the way to a boat with flaring sides and two pairs of heavy oars and some pegs in place of rowlocks. I paid him and took my time about shoving off so as to do it in privacy. Then I thought of lunch; I ran up-town and came back with raisins and bread and a bottle of milk. I'd been in boats before, but only on lakes and never alone. I did not hurry as I drifted around a corner and out of sight of the captain.

Then I inspected my first command. Laird stood stiff-legged, with water over his paws. I fixed him a place to lie down, then bailed out the water and watched the village drift by. I was lost in contentment in a world all my own. There were noises onshore—of gears clashing and children calling, and there was hammering up on a hill—but none of this had a thing to do with me. I was off on the path to the ocean, and when I lay down along the bottom all I could see were the clouds and the clean-lined curve of the boards as they swept from bow to stern. We drifted. The wind was laden with salt and pine, and I knew if I just lay still I'd go drifting right out to the ocean.

I roused myself and pulled toward the big four-master. She had her head toward the land. She was dirty and scarred but full of romance. I passed close under her bows; a ladder hung from the rail. No one moved on deck. I wanted to go on board but something scared me away. The wind came down and I smelled the windjammer smell—all tar and rot and wood smoke mixed with the odor of canvas and hemp baking in the morning sun. The breeze was light but full of a twisting tang, and I swallowed it whole as I pulled back and dragged at the oars.

The town lay open now in a crescent about the head of the harbor. It was lovely and simple: crumbling wharves and shaded homes with tree-lined margins of wall and picket fence. I looked for our tavern, but it was hidden, I guessed, by the hill —and I thought of my folks back there: he'd be pacing the bedroom or reading the Portland paper.

The palms of my hands felt raw as I pulled toward the derelicts. In spite of the sunlight, they seemed to lie in a cloud— a ghost of a cloud—and their paintwork was peeling and blotches of pine showed through. But you could still read the names on their bows—*Josiah B. Chase, Courtney C. Houck, Maude M. Morey*—and under each name, the single word: *Boston.*

A ladder trailed to the water's edge with jellyfish like red mushrooms between streamers of kelp. "KEEP OFF" said a sign.

"Hello up there," I called in a soft voice. "Hello! Hello!"—this time with more force. No one answered.

I climbed to the rail of the *Chase* with some chocolate stuck in my mouth. The dog whined. I recalled the painting in a boy-hood copy of *Treasure Island*—the boy aloft pursued by a blood-

stained pirate with a knife between his teeth. . . . I peered down
the line of the deck. Each ship was a desert island. I ran to a
place down out of the wind and the sun poured down and the
feeling of danger was gone.

I paced the length of the deck. Two hundred and fifty feet
long, she was, with a breadth of just over forty. Three ships
side to side (like a maritime village square) measuring one
hundred and twenty by two hundred and fifty feet, with twelve
masts between them. The bulwarks were six feet high. I heard
a noise and turned around—to a door that swung in the wind.

The cabins were more comfortable than half the houses I'd
seen. A central room was paneled in maple with white-painted
gingerbread work; six staterooms opened from this, with bath,
chartroom, and pantry. I sat in a swivel chair at the head of a
narrow table. Through the skylight over my head the masts
reached toward the sky. A bird cage hung in one corner and
the lamps smelled of kerosene. A calendar on one wall was dated
November 1927. The girl in the picture had long smooth legs,
and she was walking her dog as some leaves blew by. Her skirt
was full of wind and shaped like a red umbrella, her panties all
pink and her thighs white right to the stockings.

I made believe we were somewhere in the tropics on a voyage
to Cape Town or Rio. I stood by the wheel: the helmsman was
stripped to the waist, with a ring in one ear and a snake tattooed
on his chest. I stalked toward the long maindeck, where the men
were at work on a sail—

I lay on my back and dreamed. Nothing but clouds through
the masts. What's wrong, I wondered, that these ships are rotting
like this? What are they worth? Could you pick one out and
buy her cheap? Make a pretty good house perhaps. . . .

I rowed away in a veil of wishful thinking. What could be
more wonderful than a year or two on a schooner? We could sell
the car and stock the vessel with food; then no matter how long
this bad luck lasted we'd be safe back aft with a fire going hard
while the winter winds howled harmlessly over our heads. And
maybe the day would come when we'd find some friends to help
us handle the boat for a trip to some foreign land.

My wrists ached, so I pulled in the oars and drank some milk
and stretched out flat in the sun. The water slapped at the
boat as she rocked in the harbor slop. I dozed.

When she bounced on the rocks, I scrambled onto a seat just
as Laird hurled himself toward the shore. I saw an island set like

a gem in the harbor. The fissured granite led gently up to a crown of sumac and blueberry bushes and out toward a point was a grove of spruce and pine. I caught a glimpse of a rooftop under the trees as I pulled around to the seaward side.

The house faced straight toward the sea. It was yellow with green shutters, and the small-paned windows lay snug in the bayberry bushes. From the front of the house to the high watermark was barely the length of my dory. I rowed on, till I came to a cove with a rude dock and a ladder chopped off at the water. Just then I spied the sign—

FOR SALE

I tied up the boat and found the path to the cottage. This— I told myself—was my first and only island; the ones on the lake didn't count. This one was small—perhaps a hundred yards long from a high barren cliff near the mainland to a shelving point that vanished beneath the buoy.

I picked a few berries all bursting with heat and juice as I found my way to a clearing under the pines. Here I made a nest in the tall green grass that rose from a carpet of needles. Then I crawled on hands and knees through a screen of shrub till I peered at the line of the sea—a cold clear line slashing from island to island beneath the rim of the sky. I closed my eyes and all I could hear was wind.

The real-estate agent wore high-laced shoes, and his eyes were laughing and kind. He smiled as I told him about the island.

"Oh yes now, yes indeed, that would be Tumbler Island." He rapped his pipe on one heel.

"Sounds like a lovely location," Mother said.

" 'Tis indeed. Like to own it myself."

"My stepson here says we ought to buy it." Daddy Jim rocked back and forth with his hands out of sight in their pockets. "What would they hold it at, offhand?"

"Asking three thousand, last I knew."

I could hear the wind, and it carried my dreams away. But the voice went on: "Expect though, Mr. Hayden, you could rent it dirt cheap this season."

"How much would that be, offhand?"

The thin man smiled as he looked toward me. "Oh, maybe a hundred dollars, now through September."

"Would they rent it through the winter?"

"Oh Lordy, Mr. Hayden, you'd freeze your wife to death. There's no heat on Tumbler Island—not that I know of."

I kept my eyes on the floor. A surge of affection went through me for this man who had gone through such a run of bad luck. He closed the deal, and out in the street I wanted to tell him I loved him but all I could do was smile.

CHAPTER 23

Wintertime suspended in the crackling air of a silent seaport town. Days of awe in which the warm small world of the child gave way to the line of a gray horizon between pine-clad islands and a gray sky swollen with snow. Sea birds wheeling, driving, riding head to wind, the short chop of the inner harbor—rustling frosted wings against drum-taut bellies, with twigs of legs treading icy waters and, fathoms below, the waving mustard fields of rockweed surging gently to the heave and scend of the dour old North Atlantic.

A day in January. The harsh north wind rides hard toward the sea. The pines nod as smoke from the yellow cottage darts through snow-packed branches. The tiny island is half submerged at the peak of each tide while the village lies with upturned collar and the coal schooners brood out by the edge of town.

Ram Island lighthouse lies to the east—rises sheer from the sea with circling stripes of black and white and an iron-railed gallery and a ramp that leads to the shore. Beyond this tower the barren bulk of Fisherman Island—shaped like a loaf of bread, with a huge stone fort of a house on top all boarded tight and useless now while its owners frolic in the gut of some city. Bearing south by east the main ship channel runs cold and free toward the jagged horizon line. On a dome of granite known as the Cuckolds another lighthouse rises. Midway down this channel and off to the west lies the fairest island of all—Burnt Island, with its whitewashed tower of stone and a covered way leading to the keeper's domain. Off to one side and facing the sea a pyramidal structure houses a huge bronze bell. A classic scene: fields of snow backed to a stand of spruce; a boathouse

under the northern point with a launching ways that leads to
a tossing whaleboat ringed with a fragile necklace of colored
lobster pots; a buoy or two; and the chimney trailing its gray
wool scarf with its back to the blustering wind.

Fourteen years of age, these sour depression days of 1931.
Lost and lonely, living in solitude with a frightened mother and
stepfather, while driftwood burns in a sheet-metal stove and
creosote plops in the empty can beneath the joints of the pipe.
The boy is curled on a window seat with his solemn eyes on
the sea . . . huddled under a quilt with fear in his mind . . .
now watching the folks as they sit by the stove coloring picture
post cards for a firm in Montreal—"You too can make BIG money
in your free time."
He dreams, the book in his hands forgotten as he turns to fix
his gaze on the lonely rim of his sea-swept island world. He
pictures himself on a windjammer's deck, lean of hip and thick
of chest, with the muscles huge in his arms, and he swings himself aloft with the easy gait of the born sailorman, and all
around the world is gold and blue and the cares of the land
don't exist.
Even as he smiles this vision is replaced by the sight of five
topmasts marching as if by magic up through the eastern
channel. "Look!" he cries.
Now the black band of her hull shows above the red waterline.
She is flying light with an empty hold and she rides high above
the water. Coming home to die. A poor time too, for she's barely
fifteen years old. That's all it has been since they punched her
with a bottle of champagne and sent her laughing down to the
cold embrace of the harbor with flags flying and the band playing
to give her a heroine's launching—and send her along to the
war. The war to end all wars.
Morning long she beats back and forth against the bullying
wind, and a mongrel dog with a big head tears around her decks
barking every time she comes near the land. The boy rushes
out to a favorite seat in a cradle of rock at the outermost end
of the island. The great gaunt box of a ship tacks back and
forth like a shuffling crab; and he hears the cries of her mates
and he sees the crew heave and haul and curse. Fists full of
bar-taut headsail sheets flog like fiends until—after five hours
of beating—there comes a shift of wind and she lays her course
toward her grave. She moves this one last time with a touch of
speed and grace, and they roll her wheel over as her headsails

drop and a rap of a maul sends an anchor down into the water. Romance? What could be less romantic? A run-down collier schooner in from Newport News, a tramp of a coaster whose ports of call have been far-flung Harlem and Calais and Chelsea, by way of Norfolk and far-off Baltimore.

How reconcile such names with the names in the storybooks? Cape Town and Madagascar, Malacca Strait and the lone Seychelles. Good God, but those are names! How long since she has worked her way past the Three Kings or lost Van Diemen's Land? When did she last run her easting down in the vise of the roaring forties? Has she been becalmed off Starbuck Island or towed up the Hooghly River to load for Copenhagen?

So why the look in the eyes of the boy? What need is he trying to fill? What solace is handed down from those towering spars of pine? Follow him now as he runs to the house and stuffs some bread in his pocket, then out to the dock and into the catboat with its sail peaked up in a flash and its mooring slipped. Over she lies with her rail not far from the harbor, and the boy stands upright, the tiller between his legs and the sheet in one hand and a chunk of bread in the other. Up the harbor they go, tack for tack, and the schoonermen wave as the boy and his boat go by.

A day in February.

A lookout tower high on a nearby hill. Spraddle-legged it stood, fifty feet from the ground to its crotch where the platform rested—rotted zigzag steps that spiraled upward, each with its crown of snow, so rotten that the boy felt his way with care till he gained the top and leaned on the railing all decorated with hand-carved tourists' initials.

Even as he rested he knew just what he would see—the clear blue line of the sea, motionless, proud and unspoiled; all around him it would curve through half the points of the compass. And he thought of the cities he'd seen—all of them alike—the pale stooped people taut, rushing with fever every way, and the crawl of the traffic and the drab stone buildings and over the whole the crust of smoke and below the subways loud and filled to the brim with people and misery . . . Off in the east he could see the blue-black bulk of Monhegan Island some eighteen miles away, while down beneath him, Boothbay slumbered in peace round its hill at the head of the harbor.

He narrowed his eyes and shut out the land till only the sea remained—that far sea line that draws like the bar of the magnet. He heard the song of the pine treetops; his world grew smiling and warm—until a lightning-like jolt struck through his mind to sear his complacency . . .

. . . How come I'm alone? Down there right now are dozens of kids my age, in school or playing together, skating and shooting at baskets, lounging around the drugstore telling stories and kidding girls . . . while high on a hilltop I sit by myself in an old tower looking out to sea with indefinable urgings and a vow of sorts to hold hard now to these sounds and sights and smells that have come to mean so much . . . What is it about that horizon? What lies on the other side? Not just ships and land and more of the same old ocean—but what is the magic that calls . . . and who am I fooling really?

. . . Oh, it's fun to gaze from a nest in the pines but I know what it's like offshore, not smooth not safe not warm like in here with the books and the land all around. Never a week goes by but that ships come in with a casing of ice halfway to the foremasthead, with sails blown out while tired men with ripped hands and bandages under the hats stand mute by the dories as they swing alongside a wharf . . . Then later down in the fo'c'sle, the thick blue air and the snatches of conversation: "Lost two dories—Cape Sable Bank—thickasnow it was—blowing a goddamned fucking gale—sea masthead high—sand on deck the next morning—two pretty good men they was—six kids—coupla bucks put aside—not much—pass the hat in Gloucester—pass the hat in the bars down on Duncan Street—aw shit now fuck it an' gimme the jug". . .

. . . What am I doing this year? Walking day after day through the woods with Laird, dreaming and planning and dreaming some more, walking and rowing and sailing . . . always alone, except for the dreams, spending hours and hours in this tower (sometimes at night under the cold pale light of the moon, with the village spread all around like the make-believe snowbank on the rug by the Christmas tree—long ago, that is), and what are these thoughts that leap from hidden places when you stare at the path of the moon, when you gaze at the lamplight from snug kitchens in farms burrowed under trees . . .

. . . Now a strident voice:

Come down from the tower, lad! Come out of the dream! Come back from the trails in the woods! Come back to the village streets with the quiet bustle of people who live as they should. People who catch and clean and sell fish, and buy food, and sing songs and dance on Saturday nights or go bowling or take in a picture show. Come on now, boy, and be like the rest! Be sociable. Don't be standoffish. What is the matter with you? If you're scared of something, what is it?

I—I don't know—I mean, I'm not scared of anything.

You're a liar.

Remember the last time ashore? Remember how you behaved? You did pretty well as you sailed your boat up the harbor. But once you left the docks, you were in trouble. You rounded a corner and up ahead the gang of high-school kids was gathered in front of the drugstore—eight or ten in all, with a few about your age—and the minute you saw them your heart sank; you debated whether to cross the street and pass on the other side or give it up and retreat.

They were laughing and horsing around, with their hands in their pockets, some of them smoking or spinning in one-legged circles each time they came up with a joke.

Something inside told you to go ahead and strike up a conversation.

But what will we talk about?

Oh? You don't like girls?

Well, sure I do, but—

Sudden retreat. A snap of the fingers for outward effect (as though reminded of some urgent errand) and the rapid reversal of steps down the winding way to a lane that led up a hill to the small department store. "Dime to Dollar," it said on the crimson sash of a sign. Hot inside, with the sweet-sick smell of cheap perfume and drowned hot dogs awash in a jar of hot water.

Look sharp. Is she here? Oh yes, she is, and her name is Genevieve—not the prettiest girl in town, but a girl with a way about her, pretty enough at that, charged with something special that makes a fellow feel those shooting pains in the groin, just ask the boys at the drugstore, they'll tell you all about her.

Her body was on exhibit this day in a purple sweater stretched wonderfully taut, and her auburn hair was held by a purple ribbon. But mostly she wore that strange half-smile with the languorous look in the eyes.

It wouldn't do, of course, to open right up and ask her out on a date. Oh no. The safe thing is to poke around with the saws and hammers and pretend you're here on business—squinting down the back of the saw with the girl lined up in your sights, then turning away in a flash the moment she looks around, and making a headlong awkward exit as though she didn't exist.

Across the street, toward a low white building set back in a little park. A friendly building, with white pillars and snug windows and the boughs of evergreen banked high all about the foundation. "Boothbay Harbor Memorial Library," says a sign by the entrance. And it's off with the boots, and the place is full of silence and warmth, and there she sits in her regular place. Her name is Esther and this is the beautiful girl, the kind of beauty a man would want in his wife, the kind you'd be proud to have by your side when you entered a foreign legation.

She is soft, sweet, and even in her low-heeled shoes her legs are handsome—though she crosses them always with care. Too much care perhaps, which is where she could learn from Ginny or some of the drugstore girls. But her eyes are kind and there's a delicate look to her ears and her sweaters aren't so tight that they make the old folks snort.

But best of all is her way of wanting to listen. Like the times you two were alone and she'd help to find a book, then you'd talk for a minute or two and you could smell her body and it made you feel like trembling. Like the time when you brought your entire collection of ship pictures in for her to examine, and she kept them a week and asked all sorts of questions.

Her name was right, too—Esther Morrison. Maybe if you stayed around for a few more years you'd grow up fast and it wouldn't make any difference that she was three years older— maybe you could be married and you'd get a job as a journalist and go off around the world on one of the big four-masted schooners with a South Sea Islands crew and every few years you could come back to Maine to show off the kids and check on the drugstore gang.

CHAPTER 24

Books and the sea, I discovered, had more than a little in common: both were distilled of silence and solitude. I was an islander now, so what could be more fitting than that my places of refuge on the mainland should be the sail loft and the public library, for these were islands too—in the turbulent social seas. Silence and solitude, books and the sea, sail loft and library. World enough for any man. Yet how few of them knew it. There were six garages sprawled about Boothbay, and they were crowded all day long and half the night as well. There were two drugstores, and both were jammed afternoon and evening. The more popular of the two had a "rental library" as well—made up of cheap fiction for the most part, with gaudy-jacketed books displayed between shelves of deodorant and gargle, not far from the soda fountain.

By mid-September all the tourists had gone. The entire coast took a good hot bath, shuttered its curio shops, and settled down for the long cold siege of winter. The wind blew hard and the leaves tossed their lives away as I went through the library doors for the first time and presented myself at a desk. A girl looked up. "Could you please tell me," I stammered, "if you have any books on the sea, on sailing ships, voyages—things like that?"

Her smile was so warm that I looked away. "Yes, I think we have; if you'll follow me, we'll see what we can find." I followed her. Her body was lithe and her ankles were slim. I could smell her hair and her voice was low and gentle. "You're the boy who lives out on the little island, I believe."

"Yes, that's right."

"Will you be with us all winter?"

"I hope so. I'd like to live here all my life."

We came to a section marked: 910.4 Voyages and Voyaging. I watched her leave; then the everyday world dissolved in a sky full of clouds and each cloud was a book of the sea and ships. They marched through my mind for hours that day as I thumbed them one by one. When I left, it was nearly dark and my arms were loaded with books. I ran up the sail and flew toward the island and after supper I curled in the window seat with my new-found world.

I liked it best in the library when the two of us were alone. When school let out and the village kids came in, I would slip away, for they giggled and clowned and played feeling games underneath the table.

From time to time my folks would go to Portland or Boston for a few days on business. I'd restrain myself till their bus was out of sight; then I'd run to the harbor and cook some beans and breathe deep of the peace and solitude. If the sun was warm I would lie among the rocks with my back to the wind and gaze

at the horizon, then read for a time, then walk or row or lie
under the pines and dream of the years ahead.

It was different when my stepfather was around. One night
—it must have been December—he dozed in his place by the
fire while Mother worked at her knitting. A full moon was due
and all day long the wind had howled from the north. I was
reading *By Way of Cape Horn*, by Alan Villiers, the story of a
voyage in the full-rigged ship *Grace Harwar* from Australia to
the British Isles:

> . . . With the blue sky cloudless overhead, the blue sea, now
> flecked to white with the strong wind, all around us, and
> we the centre ever of our unending circle of blue beneath
> our unending dome of blue above, we came on with a bone
> in our teeth, and we must have been a sight for all the gods.
> The boys sang as they worked upon the reeling yards high
> aloft making good the damage that the passing of strong
> winds had left; the cook sang as he peeled his potatoes in
> the galley; the stowaway hummed English songs to herself
> as she painted the ship's name upon the lifebuoys. The
> fresh wind drove away the heat; we did not need, once
> we had checked yards a little in from the backstays, to touch
> sail or brace or sheet or halliard. We only had to hang on
> to the wheel, and sail on! None may know the beauty of the
> sea who has not made a voyage in square-rigged sail. . . .

I closed the book and gazed at the moon all mellow and
amber as it came rising out of the sea, and it seemed I couldn't
wait until my life at sea began. I bundled up and said to my
mother: "I'm going on watch."

I stepped into the night. The island became a tall ship on a
moonlit sea with her granite stem tossing the groundswell aside
and the wind in her pine-boughed sails. I studied the path of
the moon, then moved to my place of command on the little dock
shaped like a quarter-deck. There was a crust of snow on the
handrails and ice on the planks and the wind blew hard from
the north northwest.

Oh how it blew! And oh how she sailed that night! I locked
my hands behind my back as I paced by the hour with never a
word to the helmsman. The lights one by one slid from sight
behind the hill of the world till we were all alone in the path of
the moon—locked in the bone-gray arms of an ever increasing
breeze. From time to time I'd stand in the lee of a tall spruce

mast and nibble my fruit or crackers; and aloft I'd see the drift of the clouds with the branches in silhouette and the star-studded sky looking down. And it came to me that this was surely the most beautiful sight in the world—the pines, the clouds, the stars, and the sky, on a windy night in the full of the moon and alone on the coast of Maine. You could hear the bells in the course of the hours, and the men took their turn at the wheel. The moon went from amber to ivory—and the pine sails raged in the wake of the wind, and I thought of holding the deck till dawn—

Then I froze at the sight of a man with his back to the sea and his hands jammed down in his pockets. "What's wrong with you, young fellow?"

"I'm standing watch," I said.

"Come in the house."

"It's not time yet—"

"I said, come in the house—"

"Not until twelve o'clock, I want to last it out—"

He stepped toward me and blew in his hands, his eyes peering up from the dark. "Do as your stepfather says."

I walked up the path and he closed the door. My room was cold as I threw off my clothes in the dark. I turned the bed around and with my coat underneath the pillow I could see the moon on the water.

JOHN HOWELL—SAILMAKER. The sign on the old wharf was so low you had to duck, but it had a way of swinging in the wind that spoke of Treasure Island and the Admiral Benbow Inn.

John Howell was my friend. It was the magic of the word "Sailmaker" that lured me up the steep-pitched steps and into the low-beamed loft with its varnished hardwood floor running out over the harbor in undulating waves, as though the sea itself ran shoreward beneath the sails.

I remember standing just inside the door. He didn't know I was there, for his eyes—I would learn—were not what they'd been in his days in the deep-water ships. There were three big iron-bellied stoves in the loft; bolts of canvas were slung overhead, and coils of rope stood like the stumps of newly felled trees between heaps of sails secured with salt-bleached line.

Three men were at work with their backs to the wall full of windows. Each man had a bench some eight feet long and low, pierced with holes for spikes and knives; and each wore overalls and a peaked cap and high-laced shoes and a necktie done in great loose knots.

I thought they might throw me out. The man nearest me was narrow of shoulder and bent forward like a fishhook. He glanced at me over the top of his spectacles; his eyes had a mischievous glint. He had a long slim pipe with a little black bowl, and he clung to the stem with yellowed teeth.

"How do you do," I began.

"How do you do be damned, boy, pull up a chair and sit down." A wicker rocker stood nearby and I felt the glow from the stove. When I glanced through a window, I could see our island between the masts of a schooner. He shook the sewing palm off his hand. "I'm John Howell." He wrapped my hand in his and all I could feel was sinew and bone. His eyes danced about till he threw his head back and coughed a terrible cough.

"My name"—when he had finished—"my name is Sterling Hayden, and I live out—"

"Pshaw boy, I know where you live, you live on the island out by the buoy; and you're spending the winter 'cause your daddy didn't pay his bills and they came and took his beautiful car and—"

"He's not really my father at all."

"He's your stepfather, I know that too. And you don't go to school and you sail all the time except when it blows too hard, then you go for your rows in the dory." He raised his eyebrows as his left arm flicked out to a coil of manila that cradled a bottle. He laughed a little. Then he drew the cork; the stuff smelled strong. "Rum," he gasped.

I smiled.

"You're sea-struck, boy, that's what you are. All you care for is ships, old ships, sailing ships, am I right? Of course I'm right, don't tell me any different."

I shook my head. "How could you tell all that?"

He leaned forward and I could see myself in his eyes. "Because I was the very same way myself—sixty years ago—on the coast of Wales, that was. When the masts were as thick as candles in the Roman Church. And I ran away to sea and I shipped in a clipper named *Thermopylae*—have you heard the name by chance?"

"Oh yes, she was built in 1867."

"Yes, she was. . . . Now you're ready to go to sea." He blew his nose through his fingers and snapped them at the stove, and he said: "You go, boy, you go, no matter what they say, you go, understand?"

I nodded and smiled.

When his men had gone home, John would fill his pipe while I threw some coal in the stoves and we'd sit there in the twilight, facing the sea. Sometimes a coasting schooner would be working her way upharbor, or, more often, a big low Gloucesterman would come in, her red and green lights proud and her diesel rumbling and her men in leather boots leaning with backs to the wind.

Out beyond the islands the lighthouse would flare and fade; the firelight would dance on the baled canvas and the overhead beams, and he'd talk of his days at sea, as his gnarled misshapen hands caressed the bottle, till at last the words grew muffled and he began to spill the rum. Then I'd get the cork and help him into his thin black coat, and down the staircase we'd go.

Sometimes he'd start to sing, with his fierce old fingers locked like teeth in my upper arm, and out on the street he'd stagger. No matter how hard I tried, he'd stagger a little going down the walk, and the elderly folk would scowl and the kids would mimic and laugh till we came to the stairs to his room over the beauty parlor. I would help him upstairs, where his daughter was always waiting with a rueful smile on her face.

Throughout the winter we lived from hand to mouth, with always one last dollar bill kept in Mother's knitting bag. Each weekly trip to market was pure adventure. Mother would face the cashier—"Mrs. Marsden, so sorry to trouble you, but Mr. Hayden's check hasn't come through yet; do you suppose we could charge a few more things, my dear?"

Mrs. Marsden would nod just a trifle without looking up, and Mother began her shopping, while out on the docks Daddy Jim paced, his fingertips atwitch for a cigarette.

Yet in spite of this I was having a glorious time—except for what happened in March. This was my birthday month; we seemed to be counterparts—so I had told myself—we both were rebellious. Whenever the wind scoured the harbor a horehound white, with the screaming gulls all around, I'd laugh out loud and, if no one was near, I'd sometimes wave to a cloud.

A fine old three-masted schooner, the *Charles Klink*, stood at the foot of the hill right by the middle of town. She was laid up for the winter, and I walked around on her decks whenever

I had the chance. I wanted secretly to buy her; it was rumored she could be had for less than three thousand dollars.

One Saturday night toward the end of the month I went into town. The stores were open and I walked up and down for a time. It must have been around nine-thirty or ten when I slipped over the schooner's rail to walk in the shadow thrown by an old warehouse. You could see her mastheads all white in the lights of the village, with the stars way beyond; and something called on me to climb aloft and see how it felt in the dark. I made my way up the mizzenmast. The wind was colder now, and a halyard drummed away on the spars. The deck was nearly lost down below.

I wedged myself against the doublings and beat my arms on my chest. A window leaped into life not thirty yards away: a naked bulb cast a yellow glow on a double bed and some pieces of furniture. A man stepped into view. He wore a singlet and pants, and he carried a drink in each hand.

A feeling of guilt engulfed me. I turned away from the window. But the light gnawed at the back of my head till I turned around, with my cap pulled down—half hoping the light would be out. He sat on the bed and pulled at a cigarette; I could tell he was talking to someone. The light shone on his bald head and his skin was the texture of putty. I remembered having seen him before—he was cook at the Tinker Tavern. He got to his feet and dropped his pants as a girl stepped into his arms. She had nothing on and her hair flowed half round her face; I knew it was Esther even before he pushed her hair to one side. He stroked her back and she turned toward me, but only to get the drink. I shrank inside myself with one shoulder up as a shield, and the window was plunged into black.

I stood for some time as though frozen fast to the mast. A million lights seemed to center on me, and I knew if I moved she would see me and think I had planned it. After a while I squeezed my way to the far side. My legs felt weak and my hands were numb, and an ache expanded throughout my chest.

I rushed to the boat and hove on the halyards like an infant throwing a tantrum. All around the town the lights were dancing with laughter. Once free of the shore, I made fast the sheet and stood up to steer and never once looked back.

CHAPTER 25

Fall again, with 1932 well on its way to the grave. The maple trees guarding the library spread their leaves about—crisp leaves curled and yellow, eaves scoured with reds and browns and the palest of April green, veined leaves tumbling down in a wind gone now into the quadrant north of west. Summer cottages one by one retired: windows shuttered, eyes closed for the long sleep. Schoonermen came clomping up the sail-loft steps to stand with their backs to the fire, while the jug of rum went round and the horizon lay cold and aloof with a glint in its steel-gray eye, awaiting the onslaught of winter.

One Saturday afternoon a pickup truck appeared at McIntyre's wharf, where the Haydens were waiting with a pair of bags and half a dozen cartons. Laird, sensing the threat of a move, sat with his leash in his mouth. The driver was cheerful but he asked for his pay in advance. I hoped no one was looking down from the prim white homes on the hill. I climbed in back with the dog. A figure stood in one of the sail-loft windows. It was stooped and white; I could see a hand moving back and forth with a pipe. I waved once or twice, then started to cry. As we rumbled over the hill, I had a final glimpse of the island. Then I lay down and pulled the tarpaulin over my head.

Hallowell was an ugly, dirty town with its back to the Kennebec River. It lay next door to the capital city of Augusta some ninety miles from the sea. Our boardinghouse was a cyst in a row of boardinghouses. Inside, the air was stagnant; you could smell the mould, and the rugs were paper-thin. The rent was a dollar a day. They had a brass bed with a screen in front, and I had a couch next to a disused fireplace.

We didn't say much as we sorted our things. Mother made coffee on a Sterno stand next to the washbasin. This room had been a parlor. Now the big sliding doors were locked and newspaper was stuffed in the cracks and light bulbs cut feebly through the gloom. I sat on the couch feeling homesick while he read the telephone book.

Within a few days Mother went to work for an outfit that sold cosmetics through salesladies who went from door to door giving "demonstration facials." She was given a list of "prospects" and a little black bag full of lubricants and—hopefully—a pad of order blanks. She was in business for herself, the hard way.

Six weeks later, he bought two new Plymouths, and I was enrolled in the most expensive preparatory school in the United States. The cars were identical in color. Hers was a convertible and his a roadster. We moved to the local hotel, which was full of salesmen and businessmen who sang at lunch and adjusted their pants as they walked through the lobby. It had a view of the river, a strip of water squeezing past some mills and junk yards.

Had it not been for an oversight on the part of Daddy Jim, these wonderful things might have happened before.

Mother had been working for a month. One night she came home half frozen, her feet soaked through and blue. She had given six demonstration facials and taken in no money. She was sobbing, and for the first time there was nothing at all to eat. He took her in his arms and patted her back. I brushed the dog, who looked at us all out of big brown eyes.

Suddenly Daddy Jim slammed his fist on the wall. "By golly, I tell you I've had just about enough! By golly, I'm going to do it. Frances, sit down."

I looked up. Mother's chin quivered. "What is it, Jim?"

"Oh I hate it, believe me I've fought against this for months. But we can, if Buzz here is willing, use his three thousand dollars to tide us over and give Dad Jim the money he needs to close the deal."

"What three thousand dollars?"

"Your trust fund, son, the one your Uncle Mont put aside when you were born."

Mother broke in: "Buzzy, you must have forgotten; Uncle Mont set up this fund to see you through college or help you get started in business when the time came."

"It's up to you, son; if you want to release that money, I know your Uncle Mont will oblige."

"Of course I do. I want you to take the money. I only wish it was more."

He took me by the arms and shook his head and tried to speak. Finally: "Son, you have the word of your Dad Jim that he'll pay this back two—three—maybe four or five times over, in just a matter of months. And if we hurry, we can make it to Western Union before it closes."

He stopped by the door, patting his pockets. "Frances, have

you?" She shook her head. "Then I guess we'll have to send this wire collect."

Wassookeag School
Dexter, Maine
Oct. 6, 1932

Dearest Mother,

You didn't notice it but I cried when you left last week. I don't know why. It is just that I love you so much I guess and you have been through so much these past few years and now that I look back those months on the island seem like the most wonderful time any boy ever had. I will always remember them no matter what.

I am glad you and Daddy Jim have the new cars. You must get a heater put in yours. I don't want to criticize but why did he have to get two new cars? Where will you live next?

I guess I am getting acquainted here very nicely. The boys are quite decent most of them though we don't have too much in common. Mostly they are very rich. One of my roommates is named John Newberry. His father owns the chain stores and he has two cars, a Chrysler Imperial Phaeton for weekends and a Plymouth sedan for in town. The other fellow is named McKay and they own a machine tool plant somewhere. The uncle of one of the boys controls the New York Central Railroad but he is all right. A fellow by the name of Campbell comes from the soup family. There are 19 boys here and they have 22 cars. Pretty good, eh?

Take care of Laird. I'm not doing well in my studies yet but will try hard so you can be proud of me and I can justify all this money you must be spending.

Thank you for all you have done for me. Say hello to DJ and all the love in the world to you from a very lucky—

Buzz

Wassookeag School
Dexter, Maine
Nov. 2, 1932

Mother Dearest,

I am terribly sorry not to have written to you this past month. I did it so as not to upset you too much. Things have

not been going too well actually. Most of the teachers seem
to be ganging up on me now. Also the headmaster
mentioned to me that he hasn't gotten his money yet as
was promised by DJ. The teachers mean well but they give
me extra work to do so I don't get to go to the hockey
matches or things like that.

I don't mean to be unfair but I do think it has something
to do with money. The other fellows seem to be kind of a
club and lots of their parents know each other and go on
vacations together and things like that. Also I guess I was
born dumb and I'll tell you right now my marks are just
terrible. I haven't passed a test since I got here. Math is
worst. Mostly I get in the middle sixties.

I do have a girl. Her name is Debra Nealley and she
comes of a nice family and they live in Bangor of all places
—up on a hill in the better part of town. She came here to
a house party and I cut in on her and we have been cor-
responding constantly so I guess I will be challenged to a
duel most any day now. You would approve of her I know.

I am distressed to hear you are still working. I detest the
thought of my wonderful mother selling cosmetics door
to door. Why do you work when he has so much money?
Is the deal closed yet? I trust so. Please answer these
questions and thank you for the macaroons and the pictures
of the island. We'll live there one fine day I bet just you
wait and see.

Loads and loads of love always,
Yours,
Buzz

The headmaster's office is above the dry-goods store near the
center of town. It is a large room with tall windows arched
beneath a high ceiling. The desk is large—so large that the
headmaster could lie on top of it and not overlap an inch. He
has a go-getter's face. He is a self-made man and full of steam.
And this afternoon he is angry.

The boy enters.

"Sit down, Hayden. Now. You are here at Wassookeag because
you need special help, because you were kept out of school the
past three years—why I don't know. You were behind when
you came here, you are behind now, and you will remain behind
unless you buckle down and get to work. You're how old?"

"Sixteen."

"Sixteen. When I was sixteen, I entered Bowdoin College on a scholarship. I married when I was seventeen. I worked my way by mowing lawns and tutoring spoiled students and doing anything I could lay a hand to. I never studied evenings because I had to work. Instead I got up at three every morning and did my homework. I graduated Phi Beta Kappa and I was captain of the track team and my daughter attended my graduation. I started this school when I was twenty-two and I intend to maintain a pretty fine record, and no student is going to interfere. I suggest you stop talking to your roommates about the glories of the Gloucester fishing fleet and the hardships encountered off Cape Horn by the square-rigged schooners. When you write to your stepfather, tell him he owes me quite a good deal of money. He said he would pay last month and I haven't received a cent. This is not a charitable institution. On your way out, tell Miss Goulart I would like to see her. That will be all."

"Yes, sir."

It was warm in the sun. The snow was thawing and water dripped from the eaves of the old brick buildings. I could hear someone bowling. A pair of local girls went by loaded with books and pimples. A crowd of local fellows in loud jackets leaned on the drugstore window.

I crossed the street and after a time found the library behind a bronze doughboy with a hand grenade. The only books under 910.4 were about *Old Ironsides* and the sinking of the *Titanic*. I walked up the hill, past the school, and sat on a rock in the sun. You could hear the wind in the trees.

> Wassookeag School
> Dexter, Maine
> Nov. 21, 1932

Debbie Darling,

I'm going to tell you something that no one else knows at all. You must keep it to yourself and don't tell a soul in the world. Promise?

Next weekend is Thanksgiving holidays and as you know we are having a house party and I know you can't make it but Debbie Darling (you don't mind if I call you that do you?) I have decided this whole school nonsense is not for me so I am going to run away. You may remember I told you how much I loved the sea. Well, I have decided to beat my way (as they say) to Portland this weekend and land a job on a ship going to South America or the South Seas or around the world.

The only thing I'll miss will be you. My folks will be upset but they'll understand one day. Now I would like you to meet me. Will you please? Can you meet me just to say goodbye? Just for a few minutes please. I have it all figured out and I will be in the railway yards of the Boston and Maine (near you) at midnight Saturday. Meet me by the Railway Express shed.

If I'm dressed like a tough don't let that frighten you as I'll be riding the rods into Portland. I know I love you and I hope you love me.

Please would you bring a snapshot of yourself (full length) and give it to me there.

With love,

P.S. Do you have one in a bathing suit???

CHAPTER 26

The bell rings and the lights go out. My roommates are already in bed. I throw open the windows—wide.

"Oh now, damn it, not so much," growls Newberry.

I lower the frames and flop into bed. They have the radio on: "This is Guy Lombardo, ladies and gentlemen, playing for your radio pleasure from the Grand Ballroom of the Roosevelt Hotel, and here we go with a medley—"

My head lies close to a window. A full moon hangs just over the brow of the hill and the snow sparkles as I glance through naked branches toward Susie Goulart's house. Her light goes on. It is off to one side where my roommates can't see it. They have Lombardo, I have Susie Goulart. She's the best-looking girl in Dexter, we all agree—black hair and tight skirts and tight sweaters, but her teeth are too big, like with most French Canucks.

. . . Miss Goulart, this is my last night in school, so please do me a favor just this once and don't pull the shade down.

Part-way down is all right, but not all the way—please? She crosses the room from time to time, fully dressed, including a scarf. My heart pounds. Not so many stars tonight, it's the full of the moon.

She steps to the window and the shade whams down—all the way. Good for you, Miss Goulart. It's better this way because tonight is the big night and won't it be a laugh when they all wake up and wonder where I've gone. I smile into the pillow and a falling star leaps across the sky.

Their breathing is slower now. I whisper as hard as I can: "John! Hey Rich! Hey John hey Rich!" Nothing. Only Carmen Lombardo singing—

The closet is huge and has a light. I have everything ready. I dress fast, in tweed pants and a woolen shirt and two sweaters. The green zipper jacket with the hood makes me look like a monk—a boy monk, if there is such a thing. Down the back staircase and out, with a brief pause just beyond the street light. Just long enough to shake my fist: . . . the hell with the lot of you—headmaster, teachers, students, New York Central and Campbell's soup and Chrysler Imperials, the whole damn she-bang—except Miss Goulart—you just sit here and look under the bed and I'll send you a wire one of these days from Rio or Port of Spain.

A diner squats by the highway with steamed windows. A truck starts out and I step in the path of its lights. "Mister, could you give me a lift into Bangor, please?"

"Please!" he says in dismay. "Sure kid, get in."

He drives too fast, what with the snow and ice. My window is stuffed with paper but still it leaks; we're both bundled up, and the small Maine towns flash by. I'm free. Free to roam and laugh and slug my way through the great big roaring world of men, free to head for blue lagoons and trade-wind seas, to grab a job on a windjammer and learn the sailorman's trade. So I tell myself, patting my wallet, with its pictures of Mother and Laird and the island, along with a two-dollar bill. Debbie darling, I hope you'll be waiting there 'cause I'm cold cold and it's going to be a long haul from Bangor to Portland for a man who's riding the rods—whatever they might be.

Bangor sleeps as a clock booms midnight. I run for the depot. Oh Debbie, please be there! Because you're my girl and it's not every night you get to meet your boy friend down in the railway yards; oh Debbie, I just want to put my arms inside your coat

and feel your body and that's all—really it is—except maybe
for a goodbye kiss—something to take with me out into the
world.

A swirl of snow whips under the depot lights. The place is
locked up and there isn't a soul in sight—just the moon behind
some trees. Off by the marshaling yards I hear a locomotive.
Maybe the thing to do is get back to school before anyone finds
out. I run around the Express shed, then jog toward the round-
house with the glow of a firebox shot up into the sky. I glance
back over my shoulder, but she's not there. Why, Debbie? Why?

As the books said to do, I let six cars go by. Then I make
for the forward end of a gondola. My feet twist on the stones.
I grab for the rail and the wheels have a horrible look as I heave
myself up and fling myself down on the floor. The depot goes by.

The wail of the whistle haunts the river valley, and I tell
myself I'm outward bound at last. I flex my knees to lessen the
jolt of the car. The engine's plume turns fiery red and I envy
the fireman his job. A shower of cinders sprinkles my face and
my body aches with cold. Farms flash by: most of them somber
under the moon save for a light in the barn. We crawl up a
grade with the engine booming as her drive wheels tear at the
rails. My hands feel numb. Portland seems a thousand miles
away and I'm suddenly scared.

I lie for a time in a corner between bars of iron and a
splintered crate. When the motion stops, I wake up. We're on a
siding. Trainmen with lanterns crunch by. The reefer hatch
flies up and three men come piling out. One of them carries a
pail, which he scoops full of sand by the ditch. They build a
fire, with the bucket on top. One of them spies me. He moves
close and looks me over. I want to slip back out of sight, but I
stand there. "Hey you, kid. Wanna spud?" I do, but I won't let
on. "Well." He has a wild rough face and his collar is turned
up. "You wanna get warm? Come down, for Jesus Christ's sake,
come down."

I wish for a rock or a knife as I climb stiffly over the side.
"Thanks very much," I say.

"Ho Christ, Harry, listen to him—'Thank you very much.'
Where the hell you from, bub?"

"I'm running away from school." They all laugh and one of
them taps his head. The lanterns are swinging toward us; I
expect the hoboes to hide. But they squat by the ditch, their eyes
alert. "Swap you a spud fer a smoke," one of them says.

The trainmen stop. The cigarettes go round. "Take a couple," the man says. I shake my head and check myself from saying thanks. The lanterns swing as they go—
"You're pretty fucking dumb, kid, you know that. Next time take the butts and if you don't want 'em some of us does—see?"

Just after dawn, the river—the mighty Kennebec pouring seaward like a coal-black snake, its scales aglint in the light. Farmhouses astir, with upright smoke and a look of warmth in the kitchen, spruce boughs banked waist-high by way of insulation. . . . Maybe home is the best thing after all; maybe if a man has a kitchen and a piece of land and some trees and a creek and he's warm and strong, then that's all he needs; maybe that's better than banging around the world. . . .

I look upriver for a long time and wonder if they're awake— there in the crummy hotel. What would they think if they knew I was rumbling down the east face of the Kennebec in a gondola this bitter goddam morning? Oh, you little redheaded runt, I'll see you one of these days. I'll knock on the door and you'll open up to a bronzed giant with calloused hands and a faraway look in the eye and it'll be me.

We crawl across the drawbridge by the Bath Iron Works. The river black and wide, cold-browed as it pours fast for the sea, fleeing the land grasp of mills, sewers, tar-paper shanties, roadhouses, billboards, and senile summer resorts—Bide-a-Wee, Dew-Drop-Inn, Dun-Rovin—"I'd walk a mile for a Camel, You Bet" . . . "The Chamber of Commerce of Bath, Maine, meets every Wednesday afternoon in the Dirigo Hotel at two PM" . . . Burma Shave!

The day breaks sullen and gray. Some flakes of snow drift down. Thank Christ for that—if it snows the temperature rises. Suddenly my spirit lifts—off to one side is a thoroughbred derelict of a once-proud clipper ship. She lies to a rotting wharf with the spike of her bowsprit rammed toward the dingy town.

The iron full-rigged ship *Coriolanus* set a record of sixty-nine days from London to Calcutta. Her hull is still sound and her seven-foot bulwarks run just as true as the day she was launched on the banks of the river Clyde. Any day now they'll put the torches to her and chop her in bits for scrap. I wave, for we've met before—when I tried to sign on as one of her crew for a voyage to the Cape Verde Islands, but the Portuguese couldn't come up with the money so the venture fell through.

All day we roll through flurries of snow till we come to the

Portland yards. I go over the side and strike through the dusk
toward the water front. I am stiff with cold so I run and jog.
The snow comes harder now, and people hurry home. The glow
from the rooming-house windows looks better by far than before. The cars by the curbs have hats of powdered snow.

At the top of a hill the wind whips at me. It comes out of
the northeast with a sorrowful moan. I can't see anything as I
slide down a long hill, but I know where I am and it gives me a
feeling of pride to be a man on his own.

I hope to find one of the fishing schooners I'd known in
Boothbay. There I'd surely have a place to sleep while I search
for a berth in a deep-water ship.

The streets are deserted. I can see the storm-warning lights
on top of the Custom House. A police patrol whines by and I
follow it to a dock, where a crowd is milling around. Lights
flash, and dozens of men stomp their feet in the lee of a lumber
shed. The tide is high. A Coast Guard lifeboat lies to the dock;
stretchers are handed from the cockpit to the ambulances standing by. Someone slips.

"Watch it, watch it!" a voice cries out.

"Shaddup fer Jesus' sake, he's dead, ain't he?"

This isn't the world I envisioned those nights in study hall.
This isn't what I dreamed of from my tower in the trees or
the nest at the end of the island. I pick up the story in pieces:
". . . Schooner *Lochinvar*—fetched up on a ledge off Peake's
Island—sunk—these guys six hours in water up to their belly—
half the crew gone—frozen. . . ."

I buck the wind to the end of the dock. No schooners. Instead, the harbor a swirling black waste; waves gnash at one
another; up on the hills, the hint of yellowish lights. Back I go
to the street; my feet are soaked and my stomach feels flat with
cramp.

I find the fish pier—broken-backed buildings on a sagging
wharf all slimy with garbage. A collier unloads across the way,
her lights shriveled in the clouds of coal dust and snow.

Half a dozen schooners clutch at one another with their tails
to the wind. I know them all: *Richard Nunan,* long and lean,
with almost a yacht-like bow; *Ethel B. Penney,* with her masts
set in the middle and a long lean snout; *Elinor & Jean, Lulu
Belle, Teazer.* Hard-case vessels in need of paint and gear,
battered little schooners one step ahead of sheriff and gale,
flogging their guts out winter after winter on the banks, their

bilges full of gurry and diesel oil and rusting wrenches along with a ballast of boiler punchings set in cement.

Near the end of the dock, three ships in a row—halyards beating aloft on black pine spars, the outer one iced up, her shrouds swollen the size of a leg in a plaster cast, iced up to the trestletrees and the vertical line of a plumb stem that gives her the look of a fighter. *Restless*—good name for a schooner.

Two men come rolling down the dock; they slam into fish carts and stagger as they skirt the tip of the dock. When they spot the *Restless*, one of them yells: "Oh there y'are, ya miser'ble bas'ard—been lookin' all o'er place fer ya, ya lousy li'l bas'ard." He leans and sways and pivots with both hands in his pockets. He cocks his head and gulps at the snow, then he belches and topples toward a web of rigging. At the last second his hands shoot out and spear the shrouds and he slobbers down to the deck.

He sees me. "Hey you, sonny boy, watcha want who ya lookin' fer hey what?"

"Albert. I'm trying to find my friend, Albert Powers."

"Albie's home wit' the wife an' kids. Come down though, boy, come down out of it up there now boy."

I follow them out to the deck and stand by the fo'c'sle hatch. I can hear a radio below. My friend fumbles around with his pants. "Jus' a sec' now you boy, jus' a sec'n—gotta sign on this son'bitch." He starts to piss on the snow between the dories. I gaze aloft and wonder what it would be like to work up there at sea, with the masts bucking you loose from your grip. He yells: "Oh no I ain' gonna make her, oh I never do make her." He flings his head toward me. "Wha's yer name, kid?"

I tell him.

"Well tha's good name, yer luckier'n me 'cause my name's Chrishen'son—tha's why I can't sign on." He pulls himself together, regains his balance, and slams down the fo'c'sle ladder. I peer down the gloom-filled hatch; across a beam, scratched with a spike or a knife, are the words: SODOMY HALL.

The Hall is wedge-shaped, with a dozen bunks two tiers to the side, a folding table forward of the mast, and a coal stove behind the pitch of the ladder. The warmth soaks in; I smile at the stink of the place. Somebody hands me a chunk of pie and a mug of coffee that burns. Some of the bunks are full of gear; others hold fully dressed men with wide-open mouths and teeth sticking out of their pockets. I'm told to find a bunk if I'm

tired, and I pick one out that looks a little clean. Oily black
bugs crawl away when I throw the blanket aside.

The bunk is nearest the bow. I curl in a blanket cave and
peer aft. Here I am in an honest-to-God fo'c'sle in the plumb-
stemmed schooner *Restless* which has been fishing out of Portland since 1888—how about that? Sterling Walter Hayden, born
Montaigu Relyea Walter, alias Buzzy—in a fo'c'sle bunk full of
bugs, with a northeast gale lashing the water front and the
rigging cased in ice. Wouldn't John Howell be proud if he came
down that ladder just now?

My friend the enginer showed up after breakfast. He was
thirty or so, with a short body and a square jaw like the heroes
in the funny papers, and not an ounce of fat. I remembered
the way his forearm muscles would flicker and ripple even when
he lit a cigarette. "Well look who's here," he said. "What're you,
kid, lost or something?"

"Albert, I'm running away from school."

"Oh? What the hell for? Knock up a girl or something?"

"No, I'm going to get a job in a ship going to Africa or South
America or some place."

I waited for a reaction, but he didn't seem surprised. Two
or three men sat on a locker. They cradled their heads in
leathery hands as they spat with care on the crumbs. He lit a
cigarette and we went on deck, where it was calm and gray—
except for the water, which was a muddy green. They were still
unloading the collier. She rode high above her dock. Al didn't
seem cold even without a coat. His hands were blunt, not thin
and genteel like mine. "Kid, you got some dough?"

"Two dollars."

"Okay. Tell you what you do. Now you listen to me, kid. Go
home, see? If you ain't got a home, then go back to that school.
Stay there. Learn a trade or learn how to dance or play ball,
but whatever you do don't come messing around the vessels,
understand?"

I started to say something.

"Shut up. Stay out of sight of the water except if you're on
vacation. Make your dough and salt it away, then do your
traveling around."

I had an answer prepared but some men came on deck and I
knew how romantic it'd sound, so I mumbled an awkward goodbye and made my way toward the dock. It was low tide. The
lower part of the ladder had rotted away, and beneath the

wharf lay twisted old wires and rubber tires and hundreds of cans stuck in the blue-black slime.

I didn't know whether to turn and wave goodbye or not. I could feel them looking at me and I wondered what they were saying. I kept my chest thrown out and made a fist to swell the size of my hand, then I swung around to wave. There was no one there.

CHAPTER 27

The wind was in the eaves of the Hallowell House Hotel as the J. Watson Haydens assembled their few belongings, tied them in cardboard cartons, and filed down the winding stairs. The desk clerk watched them go. They boarded a bus that said BOSTON—EXPRESS; out in the river, islands of ice meandered toward the sea.

They rode in silence. The man was sallow and the woman cowed; the boy slumped low in the seat with his eyes vague.

It had been a hard time: the cars had been impounded and sold for debts; the boy had been sent home from school because of their failure to pay the tuition and his failure to study and give his word that he'd run away no more.

Across the Kennebec a long freight crawled down the cliffs toward Bath. The bus had a smell all its own, compounded of sweat and smoke and unwashed feet. The boy looked at his folks. They rode with eyes half closed. Do they really hate each other? Yesterday they argued right out in the open for the first time.

"Where will we go, Jim?"

"Cambridge."

"Why?"

"We'll stay with sister Emma—stay just as long as we please."

"Jim, why won't you go to work?"

"I warn you, don't you ever say that to me again, do you hear?"

"I'm sorry, Jim."

"Why doesn't your precious Buzzy go to work?"

"He's only sixteen."

"I started work at twelve."

The boy had left them like that—glowering and speaking in venomous tones. Down to the river he had run and for hours waded through drifts just to feel the surge of water, just to know that this water might in a day or so find itself basking in Boothbay Harbor. That was important just then. Boothbay was a legend now, a golden dream of a golden time that might never come again.

The bus pulled up by a roadhouse in the country. The passengers filed indoors to stand in line in front of the rest rooms, then again while they waited for hot dogs and coffee. The boy went across the highway and sat on a fence with his back to the bus and the people.

Emma was a swart spinster forty-four years old who had been dead since puberty. She was plump and firm as a porpoise, with beads for eyes and biceps like a man's. She had a nun-like face and her hands looked as though someone had taken a cleaver and splintered the stumps of her arms into five pudgy pads apiece. Her rooming house was one among a swampful of rooming houses. The alley out back was a carpet of trash and the house itself was choked with the boardinghouse smell.

The occupants were rejects and also-rans; they were withered and wan but reluctant somehow to die for a few years yet. They clung to the fringe of life and sold themselves to the money machine in return for a handful of crumbs. Year after year they scuttled from room to trolley to an office buried deep in the city's bowels; daylong they worked and at night came home to sit through the evening hours with popular papers and magazines and maybe some latest novel. And always their friend Mister Radio lounged close at hand, singing his soft love songs and telling of wondrous wares to be had from a credit man, telling of how they could make themselves seductive and beautiful like the queens out in Hollywoodland; oh he was their loyal friend for sure—if something went wrong with his tubes they'd have him fixed right quick, no matter what that cost. They couldn't take him to bed but he waited there by the side of the bed within arm's reach of his mistress; nightlong he mounted guard on the wasted body where it lay on a wasted bed —so the wasted years dragged by.

The curious part was if you wanted a job you had to beg almost. Not that it did any good.

Every morning I awoke before it was light. I would lie in bed for a bit, tasting the cold in the attic room, watching the sky turn pale. When I stumbled downstairs to the kitchen, the clock on the breadbox would stand at six and Emma would be by the window reading the *Herald*. It was always cold in that kitchen, and she was always bare-armed. Then my stepfather would appear.

"Morning, Emma," he would say, chafing his hands.

"Morning to you, Watson."

He took his coffee while I stood with my back to the boiler. "Go ahead and eat, young man."

"Thanks, but I'll wait for Mother."

"Your mother's tardy this morning, as usual." Emma would heft herself to the oven and turn the toast, then she ladled out a little oatmeal. "Don't waste sugar and milk."

Mother came in carrying her samples bag. "Good morning, everybody. Isn't this going to be a perfectly gorgeous day?"

Emma would eye her up and down to make sure she wasn't wearing new stockings, while Daddy Jim inhaled on a cigarette and studied the morning news. You could hear the folks upstairs taking turns with the bathroom and the pipes banged and the houses next door were coming to life.

"Lots of appointments today, Frances?" Emma's toothpick would jiggle.

"Just one or two so far."

"How about you, young man?" Daddy Jim remarked. "Anything lined up yet, in the way of a job, I mean?"

"No. How about yourself?"

"Emma, did you hear that? What do you think of a boy talks to his dad like that?"

"You're not my father."

"Watson, I wouldn't stand for it if I was you, I wouldn't. Shame on you, a big strapping boy, talking to your Dad Jim like that."

I borrow the paper and turn to the classified section, page 29 —Positions Wanted, Male. It runs for three columns: "Young man. Must have work. Strong. Intelligent, one year college, do anything, salary secondary." "Young man. Hi-School grad. Needs work desperately, day or night, do anything. Salary open."

Young men here young men there everywhere, hundreds of young men, thousands on thousands of fine young men bright young men all strong and willing, yes dying, to go to work . . . and not a damn thing to do. All over town this morning—

young men searching for work, folding some paper with care
to stuff it into shoes with soles worn through, ready to go
tramping around uptown downtown crosstown ringing door-
bells and haunting the agencies and scanning the blackboards.
Yes sir just dying to go to work we are sir; I'll work a day or
two free for nothing just to show you what I can do sir and a
buck and a half a day would be fine sir if you could see your
way to putting me on, even just for a week or two would help
sir, please.

I zip my jacket high, put the peanut-butter sandwich in one
pocket, my red rubber ball in the other, and reach out a hand
toward the folks. "May I have the dime please, somebody?"

Mother looks at him; he looks at the financial page; Emma
looks at us all. No one speaks. "Someone must have the dime,"
I repeat.

"Do you look for work in the city, or just what do you do,
sit in the library maybe?" His voice is harsh.

"Oh I have a lot of good jobs lined up. I just can't decide
which has the brightest future."

"You know something, young man? You're going to be a big
man when you grow up; you're going to grow up and have a
46-inch chest and a size-three hat." He stomps out back to look
at the weather.

Emma cackles and slaps her knee as I kiss Mother goodbye.

Five miles to Boston. Walk a block jog a block run a block,
round and round it goes, taking pains to stay on the side with
trees if any, breathing deep, squeezing my red rubber ball to
warm my hand and develop a manly grip. Horses pound by
and the streets are bordered with dingy buildings all the way
to the river.

I see her masts shining over the top of a warehouse roof. My
spirits sing as I jog through the lumberyard with the sweep of
her pilot-schooner hull in plain sight. She has a lantern-jawed
bow and a tapering stern with the legend *Wander Bird—San
Francisco* in bold black ice-free letters. Smoke streams from
stacks fore and aft as I step on board and rap on the hatch.

"Hello!" cries a voice. "Come down, whoever you are."

I stomp off the snow and follow the gentle curve of the steps.
A man appears; his brazen eyes are deep-set under an angry
brow, and his forehead slopes high and his jaw juts out—just
like the bow of his ship.

"Go help yourself to some chocolate, lad, and stay as long as you wish." He vanishes aft and I hear his typewriter rattle. I step with reverence into a bunk-lined cabin. Copper trays hold flowers and brass lamps swing from massive waxed oak beams. Woodcuts hang on paneled walls and a fire burns low behind the tiles of an old Dutch stove.

The chocolate is hot and I bask in the warmth of the ship. This is the finest life in the world: a ship of one's own, with no engines of any description, and a trip each year to Europe with a gang of college students, led by a man and his wife, with a pair of kids and a crew of West Indian seamen. No subways and trolleys and buses, no time clocks or bosses or standardized routine.

A shaft of sun floods the cabin table and dances through the flowers. Everything is clean and good and loving and I'd like to remain, but I'm outward bound myself—trying to find the road that will lead to a ship of my own, some day.

"So long, Captain Tompkins. Thank you very much."

The typing stops for a moment. "Come again, come again, you're welcome any time." The voice high, imperious, yet plaintive.

By the gate I pause for one glance of farewell, then I break toward the bridge on the run. It's going to be all right, I know that now. There's a ship for me somewhere—there's a job too, right now, this very day. I make up my mind: today is waterfront day. No making the rounds in the business section, no man-of-the-office routine:

"Whaddaya want, kid?"

"Well, I was wondering if—"

"There ain't no jobs here, sonny. There ain't been no jobs here in years and there ain't never gonna be no jobs again—okay?"

"Sure, lady, okay, thank you."

I start up Beacon Hill, where the houses are proud of the Yankee tradition: lovely red-brick mansions with prim black shutters and small-paned windows full of ivy and porcelain figurines. Hitching posts from the olden days by the flagstone steps—funny little nigger boys in red pants with green vests and rich red lips, hand extended of course. And atop the hill the State House itself, with its gilt dome.

Plenty of manpower in the park: fellows decked out in brown-paper capes, with morning-paper cushions and evening-paper pillows, bundled in old overcoats down to the ground.

All day long I wander. Just as I've been wandering now for more than two months: along Atlantic Avenue to check each wharf—Rowe's Wharf, T Wharf, Long Wharf (home of United Fruit and the Great White Fleet, where the cops will run you in if you go on board looking for work).

The wind is fresh off the sea. I squeeze my ball and change my paper soles and charge through the tunnel that leads to East Boston, where the Blue Funnel ships lie, with their coolie crews from Londontown, Singapore, Bombay, Rangoon.

"Hey! Hey, you kid!"

"Is the mate on board just now?"

"Beat it. I said beat it before I run ya in."

East Boston is tenement town. The sunlight is swallowed by mounds of blackened snow; the gutters are full of trash; and the pawnshop balls swing in the gusts. Movie houses and cafés and the roar of wheels, and everywhere men looking up and down, trying to stay in the sunlight, passing a cigarette from hand to hand.

Under the harbor again and past the hulk of the South Station to the fish pier, where trawlers are moored. My eye is alert for schooners, but I don't dare ask for a job. Too tough, this life. I don't mind reading about it, but when I ship out I'd like to be headed south—down where the trade winds blow. So I ramble around the pier, not knowing where or how to pass the time . . . something must be wrong after all . . . I'm not of the sea and I'm not of the land . . . I'm sworn and anxious to go, yet scared to go, so all I do is tramp the water front.

It's getting late and my face is shriveled with cold. Time to head for home. I feel for the dime. Under the El the cinders fly. I turn my back on the harbor at State Street. Office lights shine feebly in the water-front district, growing brighter as I go uptown with the rush-hour traffic.

I pause at my favorite shop: "Kelvin & Wilfred O. White—Nautical Instruments." The window is pure enchantment: sextants, barometers, and ship's bell clocks; taffrail logs, signal flags, parallel rules, binoculars and charts and shining binnacles with legs like dolphins cast in brass. The window is a magnet; it draws the gaze of countless commuters on the way to the subway. We stand in a row with our noses close to the glass and—I would guess—a distant look in our eyes. You can hear the subway growling below the walk.

When I look into the store, a man beckons me to come in. I

look around, but the man is pointing at me. This is the first time anyone has noticed me since I left the *Wander Bird*. A bell sounds as I close the door; it reminds me of the many times I have come here looking for work.

He draws me off to a corner near the chronometer case. "Well, Sterling, you haven't found a ship yet, have you?"

"I'm afraid not, Mr. White."

"How would you like to work on a big schooner sailing from New London to California?"

I'm afraid to say a word.

His face is round and kind, with a fringe of white hair above the ears, and you know he is a man you can trust. "The captain was in for his charts this afternoon. I told him you were a good lad. He sails in ten days and he'll sign you on as the ship's boy and give you ten dollars a month. How does that sound?"

I stammer. "When will you leave?" he asks.

"Right now. Tonight. As soon as I get my things I'll grab a freight from the yards in South Boston."

He reaches down in a pocket. One of the clerks is locking up, but the window is still full of faces.

"Here, this will buy a bus ticket, anyway. Pay me back if you wish—when you get a ship of your own."

BOOK III

———

EXILE FROM OBLIVION

CHAPTER 28

It was a wind-laced golden day when the schooner *Wanderer,* twenty-four days out of San Francisco, stood in from the sea to lie becalmed for a time in the lee of Nuku Hiva. Then, grasping at cat's-paws with canvas-gloved hands, she laboriously beat up into the Bay of Taiohae. Her anchor plunged and her chain roared after, and she came to rest (in nine fathoms—soft sand bottom), with the ruined fort atop Calaboose Hill in line with a string of laundry all but becalmed in the lee of Government House.

The midday heat fell like a sledge on the deck. We rigged the awning aft and the kids dove over the rails. Some officials put out from the old stone quay in a leaky pirogue dwarfed by a great French flag. They nosed through our documents, smiled at the girls, tossed off some whiskey, and left—stepping ashore, they hurried off in the shade, in time for the long siesta.

"Very well," I said to the crew, "you can take the rest of the day off. Beginning tomorrow morning I want all hands up and around by six sharp. We'll wash her down and then you can work until noon and take the rest of the day off. Fair enough?"

No one had any complaints.

"And while we're at it," I went on, "let me just say this. You've had it pretty easy on this passage. You've had things pretty much your own way. I've tried to ram it home to some of you that a ship like this needs a lot of hard work and a lot of loving care. Some of you obviously don't care much for this. Well, let me tell you that as of now the honeymoon is over. I came to the Marquesas not because I wanted to but because most of you wanted to. So far as I'm concerned, I'd like to clear out of here tonight and shove on through to Papeete. But we're here, so I guess we'll hang around for a week or so. This gives us a chance to compromise. You can go on acting like adventurers: killing goats and cows with high-powered rifles. And I'll expect by way of return that you put out some work so that when we slam in through the pass at Papeete this vessel will look sharp—not like some yacht in the hands of dudes. Any comment?" I looked at each of them in turn. No one spoke, so I turned away.

There was an odor of decay all around the ship. The curving beach peeled back to reveal clusters of huts peeking from thickets and shrubs, and the foothills ran fast inland to become engulfed in the folds of spinal ramparts that soared high overhead and formed great crumbling amphitheaters, half lost in some cloud.

These were the Marquesas: the desolate isles, the wilderness isles, the islands that always were outcasts—yet never more so than now. Far more than most of Oceania, this land had known the wrath of the white man, for the Marquesan had resented being enslaved. He fought back when they chained him and shipped him to the hellish guanoa islands off Peru. He fought back when the pious Yankee whaleships came in quest of brawny harpooners and moist warm island girls. And he fought back when the traders swindled him out of his land and the missions laid siege to his soul.

In less than a hundred years the Marquesans were all but extinguished. In 1800, the population of the islands was estimated at eighty-five thousand. A century later, because of disease, debauch, suppression, and outright slaughter, the pitiful remnant numbered less than twenty-six hundred among the dozen islands that comprise the archipelago.

And so today this might well be an island domain set apart from the modern world, consecrated to the loners, to the wanderers whose lives had been mutilated by progress, to the men who scorn progress absolute—and are scorned in turn by the drones of commerce—to the men in need of escape.

If I had been truly a rebel, I would have felt at ease in this ravaged island outpost. What I felt was, instead, a vast impatience, a desire to run free with my ship from the pall of these green-drenched isles lying like a barricade across the blue sea-road that led from the north to the sensuous citadel of the Great South Sea, Tahiti. What I wanted just then was to pick up my mail in Papeete and bask for a time in the indolent glow of some distant applause.

I paced by the hour. The ship was deserted and silent. I had nothing to do but think, though from time to time I would seize a bucket's lanyard and draw water from the bay which I'd slosh on the vessel's deck, to keep the planks from shrinking. I thought of my years of servitude on shore. Had it been so bad, after all? Or was this just a pose to cushion the inner turbulence that led me from girl to girl, from ship to ship, from job to job and film to film, from dream to dream, while the years spun by?

The sun beats down and you pace, you pace and you pace. Your mind flies free and you see yourself as an actor, condemned to a treadmill wherein men and women conspire to breathe life into a screenplay that allegedly depicts life as it was in the old wild West. You see yourself coming awake any one of a thousand mornings between the spring of 1954 and that of 1958: alone in a double bed in a big white house deep in suburban Sherman Oaks, not far from Hollywood.

The windows are open wide, and beyond these is the backyard swimming pool inert and green, within a picket fence. You turn and gaze at a pair of desks not far from the double bed. This is your private office, the place that shelters your fondest hopes: these desks so neat, patiently waiting for the day that never comes, the day you'll sit down at last and begin to write.

Why did you never write? Why, instead, did you grovel along, through the endless months and years, as a motion-picture actor? What held you to it, to something you so vehemently professed to despise? Could it be that you secretly liked it— that the big dough and the big house and the high life meant more than the aura you spun for those around you to see?

"Hayden's wild," they said. "He's kind of nuts—but you've got to hand it to him. He doesn't give a damn about the loot or the stardom or things like that—something to do with his seafaring, or maybe what he went through in the war . . ."

Sure you liked it, part of it at least. The latitude this life gave you, the opportunity to pose perhaps; the chance to indulge in talk about "convictions—values—basic principles." Maybe what kept you from writing was the fact that you knew it was tough. Maybe what held you to acting was the fact that you couldn't lose—not really lose, because you could not be considered a failure if you had not set out to succeed . . . and you made it quite plain that you didn't give a damn.

And yet, you did hate it. Perhaps you were weak, that's all. You hated it because you knew you were capable of far more. You hated the role of an actor because, in the final analysis, an actor is only a pawn—brilliant sometimes, rare and talented, capable of bringing pleasure and even inspiration to others, but no less a pawn for that: a man who at best expresses the yearnings and actions of others. Could it be that you thought too much of yourself—that you could not accept sublimating yourself to a mold conceived by others, by anyone else on earth?

Where then did the weakness lie, the weakness that forced you to give up ten or twelve of what might have been the most vital years of your life? It lay, did it not, in the fact that you were flawed. You were big and strong on the surface, but something was wrong inside. You were strong enough to rebel—not strong enough to revolt.

And so those years spun by and the more you clawed the deeper you sank. You were shunted from picture to picture; you reported for work each day consumed with revulsion. You managed to get along because most of the work you did demanded little talent. And, unlike most actors, your surface ego was small, and no one who worked with you ever called you a prima donna.

There were times when you tried to accept and adjust. After all—so the reasoning went—you were a part of the business world: what was so different about selling out as an actor? Was it in any way worse than selling out as a merchant or tradesman involved with more prosaic merchandise? Everyone was supposed to sell out, one way or another. This had been dinned into you since childhood. Everyone did it, so why not you?

Toward dusk that day two dove-gray training ships hove over the hill of the sea and came to anchor not far from the *Wanderer*—not far enough, I thought. They were "showing the flag" to this isolate island world that for more than a century has been down on the maps as "French Oceania." They had been in Tahiti a month and now were bound for France, by way of Panama. It seemed a dismal show, a travesty on *Liberté— Egalité—Fraternité*. I paced by myself some more, midway between the gun-gray ships and the land, and I thought what a gesture a man might make if he had the guts to settle in these islands, win the people's trust, and stir in them some slivers of revolt; for the native Polynesian now stands at the end of the line.

The thoughts that followed were harsh: the man who would deal in dissent should work in his own back yard, should protest, lash out, challenge—no matter how puny his voice—the forces of occupation that held his homeland all but submissive to a shallow concept of the meaning and purpose of life.

But how? How? Simple enough, you stupid sonofabitch. Write! Blaze away through the pages of a book. Draw from the only thing that you know, the life you hold in your two hands, this life of yours that has gone so far astray from the things originally planned.

Nonsense. Who are you to be writing a book? This is only a dream you nourish, a dream conceived twenty-six years ago, when you were a freshman wintering at the Academy of the Grand Banks (not far from Newfoundland), hauling your guts out in the bows of a dancing dory, with the sea as your dread headmaster. How many times in the course of the lost decade did you swear yourself in as a writer, safely ensconced in your bedroom-office, surrounded by charts and books and inspirational quotations? How many times did you pound out a title page, only to have your mind grow soft and retract within itself while you smoked and paced and cursed, with the sounds of some neighbor's hi-fi barreling through the air? How many pictures did you make without once looking at the script you kept by your side, turned upside down in a tooled-leather binder, the script you used as a notebook, filling it with notes addressed to yourself and concerned with this or that sea story you would one day write (you hoped)? And wasn't it strange that never in all that time were you able to draw from your own mind? Instead, you adapted stories written by others. You were, it seems, only a plagiarist, an actor-pirate, good for melting down other men's thoughts and words.

Remember *Denver and Rio Grande*? You were cast in the

role of a hard-boiled railroad man in charge of a track-laying gang. So you turned your back on the filming, and facing the Rockies, you wrote your first screenplay: *"The Sea Wolf,* by Jack London. Screenplay by Sterling Hayden."* It wasn't so bad, they said, when you hawked it around the town. So you adapted other stories: *Two Years Before the Mast—The Story of Donner Pass—Pitcairn's Island—The Whaleship Essex—Slave Mutiny —The Real McCoy—John Barleycorn*—none of them yours.

Now the sun lies low in the west and the crew comes off from the shore. The training ships scowl at the hills with sweeping radar eyes. The kids demolish some food, then plunge headlong into a game of "follow the leader." They squirm through the bilge, they squeeze through folds of loose-furled sail, they scamper aloft to starboard, then down to port and out on the jibboom's gear. Tiring of this, they come aft demanding you tell them a story. "No," you say, with your bare feet braced on the bulwarks. "Not tonight. Ask me some other time."

"Why, Daddy?" Gretchen asks, hands clasped behind her pajamas."

"Because I'm busy."

"No, you're not, Daddy. All you're doing is sitting in that old chair with a drink."

"That's right. I'm busy thinking, you should try it sometime and find out how it feels."

"Give me a glass of whiskey and I will." She throws back her head and stomps up the deck toward the fo'c'sle.

CHAPTER 29

It was half past four that morning when I dropped from the schooner's rail to the tethered whaleboat and, casting myself adrift, pulled southward and seaward hard. Two thousand Frenchmen lay encased in their steelclad ships, yet no sign of a man did I see on their cluttered decks. I gave them a wide berth, and when I had them abeam I spun the boat around and, facing the open sea, shoved my way out free of the land.

Under a riot of cloud the Pacific surged by in long purple ridges. The small boat rose and fell, sometimes with all but the mountains obscured. I stripped in the chill gray air and dove over the stern. After swimming for a time, I hove myself on board; I braced my heels on the riser, stiffened my spine, and swung toward the schooner. I rolled on board with the eastern sky ablaze like a fan thrust up from the hills. The long damp deck was deserted except for Doc Garvey, who stood in the bows dressed in shorts and his Hopalong hat, wielding a deck-broom. "Where in hell is everybody?" I said.

"Don't ask me," he shrugged. "Why not try looking below?"

I dropped down the ladder aft and slammed the mate's door with my fist. "Goddamit, Spike, rise up out of it quick. If you're going to be mate around here, why not act like it for a change." I barged on forward, rousing all hands as I went. The galley sink was submerged in a glacier of plates. The kids were all dressed and at work in the cool of their fo'c'sle classroom; Tryna, their teacher, looked up with something of a smile. I stormed back aft to encounter the mate as he staggered out into the open with a face like a concertina, clutching his pants and gulping great drafts of air. Ray still slept; grabbing his waist, I spun him out of his locker onto the floor. He threw off my hand and, climbing back up, he muttered: "Ya ya ya all right."

"Ya ya ya yourself. Get up. You hear me? Get up and turn-to on deck." His eyes looked up in anger. "I think—maybe—I leave this ship right now."

"Yeah, you do that; pack up your gear and I'll set you in on the beach." I rammed on up to the deck, feeling ashamed of myself. Hayden, you jerk, I thought. You're not content to condemn yourself, you have to go blasting the crew. So what if they'd like to sleep in for a change?

I paced in the bowl of the cockpit as they scrubbed down fore and aft with something less than a will. Honor where due, I thought; for they worked no harder under what I liked to think were the guns of my eyes than they would were I not around. The buckets came up scraping the side of the hull, and the brooms didn't buckle from pressure. "All right," I said. "When you've had your breakfast, come aft and we'll have us another talk."

Nothing feels right just now. Here I am, the self-styled champion of the individual, about to browbeat some men who can't fight back. Here I am, for years ready to sound off about a man's obligation to defy routine and tradition—and I'm about to rasp away at a docile crew who ask no more than a chance to relax as the old windship meanders on down to Tahiti. Well, having come this far, there's nothing to do but brazen it out. To hell with the merits; I'll put on some pressure and figure it all out later.

Once more we meet—under the awning aft—minus fanfare —once more the confrontation. A flick of a match, and a deep drag—then: "Okay, boys, let's make it simple. In a way I'm sorry I blew up as I did—and in a way I'm not. You've got to understand something: this ship is run without any formal discipline. When I holler, it's because I have to. I've often thought how simple it must have been, fifty or a hundred years ago, to run a ship like this; because in those days the men in charge never gave a damn for the feelings of the crew—if something had to be done, it was ordered done, and that was the end of it.

"Now, I'm not going to mention any names because we know each other pretty well and you know who I mean when I say that there are two or three of you don't give a good god damn about this ship— By the way," I look around in surprise, "where in hell is Jerry?"

"Jerry took off." It is Russ who speaks. "Took his blanket and cameras and a machete and lit out for the mountains; said he needed a little relief."

I smile in spite of myself. "Well, I'll be a sonofabitch." So we have an Ishmael among us, a genuine cigarette-age Melville, bound for the far side of nowhere—or maybe Typee Valley.

"Boys, let me tell you something. This is a big ship, as I guess you've found out in recent weeks. I run her the only way I know how. And it isn't my way so much as a way that has been developed and passed down through one hell of a long line of men. This is no half-assed yacht. And like I said back by the lightship, a sailing ship is no democracy either. Ten per cent of this crew has done ninety per cent of the work; and that's wrong, and it can't go on—and I guess you know that, too. So maybe this is our last chance to work things out. We'll be in Papeete in a couple of weeks and so far as I'm concerned any one of you doesn't want to shape up can figure right now on packing up and moving ashore—for good. Now let me hear it—what in hell is it bothers you all so much?"

Don Bahl speaks first. His big arms are folded, and a full black beard gives him a Biblical look. "Well, this may be the sailing-ship way of doing things, but it's not what I had in mind when I quit working for the First National Bank of San Jose. Nobody ever accused me of being lazy, but I'll be doggoned if I feel like going through the South Seas, or wherever we're going, stuck down in that engine room half the time we're in port." His voice trails off and he nods to himself.

I look around. "Who's next?"

Russ clears his throat and, looking off, speaks: "I agree with Don. I've no complaints about anything you do at sea—far from it. But I've been working since I was sixteen, and I've wanted to see these islands for a long time. Never thought I'd make it— but now that I'm here, why, I'd like to take a pack and shove off inland for a couple of nights, and forget about this ship, and the whole blamed world—up there." He nods to the north. "Something like that."

Doc's voice rumbles out through a hang-over. "That goes for me, too. As you know, I can't get too wound up over this Sinbad routine; and handling this—this nautical factory of yours is a little less glamorous than what I had in mind." He flicks some ash on deck. "Also, there seem to be one or two things about this operation that you didn't make clear when we talked back in Beverly Hills. I spent three years attached to the Marine Corps, and I came on this hayride to get away from discipline— but the way it's working out, there's more crap—skip that. . . . Also, I think it might help some of us if we knew where in hell we were going. I understand the girls in Tahiti aren't hard to take; but we were bound for Copenhagen; and now I hear rumors about going to Chile, and Indonesia, and Christ only knows where. It's all a little confusing to a boy like me from Olean, New York."

As I look at the doctor, I think of the day we met. Late in July it was; in a fancy sidewalk café near the heart of Beverly Hills. The place was full of splendid-looking girls sitting erect like frightened fawns, dabbling with diet salads, shaking their hair to the wind, gazing around the terrace—while across from each one, it seemed, sat a pasty agent with nipped collar tabs, peering down the dresses of these breathless girls. I had taken to Garvey at once. We hadn't intended to drink—we said; so we had some beer, and then same aquavit. He didn't know any girls, so (always the big operator) I pulled out a notebook, and went to the phone, and—

Dennis is next: "What the others just said—well, that goes for me too, I guess."

"Ray?" I light another cigarette.

"Well now—I'm sorry I didn't wake up. And I'm sorry I talked back; but it—well, this just isn't what I expected, that's all. And when I worked for Standard Oil, they didn't bawl me out or get sarcastic if I happened to make some mistakes." He covers his mouth as he coughs. "We'll see . . . maybe in Tahiti you, you get someone else—to take my place."

Red appears in the hatch, wiping the sweat from her eyes. "If you don't object to hearing from the so-called weaker sex, there's something I'd like to say." She turns to the crew with her arms spread wide on the scuttle. "You should—some of you, that is—should be ashamed of yourselves. That's what I think. You don't know what work is. You're spoiled. This trip is the best thing that ever happened to some of you, and you're letting the ship down. You're bored, you say. All right, so you're bored; you're bored because you're lazy. And some day you're going to wake up to the fact that this voyage was the best thing ever happened to you—but then it will be too late. Thank you. I will now return below and do the dishes—your dishes."

It is quiet. I'm waiting to hear from Spike, and I feel some remorse as I look at his visceral face. He stands alone by the rail. Now he stuffs some snoose in his mouth and cinches up his belt. "Well, I'm all for you and I'm all for this ship, and I guess you know that by now. There's some mighty damn good men in this ship. . . . Also there's a couple I wouldn't hire as towel boys. . . ."

His jaws work hard as he follows a bird with his eyes. "Now, I'm not trying to win any popularity contest around here, but I don't think you're giving some of this gang a chance. You expect everyone to feel like you and I do about this ship. It won't work. It won't work because this is 1959 and people don't know what these ships mean. . . . And I want to say one more thing." He hocks, spits, and wipes his chin. "The next time you can't sleep and you get up in the middle of the night and row halfway to Bikini and back—and then you feel like chewing me out, I wish you'd take me ashore to do it. I've been chewed out by some experts, believe me. But never in front of my crew. It's not right. It's bad—bad for a man's self-respect. And that is all I have to say at this time." He turns and shuffles forward, his slippers patting the deck.

Well, I think, that's it. A feeling of vast relief comes over me now—a feeling I'd hoped was dead, yet here it is again. The voyage is foundering; the escape hatch is open wide.

I turn to the crew and smile. "Okay. We'll try it your way. Take the whole day off. Take tomorrow off. Just work it out between you so that one man stays aboard. Wash her down when you feel like it. This old bastard has survived for a good many years so I guess a little neglect on your part isn't going to kill her." I turn away and lock my arms on the wheel.

And so, for the rest of that day, with the voyage consigned to failure and the burden of battle lifted, I swore off smoking, scoured my teeth, and surrendered myself to my kids. The thought swept through my mind that we hadn't been together for a long long time. With the rest of the crew gone ashore, we had the ship to ourselves.

Down from the hills came a whistling squall of wind; and after the wind the rain, and the air turned chill so each of the kids rigged a shallow tent of canvas and blankets beneath the drum-tight roof of the awning. This camp was arranged in a rough circle around the thick teak base of the cabin skylight. I squeezed some limes in a pitcher of lukewarm water, ransacked the galley for crackers, and then, much to my own surprise, managed to produce—from deep in my laundry locker—a mildewed bar of chocolate.

The rain hung on, so I gave them each a lantern, and there we sat in a circle, like castaways, munching and sipping and chatting, with the world shut out.

Dana kept eying me, his legs crossed tailor-fashion. "Popso, I don't get it. Something's wrong. Cuckoo."

"What do you mean?"

"What's got into you all of a sudden? You—you seem like you used to seem. You even look different."

Gretchen chimed in: "I'll say. He looks like he's ten years younger."

"Well, I'll tell you something; I decided to relax for a change."

"About time." Christian peered out from his cave.

Matthew lay curled out of sight in a blanket. "Hey, Matt," I called. "Tell me what you're thinking." The blanket stirred but the boy had nothing to say. I shared out the last of the chocolate, one square apiece. "Make it last," I cautioned. "Now here's what we're going to do. I'm going to give you three minutes to get ready, and then each of you is going to have another three minutes to describe exactly where you would like to be, and what you would like to be doing, if you had the power to be any place on earth—"

Matt's head popped out of the blanket. "I know, I'd like to be back in the big house in California, I'd like—"

"Hold it. Take your time and think it out carefully. Then we'll go in turns, beginning with Gretchen." I slide down flat on deck, cross my legs on the skylight, cradle my head in my palms, and listen to the rain thrumming away on the canvas. "Christian old boy," I say, "excuse the interruption, but if you don't mind, just drop down into my cabin and fetch me my cigarettes."

Even before the recital began, I knew what they would say. For this was a grown-up's world, this hundred-foot sliver of fir and oak and iron all garnished with bells and watches and hundreds of regulations—with never a moment, it seemed, when a child on deck was out from under the cynical eye of some adult.

It had looked so good from a distance, from the land in the years gone by—and the strange thing was it would look even better one day, when the voyage was done and gone. Why not? Wasn't it always that way? Where was the dream that didn't shrivel when you pierced it with reality?

The kids spoke one by one and their words were all the same: You may not like it in Los Angeles, Daddy, but it was so comfortable in that nice house and we had so much fun in the pool and remember the way we could play baseball in the back yard . . . we had so much room to keep our things and there was the tree house out back and the observatory on the roof and the dogs even liked it and we all had our own friends and you used to tell us stories all the time and we were always taking trips some place and—

I closed my eyes and let their voices drone on, and I thought how odd it was that even for these kids the goal of life seemed to be comfort and ease. But then, these weren't average kids; they had been exposed to a savage custody fight; they had gone through "visitation," the ritual whereby, for more than a year, their father came each weekend to pick them up and take them to neutral territory; and then, all of a sudden, they had changed worlds. At ages six, five, four, and two, they found themselves slung from mother to father on a permanent basis, and for reasons far beyond their comprehension. No wonder they yearned for a stable world—motionless beds and rugs and lawns; clamorous birthday parties, picnics.

The rain squalls passed and the wind died down and the decks steamed under the sun. A dory poked out from the shore deep-laden with some of the crew, so we struck the tents and broke up camp. Life on board went on as before—but with a subtle difference. Something was gone, some vital bond that had held the whole venture together.

I felt confined aboard ship, so, stuffing the rucksack with raisins and a dog-eared copy of Thoreau's writings (and some blank paper), I sculled myself ashore and headed toward the hills. I climbed for perhaps two hours, until I came to a stream with a pool, and there I sprawled in some ferns. After a half hour's nap, I opened the book to the essay entitled "Life Without Principle"—for me the most enchanting, challenging, and altogether cogent passage ever written, and one that is far more appropriate today than when it was conceived, ninety-four years ago.

It is remarkable that there is little or nothing to be remembered written on the subject of getting a living; how to make getting a living not merely honest and honorable, but altogether inviting and glorious; for if *getting* a living is not so, then living is not. . . . The ways by which you may get money almost without exception lead downward. . . . If you would get money as a writer or lecturer, you must be popular, which is to go down perpendicularly. . . . You are paid for being something less than a man. . . . There is no more fatal blunderer than he who consumes the greater part of his life getting a living. . . . If a man walk in the woods for love of them half of each day, he is in danger of being regarded as a loafer; but if he spends his whole day as a speculator, shearing off those woods and making earth bald before her time, he is esteemed as an industrious and enterprising citizen. . . . Wherever a man separates from the multitude and goes his own way in this mood, there indeed is a fork in the road, though ordinary travelers may see only a gap in the paling. His solitary path across-lots will turn out the *higher way* of the two. . . .

I read till the light grew faint. I fondled the book as I slipped it into the sack with some of it syphoned off into my mind. I stumbled back down to the shore and, shoving free from the beach, stood erect in the night with the land breeze fanning me out to the ship. She stood tall and proud with her spars raked aft, their trucks pointing up at the stars. The light of her lantern threw an amber glow on the folds of the outer jib.

Moved by a long-dormant urge, I settled down in the arm-chair and started a letter home, and it came to me then that perhaps I too was playing the game "Where would you like to be?"

Schooner WANDERER
Taiohae Bay
Marquesas Islands
March 13, 1959

Dearest Lorna,

This is the letter I said I never would write. You have, I know, heard a little about this voyage. I can't help writing you now. A French training ship is anchored nearby to-night, she will carry this letter and mail it in Panama.

It is lonely out here, believe me. I feel well these days, better by far than I have in a long lone time. Yet something is terribly wrong. Something within me aches whenever I think of you—which is very often indeed.

And I'm wondering how you feel. Do you think—very often—of some of those things we shared? Is there enough of a spark still left where you are concerned to give us a chance in the future—together? We almost made it, Lorna, we both know that. We might—no, we *would* be married now—were it not for the ogre that plagued me all through those miserable Hollywood years. I wish you were with me tonight—tonight and every night and all the days between.

This voyage is coming apart already. And yet I honestly believe that I'm free of the rut at last, and the feeling per-sists that if only we could meet once again we would at last be able to find our way together. I hiked in the moun-tains this afternoon, and I looked for a long time toward the north and east where I know you are. And—don't laugh—I even went so far as to think of jumping a plane out of Papeete and flying back to see you.

I love you very much, and I guess you know that too. I only hope that—

I rise to my feet and pick my way through the slumbering forms on deck and drain some wine from a bottle uncorked on the workbench. And then I go aft and crumple the pages and hold one edge to the mouth of the lamp's long chimney. They smoke, then flame, and I drop them over the rail. She went from my life like this, and nothing will bring her back; not letters or cables or wild-eyed jaunts on a plane.

There is dew on the rail as I ease out over the bows and bury my body deep in the folds of a jib. I stare at the stars and I know that this is my final voyage—this is the end of the long sea-road that I started to tramp as a kid.

I close my eyes and it all comes drifting back, and the kid that I was is outward bound with his seabag slung on a shoulder as he strides like a man through the railroad yards in Boston a long, long watch ago.

CHAPTER 30

Along the river that morning the fog lay drifted and gray and dank as a lungful of smoke. You heard the night freight crawl up the curve of the grade to paw with some doubt at the sill of the trestle before snaking out onto the bridge. Downstream a foghorn boomed. There wasn't much snow for March, just some chunks in the woods and the remnants of roadside drifts all pocked and black as a lava flow.

You saw the man—as he leaped from a boxcar door. He waved both arms as he spun around and rolled out of sight in a ditch, and when he rose up you saw he was wearing a knit wool cap and wasn't a man but a boy, with a white canvas bag that he slung on one shoulder before walking off down the road, toward the barn. He cut through an alley that led to a dump heap pitching down to the river and paused. You heard the clang of a bell buoy lost out on the stream somewhere.

From ahead came the sound of the riveting guns, the shipyard sound of hammers and engines and the screech of a circular saw. He looked toward the sounds and kicked at some old tin cans, and he scaled a few stones and counted the skips that they made.

Now he shouldered his bag and moved along toward the shipyard. The trail was a winding one lined with the wreckage of cars, with busted sofas and pieces of basins and toilets. All of a sudden he stopped. A long dock jutted through the fog and right at its end stood a tall two-masted schooner. He could barely make out her hull, which was painted white, but her spars stood out like trees on top of a hill.

Spiral Notebook　　Entry #1
Schooner *Puritan*—New London, Conn.—March 23, 1933
Something is wrong. Something I never expected. Now that I am really here at last I wish I hadn't left home. Why is this? I don't know. The feeling began when I jumped on the freight in the yards at South Boston. It got even worse when I jumped off here by the river and found the PURITAN lying at the shipyard dock.

I suppose the day will come and I will get over this but somehow I don't think so. Life on shore seems very desirable now. Thick fog nights and mornings too. I am alone on the ship nights. This forecastle very cramped. Dirty too. My pipe bunk only five feet ten inches over all. I have a lower. None of the men have unpacked or anything. Cook is very nice. Also man named Bill. Mate not so good.

At least I know I can quit and *walk* back to Boston so long as we are tied to the land. But what about later??? These men don't understand anything about the sea. To them this is just a job. They get forty dollars a month. The mate gets seventy-five.

I hope nobody ever sees these words. I would not write them down but I want them to serve as a reminder if I ever do anything stupid like this ever again!!! Never again!! I wonder if these men are good sailors? The ship is okay I guess but maybe not too strong in the rig.

Two days ago I landed here at lunchtime (hurt back a little jumping off freight). . . .

Along the river that morning the fog had thinned out by noon. He had hidden his bag in a pile of timber, and now he stood on the dock by the ship. Three men were at work on deck. When one of them looked at him, he shifted his gaze to the rigging aloft.

The tallest man was called Frank. He seemed easygoing enough. Bill was a short husky guy with a brilliant red face and a high-pitched voice. He had the habit of snapping his fingers if a job didn't go good and fast. His eyes danced and he swore a lot, and once he winked at the boy. He wore a belt full of spikes and knives and a cow's horn full of tallow.

The mate was dressed in faded dungarees carefully patched, and his sleeves were rolled up all the way, revealing huge muscles under taut reddish-blue tattoos. His eyes were too close together.

"Sir." The boy held a note in his hand. "This is for you, I believe." Reaching one hand toward the ship—

The mate grimaced. His hands were busy with rope. "Well, bring it down here, for Christ's sake." He took the note and probed his teeth with a toothpick. Even as he held the paper, his biceps twitched.

He looked at the boy, then handed the paper to Bill. "Jesus Christ. The new man. Fresh from kindergarten. Here's your watchmate, Bill. You an' the kid can furl the topsails together." He turned to the boy and said: "Kid, lemme see your hands." The boy held them out—white and clean and soft—knuckles that protruded and white-blotched palms. The mate flung the hands away. "Here!" His voice had a knife edge now. He shoved one hand right under the face of the boy. It seemed to be made of bark—rough bark on the inside, smoother bark on the back. The tip of a finger was gone. A tattooed star clung to the trunk of the thumb. He fished for a wooden match and struck it across one palm, his eyes burning up at the boy.

Schooner   PURITAN
New London
March 29, 1933

Dearest Mother,

Well here I am at last. In the fo'c'sle of a real schooner. And three days ago was my seventeenth birthday. I am alone on board and it is evening and all the crew are on shore saying goodbye to their wives or sweethearts. I don't mind telling you that I miss you very much. I am only now beginning to appreciate all the thousands of things you have done for me.

Mother, it makes me very sad to think of how I treated you. If I ever get home I will do my best to make it up to you.

There are seven men in the crew not including myself: 3 AB seamen, Mate, cook, engineer, and Captain. The cook is named Harvey. He is my friend. He is a very powerful man with a face like a bookkeeper. He weighs over two

hundred and forty pounds all muscle. The rest are all okay
not counting the Mate.

I miss you very much. I don't know what the matter
with me is. When I think of what you went through I am
sad. I swear I will do nothing for you to be ashamed of, and
will try to conduct myself as a gentleman should.

Some day the time will come when I can buy a little
house on the coast of Maine or in East Gloucester and we
can live together with Laird and I will buy a shipyard or
run a schooner up and down the New England coast.
How would you like that?

I still have the five dollars. I hope your work goes well.
Take care of Laird and I will see you before too long. Will
write from the Panama Canal. Don't worry, it is safer here
than on the Boston Post Road.

Good night. I love you.

Spiral Notebook   Entry #7   March 29, 1933

Have decided to stick it out. I will think of Von Luckner
and Jack London and the men in the Cape Horners and in
the Grain Races and then this will not perhaps seem quite
so bad. This will be something to tell the children about
one day. Captain due tonight from his home in Nova Scotia.
Letters to Mother and Debbie and John Howell.

CHAPTER 31

Along the Mole that night the sea tossed buckets of spray into
the face of the wind. The docks were a blaze of light with a pair
of steamers working cargo. Half-naked stevedores sweated deep
in steel cells choked with Panama heat.

The American Zone lay serenely aloof from its gutter-born
sister Colón. The lawns were lush with shrubs and flowering
beds, and fountains played. The kid came on shore from the
launch. The men he was with made a row as they hailed a
carriage. They swore and swaggered and clowned like high-
school kids in a crowd.

"Colón, Sambo, Colón!" yelled the man with the rough red face.

"Ask him how much," called Farish, the seaman from Newfoundland.

"Fuck you, Jack. He ain't gonna fool Bill White."

The boy sat erect with his arms crossed on his chest, muscles pushed out just so. The street lamps glowed and people in soft clean clothes moved quietly along the walks. A girl moved by with long blonde hair all ribboned and braided, and her dress belled out, crisp with starch. The kid in the carriage looked back to see what her face was like.

"The hell with that stuff, kid." Farish wiped his nose on a sleeve. "Where we're takin' you is the real thing."

But what the kid wanted was to leap from the carriage and go back to the big clubhouse with the red tin roof, and sit reading magazines or drinking an ice-cream soda; or maybe he'd just go out and lie on his back, with the grass like a cool green cushion, and over his head he'd see the stars shining through the lattice of palms.

And then, up ahead, he heard the growl of Colón, a cauldron boiling with life, and the wail of a thousand radios; sweatshops and honky-tonks and canteens sprawled by the side of the narrow streets, gutters choked with refuse. A sweet stench hung in the air like fog in a river bed, and the glare of the place erased the stars from the sky.

"Whoa boy! Whoa!" Bill took up the slack on the reins.

"What do we owe you, Snowball?" Farish hitched at his pants and thrust out his egg-shaped chin.

"Five fellas—one dolla each man, that's all."

"Why you lousy—" said Farish as he drew the curve of his arm toward his face.

"Aw, Farish, for Christ's sake shaddup, you goddam tightwad." Bill peeled off a five-dollar bill and thrust it deep in the outstretched hat. "For the horse, get it? For the feed for the frigging horse. Not for the rum but the horse, okay?"

The girl was possibly twelve years old. She was scrawny, her bright red dress was covered with spots, and you could see the sores on her legs. She slid up to the kid as he stood in a corner saloon. She arched her back and pressed the muzzle of her crotch against his legs. He was so tall the crowd laughed. She laughed too. As she dragged on her cigarette, she looked at him

with a funny face and started to weave her body round and
round in little taut circles. The boy tried to laugh and he gazed
at the fan up over his head. The cook, Harvey, stepped up and
put one paw on the girl's shoulder and moved her gently aside.
She grabbed for his crotch and said: "C'mon Charlie. C'mon
Yank, you'n me, hey boy hey? Hot stuff Charlie, two bits
Charlie, hey now hey?" The girl squirmed around and made the
hissing noise that you heard all up and down the street. The
cook reached down in one pocket and gave her what change he
had. She shook her hair like a dog just out of the water.

"I tell you, kid," said Harvey, "you'd better go to the show or
the boys'll think you're a queer or somethin'."
"Sure, Harvey, that's fine with me. What do they want to see?"
It wasn't much of a picture house. Just a slit in a wall with
some posters out front of a girl on her back holding a parasol
while a midget wearing a tall silk hat squatted between her
knees.
Inside were nothing but benches. Row on row, some of them
half tipped over. Farish was so drunk he fell off one of them
and started to cough and then all of a sudden he began to snore.
The place was half empty when the lights went out.
The titles were in Spanish and there wasn't any sound. The
film was old and scratched, but you could see an esplanade with
the sea in the background and all kinds of flowers and palms.
A carriage came by, with a handsome woman beneath a parasol. She wore a wide-brimmed hat like those in the wedding
pictures that used to be in the hall. She was obviously very
popular. Everyone waved as she rolled down the esplanade.
Then she signaled the driver to stop. He was dressed like a
man in the circus, with fancy breeches and a long brass-but-
toned coat. She saw somebody in the crowd who attracted her
attention. She pointed him out and the driver jumped down
and came back with a little midget who couldn't believe he was
invited to ride with the great lady. Away they went, with everyone waving and laughing, and some even handed her bouquets,
one of which she gave to the dwarf. His name was "Stumpy"
(so the titles said).
The screen went black. Nobody said a word. Farish still slept
on the floor. The place was full of flies and smoke. The screen
lit up once more and there was the grand lady in a huge bedroom with mirrors on three sides and a big brass bed. She called

to the dwarf, but he shook his head. She patted the bed and beckoned to him with her finger. He tried to leave, but the door was locked. Now she jumped toward him and picked him up and dumped him down on the bed. She held him there with one hand while she started to take off her dress. She wore corsets and petticoats just like back home.

Now she had everything off but her stockings. She stood him up on the bed and told him to take off his pants. He wouldn't do this and he squeezed his hands with his legs. She dumped him down and ripped off his clothes and pretty soon he became excited so she lay down but he couldn't get anywhere. She kept making faces and laughing at him and yelling to him.

The screen went black. Nobody said a word. You could hear some music next door. The kid wondered what time it was. He wanted to leave but he hadn't the nerve.

The screen lit up and there was Stumpy, with nothing on, lashed to the foot of the bed. The woman sat up when she heard a knock at the door. She flung it wide and a man came in with a black mustache and she grabbed him between the legs. He looked like an old-time river-boat gambler with his tall silk hat, which he placed on Stumpy's head.

This time she laughed and screamed and clawed at the bed, and the camera jumped all around from mirror to mirror and then in close, and all this while Stumpy was left to amuse himself as best he could there at the foot of the bed.

The lights went on and they called to Farish to get up. He lay in a pool of vomit. Harvey and the kid walked back and it rained and the air tasted fresh.

It was three when they reached the ship. There was no wind but you heard the surf washing at the shore, and beyond the Mole the sea was quiet and black. He stripped and plunged off the bow and wallowed and scoured at his body with the palms of his hands, trying to rid himself of all the things he'd seen.

Harvey sat on the fo'c'sle hatch, watching the lights on shore, smoking. His voice dragged. "You know, kid, I'm twenty-nine years old. I been working ever since I was twelve. I got a good wife an' three good kids an' twenty bucks to my name." The voice trailed off and he stared at the cigarette stub. They heard Farish screaming in his sleep. They had lashed him down in his bunk—the way Stumpy was lashed to the bed.

"So, kid, I tell you what you do; you stick with me an' we'll beat our way back from California by freight an' then you go

back to school, see? Go back to school an' make somethin' out
of yourself and then if you wanna sail buy yourself a yacht. But
for Jesus' sake quit going to sea."

"Yes, Harvey, I think you're right."

"You're goddam right I am."

CHAPTER 32

Twenty-three days after leaving the Panama Canal, the schooner
Puritan powered in between a pair of almost endless break-
waters and let go her anchor in Los Angeles outer harbor. A
boatload of officials boarded her and gave her clearance, and the
kid hauled down her quarantine flag.

A few hours later, a yacht-club launch ran alongside and
the son of the schooner's new owner came aboard with some
of his friends. They were modishly dressed, the boys decked
out in non-skid sneakers and flannel pants, and shiny-buttoned
blazers with what looked like a coat-of-arms. The host himself
wore a yachting cap emblazoned with small crossed flags.

"Commence fucking yachting," muttered Bill the rigger to the
tall kid, as he swaggered the length of the deck and, squatting
next to the anchor windlass, pressed on a button that brought
the chain rattling in over the bows. The kid was at work shining
brass. His face showed signs of dismay as he turned from his
work to the guests back aft. A red-headed girl in a bright green
dress moved forward and stood next to Bill, watching the chain
come in. She sat on the rail with her legs apart and the kid
looked away with his head, but his eyes turned back and he
polished fast.

They steamed down the coast for twenty or thirty miles and
then turned to enter a sprawling man-made bay all lined with
yachts and houses jammed in close. The kid was disturbed because he couldn't decide which of these groups he belonged to.
Of course he was one of the crew; and yet, given the clothes
and the money, he could fit just as well with the guests—not
that he would. They gave him a pain . . . with their soft white
hands and their endless cigarettes and their way of looking not
at anything but *through* it.

At one point the kid dropped down into the empty fo'c'sle,

where he did fifty fast push-ups. Then he chinned himself a dozen times on the topmost rung of the ladder, and sauntering back aft to take the wheel, he could feel the blood swelled out through his muscles. The girl in the green dress didn't even recognize that he was not like the rest of the crew. She looked right through him.

Harvey appeared from below wearing a chef's hat and an apron and pointed white shoes. He looked at the kid and they both broke out laughing. Then the cook compressed his lips, took a drag from his cigarette, and swept it over the rail, as though fed up with himself. The kid was pretty upset because the trip hadn't panned out as he thought it would. He had in fact been on the verge of jumping ship in Mazatlán. But Harvey had said: "Boy, you stick it out. Then when we pay off in Pedro, you an' me, we'll bum our way home on the freights; I'll see you clear through to New London and you can give your folks a ring and tell 'em you're ready to go ahead on your education."

The trouble was, he didn't want to go home and he didn't want to stay with the schooner, and according to all the gang, jobs were tougher to find in California than back East. He knew he was a quitter; he knew he was licked and it hurt.

They went by a big old ugly pavilion and tied up alongside a shipyard, and that was the end of the voyage. Harvey was shuffling around among the guests, passing out small diced sandwiches from a tray. When it was over, he took off the apron and the queer hat and the pointed shoes and rolled them up and stuffed them in with the garbage.

Then he and the kid threw their bags on the dock and went aft to be discharged. The Old Man was happy because this place was going to be his new home, and the new owner was the president of a gas company and very rich. He handed the kid two ten-dollar bills and a piece of paper that said: "This is to certify that the bearer, S. Hayden, served for four months as ordinary seaman in the schooner yacht PURITAN. He is very strong and at all times willing and it gives me pleasure to give him this recommendation." It was signed: "Captain Howard T. Horton." The rest of the crew had disappeared, so there weren't any goodbyes. The cook and the kid just walked off up the dock, went through a shipyard gate, and stood on the sidewalk looking around, not knowing which way to turn.

Under a heavy overcast, with rain, the boxcar dragged its creaking joints into the Saint Louis marshaling yards. The

couplings clash and all you can see as you lean out the door is
a wilderness of pipe and girders and monstrous piles of scrap
iron. Way up ahead the locomotive chants and above the little
switch shanties the smoke stands straight up.

In town after town, as the freights dragged through, you
were met by a hard-mouthed string of locals armed with gun-
belts and clubs, or maybe with cut-down shotguns. You would
have given up after that first night in the mission just off Main
Street in downtown Los Angeles. You sang "Washed in the
blood of the lamb," and they gave you some mucus-tasting
soup and you all filed into a corridor lined with chairs. There
you sat all night trying to sleep, with a length of old manila
rope stretched bar-taut in front of you for a pillow . . . and at
half past five in the morning some bastard at the end of the
line cast the rope adrift, pitching half a dozen men flat on their
faces on the floor.

Come to think of it, your age of enlightenment really began
that night in Newport Beach. Harvey decided to make a quick
trip to San Diego, where he had a relative of some sort, so you
were on your own for two or three days. You were about to rent
a room when you met a man who said that he and his wife didn't
have any kids but they had a spare room in the basement. They
gave you a big dinner and you talked about the voyage, and
after that you soaked in a hot bath, then turned in and fell
asleep. Your last waking thoughts were about the strange way
his wife kept looking at you during dinner. All she was drinking
was beer but she seemed drunk, and she kept two cigarettes
going at once half the time. She wore skin-tight pants and very
high spiked heels, and she had a bracelet around each ankle.

The man's name was Gus. He went to bed before you did because he was captain of a sport fishing boat and had to get up
early.

"How old are you?" she asked, after her husband had left.
"Seventeen." She shivered a little. "My, but you're big for your
age. When will you be eighteen?" "Next March." "Do you like
to dance? I love to dance—" She put on a record and held out
her arms, but you just shrugged—because she was married—
and you quickly went downstairs to bed. The music was playing
as you drifted off to sleep.

The next morning you woke up because somebody was in
the room. The room was full of sunshine. With her back to you
she closed the door and you heard the click as she locked it.
You kept on breathing deeply. She wore a pink kimono.

She crossed to your side and whispered your name. You feigned a small stir, just enough to roll you onto your back with your legs and arms spread wide. Very gently she sat on the bed, saying your name' again, out loud. You sighed and said, half under your breath: "Okay, Bill, okay. My watch? Okay." And all this time you could see her. Her eyes were puffy, and when she lit a cigarette her hands shook.

She took your hand and kissed it in the palm, with her tongue. You wondered if she tasted the tar. You didn't need your eyes any more because she took your hand and put it between her legs. You had been thinking about all this for a long time and now you were going to find out and this was a funny damn way for it to happen, and if you were really a man you would stop acting and wake up and go to work.

You remembered just then the way her husband had looked after supper as he went through the kitchen on his way to the bathroom. He had a barrel chest covered with thick black hair. Suppose he came back, just now? Suppose he'd forgotten his hat, or the engine in his boat wouldn't start.

She threw the cigarette in the corner and started to mess with your hair, then her hand drifted down across your eyes and your face and you brushed it away. She flung back the sheet and not taking her time very much at all swung around on top of you. You wanted to look down but instead you looked at her face but not in her eyes. It was going to happen quick, which wasn't good you knew. But it was happening quick for her too. You held each other close and her breath was bad and all you could think of was the lady down in Panama in the movie who had picked up poor old Stumpy. She whimpered and you knew what you had to do. It was almost noontime before you slipped out the back way while she was upstairs getting a beer.

On toward the eastern seaboard they rolled, under a full moon now, through Illinois, through the level farmland of Indiana, and the world for a time wore a warm and friendly look, with the towns on either hand strung out, their street lamps flickering through gently tossing leaves.

Once more it rained, but the journey was almost over. They sat strung out, thirty or forty men and a couple of girls, in an empty gondola, with burlap capes and cardboard bonnets, crawling toward Jersey City, or maybe Hoboken. Nobody spoke. Some were half asleep. The cook just looked at his feet, with his jaw gone slack, teasing a cold cigarette, his glasses all bleary with water.

They were met by a guard who glistened and flapped like a bat. The cook, bending low, came up with a rock from the road-bed and the two of them marched right past the guard and on toward a hole in the fence. "Fuck you," said the cook out loud.

They walked till they came to a ferry, and the years peeled back when the kid realized that he'd been on this boat before, maybe a decade ago. Once again he stood, in spite of the nagging drizzle, on the outermost open deck, watching the harbor traffic, watching the North River pouring seaward past the blackened stubs of docks clinging like death to a mutilated shore.

They said goodbye standing in the rain outside a bus depot on Thirty-fourth Street. The cook's suitcase was made of paste-board so he kicked it out of the wet. The bus driver punched his horn.

"Good luck, Harvey. I hope your family is fine."

"Yeah, sure, kid. Drop us a line sometime."

"I will, Harvey." The hand of the kid disappeared in the cook's big mitt.

"You're gonna make out, kid, don't ever forget it neither. You ain't like the rest of us humps." He closed his lips and worried the cigarette stub till it fell down on the sidewalk.

The kid found a seat and cleared the mist from the window. Craning his neck, he watched the burly shoulders plow out of sight in the crowd.

CHAPTER 33

Riding the subway that day from Boston to Harvard Square, the boy was quenched with a hundred fears, but he managed to bury them all beneath an act that said: Take a look, you poor city dwellers, take a look at the shape of a man.

And the funny part of it was, they did. Not just the girls, but some of the men. Over their shoulders they glanced, and over the rims of their papers. He pretended, of course, to be totally unaware, and he stood stiff-backed with his head high.

Fat Emma opens the door, and she frowns, wiping red hands on her chest. "Well?"

"Hello, Aunt Emma. I'm back. I'm looking—"

"They ain't here. Gone down to Rhode Island someplace." She moves to close the door and he thrusts one foot in the threshold.

"Could you tell me where?"

"Sure. Woonsocket. Some place on Oak Street that takes in boarders."

"Thank you, Aunt Emma."

"And tell that mother of yours I need the money they owe me."

The mill town bakes in the summer sun. Main Street is dowdy, with ugly brick stores swamped in advertising. He shoulders his beat-up bag and tramps till he comes to a tidy white house with a screeened-in porch and a swing. His mother recoils in the doorway, then flings herself in his arms. He pats her shoulder with dutiful tenderness. She seems to be sobbing with joy. "Oh Buzz Buzz Buzz, I can't believe you're home."

"I'm home all right, Mother. It's wonderful to see you and you look very well and—"

She holds him at arm's length, laughing tautly through her tears. "Let me look at you, son. My, but you're brown. And you've grown so much and—"

The landlady bursts through the door. She looks like a keg in an organdy smock. "So this is Buzz," she says. "My, Frances, but isn't he a splendid-looking young fellow."

"I think so." She is drying her eyes. He feels dulled inside until, turning, he sees Laird, the old collie, sitting up in front of the swing, his ears pressed back, his clean paws limp, and a look of devotion deep in the dark brown eyes.

"Jim!" calls the mother. "Buzzy is back home safely." Footsteps sound on a floor. The boy is bracing himself. "I'll call him Stumpy," he thinks. The stepfather swings through the door. Two sores stand out on his chin. He is smoking a cigarette, and his knickers look thin in places, but his calves still lock and expand as he rocks from his toes to his heels. "Well now, son, good to see you again."

"It's good to see you, too—Daddy Jim."

Nothing to speak of was changed: the mother still peddled cosmetics; the father was looking for work (with an eye cocked on a big deal in Boston); the dog was slower and softer; and the boy felt lost and bewildered.

He walked in the hills and he walked through the town and

always he felt like an exile, for there wasn't any sea and there weren't any gulls, and the air seemed to droop on the land. For a time he worked in an apple orchard, and then in a lumberyard, but most of the time he loafed. And then he met Leonard Raynor.

It was just after lunch one day when he entered the public library, returned an armload of books, and moved through the stacks till he came to his stamping ground: 910.4 Voyages and Voyaging. A thin dark older boy who looked to be twenty or so stood down the aisle by a window, leafing through a book. Their eyes met and the stranger smiled. "Excuse me, my name is Leonard Raynor, aren't you a stranger in here?"

"Yes, I am, and the quicker I get out the better I'll like it. My name is Sterling Hayden." They shook hands. "My goodness," said Leonard, "let me look at your hands, I've never felt such a grip."

The boy laughed. "Just helped deliver a big steel schooner from New London to San Pedro; then beat my way east on some freights. My stepfather is here on business."

"I'm from New York City. I'm studying music, to be a concert pianist."

The older boy had a habit of standing so close that your arms touched a lot of the time. He had long tapering fingers and a very thin neck. But at least he was friendly. He wanted to hear all about the trip under sail, so they left the library together, crossed the main street, picked out a shady place behind the war memorial, and lay in the grass.

Later, walking alone up the hill, the boy kept thinking about his new friend. There was something fishy about him, but this didn't matter too much—it was pleasant to have someone you could talk to. Also, and he wasn't so sure about this, he had promised to meet Leonard the next day because, as the older boy had said, maybe they could be friends and defeat Woonsocket.

A week or so later, he had introduced Leonard to his parents. His mother semed favorably impressed, perhaps because of the piano business, or the fact that his friend was so polite. But his stepfather had certain reservations. "I'd go easy, young man, if I were you."

"Why?"

"Oh . . . no particular reason, I'd just go easy, that's all."

"I wish you'd tell me why."

"Dont ask me why. Just mind what I say, or the first thing you know you'll get into trouble."

Early in the fall they moved to Providence because his mother was promoted. The big deal in Boston was to be closed any day, but they ended up in another stale rooming house, with the boy and the dog in a tiny room on the fourth floor. From the window he could look out across a fine formal garden to a huge stone house shaped like an armory. The people who owned it must have been very rich because often in the evenings they had lawn parties with a live orchestra under an awning and a whole slew of well-dressed folks laughing and dancing and talking most politely. The boy enjoyed watching these parties because he knew that someday he too would be part of just such a world.

His days were spent looking for a job, but he didn't try very hard. Mostly he lived in the library. Three nights a week he went to night school to study typing, short-story writing, and French, which, according to Leonard, was the language of international diplomacy. The girls in these classes weren't pretty. They wore horn-rimmed glasses and all of them were serious.

One day, coming down the library steps with some books about the South Seas, he met Leonard.

"Hi there, skipper."

"Jesus, please don't call me 'skipper,' call me anything you want but not that, it sounds like the Toonerville trolley."

Leonard laughed. "Living in Providence now, and Saturday night there's going to be a party in Boston. I'm going with some friends, and I'd love it if you were my guest."

"Sounds pretty good. What kind of a party?"

"Well, there's this place called 'The Empty Barrel,' where painters, writers, and artists go. Charles and Curly are going and—"

"Who are Charles and Curly?"

"Well, Charles is in charge of draperies for a big store here in Providence, and Curly is a tackle or something at Holy Cross— he's Charles's friend, so I don't know him very well."

"He is?" The boy swung around in surpise. "You mean to say he's really playing for Holy Cross?"

"He's supposed to be. Charles says he is; he's big enough all right."

"Okay, fine. Where should we meet?"

"Tell me your address."

"No, we're moving. Tell you what—I'll meet you right here. What time?"

"Five o'clock. Promise you'll be here?"

"Word of honor, I will."

He sat in back with Leonard. Charles drove, and Curly kept turning the radio, trying to get something classical. Charles had curly blond hair and rounded hips that he tried to conceal under a tight double-breasted suit. Curly looked like the real thing, no doubt about that, with his crewcut, low forehead, and big shoulders.

The boy felt conspicuous as the four of them rolled slowly through the wayside towns, but it soon grew dark, which made him feel more at ease. It was chilly in the rumble seat and Leonard pressed against him as they rounded the curves. Every once in a while he rested one hand on the boy's leg. To complicate matters, Charles kept staring at him in the rear-view mirror, and sometimes he winked. But the boy ignored all this. He was good and warm. He wore his old tweed suit, with the legs and sleeves let out; only the day before, his mother had sewn a lining made of silk stockings inside the legs to keep them from scratching him indoors when it was hot. There was a patch across the seat where the tweed was tissue-thin.

Above, a harvest moon raced through the branches. "Isn't this fun?" asked Leonard. "You bet," the boy replied. As they were nearing Boston, Charles called back: "We'll go to Harry's first and change."

"All righty," said Leonard.

"Change into what?" The boy didn't understand.

"Oh, not you; just some of us. I didn't tell you before, but, you see, they're having a masquerade. And now let me ask you something." His face came close. "I thought I might dress up too, as a girl?"

"As a girl? Jesus, what for?"

"Oh never mind. I just thought you might like it, that's all."

"Go right ahead, it's got nothing to do with me."

The apartment was large and carpeted wall to wall and it was lit in such a way that you had trouble telling who was who or what was going on. The place was alive with people but he didn't see any girls. Someone gave him a drink that looked like grapefruit juice in a tall glass. He sniffed it first, then tossed some off.

A victrola was playing one of his favorite songs, all about the depth of the ocean and the height of the sky. The lights were low and couples went rustling by. A blonde swept past, her long hair brushing a rust-colored gown. She looked at the boy. Good Christ, he thought, it's Charles.

Then Leonard appeared by his side. "Skipper, let's try dancing together, just for a little bit. I know you think we're mad, but won't you try it . . . please."

"Maybe later." He wasn't worried about the dancing so much as about the way he felt. His glass was empty and the room was beginning to whirl. Leonard took his glass and handed him a fresh new drink and for no good reason he downed it.

"Time to go." A voice rings out through the rooms.

Everything whirls and he feels like a goon repeating a grade in school. His head towers over the rest of the class and someone is pinching his leg. But they sweep out into the night, where the clowning stops and they all become model children and scatter in pairs toward cars.

He finds himself in a strange closed car, with Leonard pressed down on his lap. He cranks the window all the way down. "Please," squeals a voice, "that wind is mussing my hair." He cranks the window halfway up and the city goes barreling past and before he knows it a sidewalk under his feet keeps tilting and pitching and his friends have hold of his arms.

He pitches down some little steps. A door swings wide and hundreds of faces cheer and yell and stamp on the floor. The walls are plastered with gaudy travel posters. The floor is made of sawdust. They give him a seat on a barrel that's none too steady. Someone hands him a foaming mug of beer. "Drink up. It'll sober you up in a hurry." He doesn't dare speak, so he drinks.

All of a sudden, without warning, the whole cellar begins to capsize. "Hold her!" he cries, clutching the table with desperate arms. No use. Over she goes, with him fighting and flailing to get on his feet, and he crashes through a table, and his head fetches up with a smash and all he can do is drown.

Faintly it comes at first, a faroff sound of singing. You cautiously open your eyes just enough, not much. You're flat on a bench by a corner. Your head is in somebody's lap, whoever it is has a hand tucked under your belt. You stir. The hand

withdraws to your chest. Your pants up top are drenched. By
straining one eye you can see the waiters go laden with trays
through a swinging door.

Then all at once you rise to your feet, suck in your gut, check
on your fly, and break toward the swinging door. The room tilts
right and then left but you bore through the door, with Leonard
calling your name. Startled faces stand in your way but, swinging your arms, you burst through and a door appears that you
kick with the flat of your foot till it springs open and down an
alley you go, tipping garbage cans upside down in your wake.

You trip on some steps, pitching headlong out on the sidewalk close to the wheel of a car. Two cops stand under a street
light down at the corner, slapping their flanks with nightsticks.
You get to your feet, march soberly into a shadow, then run like
hell for the harbor.

You taste the salt night air and the harbor buoys pulse, and
low on the seaward quadrant the primary beacons keep stabbing away at the dark. A tall-stacked tug lies snubbed to wooden
pilings, with her watchman asleep in the galley. You slip on
board and rap on the varnished door and offer to pay for some
milk. The watchman looks you over, gives you some milk and
says you can sleep on a locker. You stretch out with a sigh
and quickly sleep.

CHAPTER 34

With Christmas out of the way all the nonsense about peace
on earth and kindly lights and brotherhood was stowed under
the counter. In came 1934—careening wildly downwind before
a howling icy gale called a Depression. We packed up our cartons, bamboozled the landlord, and cleared out of Providence for
Boston. Things were looking up: the promised deal on the
fabulous summer resort was, so Daddy Jim said, about to be
closed. I thought of the perfect epitaph to go on his grave: The
Deal Is Closed.

Riding in on the bus, he explained how important it was
that, in the weeks ahead, he have a proper address with which
to impress his "financial associates." So after some frenzied

scouting we freshened up in the rest rooms next to the subway, combed the collie's coat, and sailed up Beacon Hill to check in at a hotel near the State House. The cartons we'd smuggle in later.

The address was fine but we were tucked away on the rear of the very top floor, where our windows commanded a view of other curtainless windows, each of which dangled a packing crate that served as an outdoor icebox. The dog stood dismayed on what passed for a rug. I unsnapped his leash and he circled around for a bit, then flopped down next to the steampipe.

Something went wrong with the deal. Each weekday was always the same, with my stepfather pacing for hours under his wide-brimmed hat, pacing and picking his face and dragging at cigarettes. Mostly my mother knitted. With her back to the airshaft she knitted, or darned his socks, or stitched away at our clothes. Sometimes she cried.

She sat with her fingers flying, looking up at his legs as he passed; then her face congealed and she worked her jaws as if something were stuck in her teeth. Her fingers would move less swiftly and at last stop altogether, and all she could do was stare at the floor in silence with her chin quivering. Then one by one the tears would go tumbling down into the yarn on her lap. I would look away, trying to read, but the sobbing would grow louder and louder till at last she simply broke down and cried.

And then his voice: "Stop it Frances. I say stop it, do you hear me, stop it. Everything is going to be all right. Now I'm going downstairs to check on my messages." And the door would softly close and his steps would pound on the worn bare boards of the corridor.

Early one morning the manager appeared with a bellboy. They gave us a week to pay or get out, and when they left, the bellboy was loaded down with most of our cartons and my mother's little black bag full of cosmetics. This was a blow; that bag supported us for a good many years. They even took my seabag, with its oilskins and boots and the sheath knife that old John Howell the sailmaker had given me back in Boothbay.

Late that afternoon the stepfather asked her for enough money to buy cigarettes, with a quarter left over for carfare to Wellesley, where he could borrow two or three hundred dollars from a man who had once been his partner. He never came back. Several days dragged by. Each time we heard footsteps out in the hall mother stood by the window, her back to the door, with one hand held close to her throat. I knew these were not his footsteps because he had a way, small as he was, of making a lot of noise as if to say: Stand back, this is J. Watson Hayden and he's bigger than he looks.

We had less than two dollars between us. I tried to explain to the manager about the little black bag but he wasn't interested. He just kept shaking his head, he did not even look up. I went down to the instrument shop and borrowed ten dollars from Mr. White. When I returned, mother was lining her shoes with cardboard. We talked of the places we'd been and the place that appealed most was Gloucester. Gloucester is a fishing town and fishermen know all there is to know about hard times.

It was cold and clear that day, with the State House dome braised in morning sunshine. Sensing a change, the dog frisked around, biting his leash and every few feet taking a squirt at a snowbank. The wind was strong northwest as we plowed through slums and icy streets toward the North Station.

The train was old and slow and warm and full of a relaxed sort of friendly feeling that had nothing to do with cities. My mother slept and the dog stood leashed in a corner and I sat by myself pressed close to a seaward window. Beyond the window, the countryside was indented with inlets and marshes and barren little harbors. As we came into Gloucester, my heart soared at the sight of sail in the distance.

We found a room in a big clean house near the top of a hill. The woman who owned it smiled as she opened the door, and the smile stayed on even when I told her that we had no baggage and no money and didn't know a soul in town.

"Come right ahead in," she said. "Your mother looks all worn down."

Without delay I headed for the docks. I came to a wharf with an office under a sign that swung in the wind: ATLANTIC SUPPLY CO. INC. CAPTAIN BEN PINE. I peered through the door at pictures of schooners covering every inch of the walls; big schooners, long low Gloucester schooners, schooners about to be launched, schooners racing and schooners fishing and schooners dismasted at docks. A thickset man in a store suit came swinging up the dock with a cloth cap shoved back from his face. "Sir," I said, "I'm looking for Captain Pine." "No, you're not, you're talking to him. Come on inside and get warm."

Two hours later, I hustled out of the office with fifty dollars in my pocket, and a note addressed to some captains who fished out of Boston in beam trawlers. "This boy is all right. He wants to go dory-trawling from a schooner but I think he should start off in the beam trawlers first. Give him a job if you can. Ben Pine." My mother was still asleep so I left a note and some money and ran like hell toward the depot.

🦅

CHAPTER 35

Gone is the bleakness and the vacillation. Still on the run you go, through tenements that belt the Boston water front; through raw red-handed kids who play with tin-can toys and old truck tires and battered whiskey barrels. Through wop and nigger kids (so called these days in other sections of town, in Back Bay and Beacon Hill, in the haughty suburbs where "the better people" are dining by candlelight, where the young folk are swathed in cashmere and camel's-hair coats).

Down along the fish pier the trawlers are slung in a webbing of wire belayed to bollards deep-set in cement. Spars of schooners probe the overcast, and drays go rattling by, drawn by horses with steaming nostrils. Saloons hang low by the cobbled street, jammed with smoke and the laughter of drunks.

Clutching the note in my pocket, I stalk the length of the pier in search of a ship. Suddenly I see her: a swart black hull with powerful ends and a cold steel deckhouse rising from a litter of nets and cables that lead to a massive winch amidships. A brute of a man leans on the rail of her bridge chewing a dead cigar, watching great baskets of fish swing out of her hold. Moving along, I peer at her stern: *Maine—Boston*; the letters are drowning in rust.

I slip unobtrusively down to her deck and enter the galley aft. Cooks are soft as a rule, more inclined than the men on deck to make you feel at home. "Excuse me, sir, but I was wondering if you needed an extra man. I'm from Gloucester and I have a letter from Ben Pine." (I was right in picking this vessel. The galley is spotless, the cook has a friendly face, and the table is laid with a red-checked tablecloth.) "Well son"—the cook is lighting a pipe—"if I was you I'd look for a job in a freighter headin' south; better yet, I'd look for a job in a laundry, where it's warm and full of females; but since I ain't you, then I guess I'd go talk to the skipper."

"Is he on board?"

"He's on board all right. He's always on board, except some- times he goes up to the Garden an' picks up a few berries wrestlin' preliminaries; name's Coffin, Clyson Coffin, an' I tell you one thing, he's a driver."

And so, up in the wheelhouse, I hand my note to the man with the cold cigar. He has a broken nose and a heavy jaw and there's something about his eyes that makes you look away. "Where's your gear?" he asks. "Well, sir, you see I lost it—a couple of months back—when I was coming east on the freights, but I've got a little dough, enough to buy what I need." He shifts his cigar and starts paring his nails with a knife. "All right, son, I'll give you a chance, if you're willing to make a couple of trips for noth- ing."

"Yes sir, I am sir."

"We'll haul-ass out of here around ten tomorrow morning. Find yourself a bunk, and never mind saying 'sir' all the time, this is a dragger, not a yacht."

Then around the clock it goes, six hours on, six hours off, seven days out of seven, week after week, till the hold is nothing but iced-down fish. Then back to Boston, where the gang spreads out to get loaded, dip into some girls—or maybe the wives for a change—get loaded some more, not just drunk but loaded full-up pass-out piss-in-the-corner plastered, then back down the bay and out past the Graves light station, and turning your ass to the lightship, you put her on east by south and let her roll for the Western Bank six hundred miles away.

Dawn now, dawn on the Western Bank, east of Georges Shoals, south of Halifax some place. A barbed-wire sky all meshed with a barbed-wire sea.

Backs to the wind, the men stand bent double almost, braced with shales of ice on bulging black rubber suits. Thick in the legs, thick in the chest, thick in the skull, and thick in the ways of the world. How else could they stand such a life? Fourteen degrees this morning in the lee of the after house, yet they work much of the time with bare red hands puckered and torn from constant intercourse with steel-wire slivers and fumbled knives, and with bones that sometimes protrude from the bloodless guts of fish.

Ice on the tubed steel masts, ice on the forecastlehead, ice on the wheelhouse, ice on the twin iron-hooded toilets that cling to the stern like monks. Black ice in the graveyard watch that lasts from twelve till dawn at last. And back to the galley where they wolf some food and slosh some coffee down and drag on a butt as they lurch to the fo'c'sle and peel off oilers and boots to roll up and die for as long as they can.

Here's what happened to Paul the big Icelander, the one with the blackened eye, the gashed cheek, and the frozen blood in his beard. It was almost midnight and Paul started aft to have a cup of coffee and maybe a wedge of pie. Down in the engine room the second engineer had just completed a bowel movement with newspaper spread on the floor. Paul was wearing a cap that his wife had made. It was thick and woolly, with long red tassels that hung clear down to his shoulders. He was passing to leeward of the house when a porthole opened and something hit his head and knocked his cap overboard. The something fell at his feet and he looked down to see the Boston *Herald* opening up like a flower. You could hear him roar halfway to Halifax, and the engineer slammed the port in a hurry. Big Paul stormed through the galley, picking a meat cleaver out of its rack as he went straight on down to the engine room. The second saw him coming and ran up a ladder that led to the escape hatch set in the side of the stack, and from there he passed to the wheelhouse and locked himself in the chartroom. Following fast, the Icelander started chopping away at the door. Just then, Coffin appeared, and yelled at the man to stop. But he was close to being berserk, so the Old Man handed his cold cigar to the kid who stood at the wheel, and spinning Paul around, drew back and struck him so hard he shot through the leeward door and almost went over the rail. Slumped on the iced-up iron, all he could say was: "Muh bonnet, muh bonnet, muh bootiful fuckin' bonnet."

Spring came late that year. Trip after trip he lasted it out. All through the summer he fished, shifting from vessel to vessel. Half of what he made went to his mother in Gloucester, to pay off the debts (it cost him two hundred dollars to get his sheath knife back).

That fall the steam trawler *Gale* was bound in for the Boston market with a hundred and seventy thousand pounds of haddock and hake and scrod—groundfish mixed. The day was thick with fog and up on the fo'c'sle head the kid clumped with his

boots on planks gone red with rust from pitted ironwork. Whalen
the skipper leaned in the wheelhouse door with a hand on the
cord of the whistle. A shovel clanged on the fireroom floor and
the stack erupted with smoke that mated with the fog.

He looked up ahead through a hundred miles of damp and
dangerous vapor to the place where the lightship lived, to the
fish pier and on through the city and up along the river, and he
thought of the autumn land, with the smell of burning leaves,
the pigskin sounds, the taste of mustardy hot dogs, and maybe
a nip from a flask. You think how the stadium banners wave
and the crowd chants and you walk with a girl tucked under
your arm, a girl so pretty that the fellows who pass you stare
and whisper among themselves and maybe whistle—but not
very loud for fear you might get angry . . . her fingers play on
your wrist and her throat looks soft and she dresses with taste,
and you wonder how come she isn't cold on a day like this with
nothing under her skirt but those tiny V-shaped panties . . .
and after the game you go to her house overlooking the river and
her father is a fine-looking man like your Uncle Mont, and you
sit by the drawing-room fire with books all around and you
know from their eyes they admire you . . .

Ed Watson borrowed his brother's car; it was a Franklin
sedan. We met near a subway station.

"Well, if it isn't the old Fisherman himself."

"Hi, Eddie, how much dough you got?"

"Three bucks and a half. You?"

"More than that. Know any girls, Eddie?"

"Sure, but they're all dated up tonight. Goddam Princeton
comes to town dates up all the goddam girls."

"What say we go to Morey Pearl's Tent?"

"Oh Jesus. My old man would boot my tail if he found out."

"How's he going to find out? Let's go. The guys on the boat
go there all the time. They tell me you can't miss with a girl
from the Tent."

"Okay. What say we buy a pint?"

The place has an armory look. It is all lit up outside and dark
as a grotto within. Morey stands five-two; he waves his baton
and bounces up and down, with an eye on the crowd, an eye
on the gate, and an eye on the new girl singer. The kid and
his friend come in, snapping their fingers to match the beat of
the band.

"Good good evening, radio fans out there, this here is Morey

Pearl the old Bag Man broadcasting from Boston's beautiful dancing arena 'Morey Pearl's Tent.' This is bag night here at the Tent [holds up paper bag, winks at his faithful fans all gathered close]. Yes sir boys, this is your night boys, Every Boy goes home with a Bag tonight [cymbals clash, Morey throws bag in air, brass section blazes]. For your dancing pleasure, folks— it's 'Deep Purple.' "

Shapes melt with shapes.

"See anybody, Eddie?"

"Not yet. You?"

"How's about those two there—see—the green one and the lavender one?"

"Geez. I dunno."

"Come on."

The kid in tweed suit steering the green shape, testing—is she a nice girl or a quick lay. "You see, Ruthie, my uncle is on the board of directors of the Bay State Fisheries—that's how come I'm fishing. I'm learning the ropes so I can take over when the time comes."

"You gotta car, Sterlin'?"

"No, but my pal does."

Hasty consultation across the urinal trough. "What say, Ed, we take these two home?"

"Where's yours live?"

"Charlestown, right near the Navy Yard."

"Jesus Christ, we'll need gas."

"Do I wanna drink? Sure, Sterlin', I wanna drink but not right outa the bot'le—whaddaya take me fer . . . oh all right. Say, he ain't goin' to Charlestown now."

"Hey, Eddie, where you going?"

"Going down to take a look at the river."

". . . You know, Ruthie, I've never done this before."

"Done what?"

"Been to the Tent, met a girl like I met you."

"Me neither."

The excitement is suddenly gone, like summer lightning. "Hey, Eddie. Drive for the Navy Yard."

"Get him!" Her voice shrill. "I ain't goin' home so soon, my old lady'd drop dead if she sees me this early—hey, Ducky, let's park by the river here."

"You heard what I said, Eddie, keep going."

"Whatsamatter, you queer? Here!" The spread of the legs and the calloused hand thrust out of sight and—far away—the thread of a voice: "So always remember, Buzz, that is the most beautiful thing in the world—"

Even before the car is stopped, the door bursts wide. Her nails rake the side of his jaw and the whiskey backs up in his throat and she holds his tie in both hands, her dress halfway to her waist. He hears the slam of the door as he runs. "Baby can't get it up baby can't get it up."

CHAPTER 36

The merchants were beating the yuletide drums again when he packed his kit and came on shore determined to taste for a time the delights of office hours and hot baths. If nothing else, at least he'd be safe for a while.

He bought a paper and sat in the sun on a windy bench in the Boston Common and studied the help-wanted ads. All around him were men in long loose coats and cracked shoes, some with a stubble of beard, and all with that vacant look that betrays the man who is down and out and full of terror.

Two days later, he went to work in Filene's Bargain Basement. First they gave him a lecture on how to behave toward the customers, then they hung a sales scorecard in his left lapel along with a paper carnation and, patting his back, turned him adrift on the floor. At nine sharp the doors flew back and a raging throng of women charged the merchandise. They waved and screamed for prompt attention; they spat on the floor and bawled at their kids, and once each hour at least two of them would stage a tug of war over a marked-down dress or blouse, or maybe a two-bit necktie. His feet grew swollen and pinched and the foul air echoed with carols and every so often a boozy Santa Claus would circumnavigate the basement clutching his belly and clucking at kids with a sharp eye fixed on the clock, while all through the mob the sales force tossed and swayed like buoys sucked under the current.

When his lunch hour came, he bolted outdoors and struck off fast through crowds and short-cut alleys till he gained the water front, and here he perched on a piling and tried to figure things out. Either you hurled yourself into commerce or you went to sea, resisting the brutalizing process that seemed always to go with the ships. There must be a better way, a middle passage.

Then one day, during the final week of the Christmas assault, he discovered a book in which was revealed the answer. Its name was *N by E*, and its author was Rockwell Kent. The copy he bought was worn. Some parts were underlined. It cost him a dollar and fifty cents, and it was the first book he had bought with his own earned money.

With the book in his hand, he went to the end of T Wharf, where he sat in the winter sunshine and, declaring the afternoon a holiday, settled down to read. The third chapter was the one that held him enthralled. Here was the solution.

A woodcut at the beginning of the chapter shows a man in a city hat and a city suit. Behind him rises the metropolis. He stands with arms flung up and out, an image of mute despair.

There was a certain man who lived in the suburbs of New York. And every week-day morning for years, he took the 7:45 train to the great city; and every day on the 5:15 came home. He owned, we guess, a little house. It had a furnace to be his winter care and a front lawn for summer. He had a radio set and a motor car, and a wife. One night they would play bridge, another they would go to the movies; and on Sunday afternoon they would go motoring. It seemed as if things would go on and on like this; always; until at last he would die. And that would have been his life.

Now there are certain islands in the South Seas so far away that everyone believes them to be paradise. Summer is eternal there. And in the cool shadows of their groves recline fair youths and maidens happy in being and through happiness forever young.

When the vision of these islands broke on the commuter, suddenly the little round of his activities became unendurable. His imagination took fire and in the aura of the conflagration he saw himself sailing the broad Pacific, landing, a sunburned mariner, on those flowering coral shores. . . . So he must build a boat. . . . It must be a small boat and a staunch boat. . . . It must be a safe boat, seaworthy and able.

Her keel was laid in a little shipyard on the Hudson; and from that day to the day of the boat's completion her de-

signer watched her growth as only a man about to sail the
seven seas for Paradise would watch his magic craft
evolve. . . .

And so in the growing excitement of the enterprise the
years flew by; the boat was nearly done. What hope must
then have beamed in the commuter's countenance, what in-
timation of approaching glory! . . . Was not the boat itself
an unfoldment of his own spirit, an opening of the book of
his own dreams, the materializing in such symbol as the
world might understand of his most secret self? . . . So, at
almost the very moment that this poor man was about to
step into his swan boat, his wife, we only guess, confronted
him.

"What,"—arms akimbo—"do you think you're going to do
in that boat?"

"I was going," he answered with quiet determination, "to
sail to Par—to the South Seas."

"You're not."

And there, true or not, ends one of the saddest stories in the
world.

The kid closed his book—the rest of the story was all beside
the point. His plan was now to return to the fishing until April,
to save every cent that he earned; then, pooling this with the
four hundred dollars already saved, he would comb the entire
New England coast for a small boat. And, after fitting her out
in the summer, he would sail alone in the fall—bound for the
South Seas and maybe around the world, earning his living by
writing. How simple. Already he had the name: Horizon.

To get the money he wouldn't go back to the beam trawlers.
He was ready to go all the way, to tackle the toughest job on this
or any sea . . . dory-trawling.

CHAPTER 37

Somewhere between the flea-bit hotel off Scollay Square and the
Boston fish pier, he changed his first name to Chris. "Sterling,"
for Christ's sake! Whoever heard of a man with a name like
that—anywhere; let alone in the fo'c'sle of a Gloucesterman.

Chris was for Fletcher Christian of H.M.S. *Bounty*, patron saint of mutineers and kids cast loose in the dismal thirties on the shores of a world so civilized a man could starve to death in a flophouse while less than a mile away toy poodles wore matching booties and jackets when they were taken riding by the chauffeur.

Jimmy Abbot had a high-pitched voice for a skipper. He looked like a New York cop: good-natured on the outside, tough as boiler plate inside. "Now where the Jaysus is my goddam engineer, anybody know?" Forms pace in the dark. The schooner's spars ram into the night as high as a four-story building. (Her topmasts are safe in Gloucester, along with her main gaff and the outboard half of her bowsprit—in honor of wintertime—their place taken by a diesel the size of an ox.) "Jaysus, he's too old to get stuck in a whorehouse."

"Think so, Skipper?" The voice on top of the wharf comes from a man with a caved-in chest. He weaves and spits, one hand clenching a three-foot Stillson wrench.

The skipper coaxes: "Come on, Angie. Jaysus, come down, boy, we're missing the ebb as it is."

The wrench sails down toward the deck. "Heads up below!" shouts the man as he flings himself at the shrouds and, slithering down to the deck, goes cursing below to crack some valves and fiddle around till minutes later comes a hiss of air and the rattling cough of the stack. The lights snap on, Big Ernie yanks on the cord, and the dock walls echo as she plows backward into the stream.

"Better let the kid stand to the wheel," Jimmy says. "He's the only one in this crowd sober enough to steer, including me, I guess."

The lights of the city recede. Off Winthrop she starts in, rising and falling, crunching the sea in her teeth. "There she feels it," says the Old Man to himself, "now, boy, let her go east by south."

"East by south, sir."

"None of that 'sir' shit; did you call Coffin and the rest 'sir'?"

"Sometimes." The kid felt good, taking the *Thebaud* to sea, nursing the four-foot wheel made of iron, galvanized and raked aft with its shaft aimed halfway aloft. Through the scuttle he could see the cabin stove standing like a little round Indian with a red gut and a headdress of mittens and sweaters and socks, its belly aglow with fire. Well, he thought, here I am; all my life I'll be able to say: When I was a kid hauling trawl in a dory, down on the Banks in the dead of wintertime. . . . He could make

out the loom of the dories nested six to a side, higher than a
mans' head. Some spray came sifting aboard. He began to feel
sick but he knew it would pass. He also began to feel scared,
thinking about how it would be in the dories.

It is half past four in the morning when a blast from the cook's
toy whistle scuttles the kid's fine dream and he opens his eyes in
the forwardmost upper bunk. Under naked lightbulbs, twenty
men hock and fart. Some of them just lie there, staring out, void
of any thought.

The room soars now above the hill of a sea. It ceases to rise,
pauses and hangs, then drops down into the trough, smashing a
hole in the sea only to be quickly flung skyward again. The kid
lies curled, one hand between his legs. His bones ache, and he
offers a little prayer. . . . Please God, make it too rough to fish.
Give us fifty miles of wind, please God, and if you could manage
somehow to keep it rough for a couple of weeks we'd quit and go
back to port and I'd find some job on the land. . . .

His pillow is wet from a leak overhead. The bow shoots up
again. "Oh now, here comes a good one, boys, hang on you
sonsofbitches, for Jaysus' sake hang on." It's the cook who gives
this warning, crouching and watching his stove. The men freeze,
to bunkboards, lockers, and ladder—whatever comes under their
hands. She drops like a roller coaster. The wood protests and the
foremast crawls under its wedges, and up on deck a cataract
breeches her bows.

The kid finds a place at the table. Across from him sits a fiery-
faced man with bulging eyes who is wolfing a load of steak and
potatoes and cornbread smothered in gravy. "How you feelin'
hey?"

"Okay, Jack, I guess."

"Eat up, boy, eat up! You ain't et enough to keep a canary
alive; eat it and puke it and eat right away some more."

"Jack—think we'll fish today?"

"Christ, boy, of course we'll be fishin' today; and every day.
Old Ben Pine's been to the auto show—got his eye hooked on a
nice new Buick—so we gotta ketch plenty of fish." And these two
are dory-mates. A kid with dreams and a trawler from Newfoundland, cocky and loud, his eyes clamped hard on command.

Polaris stands firm in the night, Orion reclines on a cloud, and
the *Thebaud*'s deck is livid with flaming torches. The boy appears
from below, looming a head taller than the rest of the men. He

sniffs at the wind and peers out into the dawn—searching for snow, fog, ice, gauging the heft of the wind and the size of the seas. He slips aft alone, intent on sneaking a look at the cabin barometer. "Hey, kid! Where the hell are you, boy?" Jack Hackett is calling his name.

"Okay, Jack, okay!"

The skipper's voice rings out: "All right, boys, I'm layin' the dories out on east-south-east—it's snow maybe in them clouds up to weather—so we'll just make a little one-tub set before you're havin' your second breakfast."

Hackett's breath shows white. The flame of his torch goes dashing about, licking the night with a long smoking orange tongue. He comes up with a cigarette, jabs it into his mouth, then plunges his face down into the flame and with watery eyes rears back, puffing and laughing at nothing.

Their dory is number nine. It is sixteen feet long, with flaring sides and a flat floor and almost identical ends. They swing it out to the vessel's rail and load it with fishing gear: two pair of oars and a spritsail, bailers and buoys and tubs of trawl, pen boards and gurdy and pitchfork and, last but far from least, a wooden bucket containing a compass, a jug of water, and thick white woolen mitts. They climb out into the dory. Hackett sits in her bows with his hands locked round a line that leads to the schooner. The kid crouches down back aft with a hand on the Spanish burton. The man now measures the sea. When a breaker comes rising under, he braces his back, with his legs straight out, and "Lemme down!" he cries. Plummeting fast, the dory is gone from the vessel's rail to a place not far from her keel. The tackles are freed and the ship rumbles off in the dark. All up and down this lonely street of the sea the torches rise and fall. Twenty-four men and twelve dories.

The hard-laid line of the trawl goes flicking out, two thousand hooks spaced at intervals of six feet, one end anchored, the other made fast to the dory. Some light labors into the east. Now for the waiting time, nothing to to do but wait, wait for an hour or more hoping the fish will bite, wait for the *Thebaud*'s horn. This is the coldest time of all. Hackett's head droops on his chest.

The ghost of a horn that intrudes brings Hackett onto his feet and, bracing himself, he locks his back and starts heaving in on the trawl. The kid coils down in an empty tub. "Boy, lemme tell you, this is a poor fuckin' way to get rich."

"Jack—that's snow, isn't it?"

"You can bet your ass it is." When the dory climbs he sets himself, when it drops he takes in the slack, swinging his shoulders in rhythm, just like a pendulum. "Tell me, kid, how much more dough you need to buy this sloop of yours?"

"Oh, four hundred bucks."

"Take me along, eh kid? We'll sit in the sun an' we'll sail to the west an' we'll chase us them brown-skinned gals an' lie under the palms drinkin' rum—say, that's the life, I bet."

"Sure, Jack, that would be fine—you're kidding me, aren't you?"

"Yeah, I guess so. You know what I am? I'm a stupid goddam Newfie what's been haulin' his ass off on these Banks since he was thirteen years old. Had me a yacht job once. Big bastard. Had me a uniform too; queer hat, white britches, white sneaks. No good; too much flag raisin' an' brass shinin' and sittin' around up in the bows while the party back aft sat on their duffs talkin' the nautical talk. . . . No good for a dumb damn Newfie like me."

It started to snow and the world turned feathery white and suddenly terribly small. "Jack . . . did you ever go astray, ever get lost in a dory?"

"Old dyin' Jayssus yes. Two winters ago it was. Right out here some place . . . Me an' Hymie Powers . . . Spent two goddamned days driftin' around in a livin' nor'west gale . . . blowin' the wee tin horn an' sayin' me beads . . . figurin' how, if I ever got back on the beach . . . I'd land me a job in the post office."

"What happened to you?"

"Oh, nothin' much; a Greek freighter come along and picked us up and took us on into Portland. . . . Hymie went to the hospital and me, like a dumb sonofabitch, I caught me a bus back to Boston an' jumped back into the fo'c'sle . . . just as the *Goulart* was pullin' out. Some smart, hey?"

The *Thebaud*'s horn lets go in the offing and the heart of the kid bursts sparkling free in his chest. "Breakfast!" he laughs, scoffing now at his fears.

"Yeah," says Hackett, "I'm like to starvin' to death."

CHAPTER 38

It was on a fine April morning that I stepped from the savings bank with five hundred dollars in cash creased in my money belt and, boarding the rented bicycle, pedaled off through Boston, bound for the coast of Maine.

And the day came when I found myself in Camden, and scanning that anchorage tucked under the hills, my eyes were drawn to a thirty-foot sloop with a sweet sheer that led to a clipper bow, and a board in her rigging that said: FOR SALE— $450. In a leaky skiff I sculled on out to circle the sloop perhaps half a dozen times. Then, with a heart that was pounding hard, I went on board and, taking my knife, I gave her the third degree.

I bought her that afternoon, with a hundred dollars to spare, and the bike went west on a truck. The rest of the day—and most of the night—I spent discovering her. She had two narrow bunks in her cabin along with a small wood-burning stove; and out in her open cockpit was a one-lung rusty engine. Her sails were nearly new and her mast was solid pine, and although I hadn't felt inclined to inquire as to her age, it somehow seemed fitting and proper that she hadn't any name.

I christened her that night—*Horizon*—leaning over the bows with my back to the dancing stars, looking down at the gentle curve of her stem. The fire in the cabin burned with a chuckling sound as I sat on a locker—scheming, planning, dreaming, and waging a constant battle with a drinkless pipe (apparently smokeless, too) purchased that afternoon in honor of total emancipation.

Then one spring day, slipping my moorings, I sped down the bay alone, with the wind northwest and the whitecaps under my feet. Then magic nights in my thirty-foot home, at rest in a westward-leading chain of safe deep island havens; nights when the moon as it rose would bathe the somber stands of nearby fir and spruce in almost a holy light. Those were the nights when I made my one hot meal of the day a feast of beans or hash, or soup and pilot biscuit, all washed down by spurts of nothing but water poured from the snout of a wicker-mantled flagon.

In the course of a week I sailed her back to Gloucester. Sculptured deep in the cocked left fist of the scarred New England shore. An ancient port, in this new-found part of the world. A tough port, gray and girdled in wharves. A wintry port built by a wintry breed. A port consecrated to fish: to vessels and men and lofts—spar lofts, rigging lofts, twine lofts, and sail lofts. A port of shipyards, ropewalks, and chandlers. A port of many men—calkers and skippers and mates, bosuns and trawlers and lumpers and engineers. A port, too, of many a man who is missing, who is drowned and won't come home. An old fish chowder, brewed in a granite bowl.

Curled in the utmost inner harbor this day rests a tongue of land that is known as Rocky Neck. A peaceful place, full-up with wharves and stiff-backed ugly houses, and flower beds laid out in busted dories, all in the shade of tall old elms and maples. Out at its northeast end lies a mouldering shipyard with low red sheds and a steam-fired winch that is fine for hauling schooners. A squared brick chimney rises not far from a clapboard office graced with harbor-facing eyes. Above its doorway a carved gilt signboard says: ROCKY NECK MARINE RAILWAYS.

This is not a formidable place; not a place that is listed in any shipowner's trade union. It isn't fat from subsidy feeding. It is, in fact, not even a moneymaker; all it is is a shipyard, run by a man who loves ships, a man named Sherman Tarr. He walks with a limp when he walks at all, and now he sits in his office surrounded by pictures of ships—watching ships glide by outside, and dreaming of ships that are gone. Moored to the end of one of his docks are two tall and graceful schooners: *Yankee*, and *Wander Bird*.

It is late in the afternoon when I in my small white sloop come ghosting into Gloucester. I curve around Rocky Neck till I come to the shipyard office, where a white-haired man pressed close to the window gives me a smile and a wave from his loose-hinged hand. Waving back, I pass under the sterns of the two tall schooners and, shooting up into the wind, come to a berth in a corner.

Summer is past and now it is fall: the fog-bound windless days, the yachts, and the tourists and artists and flat-heeled girls who haunted the Little Theatre are gone. Now the mornings come in raw-edged, the leaves lose their grasp, and the smoke lies low.

All summer long you sailed and puttered around, and every so often picked up some change taking tourists on sailing parties. But, just as the summer waned, so did your fine resolve to tackle the world alone with your ship. To make things worse, the ship was a failure. A third of her frames were rotten (you knew this when you bought her); some of her planks were spongy; and she leaked so much, even in port, that you slept each night with a hand trailing down on her floorboards and when the water rose to your fingers you got to your feet and you pumped.

One day in late September a thunderstorm came pouncing down on Gloucester, driving my anchored sloop, stern first, directly toward the serene white hull of the schooner *Yankee*. I hadn't known it was coming because that afternoon I was asleep in the cabin. Rousing out in a rush, I went to work on the flywheel of a one-lung engine. No luck; so, slamming the lid with a curse, I went to work on my mainsail. A knot of spectators stood in the rain on the nearby dock, wishing they had their cameras. The hulls were about to collide when the schooner's master, stripped to the waist, came flying over the rail to land like a cat on my deck. Not a word was spoken. With a long slow heave he fended off and we went to work together; and moments later, the little *Horizon* was scorching across the harbor. We sailed for almost an hour, just for the hell of the thing. Then, with the squall taking off, we ran back in and moored in the lee of the shipyard. As he started up the dock, he paused and, turning back, called out: "Say, why don't you come on board and have supper with us?"

"Thanks," I said, "I'd like to."

The big main cabin was warm and my eyes were full of a ship that was really a ship. It was painted out in ivory and trimmed with varnished teak; the beams were big and each of the fourteen bunks had curtains covered with flowers. One wall was solid books. A halyard tapped on the mainmast, far up aloft; and Gloucester lay all around, unseen, yet felt somehow.

The master's name was Irving Johnson and they broke the mold when they made him. He was owner of the *Yankee*, a former North Sea pilot boat built by the Dutch in 1896. He was commonly regarded as the finest all-around schooner master on the face of the earth. That fall he was beginning to carve out for himself an altogether unique way of life—sailing around the world, at three-year intervals, for pleasure and for the benefit of a select group of young people who were willing and able to pay something like three thousand dollars.

Johnson didn't smoke and he didn't drink—not even tea or coffee, and over a wasp waist he had a tremendous muscular development extending from a bull neck down through corded arms and small wrists to a pair of big blunt hands. He could chin himself half a dozen times with the middle finger of either one. There was, when it came to a sailing ship, nothing he couldn't do; he was a rigger, marline-spike-seaman, sailmaker, helmsman, engineer, navigator, and clinical psychologist, all rolled-up in a gaunt-nosed bundle secured by a catgut ribbon of Yankee thrift.

In the cabin that evening, I sat very straight and quiet. With the dishes cleared, Mrs. Johnson turned to her knitting—a baby was due that winter. "And so," he says, "Sterling here plans to start off in the next few weeks, and sail around the world alone."

Mrs. Johnson's fingers rest and she looks up, and our eyes meet, and after a moment she sighs: "It's an awfully big world." She has no idea, I think, how big it looks to me. Johnson leans back, rocking slowly, one knee locked in his palms. "I'm going to say something now that might be of interest to you." His wife's hands rest once more. "A year from now, we start on our second voyage around the world. I'll be needing a mate . . . to join the ship in the spring . . . I can't pay much; maybe a hundred a month during the summer cruises along this coast . . . nothing at all on the voyage around the world."

"Now," he goes on, "this isn't a promise—only a thought, or maybe a hunch. But perhaps if you worked for the winter down in the West Indies . . . picked up some more schooner experience; then you might come on board here in March, and if things worked out all around . . . you could go mate around the world."

"I—I don't know what to say."

Johnson stretches and yawns and the sleeves of his shirt bulge out. He looks at the cabin clock. "It's getting late. Past my bed-time." The clock shows five past nine.

"That's funny," I say, "I never heard it strike."

Gloucester rests in silence. You can count the trees on the hills. The planks on the dock are wet. Without looking back at first, I walk to a place near the office. Then all at once I turn to look at the big white ship. It comes to me now that I didn't even say thanks for supper.

The sloop seems forlorn, lost in the lee of the dock. The cabin is damp. When I turn up the lantern, I can see the glint of water beneath the floorboards. I dig out a piece of scrap and a brush and some paint, and carefully work at the letters:

FOR SALE
BARGAIN!
OWNER GOING SOUTH

CHAPTER 39

Without waiting for the sloop to be sold, you cleared out of Gloucester bound for Palm Beach in a 46-foot fishing schooner by the name of *Blue Lagoon*. She was owned by Captain Bill McCoy, who had come into port looking for a crew to take his new boat south. He was fond of telling how, back in the Roaring Twenties, he had founded an institution known as "Run Row."

We sailed in late October. Red Baker was running the show; he had just been fired off the bridge of a Texaco tanker because he was a drunk. The schooner was pretty enough, but we soon found out that she leaked like a dime-store basket. She was so loose in her ribs that she worked back and forth whenever the going was rough. And rough it was, all the way from Nantucket Shoals to the mouth of Chesapeake Bay. To pass the time, Red slept every minute he could; and the bottom half of his seabag was ballasted with bourbon to hold the cold at bay.

Like an arrow shot from the bow of Cape Cod, the schooner went tumbling south in a driving northerly gale. We took in the mainsail and reefed her down and with the cresting seas breaking on board you would stand back aft for a third of a day at a stretch with one foot working the tiller and both arms working the pump. The seas kept hurling you on, and every few hours the scuttle would open part way and Red would come up just far enough to exclaim: "Oh good Jesus H. Christ, take a look at them goddamned seas." And then he would say: "You aren't tired, are you?" "Hell no, Red. I like it rough this way." "You're all right, kid. I'll give you a good recommend—next time I see Irving Johnson." And with that he would vanish below.

McCoy and the girl joined the ship in Savannah, along with his brother Ben, who looked like Trotsky and was one hell of an engineer. So the rest of the way you steamed on down through the Inland Waterway. Whenever you were able, you escaped to the top of a mast, where you sat by the hour, watching the cows go by. Maybe, after two or three years with Johnson, you would at last be good enough to merit a ship of your own. You might even follow in his footsteps, and the rest of your life go sailing to distant places with dudes for cargo.

In mid-November you barged into Palm Beach, along with a hurricane. Bill and the others jumped ashore, while you and Red powered back up the Indian River a few miles and there you rammed her nose up on a beach and tied her up to some palm trees. Red turned in and slept and you waded through miles of swamp till you came to the outer shore, where you lay in the dunes and watched the storm at work. So far at least, your luck was holding well.

McCoy gave you fifty bucks for the run and you hitchhiked down to Miami, where, if Biscayne Park was any index, half the unemployed of the nation were hard at work reading want ads under the sun.

The Miami River was choked with yachts. So were the bays and the piers and the basins. Each of these you combed in search of a job, offering to work for nothing more than your found, till you could come up with a paying job. They grunted and waved you away.

Finally, there was a week's work in a boatyard, hauling timbers, cleaning up the debris left by the hurricane. Forty cents an hour they paid you, the same for overtime. Then the lay-off came, on a "Yankees first" basis. Once more you went to the post office and sent some money to Gloucester, but then your luck ran out. The crowds that collected each morning in front of the employment offices were nearly as large as those at the race track, where you almost landed a job as a parking-lot attendant.

In Biscayne Park you staked a claim on a length of grass next to an ersatz brook. Zipping a one-dollar bill in your belt, you blew what was left on three loaves of bread and a jar of peanut butter. This carried you for three and a half days. Then you got a job as dishwasher at the University Club, atop the Biscayne Building. The sinks faced the sea: all day long the northbound tankers marched past on the blue horizon. You were given a cot next to the winch at the top of the elevator shaft, that and four dollars a week. You started to put on weight.

After about a week a busboy named Mario took you under his wing. Mario hailed from a village lost in the mountains of Cuba —even he wasn't sure just where. He would sit on a table nearby, smoking and swinging his legs, his big eyes snapping: "Beeg Yank, next Thursday you come with Mario down to steamship Florida. Ver-ree fine sheep, runs two times each week to Havana for P and O. Mario knows you too good for thees job, Beeg Yank, so he feex you up with job in en-geen room."

"Golly, Mario, that would be great, but I tried to get on that boat, two or three times I tried it."

"Non-sense, Mario has many many friends, that sheep. Most all mens work on sheep come from Havana too. Also, the brother of Mario, he run the ver-ree special girly house in Havana; extra special whorehouse, plenty new young girls come down from mountains to these nice fine whorehouse. Officers from sheep— they come whorehouse alzo. . . . So? Mario feex up Beeg Yank, is good?"

"Sounds great, Mario."

You and Mario joined the ship together. You signed on as Fireman No. 6. Mario went back to his former job as waiter in the Officer's Mess.

The fireman's fo'c'sle was set right over a boiler. Fifteen men lived in this steel-walled cage with the bunks five deep, and you of course wound up in a bottom berth. During your off-watch hours, the guy in the bunk above kept hocking great yellow oysters down into a coffee can by your pillow. But the job wasn't bad, for the ship burned oil, not coal. And the long-stemmed Yankee girls would come down each night after supper, guided by Junior Officers with braid on their shoulders, and the girls would say: "Wheee, isn't it hot down here"—all the while standing under one of the big ventilators. And climbing back up the steep pitched ladders, they'd clutch at their skirts while the gang from the engine room maneuvered around for a look.

It was coming on toward Christmas again and what was most upsetting was your mother's attitude. She wrote so often that you came to dread each trip to the post office in Miami. She wanted you home for Christmas. While you were off at sea you wrote long letters, saying you really loved her, saying you couldn't explain your behavior that last visit you had together, saying it would all be fine "next time." And the next time, you held yourself in check for maybe the first full hour. Then the conversation lagged, faded, and died to the clink of forks on plates. And there you sat, angrily munching your food. And her eyes clouded and her chin began to quiver, and the rest of your time together (never more than two days) was a nightmare.

But your vivid childhood memory, reaching back almost to kindergarten, was of always thinking: How come I have the most wonderful mother in all the world? I shall always love my mother.

One day in Havana, after you'd been in the ship for almost a month, Mario took you inland to his home town. The bus was smelly and dirty and kept breaking down, but all the passengers seemed to know one another. All of you jolted along laughing and talking, and when the engine quit somebody brought out the beer and there you all sat, kidding the driver or snoozing besides a bush.

You climbed far into the hills and Mario said with pride: "You are the first Yankee man ever visits in my home town." It seemed he was right, for all the villagers stared as you swung down the street to Mario's house. The place was small and clean. They gave you the special chair and plied you with beer and food, and Mario's mother and father gazed at their son with proud eyes and everything seemed so relaxed that you envied this life of theirs. Mario was blessed in one way and you in another. You were able to stiff-arm the surface world, yet were torn inside with conflicts. On the other hand, life seemed to stiff-arm Mario, but he seemed quite able to accept his fate and go floundering down the years without inner torment. Why couldn't the scales be balanced?

Early one Sunday morning a lifeboat drill was called. Three lifeboats jerked dangling down till they came to the water, resting there with crewmen like monkeys scrambling down knotted lines—laughing, losing their shoes, then hefting great oars eighteen feet long, trying to master the alien art of rowing.

You saw your chance and, shipping your oar, spit in your hands and rowed. Rowed till your wrists ached and your eyes were swimming with sweat. When the chore was done you heard the voice of the chief mate: "You! You kid. Come here."

"Yes sir?"

"What's your name, lad?"

"Hayden, sir."

"I haven't seen you before. What are you doing in this crew?"

"I'm a fireman."

"Where in hell did you learn to row like that?"

"Dory-trawling on the Grand Banks, sir."

"Get your gear and move into the seaman's fo'c'sle; you don't belong in no goddamed fire-room."

"Yes sir. Thank you sir."

A few weeks later, you were shining the ship's bell one morning, with the sun slanting off the new cars on the Miami Beach causeway that led past the giant yachtboats off Poorhouse Flats. A yacht broker tapped you on the shoulder: "Hayden, I've got you a job as ordinary seaman in a schooner yacht named *Chiva*. They'll pay sixty dollars a month."

"Where are they bound, Palm Beach?"

"Not on your life. They're leaving in three days for Saint Lucia, Martinique, the Grenadines, and Barbados—and maybe even down to Rio."

"Good God."

"You want the job?"

"Yes sir."

The *Chiva* turned out to be a tough little wagon, a vest-pocket version of a genuine Gloucesterman. Her owner was a man from New York City named Wittaker, who had a confused yet gentle face and who knew nothing about the sea.

Pushing *Chiva* through the tropics was a listless affair. The guests smiled and the crew worked and the sea was indigo, stippled sometimes with golden strands of gulfweed. Wherever you went, the islands were acrawl with shuffling Negroes who had nothing but raggedy clothes and fine big calloused hands— and maybe a shack somewhere with some tin utensils, a gaunt wife, and a swarm of bubbling children.

Before you knew it, this little voyage ended. You were paid off, and you grabbed a freight up to Jacksonville because the papers said that the four-mast schooner *J.W. Clise* was there—loading secondhand trucks and jalopies for Dakar. But she had a full crew of Negroes in her fo'c'sle who were drawing twenty-five dollars a month for a fourteen-hour day.

You hitchhiked back toward Miami. Not far from Hobe Sound a car with its steering wheel on the wrong side pulled over and gave you a ride. The man behind the wheel kept turning to stare at you with a quizzical smile. His name was Kenneth.

Morton and Ken were friends. Both were in their early thirties and both were very rich. Morton was bored and instructed a broker to pick him out a yacht, a nice-looking yacht with sails. Ken had an office in Wall Street, where he managed the family's fortune. He was bored too, so he agreed to go for a West Indies cruise with Morton. Papers were signed and Morton became the nattily dressed owner of a sixty-foot schooner, named—of all things—*Pandora*.

The broker also engaged a three-man crew. The captain was Williams; the cook was a Swede named Sven; and the deckhand was Hayden. They were due to sail on a Sunday afternoon. That Saturday night Morton went to a party and became infatuated with a big ex-gob whose name was Ross. He was added to the guest list, which made Ken unhappy. For three days they quarreled and made up till at last the *Pandora* slipped down the channel, with three men aft and three men forward, bound for Nassau, Haiti, Jamaica, and the chain of the Lesser Antilles. They were due back in Miami March first.

Things didn't go well. The skipper—in spite of a fierce countenance and a stark white scar from ear to jaw, a long experience in yachts, and a proper reputation—proved to be not only a bad navigator but much given to flying into tantrums. Morton and Ken were both seasick. Ross lounged below all day, listening to the radio and plying the cook with whiskey. Hayden was seasick too, but he had the deck pretty much to himself and he ran the ship as he pleased.

The skipper was proud of his body and enjoyed moving around without any clothes on. Sometimes he stood in the bows and poured buckets of water over his head for an hour at a time. Morton and Ken watched him. "Ken, now really, I ask you, did you ever see anything the size of that?" They were dressed in pastel shades—contrasting, of course; both wore wide sink ties tied sideways and rope-soled sandals tied with cotton cord; both were tanned and neither seemed very happy. "No, Mort, I must say I never did."

They anchored in Nassau's Hurricane Hole, where the party aft moved into a big hotel, and then sailed to Port-au-Prince and there rented a house on a hill. But the call of the sea had soured, so the *Pandora* swung off for home, by way of Montego Bay and the Cayman Islands. The night they entered Miami's main ship channel the skipper almost ran the ship on the jetty. In the course of the tantrum that followed, he sang out in his high-pitched voice: "Here I am on this clambake with nothing but a bunch of fucking queers!"

The yacht's owner fired him the following morning and hired the deckhand in his place. Three times in the months that followed, the *Pandora* cruised through the Bahamas, now with a Negro crew. And then on the last day of February the kid in command was handed a telegram: "LOOKING FORWARD YOUR ARRIVAL SCHOONER YANKEE AS MATE VESSEL LAID UP AT RUDDOCK'S SHIPYARD GREENWICH REGARDS JOHNSON."

That night the northbound freight had a guest in a reefer compartment.

CHAPTER 40

Down the winding road to the harbor I trudged with the seabag slung on my shoulder, my eyes fixed on the *Yankee,* which lay to the end of a wharf. And I wouldn't have traded places with any man on earth. It was March 26, 1936—and I was twenty years old that day.

An idyl was in the making. For thirty months I dwelled in a land so bathed in golden sunshine, so placid, so laden with charms and new sensations, that I was all but entranced.

Mine in a way was a minor role in the passive life aboard the *Yankee.* Johnson supplied the driving force; the crew supplied the cash and whatever muscle was needed; and I was a go-between, an interpreter of the ways of the sea to this assortment of well-heeled vagabonds. The lure of the life rested on a foundation of utter simplicity. My home was a lower bunk six and a half feet long and maybe three feet wide, with thirty inches of space between its thin mattress and the slats of a bunk overhead. I had one shelf for my clothing, and above my feet was a hinged box that held my books and papers and letters. In the course of the voyage around the world, which lasted eighteen months, I spent the grand sum of one hundred and sixty dollars.

Sterling Hayden of Gloucester, the first mate, was that rare find, a born sailor, a "natural." This is the greatest quality a man can hope to find in the man to whom he will at times

have to entrust the command of his ship. In addition he had
the ability to assume authority, and apparently that too was
innate. He gave orders easily and they were followed un-
questioningly, though most of those under him were older
than this twenty-year-old mate.—*Sailing to See* by Irving
Johnson

Throughout the summer we cruised the New England coast
from Manhattan to Nova Scotia, under charter, a week or two at
a time, to various groups. Gloucester was the base of the operation, and we returned there for a few hours each Saturday to take
on provisions, fuel, and water, and pick up mail.

Few things can be more conducive to contentment than coastwise cruising in a deep-water vessel. Day after day you laze
through islands and thoroughfares, seldom out of sight of land
and always with safe anchorage within reach should a breeze of
wind come down. The glory days of seafaring New England are
a thing of the past and so the big white schooner with the square-
yard fixed to her foremast was by way of being a legend. She cast
a long romantic shadow across the scrawny sailing and power
yachts assembled in those late afternoon anchorages.

Sometimes it troubled me a little that I was part of an anach-
ronism. It bothered me that we weren't carrying cargo or catch-
ing fish. But I wanted, or needed, to stay in sail, and where else
could I go? And so the summer passed, and the big trip lay in
the offing.

On the first of November we sailed from Gloucester, bound
outward around the world. We had a paying crew of twelve
young men and two girls, and stashed behind a collapsible fish-
net barrier was the year-old Johnson baby, with a cabin all to himself. I was working my way; only the cook was salaried, and he
was my special friend. His name was Fritz Vollmecke. He hailed
from Hamburg, Germany, and he was twenty-nine. He had a
deep rumbling voice, a cleft chin, and wild green eyes, and he
knew all there was to know about work. He could smile and
swear and laugh and stay on his feet in a maddened galley
through a protracted bout of seasickness. He dressed like a used-
car salesman, he couldn't swim a stroke, and he had a low
opinion of all paying guests.

Beyond Eastern Point we shut down the engine and lay for a
time becalmed. Along with Fritz I stood on the deck back aft,

watching Gloucester grow dim in the dusk. I thought of a girl who even now must be driving home toward Boston. Her name was Sarah and we had been together a lot that summer. Only the night before, we had dined in a little hideaway and then I had driven her car to the top of a hill, where we had parked for hours. I thought I should feel sad, but didn't—perhaps because of my mother, who was waiting for me to come to her little apartment, where, as she said, "we can say goodbye in private . . . and you can have a last hot bath and some of your favorite molasses cake."

The wind blew and the ports reeled into our wake: Cap-Haïtien, Panama, half a dozen roadsteads in the Galapagos Islands; then a long reach across the southeast trades to desolate Easter Island, until, early in February of 1937, we swung her off for Tahiti, by way of Pitcairn Island, eight hundred miles to the westward.

This was the tranquil time. The Depression didn't exist. Week after week the ship soughed on. The crew had settled down well enough, the food was fine, and the sea was content to shimmer under the sun like those endless western wheat fields. I kept a special journal in which I recorded a mass of data concerning the behavior of three imagined craft that voyaged with us. By the time this voyage ended, I reasoned, one of the ships would emerge triumphant as the perfect ship for my life at sea. I also knew that the ship was the least of my worries. Money was the headache. But never mind that now; I had the will, so there must be a way somehow.

Something else troubled me. Was I, as it sometimes seemed, cut out to be a mate rather than master? Was it Johnson's presence that enabled me to function so freely? It wasn't the ship that concerned me so much as the essential traffic with land: with matters of finance, organization, lectures, films, and the endless patient contact with hundreds of prospective crewmen. He was phlegmatic and I was a romantic. He was practical; I couldn't balance a checkbook. He was tolerant, even of those he didn't respect; I prided myself on harshness, when it came to the ones with the silver spoons. He was apparently immune to the blandishments of tobacco and booze and each new girl with a certain set to her body. I wasn't, not for a minute—except for this voyage, during which I was doing my best to emulate the master.

Tahiti lay up ahead, the Tahiti of a thousand library dreams, envisioned through boxcar doors and during nights on iced-up trawlers. The Tahiti of Stevenson and Jack London and Fletcher Christian. And facing this prospect, I smiled, with the doubts now banished.

The days dissolved and the islands streamed by: Pitcairn, Ducie, and Henderson; Mehetia, Bora Bora, Huahiné, and Maupiti. Tahiti too, where nothing much had happened, perhaps because Johnson—wise in the ways of youth—hadn't seen fit to remain in Papeete for even so much as a week.

West and north of Tahiti itself lie a group of high islands known as (surely one of the most magical place names of all) "Les Isles-sous-le-Vent"—The Islands Under the Wind. Among them is Raïatéa, a somewhat diminished Tahiti.

For a week and more we had been sailing among those islands. The crew explored and snapped pictures, dove from reefs, or whanged away at goats and boar, with high-priced rifles. One night the *Yankee* lay to a grassy timbered quay. I lingered over supper and joked with the cook and thought about writing letters. Through the open skylight above my head came the drawn-out words: "Oh-h . . . Hah!" softly intoned by the skipper. Something was brewing. As I rose to my feet, his face came framed in the skylight and his voice was tense this time. "Hey, Sterling, better take a look here quick."

I shot from the hatch expecting to find the ship beset by an arched squall or maybe a tidal bore. Instead, moving toward us across the lagoon, was a broad-beamed copra schooner with a cargo of beautiful girls. There must have been twenty of them; they lined the rail nearest us, they clung to the rigging, they stood on top of the cabins. And at the outermost end of the bowsprit, framed against a cloud, stood the most ravishing creature I had ever seen. Her long black hair lifted and fell in the wind. She wore a two-piece bathing suit made of *pareu* cloth and incredibly brief. I simply stood still and stared. Then I felt the cook by my side, and heard him catch his breath. "Kee-r-r-ist! Pee Wee, yust take a look at that!" The schooner passed close by and moored right under our stern. From beneath her awning came the plunk of an old guitar. I dropped below and brushed my teeth and changed to a clean white shirt.

The schooner was named *Moana*. She hailed from Papeete and for several weeks had been cruising among the islands under charter to a planter named Pedro Miller, a friend of Nordhoff's and Hall's. And all at once the *Yankee* seemed to me an antiseptic craft on a mundane cruise, quietly moored with a baby asleep in her belly and family pictures pinned to the walls of her bunks.

Whereas from the *Moana* flowed ripples of high-pitched laughter. A long board table was spread with a red-checked cloth. Bottles of wine appeared. Oil lamps were lit and lanterns glowed in her shrouds. Hurdling the *Yankee*'s bulwarks, I sauntered toward the sound of music and laughter. I glanced back just once: I could see our skipper standing not far from the wheel. His arms were crossed; his wife sat on a skylight; and I wondered what he was thinking.

The dancing exploded as soon as dinner was finished. The quay was packed by this time with people from Raïatéa. I went on board the *Moana,* where I found a place right next to a flickering lantern. I looked for the girl I had singled out earlier. Our eyes met briefly. And all at once she was dancing alone. Her hips swung and the grass skirt was thrust aside by her thighs. I reached for a bottle of wine. With a final spasm, the music stopped and the girl was by my side. I could smell the flowers that cradled her breasts. I poured some wine in a trembling glass and gave it to her. "Oh," she laughed, "just a taste." She touched the glass to her lips. "Thank you very much."

"Why, you speak perfect English—"

"And why not? My father is the—is your American consul in Papeete."

"Oh—oh, I see." And I told her my name.

Later that evening we walked to the house of her aunt in the village, and she got permission to stay out until eleven o'clock. Then we walked for a long time down a rutted sand road that bordered the dark lagoon. Our hands touched and at last held. Save for the surf on the reef, the night was silent. Some dogs barked as we slipped back through the village to her aunt's house, where a tall white candle stood watch in a glass chimney next to an old alarm clock. We kissed good night quickly and I swaggered back to the quay. I stood for a long time midway between the two schooners.

Then the elation was suddenly gone. I looked from ship to ship: *Yankee—Gloucester, Moana—Papeete.* Take your choice, I thought, you can't have them both. For what seemed a long time I lay in my hammock under the stars. And I think that perhaps I sensed then that from that night on the voyage around the world would all be downhill.

Emerging from Polynesia by way of Christmas Island, Pago Pago, and Apia, we passed through Melanesia, skirted Micronesia, slipped through Torres Straits south of New Guinea, and pottered around in the Dutch East Indies till we came to Singapore. During the entire voyage I slept ashore only one night—on Pitcairn's Island—and that because I was sick.

We crossed the Indian Ocean in twenty-eight days or so (from Sumatra to Zanzibar); rode out a gale off the Cape of Good Hope, looked in at Cape Town; and then, taking the brawling southeast trades of the Atlantic broad on our starboard quarter, the *Yankee* ran for almost a month unchecked till she came to Rio—where a giant GOODYEAR sign on the crest of a hill, not far from the statue of Christ, was a reminder of home.

On the first day of May 1938, the *Yankee* raised Eastern Point, and at two in the afternoon I stood in the bows. I took a deep breath and, with a suitable pause for the cameras, rifled a bowline into the lap of a welcoming crowd. My mother looked on with pride, and that was the end of the voyage.

CHAPTER 41

The Coast of Maine. Blues and grays and greens. White clouds sailing, throwing shadows that glide like great sea bats just below the surface. A windy day—Penobscot Bay, far east of Portland, alive with laughing whitecaps, islands incised on the rim of the sea.

Close inshore a lighthouse, Owls Head, its back to a stand of silver spruce, and off to its north Rockland Harbor. This is an ugly place, a scar on the breast of Maine: commercial, full of wart-shaped buildings—garages and filling stations, blue-eyed cafés and such.

The *Yankee* beats in, past the long stone breakwater's flank. On her decks are nearly two dozen Girl Scouts, shapeless and unformed—almost all—in royal-blue dresses and slacks. A launch from the town runs to join with the schooner. She carries a special stranger, standing with his hands thrust deep in a pilot coat; the brim of his hat bats away in the wind. He springs on board and waves the launch away.

Up with the helm and back your jibs and ease your sheet! The ship pays off and runs back into the Bay, where she hauls her wind and begins to thrash up the Camden shore, bound for Searsport.

The stranger hails from there. He stands now with his head thrown back, checking the lead of the gear; his eye runs around on the mainmasthead, then crosses along to the fore and down again to the bows. He stamps on the deck and you'd swear he was tempted to smile. His eyes, mouth, and jaws shine with arrogance. The face is sharp, and handsome too, in a jaundiced way as befits a man with his background. Born off Cape Horn in his father's full-rigged ship, he has been, in turn, civil engineer, Washington correspondent, editor of a radical journal —and the author of a dozen novels about the sea. His name is Lincoln Colcord.

The mate and he shake hands and size each other up. (The mate is envious—if only he too had been born off the pitch of the Horn, or down here on the coast of Maine, or in Gloucester.)

Captain Johnson is honored that the older man is aboard. "Mister Colcord"—pointing aft—"how would you like to take the helm for a while?"

"Well, I tell you, Johnson, I'd a damn sight rather have some rum."

Johnson shakes his head with a half laugh. "Sorry. Dry ship. Don't keep a drop on board. Better this way when you sail round the world the way we do." His smile is mostly on the left side of his face.

The stranger blinks in the wind. "No!" A hoarse whisper, head thrust forward. "You don't say. A dry ship. Well, I'll be goddamned!" His enunciation is tinged with the twang that comes with the coast down here. He looks into the wind, where—faroff—you can see some low-lying hills and the spire or two of a town. It won't be long till the anchor is down and he's snug in his home by the fire.

They strode through the village together, mate and friend, aged twenty-two and fifty-five that July day in 1938. The mate felt pleased—honored really—that he was the only guest of this querulous man who delighted in speaking with ruthless honesty.

The house was old and white, with a giant elm to one side and a view down the length of the Bay. Off to the right you could see the masts of the *Yankee* beyond the rise of a hill.

The living room was full of pictures of ships and oil paintings done in Hong Kong, and books everywhere, from ceiling to floor, under and over windows, piled under tables, on top of tables. The mate was awed. This is a home . . . this is what people mean when they talk about home, not the houses in the suburbs like we used to have, not the hotels and the fancy apartments and all that—just an old white house by the water —feeling its way into the life of a village.

"Now," said the man, "you and I are going to have some rum."

"Thanks just the same, Mr. Colcord, but I don't drink."

"Why not?"

"Oh, I just don't care for the stuff, I guess."

"Nonsense. You don't drink because you've been taught it was wrong. You don't drink because that goddam Boy Scout of a skipper—he's a good seaman, understand—he doesn't drink. Right?"

"Right," smiles the lad.

"Do you smoke?"

"No sir."

"Don't call me Mister and don't call me Sir. Now, you build a fire while I wash up. Then you and I are going to have a talk. I've had my eye on you all afternoon. Johnson tells me you're the best mate he ever had. That may be. But you're all tensed up. That's bad. The wood is under those papers."

His wife Frances came in. She was a plain woman with the warmth given only to those who are plain. She smiled as she put the rum and lime juice next to his big armchair.

The fire crackles. The mate turns and sits on a low stool, watching the flames, smelling the smoke, and thinking.

"Frances, draw young Hayden here a tub of water. If I'm any judge, he'd like a good hot bath."

The mate laughs, a habit he has. "I went around the world and never once had a hot bath—except on Pitcairn."

"You did, eh? Well that's too damn bad, isn't it. No hot water in the whorehouses any more. There was in my time."

Two and a half years on the *Yankee* reading the *Geographic* and the *Digest,* no drink no smoke. Skimming the world, looking at it from a distance.

"Might I try just a bit of that rum?"

"Of course." Shoving the bottle across. Smiling. For the first time really smiling. "You see, son, I'm not against being teetotal, but I do hate hypocrisy." He stands by the window, sipping rum, watching the Bay grow dark.

The rum tastes good.

"Tell me about Tahiti. Anyone fall off the wagon there? Anyone sit on the porch of the Cercle Bougainville and get plastered, with the schooners laying off and the girls going by, eh, how about that?"

"Well no. Mostly the crew went for ice cream. Ice cream and milk."

A look convulses his face. "Ice cream and milk! Frances! Did you hear that? Hayden here says while they were in Tahiti there wasn't any drinking. Instead they went for milk and ice cream. Good God!" He freshens his glass—and his guest's.

A new log thrown in the fire—black and tough.

"What did you think about Austria?"

"About Austria?" Again the awkward laugh. "Well. What about Austria?"

"Forget it. What do you think of Roosevelt?"

"Gee, I don't know. We never talk politics on the ship. Politics or religion. I remember the guys in the fishing fleet used to think he was God, mostly."

"He's a god, all right. A war god. I tell you that right now. I used to be a pretty radical man in my youth. But I tell you, Hayden, this man is mad. He's going too far. He'll have us at war before you know it. Mark my words."

"Mr. Colcord, if you were going around the world in your own ship, would you want a ship like the *Yankee* or a big Gloucester fisherman or a small square-rigger like the *Conrad?*"

"Square-rig. Every time square-rig. I was born under it, you know. Finest thing man ever created." He fills his glass. "So. What will you do with yourself in the future—any ideas?"

"I'd hoped to get some financing. No luck. Nothing to do but keep working away for other people, I guess. Trying to save some money. Hard to do. Seemed easy once—back in Singapore. Now I'm home, it seems tough."

The older man spits into the fire. "You can take that life and shove it. In my opinion, there could be nothing worse than farting around the world with a group of spoiled kids fresh from school in search of pleasure. Gawd!"

"I'm inclined to think you're right."

"Of course I'm right. You'd be better off hauling lobster traps and living your own life. Being your own man. You say you'd like to write. Well damn it, son, go ahead. Write. But I warn you—you'll go hungry if you do." His eyes shine. "Pass that bottle, will you? There. On the other hand, if I were you I might just go out to the South Seas and get a little girl and put up in one of the Tuamotus while this madman leads us into war and the blood flows all over the world. Mark well my words—

"All right, what about sex? Any good-looking girls on that trip? Anbody get fucked in the folds of the jib?"

"Lincoln." His wife smiles.

"Well I'm worried about our young friend here. I'm very much afraid he's a hell of a good mate but he's long overdue when it comes to discovering life. Wouldn't you say?"

She is sewing at a piece of cloth stretched on a little hoop. "What were you doing, Linc, when you were his age? Still in the university?"

"Sure I was. Writing songs and making socialist speeches and screwing girls and getting drunk and laughing like hell and getting mad. That's good. That's life. This boy has been working his ass off ever since he was fifteen and he's still just a child inside."

"Lincoln, now please."

The mate feels ready for bed. It will be good to get back to his bunk in the schooner's deckhouse. Good to see Johnson, moving quietly around on the deck. "Well, Mister Colcord, I guess I've had too much to drink of this rum. I do know you don't sound like any socialist to me and maybe I'll just have to do some thinking about these things."

Together they walk through the village. The older man keeps a fierce hold on his arm. When they come to the turn that leads to the wharf, they pause and shake hands.

"Don't feel bad, son, about anything I said."

"Oh I won't." A smile in the night.

"No. Don't. Because let me tell you this. You know how to sail a ship, see? You're a damn good sailorman, from what I hear. Anybody can handle a woman, see? But not just anybody can handle a vessel." He taps the boy on the chest. "Remember this, what I say. You can't fuck a ship off a lee shore!" Straightening up and stepping back: "Good night."

CHAPTER 42

High water. A schooner lies to a wharf. Her sheer is proud as it runs up to her bows from a low point amidships. Old men lounge in late September sunshine, fiddling with pipes and knives, admiring the look of the vessel, spitting and scanning the sky.

Against this sky is a man at work on the mainmasthead. He wears a checked wool shirt, one sleeve ragged. Ninety feet from the deck he works, wearing a rigger's knife—homemade from the blade of a file—with a bucket of tar dangling near his hands.

Gloucester somnolent and warm. He basks in the glow of the scene—in the crowding of masts, the wheeling of gulls, the lift of a sail in the distance. His world begins and ends with just such things as these. The ship is the *Gertrude L. Thebaud,* fitting out now for a challenge match against the Canadian *Bluenose* (best three out of five races, no handicap, no shifting of ballast, plenty of good hard feelings). His job is that of mastheadsman—he on the main, Jack Hackett aloft on the fore. What more could a sailorman ask?

His hands now thick with tar. Gingerly he reaches with careful fingers, wary and tuned to the wind, cups the match and bends his head. And looking up he sees her. Along the dock she comes with a dogged gait, plowing through bystanders and fishermen mixed. He shakes his head slightly, and down from aloft he clomps, slapping his hands on the shrouds, dreading what lies ahead.

"Well—Buzz—how good to see you, my dear."

"Hello, Mother, how are you?" They move to the lee of a shed.

"So you're going to be in the race."

"Seems that way."

"And afterwards? Any idea—what you'll do and where you'll be, once the races are over?"

"Mother, I don't know. Back to sea, I guess, assuming I find a ship. Nothing for me on shore."

"Oh Buzz, is it any use my staying in Gloucester? All summer long I was here. We saw each other twice."

"Mother, I know. And I'm sorry, believe me I am, but—"

He looks around in despair. Busy men everywhere. Men at work—painting, chipping, scrubbing and mending and splicing. Across the harbor lies Rocky Neck. Leaves are turning—reds like rust, golds and browns.

Without a word she is gone. Her head is bowed. She is crying. Farther apart now than when he was halfway across the world. She pauses at the corner, starts to turn around, checks herself. Then out of sight.

He clomps aloft once again.

Out of Gloucester, a week before the first race, forty men and one tall ship bound on a trial run. Pitted against the clock. Against some wind as well—ragged brawling wind blowing a southeast gale. Storm warnings fly beneath a dull gray sky, and leaves skirmish. (Out on the Banks no dories will work this day, and up in Boston girls clutch skirts and hats go tumbling to leeward.)

Half past ten, says a belfry clock. Captain Ben Pine stands by the wheel. You would swear he was part of his ship—in spite of the blue vested suit, the brown felt hat, and a red bow tie. More like a coach he looks than like a racing-schooner skipper.

A motor launch tows the *Thebaud* free of the wharves and holds her head to the wind. "You can set your mainsail now," Ben says softly. Forty men to the halyards—peak to starboard, throat to port. Twenty men to a side—to lay back hauling, grunting at first, then gasping. Big new halyards an inch and a half in diameter. The canvas flogs. All over the harbor you hear it. (Plenty of empty seats in Gloucester's schools. Plenty of hooky-players hiding out in wharves.)

"Now go ahead on your foresail." Ben spits in his hands and paces in front of the wheel, feeling the wind and gauging the heft of the ship. Putting pieces together like an artist, working with wood and wind, buoys and rocks and anchored vessels, painting a wind-blown scene.

"Run up your jumbo and jib." His voice edged now, the coach look lost. The decks a tangle of gear: of mooring warps, gaskets, lifts, sheets, runners, tackles, and halyards. (Paid for by townsmen who donated money or labor, by riggers and ship-wrights and sailmakers who worked for almost nothing.) Ben spits as he gauges and measures. The towline is gone, and the bow cants fast to starboard. She starts to move through the water. Most skippers would be content to run for the open sea, but not Ben Pine.

Cordage bites into grooved oak rails. Like an iron-capped lance, her bowsprit flies toward Sherm Tarr's office window. A sharp puff rams home in her sails and lays the vessel over. Her rail smokes. Dead toward the dock she goes. Anyone who doesn't know schooners would swear something is wrong.

She goes now. Better than ten she goes. Up aloft, you hear a deep rumbling roar—and the hissing of spray. Square in mid-channel lies an old-time sailing vessel—a brigantine with a lascar crew, hailing from Ceylon. Her name stands out—*Florence C. Robinson.*

With a thrust of his fist, Ben orders a man aloft. Up he goes on the run till he reaches the masthead, where he heaves himself over the hounds, breathing hard, and goes to work with the topsail. "Stand by!" Ben's voice betrays his calm. One final look—full circle—with an arm flung wide for balance. Now he claws at the wheel, fighting it over. "Helm's alee!" For the first time he really yells out.

She slashes into the wind. Canvas booms and sheet blocks dance under booms. Straight into the eye of the wind. (Not six feet separate her from the queer brig with the crew all wrapped in skirts and blankets—tumbling up on deck in response to a shipmate's warning.)

She passes across the wind, flung down to port. "Leggo your main sheet, boys." Ben is right where he wants to be. "Clear that coil—now let her run to the knot." The sheet runs snaking out till the knot fetches up in the block.

She swings toward the harbor entrance, and all around the harborside spurts of white stab from whistles—a pleasant sound, on a southeast day with rain.

Half a mile inside the breakwater she really begins to pitch, though the force of the wind is blunted. Both topsails are set. Down in the galley, they're mixing hot water with rum, butter, and cinnamon.

Up aloft you hang on. Beyond the breakwater the wild Atlantic growls. Plumes of spray pounce on lighthouse windows. Your mainmasthead is six feet higher than where Jack Hackett lives, thirty feet away. His voice is high and loud. "Oh dyin' Jaysus, boy, if she catches one o' them seas just right she'll pitch us clear to New-found-land!" Up here you feel the motion more. You feel her reach out over a sea and hang; then down she goes with a sickening rush, and the second after the crash your mast goes buckling forward with a sideways motion. You

wonder how wood can take it. (This goes on for an hour and
more. Then both topsails are furled so as not to do any damage.)

Boudreau comes up from the galley, wiping his lips, leaning
in to the weather rail, shoulders hunched. His yellow oilskins
shine. He rests one knee on the deck and jams one booted leg
out stiff against a hatch as he watches the vessel go. Low in
the water she flies; two feet of sifting water conceal her rail.
Her long bow threads through breaking seas, reaching high,
plunging down, always with the roar in the shrouds. He
thrashes his arms and screams: "Fourteen, goddam it, boys,
fourteen she goes, or I hope to die with a hard-on!"

Ben by the lee of the wheel, fondling the spokes, feeling her
go—knee-deep in water. Satisfied.

CHAPTER 43

Captain Angus Walters swung his big salt-banker *Bluenose* in
past the Boston lightship, strapped her down, and sent her
rampaging up harbor in time for a welcoming luncheon thrown
by the governor on behalf of the Commonwealth. Those who
were there pronounced it a dandy affair: plenty of dames,
plenty of booze, plenty of platitudes. Captain Angus wasn't
there. He stayed by his vessel instead. "Let 'em spout," he
barked. "I'm gettin' ready to race."

The mayor of Gloucester passed the word to the better
saloons down on Duncan Street that he expected a little decorum, a little restraint . . . during the racing. When they heard
this, the boys in the red jack boots and the checked shirts
smiled. Saloon keepers are smart: by the time the *Bluenose*
arrived there wasn't a piece of moveable furniture in a single
water-front bar.

October came in like a lamb, mewed for a few days, roared
like a lion for the better part of two weeks, then trailed off into
November. The first two races were sailed in moderate winds
and sunshine. *Thebaud* took the first one by thirty seconds,
and *Bluenose* waltzed off with the second. During the scheduled
three-day hiatus that followed, Gloucester got down on its knees
and prayed for a living gale. While Gloucester was busy pray-

ing, Angus Walters took advantage of the moonless midnight hours to scan the weather forecasts and juggle around with his ballast. When the Clerk of the Weather predicted a breeze of wind—into the *Bluenose* went an extra ton or two of pig-iron ballast. When the Clerk called for light airs—back on the wharf went the pigs. Pretty clever. It was also against the rules that governed the races. But Captain Elroy Proctor of the Master Mariners Association and Miss Ray Adams, Ben Pine's partner, were pretty clever too. They sprinkled a layer of sand over the ballast pile, and Angie was caught red-handed. "Some cute," said Gloucester. What Angus said did not appear in the Glouces-ter *Times*. Everybody shrugged. After all, the little Lunen-burger was more than just a crack racing skipper: he was renowned as a dairyman, and like all businessmen he wanted to win and to hell with your goddam rules.

The day of the third race dawned with rain and a driving easterly gale. All but one of the *Thebaud*'s crew smiled, and I was the one who didn't. The reason was simple enough: only the day before, I had been turned from mastheadman to naviga-tor because my predecessor had got all but lost in the second race. To make things worse, Captain Pine was in the hospital with a sinus attack.

A cannon on the Coast Guard boat let go with a puff of smoke and the race was on. Both schooners hit the starting line going twelve knots and the Canadian pulled ahead. Captain Cecil Moulton hung to the *Thebaud*'s wheel with his boots full of water and his cap rammed down on his eyes. We averaged thirteen and a half to the first mark, where forty brawny Glouces-termen lay back chanting and straining on swollen manila sheets. "Haul, you bastards, haul!" cried Harry the cook, buried waist deep in the hatch, clutching his derby in one hand, a mug of rum in the other.

The *Bluenose* tore past the plunging buoy two lengths ahead of us and swung hard on the wind. Her long black snout, streaming spray, reached over a steep sea, then fell like a maul into the trench beyond. Her scarred old timbers shuddered. Her spars pitched hard against their tracery of shrouds. High far aloft, her foretopmast backstay parted and the wire rained down on deck. Fiery Angus—never a man noted for patience —laid down on the wind-honed waters a savage barrage of four-letter words.

With this stay gone, they were forced to strike their big jib

topsail. The smaller *Thebaud* forged by to windward, slogging
her way uphill now, through charging white-plumed seas. This
was the windward leg. Fifteen miles away, dead into the eye of
the wind, lay a small white buoy. The visibility was about two
hundred yards at best—less in the squalls, of course. Back and
forth the two great wagons tacked, sawing away at the base
course. When they came about, you could hear the flogging of
canvas halfway to Scollay Square. I'm all right, I kept reassuring myself, so long as the wind doesn't shift. If we can't find the
buoy, they'll not blame me too much, what with this horsing
around, first to the southeast, then to the northeast—with Christ
knows what for a current setting beneath the keel. But if the
wind should haul and we run for the mark—and I have to
conjure a fixed course—what in hell then?

The wind hauled. I pored over the chart, gauging and guessing and praying. I crossed myself twice, exhaled with resignation, and called out to Cecil: "Let her go east by south and a
quarter south."

"East by south and a quarter south it is!" his voice came
through the hatch. I wished I were Irving Johnson. I wished
myself back on the masthead, where there was nothing to do
but curse, work, and spit downwind—all the while thinking
how tough you were. I took the binoculars and made my way
forward past the prone bodies of thirty men—half of whom
were skippers of lesser craft. I climbed halfway up the lee fore
rigging, locked my legs through the ratlines, and smoked. For
forty minutes she blazed a trail with her rail buried deep in
foam. The harder I looked, the less I saw. Either that, or there
were buoys everywhere: dozens of baby bouys bouncing around,
plunging like pistons between helmeted seas.

"That's it, isn't it, Hayden?" Cooney the sailmaker called
from his place in the bows.

"I think so," I called back calmly, seeing nothing yet, steal-
ing a glance at him, from under my binoculars. The *Bluenose*
was far astern. The buoy lay dead ahead. If Cecil hadn't
knocked her off a touch, we might have run it down. You lucky
bastard, I muttered under my breath; and swinging down to
the deck, I sauntered aft, looking the world in the eye, vindi-
cated, my belly afire with pride.

Rounding the mark, we flew downwind like a gull, bound for
the finish line. The Coast Guard boat, with its cargo of seasick
race committeemen, had quit and run for the cover of Boston.

We clocked ourselves across the line. But fishermen are casual about some things. Nobody knew for certain whether we should leave the marker to port or starboard; so we finished twice for good measure, then jogged along slowly, the gang all on their feet, tired—but not too tired to line the rail and give three cheers when the big Queen of the North Atlantic came booming down on the line.

A late October day and the racing is finished, forever. Five thousand people are gathered under the Gloucester sun, with Legion and high-school bands, with the governor himself on hand, along with half a dozen sub-governors, surplus mayors, and councilmen. Natives mingle with tourists in for the day, newsmen audit the scene with cameras and pencils and cabled microphones. This is an occasion: it marks the formal dedication of the big new red-brick fish pier, financed in part by the PWA—with greetings from F.D.R.

Moored to the dock in the place of honor lie the two great racing schooners, victor and vanquished: *Bluenose* and *Thebaud*. The former had retained her title as champion of the North Atlantic, taking the last two races by a wide margin in what Gloucester called with contempt "New York yacht club weather." Both ships are dressed in flags this hot and windless day, and the traffic on Main Street is snarled. Tomorrow it will all be over and the saloons will blossom with tables and chairs and benches.

A politician speaks. Hear him now, a comical cutout figure, full of brass, tempered in booze, bursting with plans for the future—his future: "And so, friends, we are met this glorious fall day, not just to dedicate this marvel of brick and mortar, but to pay our respects to those men, living and dead, who for more than three hundred years have gone down to the terrible sea in frail barks to reap from it a harvest of fish. Now, friends, and fellow citizens of this great Commonwealth, and our neighbors from across the Gulf, it is altogether fitting that—"

From the fish hold of the *Bluenose* comes the sound of a trumpet muted by three-inch pine. A journalist stalks through the mob. His shirt is drenched and he harbors a terrible thirst as he swings to the deck of the *Bluenose*. Fishermen guard each hatch, for the party below is by invitation only—given by the crews of the schooners in their own honor, and maybe that of the press. No one else is welcome.

He shows his card: "Tom Horgan, Associated Press." They
give him a nod and down the ladder he goes to the cavernous
hold. Here ninety men are assembled out of the sun, away from
the politicians and tourists, the kids and the wives. They're
assembled this day to bury some hatchets and kill a few kegs of
rum. Up and down this cave long bundles of sail are spread,
with flags nailed to the inner hull. Hymie Rodenhauser, one of
the *Bluenose*'s mastheadsmen, straddling a keg in a cradle, is
blasting loose with his trumpet. A bedlam of laughter and singing and wild gesticulations seen through a pall of smoke.

Horgan is handed a cup. He raises his fist. "To the *Bluenose*!
I say we drink to this ship!" A hand is slammed on his back. "I
say we pretty damn well better drink to this ship, Tom, or else
get our ass knocked off." The man who says this is pleasantly
drunk. His head is large, with a domed brow and bright eyes, a
big nose that leads to an upturned mouth. His hands are those
of an artist. His name is Lawrence Patrick Joseph O'Toole ("of
the South Boston O'Tooles," he says). Along this coast he is a
legend; if you want him any time, look down on T Wharf,
where he hangs out, living with Horgan sometimes, or with any
one of a thousand friends. People like to have him around because he makes them happy. He doesn't drive a car and he is
always broke, and the worse things are, the more he laughs,
painting away at his pictures of people and ships, or carving a
figurehead.

Tom Horgan drains his cup. "Larry, you miserable bastard,
why aren't you up on the dock making a speech or something?"
O'Toole looks around and places a finger to his lips. "Sh-h-h," he
whispers, "to the health of the poor old *Thebaud*." Their cups
meet. A man comes by with a pail full of rum. It slops when he
ladles it out. O'Toole scoops deep with his cup.

Now they edge their way to a corner where a friend sits
mute on a blown-out stays'l. "All right," says Tom, "I shall
now propose a toast: To the best damn man to sail out of
Gloucester in many a fucked-up year."

"Hear Hear," says O'Toole, "that's right."

The friend seems a little embarrassed. "Oh no," he smiles
with a deprecatory nod, "don't say that."

"Whaddaya mean, 'Oh no'? You know who said that? Ben
Pine said that. Don't be so goddamed modest."

"Then, I drink to Ben," says the friend, killing what's left in
his cup.

A figure bursts into the hold, blowing the cook's tin whistle.

"All right, you bassards, up, up, everybo'y up on the goddam
deck! Hear me? The governor's gonna make us his honorin'
speech, an' the mayor wants every friggin' one o' you on th' deck
... An leave the booze down here ... An' no more friggin' noise!
Hear?"

No one moves. "Drink up!" roars O'Toole. You can hear the
Legion band playing the National Anthem. All rise. When the
Anthem expires, they sit—among them, three friends: Horgan,
O'Toole, and Hayden.

Requiem. Midnight. The dock is deserted, the flags make an
arch in the rigging, and the night around is cool, calm, and
clear. Aloft on the *Thebaud*'s mainmast a man lies flat in the
crosstrees, staring up at the stars. His legs are crossed at the
ankles, one fist is full of a halyard. Up past the head of the pier
the street lights blink when crossed by nodding branches.

(We approach this man ... gently ... intent on asking some
questions ... on probing his mind just a little.)

Hey. [softly] Hey, you on a mainmasthead—

"Yes?"

You're sober, we trust.

"I'm sober enough."

Where, if you don't mind the asking, where will you go from
here, now that the racing is ended?

"Oh hell," he sighs heavily, "I don't have the least idea." His
eyes keep staring up.

They say that, during the course of the races, you really distinguished yourself.

"Do they?"

Yes. [A rustling of paper is heard] Yes, they do. We quote
from the Boston *Post*, dated October 24, 1938: "The mettle of
the THEBAUD's crew was tested when a block on the end of the
main gaff began tearing out under the pressure of wind-tautened
wet canvas. Sterling W. Hayden, the youngest and tallest of
the Gloucesterman's crew, went inching out along the spar to
secure the block along with Jack Hackett. The two men
struggled there on this perilous perch, clinging against the blast
of the gale, and—"

A hand is raised in the darkness. "Stop. That's enough."

But there's more.

"I know; I read it all right, don't worry about that; made me
feel good, I admit."

Well, of course. [Now a further rustling is heard] And how

about this? Again from the *Post*—under a big headline at the top of the second page, next to a picture of a face, close-up and grinning, showing some wind-tossed hair. "THEBAUD SAILOR LIKE MOVIE IDOL. Gloucester Youth, 22, Born Sea Rover . . . Fine Masculine Specimen . . . Neat seamanship may decide the victor of the fishermen's races, but when it comes to masculine pulchritude, Sterling W. Hayden, tall, blond, and lithe, wins by 100 fathoms over fellow members of both crews. He stands straight as a ramrod and is six feet five inches tall . . . More than a few of the scores of women who viewed the vessels yesterday at the fish pier inquired as to his identity . . ."

"They did, eh?"

That's what it says in the paper.

The figure sweeps to an upright position and strikes a match off a shackle. "Yeah, yeah. I read that one, too. They shouldn't print stuff like that."

Oh? Why not?

"Because it makes you feel embarrassed. Besides, it's not even true."

What do you mean?

"Never you mind what I mean."

CHAPTER 44

Rapt in thoughts of the future, I was hurrying toward the depot when, as I passed the office of the Atlantic Supply Company, Miss Ray Adams rapped with her ring so hard on the window I could see the lettering quiver. I stepped through the door and dropped my pawnshop Gladstone. "Whew," she smiled, brushing some hair from her temple. "That was a close one. Mr. Robinson over to Ipswich just telephoned and you're supposed to call him back right away."

"Well, I'm in a hurry to catch the train. I'll call him up after I get back from New York." I started to open the door.

"Wait. I wasn't supposed to tell you this, but seeing you've worked so hard for us, I'll tell you what it's about." She paused for breath. "Mr. Robinson is going to ask you if you will take command of the *Florence C. Robinson* and deliver her out to

Tahiti." She cocked her head to one side, widened her eyes, and looked at me.

The office dissolved into a mirage of reefs and palms and the lascar brig running westward under the sun. I shook my head a little. "You . . . you aren't kidding with me . . . are you?"

"Of course not, Sterling. We've known for weeks that he had it in mind. Why, he talked with Captain Pine about you, and he spoke with Irving Johnson and—well, it's been all we could do to keep it a secret, I tell you."

I picked up the phone and called; and five minutes later I was given my first command.

An hour later I stood on the Rocky Neck Railways wharf, and in stentorian tones let go with a hail toward the brig. A turbaned figure came on deck and I beckoned him to the ladder. The *Robinson* had been in Gloucester all summer, having appeared one day, ninety-nine days out of Gibraltar, under the irate command of Captain Dan McCuish, a hard-bitten Gloucesterman who, as he stepped on shore, exclaimed: "Not for ten thousand dollars would I sail to Provincetown in that miserable sonofawhore!"

She was, by Gloucester standards, a cumbersome old vessel, having been built on the northwest coast of Ceylon for the Indian Ocean rice trade. She was, in fact, a faithful, if rough-hewn, replica of the British East Indiamen of a hundred years ago. Her size was about that of the *Yankee*. She was square-rigged on the foremast and her mainmast looked like a schooner's. Robinson had it in mind to convert her into a yacht; and throughout the summer her eight-man Hindu crew whiled away the time by flying elaborate kites off her afterdeck.

One of these kites was bounding around in the sky as I climbed up and over her bulwarks and looked around for the mate. It was he who was flying the kite. I told him why I was there, and then I inspected my ship. He didn't seem much impressed and I made a note to roust him, the moment he gave me the chance. The chance wasn't long in coming. "Serang," I said, with a mental assist from Conrad, "I want you to put your crew to work hoisting that sand ballast out on deck. The bags are rotten, so shovel it out, shouldn't take you more than two days. Okay?"

"Captain"—he gave his kite some slack—"we will finish some other work first, then we will work with the ballast, perhaps in two days we shall start."

"Start now. Haul that box down out of the sky and get to work. You hear me?"

He gave the kite more slack, shaking his head. I was about to take him in hand when a better idea struck me: to hell with this nonsense. I'd get on the phone to the owner and he could choose between the crew and me; and if he gave me permission I would round up a crew of men I knew who would work. A man with a beard and a deck-length sash rowed me into the dock.

Boston hasn't changed, Boston will never change . . . still full of crowds and noise and dirt; stumbling along with its back to the future, gorging itself on tradition with a belly full of corruption. These are my thoughts as I charge along under the El, bound for T Wharf on a mission.

I take some steps two at a time, then pound on a door.

"All right, you bastard, open it, don't knock it down." The Irishman's voice is harsh. This loft is number 15 and is owned by a man named Homer who once worked as a guide and a trapper in the woods of Maine.

It blows so hard the windows rattle, and gulls flash by outside. O'Toole is at work carving a figurehead for his friend Herb Talbot's schooner. "Well whaddaya know, it's the movie idol himself. Thought you were in New York by now, or maybe robbing a bank."

"Larry, I have some wonderful news."

"The hell you have."

"Larry, listen, I'm taking the little brig, the *Florence C. Robinson*, out to Tahiti. Right now. And I'm here rounding up a crew and you're the man I want first."

"You serious?" He goes back to work with his mallet. "Nah, of course you're not. Ben must have put you up to this, or something."

"No! So help me God, I'm serious."

"You're standin' there like a big fuckin' boob asking me, do I want to sail to Tahiti in that thing?"

"Right. No wages. You work your way out. Robinson pays for your passage home. Should take us . . . five, maybe six months at the outside. Now, what do you say?"

For a moment he doesn't move. Then he puts his tools down on the bench, and reaches for a bottle of rum. A gust of wind goes by, shaking the wharf. Our glasses clink and we drink to the trip. "When do you want me aboard?" He is pouring another drink. "The sooner the better. Tomorrow. Today. Right now. Let's go."

He pats his belly and belches. "Gimme a pencil. Gotta leave a note for Homer."

We warped her into the dock. Right next to the *Yankee* she lay. And the late-fall days flew past, slashing cold windbound days choked with work, with sails to be bent, gear to be rove, three tons of food to be stowed, and a cargo of case oil to be levered down into the hold.

The crew came fast. Horgan saw to that with his typewriter, breaking story after story over the AP wire. Big Dick Hemingway heard about it as he was driving a tractor, yanking stumps for the PWA. Grabbing his coat, he lit out fast for Gloucester and I signed him on that night. Art Hansen was a photographer for the Boston *Traveler* and a friend of O'Toole's. He took a leave of absence. Down in lower Manhattan, Bill Shepard and Bill Butler heard about it, too. First they wired, then they phoned, then they drove all night and presented themselves on the brig . . . then they wired farewell to the boss. Emil Huddy quit work as engineer on a dragger to join up. Ken Butler walked out on a good job as a linotype operator. Don Langley had been selling trucks until the news came in. Taking a truck and a brother, he drove to Gloucester, and the brother went home alone in the truck. Eddie Ruggles was a cog in the Nashua Gum Paper and Envelope Company—until the fifteenth of November, when he settled down in a fo'c'sle. Eleven men all told, with an average age of twenty-six. O'Toole was the oldest and he was not quite thirty. All save one were landsmen, though Bill Butler and Ruggles had played with some yachts, and Hansen for years had amused himself, and others, by rigging scraps of worn-out sail on leaky skiffs, then sailing off into the night, with his dog and his flute and some biscuits. But never mind, the sea is a skillful teacher.

ADVENTURERS SAIL FROM GLOUCESTER
FOR TAHITI IN 89-FOOT BRIGANTINE
Gloucester, Nov. 22, 1938 (AP). At sunset today 11 young adventurers sailed into the dusk, bound on a 7,000-mile voyage to the South Sea Islands and Tahiti.

They are the crew of the awkward, antiquated little brig FLORENCE C. ROBINSON and they traveled in a style little different than seamen a century ago.

Youngest and biggest of the ship's company is her skipper, Sterling Hayden, 22, taking his first command. Oldest of the crew is Lawrence O'Toole, Boston artist, and he is only 30.

The little ship—she is only 89 feet long—was built in Ceylon of teak and other native woods, and her original name, carved so deep in her topsides that paint could not obscure it, was ANNAPOORANYAMMA of JAFFNA. . . . The purpose of the voyage is a workaday assignment to deliver the brig to a copra trader in Papeete. Her skipper believes she should reach her destination in time for him to catch a steamer for home April 6 next spring.

OFF TO THE SOUTH SEAS

Are there not, dear Michael,
Two points in the adventure of the diver,
One—when, a beggar, he prepares to plunge,
One—when, a prince, he rises with his pearl?

The departure of the Ceylon-built brigantine FLORENCE C. ROBINSON from Gloucester Tuesday was suggestive of Browning's lines. Her crew of eleven young Americans— their skipper a salt-hardened lad of 22—were not, to be sure, precisely beggars. But the unharnessing of their auxiliary engine because of bureaucratic regulations, the handling of an hermaphrodite rig which none of them seemed to be too familiar with—these were the vicissitudes capable of shaking the adventurer's spirit. Then there must follow several days, perhaps weeks, of slow, stormy progress down the North Atlantic before the tropics are struck. But in the end—if all goes well—Tahiti, and every man a prince.

Eleven ill-advised young men, without question. The sea can be not only a hard and brutal taskmaster, but a dull and boring one as well. There is no money in its service, as any sailor will tell you. It means loneliness, laziness, lovelessness. But always—just beyond the horizon—there lies a vision or an experience worth a king's ramsom. . . .

Eleven visionary young men, without question. But what young men would not be with them?

Editorial,

Boston *Herald,* November 24, 1938

On the twenty-fifth of November, 1938, the Cunard liner *Queen Mary,* having passed south of the Grand Banks, bound for New York City, reported herself embroiled with a savage storm of hurricane proportions that would, it was estimated, delay her arrival for some eighteen or twenty hours.

That same day the *Robinson,* three hundred miles east of New York and bound for Panama, lay hove-to not far from the Gulf Stream, fighting for her life in the same storm—which would later be known as "the second New England hurricane of 1938." Afterwards O'Toole reported by letter to his constituents on T Wharf: "The barometer decided to drop from 29.99 to 28.88 and an honest-to-God hurricane started to blow. I hope I never see another as long as I live. . . . Cold, hailstones, seas forty feet high, wind blowing 70 miles and 75 in the blasts. We got the foresail furled before it started. We got up during the worst wind I have ever seen (all hands) and furled the topsail and topgallant—at night too. Wow, it would give you the creeps, for 24 hours it was all of us against it. We rolled so bad that the pumps wouldn't work. Finally we get a little storm trysail on the mainmast, but she won't head up very well—we all go aft and hang on for life—I thought we were through several times. When all of a sudden the topsail breaks loose with an explosion and flies out in shreds. Seas come in over the rail and she settles down after one of those long roller-coasters, down a forty footer of raging rich blue (real blue like I have never seen). When it looked like as if she would not come back on an even keel, the Capt. turns and screams to me: 'Just like that picture up on Bromfield Street.' I could have kicked him overboard. . . . This keeps up for a day and a half, never letting up. All hands got seasick, except the Capt. and, luckily, myself. One time the foresail got away and started to balloon out—Well, Sterling couldn't stand it and he and Art went aloft to furled it—they were standing on the footrope and getting it in fairly good when a terrible blast fills it out and threw them off backward into the rigging. But as lucky they are, neither got hurt. Some of those seas that we were riding on threw us a hundred yards at a clip sideways. Well . . . if I were Masefield or Conrad I could describe

it better . . . but to end this miserable affair we were hove-to
fifty hours . . . wheel lashed . . . Jesus!!!!!"

Why, I wondered, seven days after going to sea with my first
true command, did I have to be bathed in the worst storm I had
ever seen on any sea? Along with the cold, fear numbed my
body and brain. I felt trapped, inadequate, and alone. After a
time the pressure was so intense that I sought escape in sleep.
O'Toole the artist never slept, whereas I lay in my bunk for
hours, attuned to the thundering roar in the rigging and the
violent gyrations of the stubborn little ship as she vaulted the
murderous seas.

Why must I go on playing this game, why not give up the sea
and live as others do; why not, once this voyage is done, take a
fling at Hollywood? Take the dough and fool around with the
starlets and read your name in the papers, and maybe, after a
couple of years, buy yourself a vessel—the finest kind of a
vessel—and then you'll have the world by the tail on a downhill
haul.

We paused for our mail in Cristobal, then passed on through
the Canal. The mail was full of clippings from the papers concerning our departure and speculations as to how we fared in
the storm. Over and over I read the write-ups when no one was
around, more concerned with the impression I was making than
with what I was doing. I thought of the girl in Tahiti and sent
off a colorful letter—along with some clippings. And one night,
before starting out into the Pacific, I swallowed my pride and
purchased some fan magazines. From cover to cover I scanned
them, I thought that those Hollywood males weren't much.

On the thirtieth of December we towed to sea on a broiling
day, sheeted home the sails, and let her go down the long blue
road to Tahiti.

The brig as she runs just now is eighty-six days out of
Gloucester. All hands are well and the ship is a perfect picture,
freshly tarred and painted, storm damage all but erased. The
western sky is a glory, yet the men on board pay it scant heed,
for their eyes are raking the sea rim dead ahead, for the goal
men dream of reaching one day before they die.

One man wrestles with the stars. Under a hooded lamp he
works, three seconds from the helm, at a chart with crosses leading back to the north and east toward Central American shores;
crosses that are, on the average, spaced 140 miles apart.

A sickle of moon this night, low in the west. Beneath the trampling forefoot, green flashes go angling off. A bird cries out—and is answered by O'Toole, who sprawls above and ahead of the ship, with his thickset body slung in the jibboom's net. High aloft sits Hansen, high as he can go, with his back to the truck of the mast, playing his flute in spite of a square-cut beard. Hemingway sways to the wheel. Ruggles works in the galley. Forms come and go—softly—under the arch of the sails. Some men sleep.

O'Toole's voice sings out: "LAND HO-O-O-O!"

The flute sounds stop.

"Hey, Cap!" The Irishman's words drift aft. "Light dead ahead —flashing every five seconds. Been watching it now for five minutes—wanted to make sure!"

Sixteen miles to Venus Point, the only light in this part of Oceania. The whole world beams down on you—you could hurdle the Southern Cross before you could sleep tonight.

February 15, 1939. Midnight. Venus Point abeam, distant three miles. Most of the crew sleep; not so two wanderers pacing side by side, pausing at times by the bulwarks. Along the Broom Road the headlights of an auto stab seaward over the reef. The wind blows off the land freighted with sensual fragrance, and you hear the boom of the reef. O'Toole is somber: "You know something, Cap, I was wrong; all that stuff I was sayin' after the storm."

"What stuff?"

"You know, about you giving up the sea . . . going to Hollywood . . . you know, all that crap."

"Yeah. I think you were. This is world enough for me."

"You're goddam right it is. . . . But for Jesus' sake, steer clear of that sonsabitchin' North Atlantic, you hear?"

"Sure, sure I hear."

Day breaks. Brushes scour at oiled teak decks. Ruggles's galley is spotless. Hansen the mate coils down, stripped to the waist and barefoot, bulging with muscle. The old brig, upright now and graceful, swings parallel to the reef, with the Stars and Stripes rippling out from the truck of the main, the Tricolor lashed to the fore, and the quarantine flag to a yardarm.

A double landfall this—one made in the night and one in the dawn. The island emerges, shot with shadow at first, then mellowing, with green hills soaring toward proud twin peaks—Aoraï and Orohena. A girdle of palms encircles her groin, shimmering beyond the cream of the reef.

The town of Papeete comes to life, pausing to stare seaward in disbelief. What her people see is the ghost of the days of the Navigators.

Off the mouth of the pass she jibes. Halyards and braces are swayed. The wheel changes hands, and the new man settles her down, working the spokes with care. More love than care, in truth. And he lets her drive for a cleft in the stone-jawed reef.

A launch runs out, sporting a huge French flag. The pilot is jovial. "Bon jour, Capitaine. You make the rapid passage, non? You are not expected before another month, non? Veree fine little vessel, sir."

"She is that."

She enters the pass. Surf booms on either hand, but suddenly it is smooth. The voyage is done. The reefs close ranks astern, growling and rumbling, a rampart of coral.

You hear a rooster crowing. The peal of church bells. A dozen trading schooners line the quay, watching men at their work— practitioners of an art that is almost lost.

No raising of voices here. All it takes is a nod, a word, or an index finger pointing. She swings in an arc and glides up the blue lagoon. They shorten her down, and she turns her face to the wind. "Let go," says a voice from aft. And they warp her into the quay.

TAHITI RIGHT ON THE NOSE

Eleven young men, most of them inexperienced in seamanship and navigation, left Gloucester last November in an 89-foot brig. Their destination was the South Sea island of Tahiti.

The master of the ship, 22-year-old Sterling Hayden, had had some sea experience. The rest had that important ingredient, intelligence.

These are not boys. They are young men. They are young men made of the stuff that makes America great. They are doers of constructive deeds. Their assignment was to deliver the brig at Tahiti. They delivered the brig at Tahiti.

America, thank God, has untold thousands of young men just like them. They are not very vocal young men. They speak with deeds. They do not stand on soapboxes and public platforms and whine and rail against the world. These young men of the little brig face the tempests of the world and grow in character as they meet the odds, and triumph. The good ship FLORENCE C. ROBINSON got safely to Tahiti because intelligent men of self-discipline cooperated with intelligent leadership, for the common good. All eleven did not try simultaneously to steer the ship.

Editorial,
Boston *Herald,* February 1939

CHAPTER 45

We were gathered one day on the broad verandah of Le Cercle Bougainville, with the trading schooners lined out along the quay, the *Robinson* among them. Their spars were half obscured by foliage, and sparrow-like birds hopped along the railing. The corner table was surrounded by men: Hansen, O'Toole and Shepard; Hall and Nordhoff and Pedro Miller, and one or two others. We were drinking and laughing and talking, but I kept an eye on the door near the head of the stairs. Nordhoff was saying: "Hayden, let me tell you what you ought to do: go back to the States and get your hands on a big fast schooner, steal the sonofabitch if you have to, then bring her back out here and open up a scheduled packet service between Papeete and Honolulu." Hall nodded his agreement, a dreamy look in his eyes. "Mark my words, boy, you'd have all the business you could handle; passengers, freight, and mail. What the hell more could you want?"

"Nothing," I said, over the top of my glass.

And all at once she was there, in high heels and a short dress, with flowers in her hair. I leaped to my feet, and she laughed as she stepped in close to slip a lei of Tiare Tahiti blossoms around my shoulders. O'Toole simply stared. Then he drained his glass and called for another round. "This one's on you," he said, giving my shoulder a crack.

For more than two months we played. We danced, bicycled around the island, almost lived in the surf and under the ironwood trees of Arue Beach. In outrigger canoes we flew across the lagoons. And at night sometimes, side by side, we drifted down a mountain stream to the sea. And there, among the dunes, I'd kindle a fire and we'd have some wine with the light on Venus Point our only chaperone.

We fell in love, both for the first time. She was nineteen and I was just twenty-three. I would return home only long enough to promote a vessel. Then I'd come driving west with the ship and launch the packet service between Papeete and Honolulu, just as Nordhoff had said.

It seemed so sound on paper, and absurdly simple. The marvel was that no one had ever done it. I armed myself with all kinds of local information; with letters from a dozen merchants endorsing the plan, one from the administration promising co-operation, one that even went so far as to mention a mail contract. And it just so happened that I knew where there was a ship: not just any ship, but a great steel schooner measuring one hundred and sixty feet on deck. She was laid up and for sale in the Panama Canal; her name was *Aldebaran*. She had been built originally for Kaiser Wilhelm in 1903. She had a paneled salon with leaded bookcase windows; and a dozen staterooms—one with a sunken bath. On the outward passage, I had spent an entire day going over her; snapping pictures, measuring, scheming, and dreaming. In April we agreed to be married. I ordered a ring made up by a Chinese craftsman—from a pearl I had found in the course of the *Yankee*'s voyage three years before, diving off Tongareva. And a night just before my departure, her parents gave a party announcing the engagement.

By the light of a dozen torches the old plantation house stands at the end of the road with its back to the sea, its windows ablaze with light. The house is large, and each of its two floors is belted with a broad verandah. Off to the left, other torches lead the way to a low pavilion and here the guests are—more than a hundred, it seems.

My suit is made of linen and I've never worn it before. For unknown reasons I feel myself faltering. Out by the parked cars I linger as long as I can. The stars are terribly clear. I feel for the ring in its little case, then start down through the torches. I pause and look at one closely, and a picture evolves in my mind of a wild black night in the land of long ago with the dories strung out in an undulant line on the unseen raw Atlantic. I clear my mind and go on.

The pavilion is small and bursting with merriment. Wives of functionaries stand in a seemly row. A bar is besieged in a corner. An island song swings through the night and I find myself with a drink—just in the nick of time. My eyes run through the crowd, in hopes of seeing one girl. I suddenly feel like a stranger. Her mother is dressed in white. An imposing woman she is: tall—almost as tall as I; she was born on Raïatéa and her forebears were kings and queens. I think of another mother, far away in a little rented apartment, tending her plants perhaps. And I know that she wouldn't approve of what her son is doing. These glasses are much too short. I accept another drink.

And now, on the heels of an island fanfare, the floor is cleared. I find myself by her side. Our hands press. Her father puts down his glass and steps to the center of the floor. A hush, and from out on the barrier reef, the sullen roar of the sea. I feel as I felt months ago at the height of the hurricane.

His wife joins him, handing him a wide-brimmed glass of champagne. The room is wreathed in smiles. Before I know it we're dancing, round and round and round. I always liked to dance, but never as much as now. The torches go spinning past and the dories rise and fall. Jack Hackett's brazen face gives way to that of my mother, rocking now in a corner, staring down at the floor. Round and round we whirl, and the music is: "J'attendrais" . . . "I will wait . . ."

Drive with care through showering palms, past blacked-out sleepy houses, past dogs stretched flat on the road. Then I veer to the right and park next to the Harbor Office. I walk down the dock till I come to what's left of the brig. High above me she rides with her spars shorn now to half their former height. Like stunted bones they stand. I pace beyond her bows, fondling the ring she gave me. The night in the east grows wan.

CHAPTER 46

A Danish freighter nosed through the fog of Lower New York Bay, surrendered herself to some tugs, and without ceremony was stuffed into a desolate corner of Brooklyn's Erie Basin. Her lone passenger, lugging two canvas bags, a roll of charts, and a sextant, said one or two farewells, and without looking back vanished into the warehouse wilderness.

Already it was happening: just as I had expected. Settling back in a cab, I felt hopelessness run through my body. Across the swarming city, in an Upper West Side hotel, I knew my mother was waiting. I checked my gear at Grand Central Station and started on foot toward Times Square. A theater marquee proclaimed: MUTINY ON THE BOUNTY CLARK GABLE CHARLES LAUGHTON . . . GORGEOUS SOUTH SEA SIRENS.

I paused. Why not, I mused, why not have a look, you've seen it half a dozen times but maybe right now it will give your spirits a boost. I bought a ticket from the blonde—to study the actors at work, and imagine myself in their place. I felt ashamed. Never mind; I'd only stay a few minutes, long enough to refresh my mind with one more look at Tahiti. I stayed for hours.

Try as I would, I couldn't get rid of the helplessness. Wherever I went, whatever I did, it plagued me. I carried it in my brief case—along with the pictures and charts and business propositions so carefully prepared on the beach at Arue. It thrived when, once or twice each day, I managed to worm my way in to see the men of capital. Tahiti seemed a nebulous world that had slipped through my hands and was gone and would never return—except on the screen of a theater.

I quit New York, with nothing accomplished. Worse. I quit with the words of my godfather, Mont Sterling, lodged in my mind like a sliver of guilt. Only two days before, we had met for lunch at his club. It was down by the Battery, overlooking the Hudson. We hadn't met in years. I discovered that he wasn't so formidable as my memories. He was, in fact, just another businessman; splendidly groomed, proud of success—and yet, there was something about the face that betrayed a sadness.

He shrugged off my plans and the luncheon deteriorated: "Gollys, young fellow, you've had quite a time for yourself, haven't you?" I guessed I had. "Here you've been sailing all over the world and some of us have been in the city all our lives. But don't you think it's about time you settled down and made something out of yourself? It seems to me you could go a long way in the business world: sales perhaps, or advertising. Your father was in the ad game, you know; and if he hadn't died so early in life, I think he might have become a prominent man."

I gazed out the window. A ferry was bound for the Hoboken shore and I saw my father as he sat, with the starched collar, and the flower in his buttonhole, reading the paper. And then I saw a towhead kid in a tidy suit standing entranced on the upper deck with . . .

"I don't suppose that appeals to you, now does it?"

"I, I'm sorry, Uncle Mont."

"I said, nothing would give me more pleasure than to take you into the firm. I have no son of my own, as you know, and, well, it would be a fine feeling to know that after I left you'd be working your way up."

"No, Uncle Mont, I'm just not cut out for that."

"Your good mother tells me you created quite a bit of interest last fall during those schooner races."

"In what way?"

"She said there was something in the papers about your being singled out as—as material for Hollywood?"

"Oh, that." And I laughed it off.

"Why not, lad? Think of the money. Gollys, from what I hear you could go out there and make more money in five years than some of us make in a lifetime. I never thought much of actors but, judging by your past adventures, I dare say you'd never fall for the wild living that seems to go on out there."

"To tell you the truth, I've never thought much about it."

"Well, do. Of course you'd have to put up with an awful lot of Hebes, but I guess you could tell them where to head in too."

"Maybe I could."

"Now, lad, this that I'm about to say isn't so pleasant, but I feel it is something you need to be told." Here it comes, I think, now we talk about my mother.

"You're breaking your mother's heart, boy. She was in to see me the other day. I don't mind telling you that she broke down. You're all she has left in this world, young fellow. She loves you, with all her heart she loves you."

"I know that."

"Well then? Why not think of her for a change. You've had your fling. You've had more adventure than all the men in this room put together. And I don't mind saying I'm envious—in a way. But you're growing into a man. And it's time that you took a man's place in this world. . . . And that's all that I'm going to say. Think it over."

"I've been thinking about it for years, believe me."

Throughout the summer I gave myself as hostage to an out-side chance. A man named Buxton was, it seemed, making a fortune manufacturing key containers and wallets. He owned a fifty-foot sailing yacht. After leaving New York, we came to an understanding: I would run the boat for him that summer, and if I proved myself capable and responsible he would, come fall, invest up to ten thousand dollars in a corporation that would buy the *Aldebaran* and operate her on the Papeete–Honolulu run. It semed like a fair-enough gamble.

Shortly after Labor Day we met in his Springfield office. He came right to the point: "Hayden, you're a mighty fine sailor, we all know that. But I'm very much afraid that you haven't much respect for money; not just for the handling of it but—if what you said to my nephews during the summer is any indication— for the entire institution of business as we know it in this coun- try. You're entitled to sneer at us businessmen if you choose, of course. But I, in return, have no choice but to terminate our relationship as of now."

I sat there looking at him, smoking and smiling a little—no longer a hostage. Somehow I felt relieved. We got to our feet. "And I wish you luck; and any time you want a job as captain of my yacht, be sure to let me know."

"I'll be sure to do that," I said. He gave me a dubious glance and handed me my final check, along with a ten-dollar bonus.

I headed back for Boston and T Wharf. One last lean chance remained. The most luxurious loft on the wharf was owned by a man named Herb Talbot. He was a great friend of O'Toole's and a casual friend of mine. He had made a killing in the wool business and he was rather susceptible to the inde- finable charm of puttering about in boats. Several times during the course of the summer we had talked about my venture. There was only one big hitch, assuming he elected to finance the operation: Herb wanted, quite naturally, to have a small hand in the proceedings. Therefore, if I did buy the *Aldebaran,* it would be with the understanding that I operate her on short hauls out of Boston or Gloucester for the first year. After that, I could go to Tahiti. I remembered the sailors' adage: "Any old port in a storm."

No decision was reached until, one evening in mid-November, a handful of men gathered before the pot-bellied stove of a water-front café. The hurricane season was gone and the winter gales stood by. And in Europe hatreds flamed and fingers nuzzled triggers (and more than a hundred bewildered Tahitians, racked with coughs, stood guard in the sump of the Maginot Line).

The men sat in a semicircle facing the stove that stared with crackling isinglass eyes. O'Toole lifted the kettle and poured some heat in the rum. Horgan and Talbot were there along with some other wharf rats. And Hansen sat in a corner playing his flute. Talbot rose rubbing his palms: "Well, I think we should give this thing a try. Let's set up the partnership, then go down to Panama and sail that vessel back."

O'Toole shouted and they drank. Horgan had pencil and paper. "Well now, boys, let's see if I have this straight. How much is this vessel going to cost?"

"Fifteen thousand dollars."

Talbot broke in: "No money down. Not a penny changes hands till we get her back here to Boston, where we can put her in drydock and have her surveyed."

"Larry," Tom asked, "you going along?"

"Christ no! Me, in the dead of wintertime, Panama to Boston? Not on your bloody life."

HAYDEN BUYS FORMER KAISER'S YACHT
Going to Panama to Sail ALDEBARAN Back to Boston by Christmas.

Boston, Nov. 21, 1939 (AP). When adventure gets into a young man's blood, there isn't much of anything can be done about it but perhaps turn him loose with a few charts and something to sail. . . . The 161-foot steel vessel is now in Gatun Lake and Captain Hayden said he would leave just as soon as he could get a crew together to sail the schooner up to Boston's T-wharf. He hopes to return by Christmas.

Launching of the METEOR at New York for the present woodchopper of Doorn was one of the events of the 1902 social season. The then Alice Roosevelt broke a bottle of champagne across the yacht's sharp prow. The Kaiser kept her until 1910, when she became the property of the Italian Baron Alberto Fassini. Her log shows she at times hit a 16½ knot clip, but Hayden says she hasn't really "been anywhere yet, never west of the Galapagos." He sounded as tho' he intended to do something about that.

Fifteen men swarmed up and over her rail that late-November day. The one in command hove his brief case onto a skylight

and slammed his hands together. An old caretaker came
shambling aft, holding his hat in his hands. "What you will have
to do, Captain, is put this ship in drydock right away."

"Like hell I will."

"But what—what about them holes?"

"What holes?"

"Come, Captain, I show you what I mean." Over the side
they go to a small skiff, then forward to a place near the waterline. The old one takes his hammer and tap-tap, tap-tap through
the hull it goes. He takes the handle and reams out a hole that
is twice the size of his fist. You can see the pantry sink.

"Well I'll be a sonofabitch"—and a soft incredulous whistle.

"Oh yes oh my yes, Captain. Very bad. Six more back aft like
this—only maybe a little worse."

He leaps to the deck and calls to his engineer: "Cliff! Never
mind that goddam engine. Here's what you do: jump ashore
and buy two hundred pounds of cement—and some heavy timbers—enough to frame out eight or ten boxes down in the
hold. . . . Then we'll shore them up, pour them full, and hold
this bastard together, got it?"

"Got it."

On the tenth of December she sails, for Boston direct, home
for Christmas. The engine is limping along, two cylinders out of
commission. They swing her off for Cape San Antonio, at the
western tip of Cuba. The trades come in with a vengeance. By
God, this devil can sail!

This is a pickup crew, sailing a pickup ship; and down in
what's left of the Kaiser's salon Talbot is hard at work installing
a stove culled from a junk-shop window. Already she leaks just
a bit. Nothing to worry her crew, but it worries her master.

Ten days pass under her keel. Off Jacksonville comes the
calm; precious time goes slipping by. Her engine is under repairs, and her crew are at work: battening down and boarding
up, passing double gripes on the launch—extra lashings all
around.

December 24, 1939. Cape Hatteras bears northwest by
north, 270 miles distant, and the glass starts falling fast, and
the old go-round begins. It is pitch black and the evening is laced
with squalls, but the wind is fair and she flies into the north.
Some wheels feel better than others: and this one is trembling

now as she runs at an ever increasing pace and after a while begins to wash. It's much too early for heavy water to bury her deck so often, and what will she do if it really comes on to blow? Cheer up, tonight is Christmas Eve.

Gray dawn breaking. Two men to the helm just now, with lashings over their shoulders, blinded at times by spume wrenched from the crests of steep black hills that charge down out of the murk. The engineer crawls aft. "Leaking bad! Four feet—at least—in the bilge!" The captain nods, and calls for all hands on deck. Three pumps now going strong.

Fifteen at least she goes; more, when a squall comes down. She's in danger of broaching now, of running away with herself and falling into the trough where the sea will take care of the rest. A voice from the hatch screams out: "Skipper! Smashed engine room—skylight—batteries flooded out—two pumps dead!"

So you spring to the deckhouse roof. And all around are low torn clouds the color of pus. What you seek is a relative lull, and a chance to lay her to. You wait and you wait and the roar of the wind increases. You see what looks like a safe stretch to windward, and now your voice rings out: "Foresheet haul-l-l!!" And then: "Hard down your goddam helm . . . hard!"

She cleaves to the wind in a slashing, driving arc. And suddenly out of nowhere looms a monstrous wall of water. Somehow the ship surmounts this, only to be confronted by a valley beyond so deep and dark that you swear the sea has been rent by a permanent scar. Crashing down, she plunges to pierce the base of the next oncoming sea. Her foremast is set back from the stem some thirty-five feet, and down to her foremast she plunges. A vast convulsion seizes the ship and shakes her (and down in the depths of her bilge some rivets are shorn like twigs in the path of an axe). Up to their waists in water, crewmen hang on for their lives. The staysail bursts, but the double-reefed foresail stands. And the ship comes back from the grave.

For twenty hours they bailed with buckets. Fifteen men all told, with two at a time down under the diesel's carcass, where rivetheads rolled in the sump. Deep in the water she lay, and deep in the water she crawled in distress toward Charleston, her flag lashed upside down to the weather main shrouds. Up to a sea buoy she crawled, four days later, where a Coast Guard boat on patrol took her line and towed her along for a time; till out

past Fort Sumpter came a commercial tug that would finish the
job. Talbot went ashore with the Coast Guard, his bag in his
hand and his hat on the back of his head. It was dark when
they reached the dock.

A salvage company threw a pair of pumps on deck and sucked
her dry before midnight. From Boston came a telegram: FIND
I CAN DEVOTE NO MORE TIME OR MONEY TO VENTURE—
GOOD LUCK—HERB. From a shipyard came a man the next
day to perform certain rites. "You want an estimate, eh Captain?
Well, now, let's just take a little look at this fine old yacht you
got here. . . ." So together you crawled through the bilge, and
tested this and thumped that, and up aloft you climbed. And
this is what you found: seventy rivets sheared, eleven plates to
be renewed, engine room a shambles, bowsprit fractured, foremast sprung at the hounds. . . . Estimated cost of repairs? Call
it eighteen thousand as a starter, give or take twenty per cent.
Insurance? None. Value of ship as scrap iron? Maybe ten
thousand. Net worth of master? Forty-five dollars.

All along T Wharf big flakes of snow are falling. A calm and
quiet night. Only the big flakes drifting—past warm loft windows—past one or two Christmas trees.

Through the snow a man comes trudging, out from a shadow,
slowly. He carries a bag on his shoulder. One hand clings to a
sextant. When he comes to number 15, he glances the length of
the dock, ducks through the doorway, mounts some steps,
and taps on a door with the sextant. Horgan works at the
stove. O'Toole swings down from a bunk. The door is closed in
silence.

Now the dishes are done and the glasses are full and Tom
keeps pacing the room. "You got to do it, kid. You're a stubborn
bastard, but the way it looks to me, you got no place left to turn."

"Okay, Tom."

O'Toole explodes. "Now you're talkin' some sense."

"Larry," says Horgan, "take a letter, quick." He picks up his
drink, moves to the window, and dictates: "This goes to Mrs.
William Hawks, care of William Hawks Agency, Beverly Hills.
Dear Virginia: This is important. There's a young fellow back
here named Hayden who, if the Boston newspapers are any
judge, is made to order for Hollywood. He is twenty-four years
old, six feet four inches tall, weighs 220. I'll enclose some pictures and clippings to show you what he looks like. Also he is

the youngest Master Mariner in this part of the world and he just had a big steel schooner knocked from under his feet by a hurricane off Cape Hatteras. Now tell that agent husband of yours to come back and take a look at this Viking and sign him up, before somebody else does. Also, he is broke. Signed, Tom Horgan."

O'Toole pours.

"To Hollywood." Horgan says it.

BOOK IV

IRONED WANDERER

BOOK IV

IRONED
WANDERER

CHAPTER 47

It was on the fourth day of March, 1959, that the schooner *Wanderer* raised the island of Tahiti.

Shortly after midnight she came to the end of the road and, with Venus Point Light bearing due south, three miles distant, we hove her to till dawn. And the ship slept under a blanket of stars and so did most of her crew. But not the one in command. He paced alone, alone and lost in memories of the time—just twenty years ago—when he and the laughing O'Toole walked all night on the deck of the lascar brig.

He stares through the darkness at a cleft in the hills where a mountain stream runs down, and he hears a voice: "Yes, I will marry you . . . as soon as you return." The voice fades and he thinks of a letter written in Boston, a long time ago:

> My Dear Mano: Things aren't going well back here. Nothing seems to be working out as we planned. And what I have to tell you now isn't easy. The engagement is off. I really don't know why, but I do know I could never make you happy. I'm sorry. Good luck.

High noon now, with Papeete sun-blasted just within the claws of the reef. And the *Wanderer* sweeps shoreward toward a nest of great steel tanks all chromate under the sun. Four in a row they stand, swollen bastards good for the storage of oil. Like fugitives they seem—from Long Beach and Texas, from North Chicago and South Philly, from Anglo-Iranian deserts, and smoky old Bayonne— Four squat carbuncular mounds they are, garnished with chevrons, and glazed by a noonday sun, a tropic sun—intransigent as hell.

Wanderer squared, the man and his ship alike: good for going places (and not much else, according to some back home). The trade blows hard as he drives her in for the pass. Spume hangs like haze on the reef. Africa the mate works his way aft with five of the crew; they sway at the gear, at halyards and sheets, flaking down as they go. Soon the pilot comes over the rail: "*Bon jour, Capitaine* . . . so thees is the Wandeureur."

"*Bon jour, Pilote.*" He looks like a clerk or a chemist.

"*Capitaine,*" glancing aloft in dismay, "you have the mo-teur, is it so?"

"*Oui, Pilote, nous avons la bonne machine.*"

"Then, you weel, if you please, take down these sails right now."

"No, *Pilote*, I am going to sail her in. All the way to the seawall I will sail her. Then, we turn on the mo-teur, and you back her in to the quay."

She bores through the pass and the spume feels cool as she takes more wind. "Now strap her down!" and Spike and the gang lie back on the sheets, and the big blocks creak, and the ship bends down to her work, while the kids bounce up and down with laughter, pointing out each new sight.

Hard on the wind she goes, and high overhead the Stars and Stripes to the main truck, the Tricolor to the fore, and the quarantine flag (moments ago a curtain, hung by the bunk of a child) lashed to a topmast shroud.

Echoes ring out of the past. Framed again against the rooftops is the old crew, strung out atop the bulwarks of the lascar brig. This landfall is for you, O'Toole! And you Ben Pine, and Jack Hackett, and the rumpot named John Howell. For Tompkins the fighter, for Harvey the cook—and that squarehead of a mate. For Hansen and Johnson and Horgan, for a rasp of a man named Colcord . . . It's for you she goes this day.

Up in the bows the mate keeps glancing aft. Through cast-iron spokes I feel the vessel tremble, her blue-stanchioned bulwarks straight in for the beach.

Now! One final glance and I snap a butt downwind. And turning my back on Papeete, I lock both arms and roll the damned wheel over till the worm gear jams on its pinions. "Hard a-lee!" I bellow over one shoulder. And the canvas flogs with the slant of her deck erased, and the jibs come thrashing down as she shoots up into the wind and I brush at my eyes with a forearm . . . Bring on your laws and your courts!

CHAPTER 48

The mail received by the ship was little short of prodigious. They brought it on board in cartons. "Nevair," said the bow-legged Bardot at the post office, "has so tiny a sheep been get-ting so many letteurs." At last, I thought, they know who I am: not Hayden the cowboy, tall in the rented saddle, king of the non-frontier. But the guy with the boat and the kids who told ex-wife and lawyers and judges and courts: You can all go fuck your-selves.

Sixteen hundred letters lay on the face of my bunk. Not a one that hadn't been read (save for a hundred with ominous windows of tissue paper). If I never sailed again, if I never looked another squall in the eye, now I could go back home and find that (at least in the eyes of some) I was a man first, and an actor incidentally.

San Diego, Calif.
January 26, 1959
Dear Mr. Hayden:

I am a male nurse and I would like to tell you how much we who work here at Mrs. Asher's Rest Home laughted at something that happened yesterday. You see, we have had this elderly gentleman with us because for almost five months he refused to say a single word to a single soul. Yesterday he was reading in the papers about your wonderful trip to Haiti. And all of a sudden he slapped me on the tail with his paper and roared out: "By God that bastard Hayden has the right idea."

Louella Parsons says:

STERLING HAYDEN ALSO
RUNS OUT ON PICTURE

Hollywood, Jan. 27. Before Sterling Hayden took the law in his own hands and sailed for the South Seas with his four children and 20-odd people in the crew, he had agreed to play a top role in "A Summer Place." He left a message for Director Delmer Daves saying he was sorry to run out on him this way but . . .

HAYDEN IS OFF TO "SHANGRI-LA"

It is all but certain that actor Sterling Hayden is off on his long projected voyage of high adventure—leaving his angry ex-wife and the law jumping up and down on the end of the pier. Hayden, the Chronicle learned yesterday, charted not one but two courses before leaving Sausalito. One was direct to Santa Barbara as announced. The other was to Santa Barbara via Southeast Asia. This other was not only the long way around, it was highly illegal.

Hayden's ex-wife seemed to have little doubt which course the WANDERER was on. Her attorney said he would go to court and "get a contempt order and intercept Hayden on the high seas." He didn't say exactly how he would serve the papers or how he would act when Hayden told him what he could do with them.

His agent said, "This man was born in the wrong century. He should have been a sea captain in the 1800's."

San Francisco *Chronicle*, Jan. 22, 1959

HAYDEN ON HIS WAY
TO SOUTH SEAS

In Hollywood, Chester Smith, attorney for Hayden's former wife and mother of the children, charged that Hayden and crew were in dangerous legal waters. He issued this statement:

To All Members of the crew of the WANDERER: "You have even sailed without a radio transmitter for use in case of emergency—a matter which the court particularly commented on. You—and each of you—are subject to the

criminal laws of the State of California for criminal conspiracy and kidnapping and for criminal contempt, in my
opinion.

"In the event of the death of any one of these children,
in view of the court's determination as to the ship's unsea-
worthiness . . . every member of the crew would be subject
to a charge of murder or manslaughter."

On hearing the news Mrs. Hayden broke down and was
placed under sedation.

United Press International, Jan. 24, 1959

AWAY IN THE WANDERER
By Harlan Trott

A small ship has stirred up a big wind by sailing very wide
of her expected course.

Few people noticed when the schooner WANDERER
slipped quietly out over the San Francisco bar. The assump-
tion was Sterling Hayden was only bound to Los Angeles
for what was to be the shakedown to a long heralded deep
sea voyage by a company of adventuresome people who are
dedicated to the solitude, the romance, and the elemental
conflict that confront those who roam the oceans in small
ships which shape their tracks by the trade winds.

. . . It sounds romantic. There's kind of a Conrad thread
to a plot that has a character by the name of Spike Africa
for Chief Mate . . . Doubtless the court knew of Mr. Hayden as a movie actor rather than as a man who went to
sea at 15 and to the Grand Banks in the winter of 1934 in
the fast fishing schooner GERTRUDE L. THEBAUD with
that tough old cod-chasing schoolmaster, flinty Ben Pine.

. . . Here, the tumult over the WANDERER's sailing has
subsided. The storm is blowing itself out on shore. Doubtless by this time the schooner is making a good run of it
down the trades to Tahiti. The children must be adapting
their inquiring focus to much more meaningful horizons
than the focus which falls on the narrow corners of Hollywood and Vine.

Doubtless too, Spike Africa will teach them some things
in the day's work that boys don't learn at school. And by
the time the WANDERER raises the reef at Tahiti, their
hands will be smeared with tar and their eyes will be full
of their first big geography lesson.

Christian Science Monitor, Feb. 3, 1959

From Turnley Walker, the closest friend of all.

Sherman Oaks, Cal.
February 23, 1959

Old Friend:

Your departure letter is one of the key communications of my life. It is a letter I will read many times. Your letter from Taiohae Bay in the Marquesas arrived an hour ago. What interests me most is your determination to write a book about all that is happening. Great! No one else can tell your story. But keep in mind that you must write and write and write! Only when you are writing hard will the important chunks begin to form and spasm out of you. Always be writing something you cannot possibly finish, this will keep the creative process balanced just a little out of your conscious mind. When you edit, try always to leave one copy raw and untouched.

You write with power and this will get stronger as you go along. You have a way of hiding at times behind style. Never consciously hide. Some of the things you resented about acting may face you now and keep facing you as you write your book. You will have to reveal yourself. Hold nothing back. That is what this voyage is all about. It is the only story there is, anywhere, for that matter.

I wonder, naturally, about your adult relationships. That you will develop some of strength and disturbance I have no doubt. It seems unlikely that *anybody*, at home, abroad, on the schooner or the island, will really approve and *understand* what you personally, egocentrically, desperately, actually are involved in now. You say you feel like an exile. What is different about that? You were an "exile" here.

You wanted to have your own ground to stand on, to do what *you* wanted to do. Your hunger to have and do this set you apart and caused, it has seemed to me, some fairly foolish sorties with —— and others. You're not "exiled." The bleakness and loneliness were always yours. Now use them.

. . . All of your letters are a delight to have. I read them to Flora, and we laughed, and shed some tears, but in a proud and hopeful way for you.

Our love to the five Haydens, and to Spike and Red . . . But not an end to anything, you understand, between you and me.

From Jean and Irvin Kershner, who were unable to make the trip—Jean a teacher; Kersh an artist, able to write, photograph, direct, edit, score—to do anything with film.

North Hollywood
February 22, 1959

Sterling:

Your letter from the Marquesas came to us five days ago. Kersh worked late on an MGM pilot film, so I read it first and cried and raved with joy at your having done what you did—at your power to communicate too. Then K. came home and he screamed and yelled at himself until I was certain the folks downstairs would think we were killing each other instead of reacting to a dream we share. . . .

Love,
Jean

North Hollywood, Cal.
February 24, 1959

Dear Sterling:

From where I stand, I find that public opinion is overwhelmingly on your side. Everywhere, tired little businessmen think you did a fine thing—and envy you the doing. . . . The only argument I had was with your business agent, a shrewd and practical man who doesn't know that he died ten years after he was born.

. . . You must *share* the experience . . . put your thoughts on paper—about Hollywood, the sea, and 20th Century U.S.A. . . . There is a growing area of frustration that may one day lead to a renewal of the quest for a life to be lived on more basic levels.

Good sailing and a whole new life to you.

Faithfully
Kersh

Sydney, Australia
February 6, 1959

Sir:

I am a newspaperman. Your breakaway to the South Seas stirred my imagination. I would like to know how you are received in Tahiti—and do you need a hand?

As an example of a man who refuses to accept compromise in the moral sense, your story is a welcome relief from the "security" reading we get hereabouts.

Bronx, New York
January 26, 1959

Dear Mr. Hayden:

I am nothing but a stenographer and I have never written a letter like this. But I had the funniest feeling when I read of your trip and how you got away. It was a feeling of pride and yet of fear. I guess it's that anyone gets a joyous feeling when freedom is expressed as decisively as you did. You think, "Bravo, there is one of us who is not afraid."

But then comes the fear. "I can't do that, the law won't allow it. I'd get in trouble. What would people say?"

Sometimes I would like to leave it all and become a bum. Not a moral bum but a vocational and financial one.

Good luck to you and your children.

We had been in Tahiti for less than a week when it happened. Our lives had been serene. There had, of course, been threats enough in the mail, not only from some attorneys but from outraged collection agencies. And in the course of those first few days I had watched, with some apprehension, the arrival from time to time of gendarmes, or other governmental figures. These, however, had been, thus far, concerned only with our firearms and films and customs manifests. Now it was different.

It was Spike who gave the alarm. "Oh oh!" he hissed. "Watch out, Ishmael, this gang means trouble." And being a little vague as to what might have happened during the previous night, he slipped forward quickly. Seconds later you could feel the vibration as he ran aloft on the foremast.

A starched white civilian came over the rail, followed by four gendarmes. He carried a brief case and, as he approached, I moved to the hatch and took out a cigarette. My heart began to pound. Three of my kids hovered under the awning. I told them to vanish. "Shucks," said Christian, moving slowly, with an eye thrown back on the scene.

"*Bon jour, Capitaine,*" said the starched one as his men fanned out by the wheelbox. They were newly arrived from

France, and were all done out in little white puttees, and helmets, and scoured white holsters—like you see on TV shows.

"*Bon jour, M'sieu'*," I smiled.

He flashed an identity card. Two words stood out: *Security Police*. Here we go, I thought.

"*Capitaine*, I am come from thze governeur's office. We have received thze tellegramme from Loz Angelez."

One of the gendarmes moved to the rail and cracked a joke with an island girl who lived on a yacht next door.

The man speaking to me seemed perplexed as he studied the paper in his hand. "Non"—biting the lower lip—"I do not comprehend thzees thzing."

I felt encouraged. Surely if this was a matter of extradition proceedings he wouldn't be so uncertain. But then again—

He thrust the paper toward me. "Pairhaps, *Capitaine*, you will comprehend."

I braced myself, and read: INASMUCH AS MR. STERLING HAYDEN OF THE AMERICAN SCHOONER WANDERER IS DELINQUENT IN THE AMOUNT OF $189.15 PAYABLE THIS OFFICE YOU ARE HEREBY AUTHORIZED AND REQUESTED TO CONFISCATE AND RETURN TO THIS ADDRESS THE CREDIT CARD IN HIS POSSESSION.

I sighed, deeply. My heart beat returned to normal, and I tried not to laugh. "This is all?"

"*Oui.*"

I dove below, rifled the plastic wallet, jumped back to the deck, and surrendered the badge of distinction. Still shaking his head, he looked first at the card, then at me, and with a meek salute he left, followed by his squad.

Stepping forward of the awning, I looked aloft on the foremast, where Spike lay flat on the crosstrees, peering out from under an arm. "Come down, Glencannon, and I'll give you one for the book."

CHAPTER 49

Day after day, and eventually month after month, the lush moist lure of Tahiti took its toll. The crew grew bored, restless, and cynical, and one by one they drifted away until mid-May; only the Africas remained.

My days were a mixture of dismay and contentment, but, as time wore on, I discovered that dismay was dominant. I was discovering that Tahiti wasn't so different from home.

I rented a car and set the Africas and all seven children up in a tremendous house, owned by an absentee countess, out in Punaavia, the Gold Coast of Tahiti. This was not the simple life I used to preach in crowded Hollywood rooms: "Americans buy themselves in, wherever they go. Take Tahiti for an example. Hundreds of Americans go out there each year. What do they do? Do they live simply? Do they get to know the land and its people? Hell no. They take a big house in the high-rent district, hire a couple of servants, rent a car, throw parties, get plastered every night, sleep until noon, and shuttle back and forth between Papeete's saloons and the bars in each other's houses. Balls.

"Now, here's how I'd do it, and by God [sipping from a drink] one of these days I will. First off I'd rent me a bike, then pedal around the island—sleeping outdoors, or maybe under a copra shed. I'd find an old canoe house not far from a village, and I'd settle down. And I'd back off and I'd think—try to gain some perspective, try to peel off a few layers of crud. I'd backpack into the mountains, sail an outrigger canoe once a week to Papeete in time for the morning market; and I'd read and write. That's what I'd do [accepting a fresh drink]." Hear hear! Stout lad.

It wasn't as though I hadn't tried. Five days after reaching Papeete, I consecrated myself to a Spartan regimen. I swore off alcohol and tobacco (always the first step), rented the bike, took an office in Dave Cave's Rampart Garage, had a Chinese coffin-maker build a stand-up desk, and went to work. And, to further enhance my legend, I took a room in a water-front hotel for ten dollars a week. It was a lively place at night, with roaches the size of cigar butts, and half a dozen Tahitian whores.

Rising regularly at half past four, I leaped on the bike and pedaled as though pursued by the district attorney of Marin County. After an hour of this I hid the bike and struck off up a steep mountain trail, with the eastern horizon paling, with cattle and goats scattering right and left, charging up my mind for the day.

Later, after tea and croissants, I stood up to the typewriter and flailed away until noon, at which time I cycled up into a small valley not far from town, where I stripped and plunged into an icy stream to lie in a shallow pool lined with watercress while blossoms went drifting by. From two until six I wrote. From six till eight I read. And at nine sharp I went to bed. And for exactly three weeks and two days, I didn't work on the book. I wrote letters, letters by the score, long letters, four, six, and ten pages long—always single-spaced. This, I told myself, was the logical preliminary to the task of hacking out my first book at the age of forty-three—a time for sifting thought, for whetting the blade of my talent. And so the book lay always around the corner. And the day came when I had a beer one noon with Big Hank Taft off the American ketch, *Blue Sea*. This led to rum and tobacco, and to other things. I was back in the groove.

Trapped in Tahiti, trapped in Hollywood—where in hell was the difference?

Rex Cole was a Hollywood business manager whose firm, the Equitable Investment Company, a venerable organization, managed the financial affairs of many of Hollywood's most prominent figures. He was a conservative and affable man. He had a Lincoln Continental, a fine home, an imposing suite of offices, and a devoted staff, withered and worn and growing old in harness. He also had a way of persistently trying to imbue me with what he termed "a little respect for money."

"Now Sterling, it simply does not make sense for you to live this way [these words exchanged any time between 1955 and the spring of '58]. Believe me, I admire your determination to bring up your children comfortably and to erase from their minds some of the unpleasantness of recent years. But here you are making five, six, sometimes seven pictures a year, and making well over a hundred thousand dollars each year; yet you persist in living beyond your means. You barely manage to meet your obligations each month. This is a difficult time in Hollywood, a time of retrenchment, what with TV and all. You have no estate, no investments, no house of your own even; all you have is a lot of drive and that boat. Where does it all lead?"

"Rex goddamit I know all this. But I don't look at life the way the rest of you people do. I don't like my work, I don't like this city. You tell me to swallow my distaste and buy a house in a tract of houses until I'm financially secure. You're wasting your time. I wouldn't live in a row of houses for anything on earth. Don't ask me why, it happens to be the way I am. I'd gladly live in a cave on top of a hill, or a tent in some woods, or a broken-down flatboat somewhere, but I'm a sonofabitch if a man can do that in this angelic part of the world. So, since I'm trapped here, I go to the other extreme. I like fine things; I like privacy and trees and grass, I like a big stone fireplace and waxed paneling and five or six hundred books backed up to the walls."

"Do you know how much the boat costs you each year?"

"Sure I know. I know all these things. The boat runs me about fourteen thousand a year, and I'm in the sixty per cent tax bracket and I pay you five per cent of my gross, and the lawyers take another five, and the agent takes ten—and I spend over two thousand dollars every month, what with a cook and a proxy-mother, and five hundred a month for the house. But I drive a Volkswagen and I never go to night clubs; I never take vacations that cost anything to speak of and I haven't knocked up any girls. What's more, I'm trying hard, believe it or not, to come around to a more practical way of thinking. No. That's a lot of bullshit. I'm not because I don't believe in it. You may have fifty clients who are worth a million bucks. So what? I wouldn't live the way they live the rest of my life—or rather I couldn't—and that's all there is to it . . . And as for 'the boat' as you put it, that old bastard means a lot to me. You want me to take out more life insurance; well, she's my insurance; and mark my words, one of these days I'm going to spring myself out of this town with that ship, and don't ask me how because I don't know. Maybe you're right, maybe all of you are right— when you tell me I'm going in circles. Well, what the hell; you've been sitting on this corner of Hollywood and Vine for twenty-three years, and that's your affair, of course. But—well—let's just sit back and see who comes out on top in the long run. And in the meantime I'll go right ahead spending more than I can afford. It's my money. Okay?"

Rex, forgive me. We had a language barrier in those days, and I guess we still do. I remember the time I paced in your office with a view beyond the window of traffic snarled on the Hollywood freeway, and I had a lawsuit going against RKO (the one my lawyer said I could never win, the one you and my agent said I could never win, remember?). Well, you were all wrong. And I quoted to you that day the words of Thoreau that kept me going all through some bitter goddam years: "If a man does not keep pace with his companions, perhaps it is because he hears a different drummer. Let him pace to the music which he hears, however measured or far away." I believed it then and I still believe it—the wisdom of those words. And wouldn't you say—looking back—maybe I was right? Tell me, Dollarman, tell me where I'm wrong.

Early in June two men arrived on the island. Both were professional writers. Here, I thought, is the real thing, men who write, not men who "want to be writers." Twenty-four hours after stepping on Tahiti for the first time, Herb Caen was calmly at work on the verandah of a beach house, pounding out his columns for the San Francisco *Chronicle*. He sat by the sea, a flower over each ear, facing the lagoon, and smiling from time to time at an island girl who waited, patient and wide-eyed. I was acutely aware that he had written more in one day than I had in four months.

When the Conrad family came ashore from the SS *Monterey*, they resembled one of those all-American families one sees in travel ads. Barnaby Conrad was immaculately tailored and suave; his domed forehead bristled in the sun. His wife looked chic and cool. And the children, tanned and blond, were hard at work trying to outmaneuver a crinkly Swiss nurse.

One night Herb and I dropped in at the estate the Conrads had rented. He met us at the door, with a drink in one hand and a story I had written in the other—a terse account of the voyage, written in response to a cable from *Life* magazine. "Congratulations," he said. "I read it and it's great. Join the club." With dinner out of the way, he kissed the children good night, dismissed his wife, cautioned the governess not to fall off her motorscooter, handed Caen and me each a bottle of Scotch, and we started to talk.

Caen shook his head: "I still don't quite get your dislike for acting. How many pictures have you made?"

"Oh, thirty, thirty-five, something like that."

"And you're telling me you never enjoyed it?"

"I won't say I never enjoyed fragments of the work. But there was never the time that I didn't want to be something more than an actor. An actor creates a character all right, and may do a damn good job of it, but he's still an interpreter."

"But you did some good work, too, and with all those films you brought a lot of happiness to a hell of a lot of people, so I don't think you should feel too badly."

"Balls! You're part a machine—an entertainment machine. It's a corporate process. Goddamit, I want to produce something that

is mine. That's egotistical and presumptuous and all that. But it's
the way I feel. And it's the reason behind my sitting here tonight feeling genuine respect for you. You've done it. And I'll tell
you something else about Hollywood that is pathetic: it's in
decline right now. Maybe decay is a better word. Some of the
best creative people were, as you know of course, driven out of
the industry during the McCarthy period—the writers, producers,
directors . . . These days the town is running scared, and television is God.

"People try to put together little womb-shows. For four or five
years, everybody holds hands and lives like drones in this or
that 'Western,' or 'private eye,' or 'happy little family' series.
The actors don't act. The director isn't a director, he's a conductor. And the producer is scared shitless of the sponsor. And
all the while they duck anything controversial. Now, you tell me,
isn't that a hell of a life for a man?"

He laughed. "I have to admit you don't make it sound too
attractive."

"And I'll tell you another thing since you're holding still.
People don't remember the pictures you make. It's all a blur. They
stop you on the street and say: 'Hiya Sterl'n. Caught you in a
pitcher the other night—you know, the one where you played the
admiral got his leg shot off?' Well, I want to write a book that
people won't forget. I want to make them take a stiff slug of
booze, or go outside and look at the stars. And I think I know how
to do it; because this book I have in mind may be about a guy
called Hayden but it will be about them too."

We drank, and when the bottles were empty, Caen and I left.

CHAPTER 50

I relished the idea of doing nothing all through that January of
1940. I was careful to complain a good deal; I was delighted to
loaf around the Boston water front all winter.

There was a place on top of T Wharf, out near the seaward
end, sheltered from the wind and exposed to the sun, sort of a
brick pocket. Here I made myself a nest, and day after day I

curled up there, lost to the world. The city lay all around and the freighters stood down channel outward-bound and the gulls wheeled and I cultivated a theory that the most captivating thing on earth was a deep-water ship moored deep in the guts of a city. I kept a notebook handy for such thoughts.

"Three weeks," O'Toole had said. "We wait three weeks for Horgan's letter to Hollywood to do some good, and then we bust loose for New York on our own."

"With what?" I asked. "We're both broke and New York takes dough."

Larry shrugged this off: "Quit worrying. Something'll turn up. I'll do a mural for somebody or paint tits on the fire curtain over to the Old Howard."

Three weeks passed. Nothing happened, and so I made one trip to the Banks in the schooner *Ethel B. Penney*. She was old and loose and it blew great guns and we came in twenty-six days later with ice to the foremasthead. Our shares of $66.43 each worked out to slightly more than twenty-one cents an hour.

We checked into the Edison Hotel in Manhattan after an all-night trip on the steamer and a wild farewell party down on the wharf with plenty of rum and noise and hula dancing. Larry wore the same things he had on when we had met two years earlier, except for a muffler of Tom's that he knotted in front. "Makes me look like Ronald Colman," he said.

I wore a new suit that Larry had selected. It had big checks and wide shoulders and he made them reduce the seat and waist so I could barely sit down without a seam or some buttons giving way.

We got a small room for twelve dollars a night. Across Forty-seventh Street was a phalanx of windows; a cat sat in one licking its paws; off to one side was a window with a green shade pulled low and a big pair of binoculars staring out. We never did see the owner.

The bellhop was old and tired. "Give this man a dollar," commanded O'Toole as he threw his coat at a chair. "And what we need, Sam, is a quick quart of rum. And take this guy's suit and throw a real good press into it right away and get it back here in an hour, okay?"

I wrapped myself up in the red and white *pareu* and began pacing back and forth. "If that gink with the binoculars catches you in that sarong, I won't dare leave you alone." He leaned back and waved across the street, then crossed the room to the telephone, put in a call, and waited a moment for the connection.

"Hello, Harry? Say, boy, this is your old pal from Boston, this is the O'Toole of the South Boston O'Tooles, now Harry how in hell are you kid, hey? Fine, glad to hear that Harry now look Harry I'm right across the street at the Edison and I got this guy with me you got to meet because he's six foot four two hundred and twenty pounds and blond and handsome as a bastard and they been trying for years up to Boston to sign him for pitchers but—what? No, he's not an actor he's a sailor, he's been around the world four times in schooners and he's been fishin' on the Grand Banks and like I said they've been tryin' to sign him but I tell him he needs a tiptop agent like you Harry and—what? Hell no, Harry, I don't want no cut, he an' me was shipmates on a little brigantine to Tahiti and—" He turns to me with the phone cupped: "Gimme a butt quick, I think we're all set."

When I hold the match, my hand shakes. "Okay, Harry, I'm on my way." Bang goes the phone. "Where's that creep with the jug?" We collide as we pace. "Lie down for Christ's sake. Save yourself, what I need is a drink." "Me squash is clear out to here this mornin'." He holds his palm a foot in front of his brow.

The buzzer rings. "Gimme a buck for the tip." He pours a tumblerful, tosses it off, pours an inch more, and hands me the drink. I shove it one side so he throws it down. "Now don't move, ya hear, don't even go out the door, you might get lost or something."

"Where in hell would I go with no pants?"

The door slams.

An alley behind the Strand Theatre is crammed with barrels of trash and snowflakes fall as we walk toward a big red door. "Keep your hands outa your pockets, stand up real straight, look this guy square in the eye and keep thinkin' over and over: 'Go fuck yourself, Harry, go fuck yourself, Harry'—like that—over an' over, got it?"

"Yeah, Larry. Okay." My voice sounds weak.

A sign says: STAGE DOOR. I feel a certain excitement because this is where the chorus girls come out. I wonder if they are all as hot as everybody says.

We go in and walk past scenery stacked against the walls, past ropes that lead down from aloft to long pinrails. I notice that the switchboard is bigger than the one on the P & O liner.

We come to a door. "Gimme a butt," says Larry. "Now listen,

kid, this guy's sharp. This guy's as sharp as they come, but he's an old pal o' mine so he won't try any fast stuff. If he takes a likin' to you, then you're as good as a star right now." He gives the door a wallop, and we enter.

A small man rises from behind a big desk. The walls are covered with glossy photographs in cheap black frames and the lights are bright and the place is very hot. O'Toole beams and smokes. "Harry, shake hands with Captain Sterling Hayden. Sterling, shake hands with my old buddy Harry Gourfain." I take his hand, my fingers close and lock gently and at the first sign of pressure I pour it on.

He goes right up on his toes. His voice is high and irate: "Jesus kid, what you doing?" He yanks his hand away and gives O'Toole a strange look.

We sit down. He has a double-breasted suit, a small waxy mustache, and glasses with no rims. "Larry tells me you done lotsa sailboatin', eh Sterlin'?"

"I guess that's right." I keep boring in with my eyes. Go fuck yourself, Harry.

"Sterlin'?" He seems quite composed. "You done any summer stock, church pageants, school theatricals, nothin' like that?"

"No."

"What makes you think you can act?"

Larry leaps to his feet: "Harry, the kid's modest, that's what. Of course he can act. I can act, you can act, anybody can act if he feels like actin', what's so tough about actin'?" He turns to me: "Hell, if you can take a brig through a ninety-mile hurricane with a bunch of ama-choors, then I guess you can act, right kid?"

"Right, Larry, I guess."

A girl comes in wearing a green sweater and a tight skirt. She hands Harry a sheaf of papers clasped in blue folders. He starts to read them over. I look around and try to relax.

All the pictures on the walls are autographed and have long inscriptions: "Thanks, Harry, for all you did to help me up the ladder." Or: "With love and fondest wishes to Harry who gave me my start in Showbiz'." The men in the pictures are smooth. They have slick hair and very broad smiles and excellent teeth all around. They must be famous stars but I don't seem to recognize them.

"Here you are, boys," says Harry spreading the folders in front of us. "Standard New York Agency contracts, read them over if you like, boys, take your time. Harry's taking a big risk, kids, but we'll see what we can do."

"What in hell are ya signin' me for?" asks Larry.

"Keep things straight," smiles the agent. O'Toole scratches his name. I count to thirty and sign carefully.

We shake hands all around. "Okay now, Skippy, you an' me are partners, now here's what I want you should do; I want you should take in lots an' lots of pictures; I want you should see four and five pictures a day; study the way the big stars act— the way they walk and talk and move and kiss the girls—the works, get it?"

"Well, all right."

He rubs his hands as we go for the door. "By the way, how much dough you guys got?"

"Plenty," says O'Toole.

"Forty bucks," I grunt.

He peels off two five-dollar bills and hands one to each of us. "The first thing you guys better do is check outa that hotel." We shake hands gently.

It is snowing hard. We turn south on Broadway. Larry seems suddenly detached, he shuffles along kicking the slush with his worn saddle shoes. He turns up his collar and we cross to the middle of Times Square, where we lean on the cold iron railing. He spits. "Look at 'em, will you? Look at the faces. Jesus kid, it's no damn good; this city's too big, too cold, too fast."

I have a picture in my mind of the water front at Papeete. The trading schooners are washed down for the day and the crew is under the awning, smoking and dreaming and passing a jug around.

A taxi passes too fast and sprays us with slush. "I'm gonna clear out, now. You're all set with an agent and I'm goin' back down to Gloucester and I'm goin' to fix up a studio out to the end of Piney's wharf and all the rest of the winter I'm goin' to paint."

I don't want him to go, but I hand him a ten-dollar bill. He shoves it away. "Too bad," I say. "Too bad all the schooners are gone. Come to think of it, there'll never be schooners out of Gloucester any more."

A wide grin breaks over his face. "Don't you worry, kid." He gives my arm a tap. "Don't you worry, the ships may be gone but I see 'em just the same."

CHAPTER 51

Look at it from his point of view. Your name was Edward H. Griffith; your friends, few in number, called you "Ned." You were a triple-threat man on the Paramount All Stars (playing in the International Filmic Conference). You were a writer-producer-director, one of the most talented men in the world— so you thought at the time. This doesn't mean you could really write, or direct, or produce. But you were riding high. You had a contract with Paramount, an impressive suite of offices, a seaside home, a loving wife, and fine clothes, and all the things that mattered.

You were, moreover, a restless man. When Howie, your agent, handed you a letter postmarked Boston, you sensed a chance to add one more bar to your Paramount sharpshooter collection. It was not, admittedly, much of a letter. Obviously, Horgan of the T Wharf Horgans was feeling no pain when he wrote it. But the clippings and snapshots struck a chord.

What you saw was a tall youth with bulging forearms, lean hips, and a faraway look in his eyes. And you fancied yourself as a sometime man of the sea. You knew some of the lingo; you dwelt in a maritime house with a store-bought cargo of red and green lights, ship models, glass balls, and ash trays made from old upper t'gallant buntline blocks. Things like that.

"Well, Ned, what do you think?" Howie your agent asked.

"I think," you said, pocketing the letter, "I'll meet with the kid in New York."

O'Toole had been gone a month. Gourfain had accomplished nothing. I was living in a four dollar a week, beaverboard-partitioned, bug-ridden room, just across the street from Twenty-One. In front of the restaurant were long lines of big black cars driven by priest-faced men in undertaker suits who snoozed over the tabloids.

The rent was two weeks overdue, and I was about to leave town and go back to sea, when I found a message one evening: "Mr. Hagen: Call Mr. Griffis at Paramount Pictures or Hampshire House . . ." Horgan's letter had finally come home to roost.

At least five times I walked past the hotel. It was early evening and cold, and Central Park looked like the Black Forest. When the time came for my appointment, I pushed through the big doors into a different world. Everything was white and soft and everyone was smiling. The man inside the door smiled as he touched his cap. The man behind the black and white desk smiled. Only one lady refused to smile; she appeared from the lee of a pillar towed by a tiny white dog in a green sweater. She puffed and chewed but she did not smile.

The man at the desk broke loose with a wonderful smile. "Go right on up, Mr. Hayden. Mr. Griffith is expecting you." Wham! He hit the call bell. "Front!" His voice had the ring of command: "Front! Show Mr. Hayden up to the Paramount Suite."

I tipped the bellhop a dime, and the door opened when I was halfway through tucking in my shirt. "Good evening, Mr. Griffith, my name is Hayden and—"

"Mr. Griffith is on the long-distance phone." The man who opened the door seemed harassed and looked a little like Harry down at the Strand Theatre. What the hell, I thought, maybe they're all related.

Griffith was different. He came loping into the room, as though he were pursued. He looked important and confused, like a small-town mayor. As we shook hands, I was careful not to overdo it. But it was no use. He turned my hand palm up. "What have you been doing, Mr. Hayden, if I may ask?"

"Well sir, for six weeks now I haven't been doing much; but before that I was hauling some trawl and—"

"Mr. Hayden, will you just walk across to the window and look down toward the park." I went to one window and looked down on the Black Forest, feeling like good King Wenceslaus . . . "Mr. Hayden, do you always stand with your hands in your pockets that way?"

I jerked them out. "No sir, only when I'm scared."

This seemed to please him. "You are nervous now?"

"You're doggone right I am." I wondered why I didn't swear.

His friend came in with some drinks. We were introduced and then they went to the other end of the room and stood looking at me and whispering. I put on the nonchalant air that O'Toole had such faith in. They returned and we ran through an acting scene with a man called Rollie reading the girl's part. It all sounded pretty stupid. Suddenly I started to laugh. I was thinking of the time in Papeete when O'Toole was soused and he danced with the governor's wife wearing his nightshirt with a big red heart sewn below the belt.

Griffith said: "I notice, Mr. Hayden, when you smile—one tooth is broken."

"Yes sir. I was in a schooner down in the Caribbean one time when I got hit in the mouth with a block, what we call a—"

"Really?" He was smiling now, almost laughing. "And, unless I am mistaken, you have a long scar on your left cheek, is that so?"

"Oh yes sir, you see—I was mastheadsman in the *Gertrude L. Thebaud* a few years back and the strop to the tops'l sheet let go and—whapp! This stranded wire come across and fetched me a crack—" He seemed to like it.

He raised his hand. Rollie was smiling. "Very well now. I think, Mr. Hayden, that we will make a screen test." He turned to his friend. "Do you agree, Rollie?"

"Yes, Ned, I certainly do."

"Are you serious?" I asked.

"Of course. I go down to Virginia tonight and come back a week from Tuesday. We will test on Wednesday. I would like to direct you myself, but there may not be time."

"Yes sir."

CHAPTER 52

A slashing northwest wind comes down off the Jersey shore. It is six a.m. and the sky is a cloudless blue as I buck my way west to a grimy building with iron screens protecting the ground-floor windows. The door is locked. I ring a bell and a sly-looking chap opens up. "My name is Hayden. They told me at Paramount to report over here this morning."

"Well, come in and close the door." He leads the way down to the basement and through a series of halls. Steam pipes bang overhead. The make-up room looks like a barber shop. "Miles," says my guide, "this one is testing first. When you've finished with him, send him to Wardrobe, right?"

"Right," says Miles. He turns down a radio "Any preference?" he asks.

"What?"

"The kind of a base we use."

"Oh. Well no, anything you say."

"You're not an actor, I take it."

"No, sir, I'm not an actor."

He tucks me in. People come and go. My face in the mirror seems lost in a sea of naked bulbs. "Just a light pancake," he says as he works, spreading some stuff on my face. "Now, make a mouth, like this." He demonstrates. I stretch my lips. "Just a little rouge, that's all." He holds a brush in his teeth.

O'Toole's voice comes blasting down the hall: "Where is the sonofawhore?" Miles looks up in distress. O'Toole bursts in. "So there you are!" Our eyes meet in the mirror. He crosses himself. "Old dyin' Jaysus, look at that. If Ben and the gang could see you now, they'd swear they was drunk or dreamin'."

He bangs his pockets in search of a match. His cheeks are red and he wears the same old clothes.

"So you got the wire all right."

"Damn well right I got it. All night I been on the friggin' bus."

"Take him away," says Miles, sweeping the sheet to one side. The wardrobe man comes in and we start down the hall. Larry nudges me and we veer off into the men's room. He produces a pint from an inside pocket. "Here! Quick! Take a blast."

I shake my head.

"Go on, you clown, this'll make ya relax an' be full of charm."

I swallow a little.

"Now here, chew on a few of these." He gives me a packet of Lifesavers.

"Now," says the director as he straightens my tie, "we do the silent test first." He steps back and looks me over, with his legs widespread, hand on chin. I can feel the bourbon working. A tall man in a suit like mine is standing by a table in a room full of light. O'Toole whispers aloud: "You're in, kid. See that guy? He's your stand-in."

"All ready for Mr. Hayden," says a voice. The stand-in leaves and I propel myself toward his place. I turn and draw myself upright, breathing deeply, hoping this will calm things down—

"Wait a minute," says a voice. "This one is half a foot taller." They mess around with the lights. I reach for a cigarette, think better of it, and stand with my knees beginning to tremble.

"Action." It is black all around but I see O'Toole perched on the top of a stepladder.

"All-l righty now, Mr. Hayden, you're doing swell; now look to your left; now look to your right—that's it. Now take off your hat." I didn't know I was wearing a hat, so I whip it off. The voice purrs: "Move slowly please, Mr. Hayden. Now turn and cross to the window. That's the way. Remember where you are now. You are on the fifteenth floor of your hotel and you have never been in New York before and you look down to a very busy street. That's the way—"

He claps his hands and stomps on the floor. "My God! Mr. Hayden, that woman, she's hit by a car. She's hurt! Yes, she is, Mr. Hayden, she's hurt bad! . . . Mr. Hayden, are you listening to me? Please react to this, if you will. What would you do if a woman was hit by a car? . . . Surely you'd do something, wouldn't you? . . . Yes, you'd take your hands from your pockets . . . You'd lean out so as to see better . . . No No No! That is a window. There is glass in that window—"

"Like hell there is. Here, look!" I shove my fist through the empty frame.

I hear some laughter now. "Well, there is supposed to be glass there, Mr. Hayden. We must imagine there is glass there. . . . Now come downstage please . . ."

Downstage, I think—which way is downstage? I turn around.

"That is right. Now walk right toward the camera. Now stop."

I stop. I don't care for his voice . . . "All right, now you are skipper of your boat. You are not in the hotel any more. You are skippering your boat and it is beginning to storm. You are at the wheel by yourself. Take your wheel in your hands and brace yourself, Skipper. Let it show in your eyes how you feel. Don't be afraid of it, let it come out. The sails are tearing and the sheets are ripping but you'll bring her through, won't you, Skipper? You won't quit, will you; ah, that's fine. Relax now, Mr. Hayden."

It is perfectly silent now. Matches flare near the camera. I flex my knees to conceal the fact that they're trembling. O'Toole sits now, with his back to me. I think I know why.

The voice of the director returns: "You are in Grand Central Station now, Mr. Hayden . . . No, leave your hat off, it looks better without that hat. You are waiting to meet your girl— but she isn't here . . . You look all around. Other couples are embracing, but you are all alone . . . Please! You must react to this. There! There she is! She sees you. She comes rushing toward you . . . What would you do, Mr. Hayden? What would you feel? No, don't step away. We're in real close on you now. Step back—that's it, one more step. There. Now you take her in your arms and you look into her eyes and—"

A deep voice fills the room: "We're out of film as of—now."

The bright lights go off. "Take an hour," says a voice. "Then we'll do the scene with the girl." O'Toole is leaning against the wall by the exit.

"C'mon," he says, leading the way. "What the two of us needs is a drink."

CHAPTER 53

Maybe two dozen men sit in the projection room, all dressed alike in grays and blacks, with here and there a tumbling kerchief to proclaim a mutinous spirit.

I sit with O'Toole close to an exit door. "Shall we roll now?" The query comes from a hole in a wall.

"Not yet," say voices in chorus.

Ten more minutes of waiting. Then Griffith and Holman, the boss of Paramount East, enter. "Let's roll," says Griffith, and the room darkens.

One late match flares. Everybody scrunches low in his chair, out of the line of fire. Flashes of light appear on a screen with wracking sound-track noises. A hand holds up a slate: SCREEN TEST # ——. SILENT—STERLING HAYDEN—PARAMOUNT PICTURES—MARCH 15, 1940.

The slate is yanked and the figure of a man at bay in a room appears. A caricature with pinned-back ears, a quavery chin, nostrils enlarged, and eyes that seem dull.

"Focus."

Labor comes and goes and each detail now is needle-sharp and painfully large. The figure shows life, and begins to move stiffly, sweat growing through pancake. I close my eyes. I press at my forehead with clammy hands, dreading to look. Finally the screen goes dark but further labor follows, and the slate: SOUND.

The form on the screen has found a girl for himself. They ride in an automobile. He works the wheel as though the road were mined. She snuggles close. Her voice is rich. His is hoarse and he clears his throat as he speaks.

Now the camera begins to prowl. In close it goes to leer for a time, then back it pulls with a zoom to the right and a zoom to the left. Each time he speaks he muffs his lines, but a voice is nearby to prompt him softly. He blinks as he parrots the words—falters—freezes—begins again.

I poke O'Toole and we slip outside, down a flight of stairs and through a door. Times Square is full of people pushing; all I can see is that form on the screen, groping for life.

We duck down a staircase to a cellar café with a French name, and order a bottle of wine. I grab the jug and pour fast and our glasses touch. "Okay goddamit okay." I like my voice this way—harsh with resolution. "I've had it, Larry. I'm going back, so here's to the Grand Banks and the South Seas and—"

"Whaddaya mean!" his voice booms out. "Wait a sec' you miserable Protestant bastard! Here's to Paramount! You're in, I tell ya—you're *in!*"

"Ah!" I swing at the air. "You're out of your mind."

O'Toole drinks and pours. "Now shut up. Finish your glass, then get on the phone and call Griffith an' stop actin' like a bloody clown."

"But, Larry, did you see how I looked? Did you—"

"Shaddup! This whole thing's a joke. Sure, you looked like a giraffe. Who gives a damn? Go along with it. Laugh for Christ's sake."

His hand is shaking. "Now get up and call."

They are trying to locate Griffith. The nickel drops. I smoke. What I see from the booth is a door that swings on a kitchen. Griffith comes on. He sounds jubilant. I tell him I'm drinking some milk. He says the contract is ready. Holman and he and some of the others are waiting. A photographer is waiting. The test was a huge success.

He says.

I barge back to the table. O'Toole is gone. I look around. The bartender speaks: "Your friend is gone. He said—tell you—tell you goodbye—good luck—have plenty of laughs."

I start for the door. "Please sir," says the man on the bar. "That will be—for the wine—two dollars."

CHAPTER 54

They moved in, this young man and his mother, early in May. She seemed ecstatic. You couldn't be sure, looking at him, just how he felt. He had a forty-two-page contract with Paramount. He was on a payroll, earning six hundred dollars a month— three times as much as he had ever earned at sea.

They lived in Laurel Canyon in a Hollywood-Spanish house that clung to a parched hillside. It had a dirt drive and a base-ment garage and a pair of tiny bedrooms. The living room was the room with the view, framed by stunted shrubs, of a barren hill across a house-pocked road.

Each morning he drove to the parking lot next to the filling station, left the car and marched through a handsome gate of ornamental ironwork with the magic words PARAMOUNT PICTURES in an arc above. The guards called him by his first name.

He had a dressing room on the second floor, overlooking the production building and Stage 23. It was directly over Mr. Gary Cooper's dressing room and it had a shower and a toilet and a couch and chairs and a dressing table under a mirror studded with light bulbs.

He plastered the walls with pictures: pictures of schooners, barks, brigs, and ships; pictures of equatorial crossings; pic-tures of dories tossed on slate-gray seas under slate-gray skies, of vessels beleaguered by storm and entranced by calm. The lady who tended the towels and keys said: "My sakes, Mr. Hayden, but you've led an adventurous life." He smiled. The folks over in Publicity were enthusiastic, and they said: "Now, Sterling, we've got a magazine interview all set for you. We'll bring the gal over here so she can take a look at your pictures, then we'll lunch in the commissary, be extra nice to her, she's in real good with Hedda."

After sucking some strength from his picture display, he would cross to the studio gym. It had a boxed-in squash court and a playroom full of barbells and wall weights and mats. There were flying rings and bars and inclined boards to shove the blood to your head (very good for hang-overs, so the boys said). Jim was in charge. He dressed like an interne but with-out the mask and cap. He had great big muscular arms, always in plain view, and he kept his radio going so as not to miss out on the world.

Even when he had a girl starlet under a sheet for a "massage," you could hear the radio going. "Slappety slappety slap," spoke Jim's big hands. "So hurry folks an' rush right down to the friendly credit corner an' the Smilin' Irishman himself will see you drive home in a brand-new bargain car," spoke a man on the radio.

Jim also had a pair of cabinets. You could climb inside and close the doors and sit there with only your head sticking out while Jim went ahead on the steam. This must have been exciting because you could listen to Jim and the radio and the gang who hung around and find out who was screwing who and how great this latest film of Bing's and Bob's and Dottie's was going to be.

So six mornings a week this budding male starlet changed into his sweatsuit and knocked weights together and grabbed the shiny bars and grunted as he hoisted them over his head. Then he lay on a bench and pushed them up from his chest. Whenever he felt foolish, he thought of Thursday. Thursday was payday there at the Pagoda.

From time to time he stepped outdoors and lay on the docile grass under a captive tree. Then he climbed to the roof and bathed in the sun. A space was reserved for top executives so they could get healthy and talk business all at the same time. There were cushions and towels and creams and eyeshades made of cotton. The place was well-screened, but even so, you could see the water tower next door that said RKO.

After the sunbath came the time to learn acting. A sign said: Talent Department. Olive had charge of the reception room. Her daughter was just dying to break into pictures. Mr. Milton Lewis was chief talent scout, and Mr. Bill Russell had charge of the coaching.

Into the waiting room of the Talent Department came lots of hopefuls. They studied their little scenes or read the fan magazines, but most of the time they looked at each other.

Milt Lewis, everybody said, was a talented talent scout. He had discovered more talent than anyone in town. They also said he was a kindly man, not just to the talent, but to total strangers who were down and out. This set him apart from most people.

Bill Russell, the coach, was different. He hailed from Amarillo, and he liked to talk about life on the outside, about what people did with their lives. With a little luck you could divert Bill from the acting work and your hour would pass, not in learning to be a hero but in keeping your feet on the ground.

But a day came when Bill was called up to Griffith's office, and after that you worked. "I'm not supposed to say this," said Bill, "but they've got special plans for you up front." And you went ahead with the four-page scene, with Bill taking the part of the girl. "Tenderly," Bill would say, "treat her tenderly. When you draw her to you, don't plunk your mitts on her shoulder—caress her arms gently—try to hold her entranced—try to lift her—gently."

At one end of the building was the Audition Room. Here Bill and Milt and the rest could relax in deep chairs in a darkened room while talented girls and boys demonstrated their prowess beyond a plate-glass window on a tiny stage flooded with good hot lights. Some of the girls were smart. They knew what talent meant and sat with their legs spread just enough apart in front of the plate-glass window.

All studio commissaries are divided in two. First there is the lunch counter reserved for carpenters, cops, electricians, along with the extras, stand-ins, stuntmen, and those actors who are unknown or over the hill, who work by the day, when they work at all.

Then there is the main dining room where the stars gather to laugh and be seen as they pick at their food. Here also are the brains behind the stars: the producers, executives, directors, and writers. This is a segregated dining hall. Where you are seated depends strictly on who you are or who you are lunching with.

"Go there and let them get a look at you. Let them wonder who the new guy is. Maybe someone'll give you a small part in their next production. And that's how stars are made."

Yessir.

I tried this once. For nearly an hour I stood in the doorway awaiting the nod from the polished blonde who doled out seats and menus. The place was full of laughter, shoptalk, gags, and broad gestures performed with ultimate ease. Dozens of people swept by. Agents scuttled from table to table with pincerlike eyes and smiles that flashed on and off. When my turn came, I took an obscure table in an obscure corner and talked to nobody.

Once was enough. For the next few weeks I ate from a sack between some piles of lumber beyond the carpenter shop. The sun poured down and the wood smelled of pine trees and I lay down and dozed in the fragrance.

With the lunch hours gone I made the rounds of the boys and girls (as they called themselves) in Publicity. Object: to stimulate their interest. Most of them hated themselves for selling out, for turning out trash about stars and films. More than the others, they were outspoken about Hollywood: "Hayden, it's like this. All of us here got this job to do. But most of us are doing some serious writing at home nights; and one of these days we'll hit with a novel and then we'll march up to that front office and tell 'em all to go screw."

And this is how the weeks passed. There were people who had lived this life for years. They held part-time jobs and studied voice and ballet and some of the boys took judo. Some had been through the same ritual at half a dozen studios. Especially some of the girls, who surprised you by driving big convertibles and living alone in fancy apartments with a small dog and a big bed.

None of them seemed to mind because each of them knew perfectly well the day would come—quite soon—when the great break would come and they would soar to stardom overnight. There was nothing much else in life.

The change, when it came, came fast.

I was in the gym lifting weights, wondering what was the use of building muscle when I no longer worked for a living. Jim stuck his head through the door. "Griffith's secretary says for you to get over to the big man's office. Says it's important."

Griffith removed his glasses as I stepped into the room. He seemed to be sizing me up. "How much did you weigh this morning, Sterling?"

"Two hundred and four and a half."

"You look very well. How do you feel?"

"Fine."

"Bill Russell tells me you're coming along nicely."

"I am?"

"The boys in Publicity think you're a natural."

"A natural what?"

When some men laugh, it seems a painful thing.

"You've been out here how long?"

"About three weeks."

"How do you feel now, about your new career?"

"Well, to tell you the truth I've been thinking of giving the whole damn thing up. I went down to the harbor Sunday and located two of the finest schooners I ever—"

He swivels his chair through a complacent arc, then he turns back and says: "You're about to receive the greatest surprise of your life." I would dearly love a cigarette but Griffith doesn't approve.

"Sterling, I am going to do something that has never been done before in Hollywood. The front office thinks I'm insane. I'm going to star you in my next picture, *Virginia*. You will play the second male lead, next to Fred MacMurray. You will be playing opposite Madeleine Carroll."

I feign surprise.

"This is a technicolor picture and the budget may come close to a million dollars, so you have an awful lot of responsibility riding on those shoulders of yours. And so do I. Your wardrobe alone will probably cost three thousand dollars. You will portray the role of a young country gentleman from the North. You will have to learn how to ride and jump a horse. Have you ever worn tails?"

"Christ no."

"You will soon. I want you to keep this absolutely quiet. When Publicity gets ahold of this, they'll go wild. I shouldn't be the least bit surprised if both Hedda and Louella played this as their lead story. There is only one possible hitch."

This is more like it.

"Miss Carroll is the star. Miss Carroll has cast approval. It is not an easy thing for a girl in her position to play opposite someone as—as inexperienced as you. She might object."

"I wouldn't blame her."

We say goodbye and I close the door with care. The outer office is jammed. The strange part is, I knew all along this would happen.

CHAPTER 55

There was a time when the world of Hollywood spun on the axis of the "star system." A brace of box-office stars, a formula story and some ballyhoo, a million dollars—more or less—and the result was a highly profitable motion picture. Never mind the story, reasoned the wizards, never mind values and ethics. Just give us the names and the Technicolor and the capital and we'll bring in the money.

Which explains that mélange of pap known as *Virginia* and why it was that a hundred and forty technicians, players, and crew rolled from west to east that broiling summer of 1940, along with seventeen boxcars of gear, all under the nominal command of E. H. Griffith.

The whole shebang went east to Charlottesville for six weeks of shooting and then was scheduled to go back to the studio for a final month of undercover work. The finished product would be released to a gullible public not later than February 1941.

A black limousine drives from the center of town toward the time-resistant island of the Farmington Hunt Club where Griffith and his stars are staying. Griffith nips at a cigarette: "Sterling, as you know, Miss Carroll flew in from Europe two days ago. She is tired, very tired. I told her about you, and she was very decent about the whole thing. When you meet her, I trust that you will be as courteous and co-operative as possible. If she seems abrupt it is because she has a great deal on her mind."

"Yes, Mr. Griffith, I understand."

"By the way, what was your weight this morning?"

"One ninety-nine and nine tenths."

"Very well. Don't let up."

We wind through a pedigreed forest. An aristocratic hush lies low on a generous expanse of lawn and gardens and fairways that roll off toward woods in the distance. The clubhouse appears, sprawling red brick with porticoes and terraces. "Adjust your tie," he orders.

Miss Carroll's suite is garnished with vases of flowers, with cards from agents and other moguls. The living room is clogged with Paramount personnel, make-up men, wardrobe women, hair stylists, and a quorum of dress designers. But no Miss Carroll. Griffith goes into a huddle with the reigning costume designer.

I turn my back on the room. There is plenty of tension now, and I pirate a cigarette. A small framed picture captures my eye. It is an old friend, a painting by Winslow Homer showing some barefoot boys on a windy day in an open boat with a

whiskered old man to the helm. The sail is taut and the spray
flies; I peer in close and see the name on the transom:
Gloucester.

A rich warm voice interrupts: "Mr. Hayden?" I pivot. "I'm
Madeleine Carroll." I knew she was lovely, but nothing like
this—"Oh, how do you do." She wears no make-up. Her hair is
soft and has the same hue as salt grass in the wintertime. It
is swept back and secured with a small blue ribbon.

She clasps her hands behind her back and nods toward the
painting. "I imagine you like that, don't you."

"Yes. I think, when we leave this place I'll be forced to take
that with me."

She laughs. O'Toole would approve of this girl. "Perhaps I
can help." We laugh, and Griffith does not seem pleased. He
edges a bit toward us. "I think, Miss Carroll, we're about to be
joined by the boss." She hands me an ash tray. "Yes. Ned is
my chaperone. We can't talk now, you know. But we could, perhaps, have dinner together."

"Where?"

"Here, later—but not too late, we've an early call in the
morning."

Some things you never expect. This is the feeling I should
have had when I was given the part in the picture. "If you're
not busy," she adds.

"No. I'm not busy." Griffith is crossing over now.

"Now," she is saying, "you see, Ned? I introduced myself."

From our place on the dining terrace the fairway rolls toward
the sunset cloud. Candles glow in fragile hurricane mounts,
and the terrace is jammed with gentry. Through open doors
comes the sound of an orchestra. The waiters file by with their
endless rounds of drinks.

We share a bottle of wine that has little in common with the
wine where I come from. Across the way I can just see Griffith.
He sits with a group of men—facing us.

Madeleine sits with her back to the crowd, facing the west.
The actresses I've seen so far would never do such a thing.
From time to time people come over to ask for an autograph,
and she smiles as she scrawls her name. When they ask me I
feel like an ass, but I sign too. "What's wrong with people like
these, asking for the signature of some jerk who has never even
been in a film?"

"You'll find out." She holds her glass with both hands, sipping slowly.

I order more wine. When the music rests we can hear the crickets. Talking with her, I find out that she feels the same as I do about Hollywood. It is, we agree, a place to be used, a means to an end, no more.

Yet our ends are a world apart. All I want is a ship, so I say, at least. She wants money enough to throw herself in the war somehow; to support some children, forty of whom even now are in occupied Paris, dependent on her for survival. There is, when I come to think about it, a lot that an adult can do.

It is nine o'clock. Griffith has gone, and we can see the stars. The bottle of wine is empty—was that the second or the third? She draws a jacket over her shoulders. Someone breaks a glass, which is good for a volley of laughter. "I think it is almost bed-time," I hear her voice.

"I'm afraid so . . . Would you like to go for a walk—just down that fairway and back? . . . Do you know something? Where I've been most of my life a fairway means a deep-water channel."

I can't believe that we're sitting here together, that she feels alone, that she isn't married. Perhaps she is. None of my damn business.

"Yes"—she clasps the hurricane glass—"I love to walk. I used to walk alone—for hours and hours, when I lived at Malibu." The touch of a shiver goes through her. "Oh, how I hate that part of the world. Let's walk; all I do these days—is run." We look at each other briefly. "You wait here, I'll run—I'll go—and change my shoes."

I ask for the check. It is all taken care of. The waiter is old and doubled forward from the belt up. "I guess you're tired," I say.

"Yes sir, I'm a little tired tonight."

"Bring me a Scotch and water, double." I hand him a five-dollar bill. "And keep the change for your trouble."

The dancing goes on inside. I don't envy them. Not tonight I don't.

CHAPTER 56

You give a lot of yourself when they pay you to act like a star. They hold a lien not just on your working hours but on much of the time that a man should have as his own. Your time is shared with the picture in work, with their plans for your future, with the agents, and with the hacks who write for the fan magazines. But from early evening till early in the morning you do as you damn well please.

The preservation of sanity came first. To remain semi-balanced in an insane job you detach whenever you can. You can go it alone if you must. You may share it with friends. But the ideal way is to share it with one person.

The Paramount auto gate is flanked by jobless extras who hope someone will spot them and put them to work. They crack jokes and study the racing form and make minor genital adjustments.

Now a limousine passes through, driven by a burly Frenchman who is really a gardener by trade. The girl whom he drives is tired. They turn south and crawl for a time in homebound rush-hour traffic. When they come to the rendezvous point, the car draws to the curb and a man comes out of the shadow under a tree.

For fifty minutes the car plods on through a sprawling maze of burgeoning prefab housing all back to back and jammed in tight. The traffic thins out and off to the west the ocean appears and the car runs alone down a winding road that skirts a silent headland. Tiny farms show coal-oil lantern eyes. A lighthouse flashes.

"Do you really think they're here?" the girl asks.

"We'll soon find out," I say.

We turn now onto a narrow road, flanked with pepper trees, fences and vines and high-banked flowers, which curls for three miles toward the crown of the darkened hills. The house appears, its lighted windows half hidden by cypress branches. A parked car shows Massachusetts license plates. "By god they are!" I lean forward. "Hey, Fred, honk your horn, give her a good long honk!"

A flagstone walk leads to a broad terrace where an old refectory table is spread with dinner things.

"O'Toole. Mac, you made it okay, I see!"

The Irishman stands with both hands thrust deep in the pockets of his old bagged pants. "Larry, this is Madeleine Carroll. Madeleine, this is Larry O'Toole and Captain Malcom MacDonald of the Boston Pilots."

O'Toole holds her hand, then he steps back. "Excuse me, ma'm, if I take a good long look at you." He shakes his head. "By god it's true, it's every bit of it true."

"What is?" She laughs.

"What this no good bastard says in his letters." He clouts the side of my arm.

From the head of the table your eyes are full of the sea. A freighter appears, bound out from Los Angeles. When she brings the lighthouse abeam, they swing her to port and she stands offshore on a great circle course to the Orient.

Fred's wife comes out with a tray. "Mr. O'Toole, would you prefer red or white wine with your dinner?" She speaks with an accent.

He wipes his mouth and his eyes expand as he looks at us each in turn. "Mac, did you hear that—would Mr. O'Toole prefer red or white wine?—sonofawhore! I've been drinking for twenty years and I've never been asked such a question." He pats the maid on the fanny. "Mommy, I'll just try a little of each." When the wine is poured, he stands for a toast. "To the two of you: good luck—not that you need it, judgin' by what I've seen."

Mac turns in early, tired from the cross-country drive. We talk for a time, then Madeleine rises. "I'll leave you two together. There's a fire in the living room." O'Toole jumps up. "Good. I'm not in the habit of eating out under the stars, fresh air and drinking don't go good together."

What's left of a polar bear is spread on the floor by the fire. Larry stretches out with the bear's big head for a pillow. I face the fire with my back to a wall full of books. O'Toole speaks first. "Is there any rum in this house?"

I fetch the bottle, and we drink to the girl upstairs.

"They'll never believe it, so there's no use my writing to Ben or the gang on the Wharf. They'd think I was drinking too much." This pleases him. "Imagine, an O'Toole drinking too much. Now, will you please tell me what a girl like this one sees in a guy like you?"

"I've been wondering the same thing. Maybe she thinks I'm

the only person out here who hates Hollywood as much as she does."

"That's a lousy word."

"You know what I mean."

"Go on. You're daft. You just got here. You're going like a train of cars, so what in hell's your trouble?"

"It's not a life for a man. Not for me, it isn't. I'll tell you something, Larry. As soon as this picture is finished, I'm clearing out, fast."

"Where in hell to? How much dough you got?"

"Five, maybe six hundred bucks."

"And you'll buy a schooner with six hundred bucks?"

"No. What I want to do is get in the war somehow."

He sits up so fast he spills rum on the beer. "What?! Get in the war? Christ, everybody I know is trying to stay clear of the sonofabitch."

"What I think I'll do is buy me a typewriter and a good camera and be a war correspondent."

He taps his head. "You've been reading Hemingway." He looks at me and then he looks toward a room overhead. "Ah, I got it now. It's the girl. You're so goofy over this dream upstairs that you"—he snaps his cigarette at the fire—"got to go get your ass shot off."

I cross to the fire and give it a kick and freshen the drinks. His face brightens. "Hey, wait a second, what about Paramount? You got yourself a contract this time, kid. Paramount's not giving you this ride for nothing; you're their fair-haired boy; why hell, there's more crap in the papers about you back home than Gable and Cooper together."

"They can't force a guy to work when he doesn't want to."

"No? Well, they can try like hell; and if they ever caught up with you, they'd sue you till you didn't have a dime to your name."

I shake my head. "You're wrong. There's just one thing these guys really respect—"

"Sure. Dough." He rubs his fingers together. "And you mean dough to them. They're banking on you to grow up someday into a big fat box-office star—"

"I don't agree. They respect you if you don't give a shit about money, if you tell them to take their dough and get lost."

He pats the bear on the head. "Well, maybe . . . But the least you can do is go for a vessel. Get them to give you a schooner.

Wait a year. Save some dough, then take the ship and clear out."

I step outside and the sea stretches out black, with Catalina Island barely visible.

Madeleine's room is dark. I jump on the wall and stare offshore, picturing a vessel tramping a sea such as this, standing in with a leading wind toward a war-torn shore.

A spark catches in my mind and I make my way indoors. "Larry, I've got it. I'll get me a ship and haul cargo with her—maybe run the blockade into England and back. What do you say about that?"

He yawns. "I say I'm tired. And you're crazier now than back in our time with the brig."

CHAPTER 57

The moment the picture was finished, Madeleine flew east and, bereft, I prowled the house for hours on end. Down below the smog line, on Sunset Strip, extras, actors, and two-bit columnists lounged in and out of Schwab's drugstore in the autumnal heat.

You could tell when Christmas was due because they hoisted monstrous plywood cutouts of fir trees atop the lampposts on Hollywood Boulevard. The studio said I should ride in the huge Santa Claus parade sponsored by the Junior Chamber of Commerce, the Legion, the Better Business Bureau, and the Motion Picture Producers Association.

I did as they said, and rode toward the end of the cavalcade, next to an unknown starlet, with our unknown names on a placard. Roy and Dale were up in front dressed like sugarplum buckaroos, waving and prancing, and Trigger went all the way from Gower Gulch to Grauman's Chinese Theatre without disgracing his name. All the stars were there, holding down the back seat of convertibles, and if they were half-crocked it didn't matter, what with the yule spirit and general pandemonium and the searchlights sweeping skyward. And the stores stayed open till nine every night from then until Christmas.

Griffith explained how *Virginia* might turn out to be the finest picture ever made and how, to be sure the public recognized this fact, they were going to send me out to accompany the film on a sweep of the big Eastern cities. MacMurray refused to go and Madeleine was beyond reach, so right after the first of the year I hit the ballyhoo trail.

It seems almost like a dream: President Roosevelt sits at the head of a long table upstairs in the White House, flanked by Lana Turner and Greer Garson. He looks like his photographs, with the strong jaw and the genial smile and the cigarette holder upthrust like a flying jibboom. Mrs. Roosevelt sits at the other end, talking intently to Danny Kaye and Gene Kelly. I am lost somewhere in the middle. The President thanks us all for participating in the 1941 campaign of the March of Dimes. Then we file out, shaking hands as we go. It is a contest to see who can best engage the President's attention. I feel very nervous. When it is my turn I clear my throat and say: "Sir, Captain Ben Pine asked me to give you his regards and—"

He rears back as though this is the most wonderful news he has heard in months. "Well, give my best to him. Tell him the *Thebaud* should have won those last two races."

Someone gives my shoulder a shake and I come awake to hear Andy from Paramount publicity saying: "Pull yourself together, kid, we're coming into Boston."

Everything looks dreary and drab and gray and the office buildings stand with feeble glowing lights, though it is mid-morning. We circle a big freighter as she hesitates in mid-channel. The fish pier is choked with trucks and dozens of trawlers lie alongside spitting steam.

I set my jaw and cinch my tie and it's no relief when the plane sets down because now I must face my public. For five miserable weeks now, we have been on the trail: Charlottesville, Richmond, Norfolk; Baltimore, Philadelphia and Washington and New York City. Boston will be the worst because I have friends here.

Andy holds my camel's-hair coat. It has raglan shoulders and a drape shape and no buttons and a wrap-around belt. My hair is so long it curls and they won't let me cut it. My hands feel soft and small, and the wind has an icy edge as we head toward the terminal, where a crowd is gathered to give me a home-town welcome. "Hi, Sterlin'—Hey, Sterlin', over here! How's it feel, Mr. Hayden, bein' a big pitcher star?" I find myself saying embarrassed words into a microphone.

A dozen motorcycles flank a huge black limousine that is shrouded in bunting and banners. A red-faced cop throws me a wide salute and we roar through the tunnel into downtown Boston with the sirens going and little gray people leaping aside and peering into where I sit like a zombie. The lead cop skids in the slush and nearly goes under a truck.

We plow to a halt in front of the Copley Plaza, where the doorman is all smiles and the manager with a white carnation in his stiff black suit rubs his hands together.

I am shot into the warmth of the lobby with the little old ladies standing back as though I were Baby Face Nelson. I see Jack Dixon, from my crew in the *Aldebaran*, with his camera: "Hold it, Skip," he barks. "Hold it just one second." O'Toole leans against a wall sideways with his hands in his pockets. I go up to him, and the girl from behind the cigar stand comes around with her arms crossed below fine big breasts and gives me a friendly look as we duck into Andy's special elevator.

"Sonofawhore!" exclaims Larry. "This is the same suite they gave DeMille when he was here with *The Ten Commandments*." There is a long table with bottles and ice, and two waiters. "Go get freshened up," says Andy. "The press will be here in ten minutes." Larry goes for the bar. I enter a huge bedroom with twin double beds and a tapestry on the wall.

O'Toole comes in with a bottle of bourbon. I draw the drapes and peer out at Copley Square, where pigeons hump around on the snow and the public library looms dark and just as forbidding as it did eight years ago when I used to sit with the unemployed battalion in the great vault of the reading room, hushed and full of that stale sick smell.

Afterwards there is a banquet and they ship me from radio station to department store to newspaper office and round and round and back to the Copley, where O'Toole has his shoes kicked off and a pile of papers nearby. I see my name in headlines and I know my picture is there but I refuse to look. I take one drink and soak in the tub and O'Toole takes telephone calls from girls I can't remember.

Late in the afternoon I borrow somebody's coat, slip out the service entrance, and take a cab to the fish pier. Nothing has changed and an icy blast comes in from the outer harbor. The men shuffle around with their breath stabbing out, the gulls cry, and I can see the glow from dozens of fo'c'sle hatches. The gear is rusted and raw and the decks are a marvel of litter. I remember walking up and down this pier for hours and weeks on end, trying to muster the nerve to ask for a job. And here I am, warm and dry, making big money, and the envy of all. But the odd part is, I'm just the same as before.

Three of us eat dinner together in a cocktail lounge on the ground floor. I would like to get drunk but I don't dare, with the Boston "premier" scheduled for half past eight. Babs is a beautiful thing with thick black hair. She was singing in Washington when I met her. The only trouble is, she wears too much lipstick and always seems to be looking for something wherever she goes.

We have the same limousine and what looks like the same escort as we go across town and down toward the searchlights stabbing the sky around the theater. Nobody says very much. Traffic is snarled and the sirens make it worse, so we crawl along. The crowds lining the street grow larger and larger, peering in the windows and waving.

This is the bad time. Up ahead the marquee flashes, and what in hell will I say when I walk out onto that stage in front of four thousand people waiting to see me make an ass of myself.

Naked white lights spell the whole thing out: PARAMOUNT PROUDLY PRESENTS NEW ENGLAND PREMIER OF ED-WARD H. GRIFFITH'S EPIC "VIRGINIA"—STARRING FRED MACMURRAY MADELEINE CARROLL . . . AND BOSTON'S OWN STERLING HAYDEN.

Boston's own, my ass. Paramount's big blond male starlet, all sold out and locked up with a seven-year contract guaranteeing $150 per week until April, then inclining upward until, at the end of the term, he will be getting $7,500 for each week of mighty endeavor—provided, of course, that he is a good little actor, does what he's told when he's told, doesn't turn down any rotten parts, co-operates with Lolly and Hedda, and sends a case of whiskey to each at Christmas, along with flowers at propitious moments, provided he's polite to the bloodsuckers who write for the fan magazines.

I knock off my hat getting out of the car and the crowd goes wild. The sidewalks are mobbed. Not a one of them has ever seen me on film, yet I'm a "star" scratching my name on bits of paper, surrounded by a police cordon. Andy looks at his watch, gives a signal, and they usher me through the theater, down the left-hand aisle, through a pair of fireproof doors.

Sam Pinanski is a very happy man. He owns the Metropolitan

Theatre and tonight it is sold out. He seems a little tense and he jots notes on his starched cuffs. A local disc-jockey stands by to act as master of ceremonies. His name is Eddie and he seems very composed as he breathes on the microphone and adjusts his collar. When we are introduced, I feel him measuring me as much as to say: "All right, you big blond bastard, you may be the star tonight, but Eddie's a guy who has been around and Eddie might just make you look like a goddamned fool."

The lights out front go down, and a fellow in an overcoat is settled behind a pair of snare drums next to a mike of his own. A spot shines, Eddie mutters something to himself, adjusts his crotch, and dashes onto the stage. He spears the mike with his right hand and swings one leg in a wide arc as though he can't slow down. The audience goes wild.

He calls out Sam, who says he is very touched and proud of "our boy" tonight, and only in America could a thing like this happen.

The rest is a little blurred. I hear my name and my knees feel weak and my throat is dry but I square up and step on. Bedlam breaks loose—stamping, whistling, and screaming, mixed with polite applause. I shake hands with Eddie and look down at my feet. When I look back up, Eddie is gone. I feel a chill draft of apprehension.

I look around and the crowd roars. Still no Eddie. I clutch at the mike and wonder what to say, my knees fluttering. Eddie races out with a stepladder, sets it up, climbs to the top, crosses his legs, revealing one calf, and leans with his elbow on top of my head.

The audience roars. I stand motionless with a fixed smile on my face. Eddie vaults down, collapses the ladder, skids it into the wings, does a little jig, and says: "Now, Sterlin', tell all these wunnerful folks how you got your break in the pitchers."

"Thanks, Eddie. Good evening everybody, uh—" (laughter and applause). "Well, it was the day before Christmas [louder laughter now] and I had command of the big steel schooner *Aldebaran*. We were two hundred miles south-southeast of Cape Hatteras and I had a fifteen-man crew from Boston here— [wild applause] and it came on to blow out of the—" Halfway through this speech I did my trick, quit bending down to the mike, picked it up with one hand, and reared back to my full height. How they loved me for it.

Eddie pretended to chin himself on my wrist as he asked:
"What's next, Sterlin'? I suppose Paramount has big plans now
that you've created such a sensation with your initial appear-
ance in this Technicolor production of *Virginia*."

"Well, Eddie, as a matter of fact they do. As a matter of fact,
Eddie, I'm going to star with Miss Madeleine Carroll [whistles
now] in a picture based on the book *Dildo Cay*. I sure am lucky
and grateful because you see, folks, as a matter of fact I am
more at sea right now than I ever was when I was going to sea
and as a matter of fact—"

When I make my exit, I go in the wrong direction. The spotlight goes right and I go left. Then we cross and meet in the
middle, everyone laughs, and I march off. I'm so full of confidence I throw a kiss to some girls near the band. I start to
mop my face but Sam shoves me back for a curtain call and
then another, for almost five minutes, which is my record up
until now.

CHAPTER 58

I saw him for the first time in August of 1941. He was lean and
tall and he looked like a man should look. He had been ferrying
bombers across the North Atlantic. We earned equal pay doing
unequal jobs.

Madeleine and he sat side by side in a darkened corner of
Stage 31. I sat alone by the helm of a Bahamian sloop with no
bottom. I was, according to the magazines, "a blond young
viking god. . . . the greatest find since Gable."

They adjusted the lights and called for Miss Madeleine
Carroll. Whatever had been between us was gone almost completely. One hundred and twenty people were milling about—
they knew what was what. Charlie rocked the boat, the wind
machines revved up and the arcs poured it on as I made like a
man of the sea. We did the scene somehow.

"It's a wrap!" called Rollie. "First thing in the morning, same
place, same scene. Be good!" I watched the two of them leave.
When I passed her dressing room, the curtains were drawn. I
climbed the stairs and flopped on the couch.

And now, suddenly and for the first time, I knew what jealousy meant. I had no desire for dinner, and instead I drove fast, out to the coast highway and south, through Laguna Beach and clear to Capistrano.

At last I turned and drove back to Los Angeles harbor. I had my mind on a vessel which lay neglected in the bowels of a Long Beach shipyard. I vaulted a fence, ducked a watchman, and made my way down the dock. She was a big Gloucesterman, the *Oretha F. Spinney*, owned now by MGM, who had used her in *Captains Courageous*.

Her spars were tall. I paced her deck and I fondled her wheel; I sprang the lock on the forward scuttle with a rusted spike and sat for a time in the fo'c'sle. The stub of a candle lay by the galley pump. You could smell the old Banks aroma of oil and gurry mixed with tar and a touch of rot. She was for sale for eighteen thousand dollars. Who in hell had eighteen thousand dollars?

I rolled into a starboard bunk and I dozed. I woke up cold, with the plan clear-cut in my mind.

On my way out of the yard, I caught my pants on the barbed wire ("Oh Buzz look, you have a winklehawk."). I put the top down on the finance company's Lincoln Zephyr and drove, very slowly, in the general direction of home.

I'll meet with Freeman first thing in the morning. Mr. Freeman is my friend. He is also the boss of Paramount. "Mr. Freeman, I know you are a busy man. I know you have been more than considerate of me this year. I also know you have a good deal of faith in my future. But, sir, there are things busting loose inside me that I simply cannot explain. You know I want to buy a schooner and you've told me to be patient. Well—I'm sorry, sir, but I just have to have that vessel. Right now!"

. . . I see him sitting there with the kindly face and the big cigar, leaning back in a swivel chair. "Sir, *Bahama Passage* will be completed in two more weeks of shooting. It so happens I appear in almost every scene. This means you cannot finish the picture without me. Unless Paramount buys the *Oretha F. Spinney* from MGM and hands her over to me, I shall refuse to report for work. . . . What? Blackmail? . . . No sir. Don't you understand? I've got to do this thing. I'll pay you back, with interest, of course. . . . Just give me the ship and I'll be the nicest, most co-operative actor ever came through these gates. And I give you my word of honor, if I can't pay off, then I'll come back and work for nothing. I mean that, sir. I never meant anything so much in all my fucked-up life." . . . He puffs hard now. He puts in a call for my agent, Bertie Allenberg. He buzzes Jack Karp, the head of the Legal Department. . . . But I stand firm.

I smoke endlessly. The Palos Verdes hills loom up under the stars. The light on Point Vicente flashes, and the night air has a taste of the sea. It is just past five a.m. I pass the turn that leads to her house on the hill, and look back to see a pair of lighted windows blurred by cypress boughs.

All morning we work, Miss Carroll and I. (Is she really tired or am I imagining it?) "Goodness sakes," she laughs, "you're a cheerful one this morning."

"I have an idea in mind, and I'm seeing Freeman at noon." Let her puzzle that one out. We're doing a scene in which I take her in my arms. I say the idiot words somehow. The bomber is nowhere around, which ought to help but doesn't.

Mr. Y. Frank Freeman is not himself. His manner is curt. His office is flooded with sunlight, and twin boxer dogs peer through a door. "Well, Sterling, what's on your mind today?"

I tramp back and forth, swinging my arms and smoking, trying to get up my courage. "Mr. Freeman"—I clear my throat—"I just wanted to have a few words with you about this schooner we were talking about last month."

"My God, Sterling, do we have to go through this again? You'll have your precious boat when the time comes. Nobody's going to run off with it. Metro has no use for it, I have no use for it, so just control yourself and concentrate on your acting."

"Yes sir, but—but—well, when I get through work two weeks from now I won't have a damn thing to do and—"

He worries the cigar. Then he rises slowly, steps outside, puts fresh water in the dogs' bowl, and returns to his big leather chair. "All right now, Sterling, I'll tell you what. I'll buy that schooner today. While you're still here, if I can. When you finish your work in *Bahama Passage*, you will get a fifty per cent interest in the boat as a—as a sort of bonus. You have some peculiar ideas but you'll outgrow them. As a matter of fact, if I was your father I'd be right proud of you."

"I don't even know how to begin to—"

"Forget it. Do your work. When you complete one more picture for us, the boat will be yours. But not until then. Is that fair, do you think?"

"Fair? It's—"

He waves this away. "You don't have to tell me how you feel, I'm not as heartless as some people think." He presses a button. "Sidney, get me Eddie Mannix at Metro." He pours a glass of water and swallows a pill. "Hello, Eddie? You've got a boat somewhere down at the harbor called the—" I supply the name. "Called the *Oretha F. Spinney*. That's right. How much do you want for her? Eighteen five? I'll buy her. Right. Jack will talk to you later. Goodbye, Eddie."

He takes some papers and swivels his back on the room, and I close the door with care.

CHAPTER 59

All through the August night the car rolled north through California's Central Valley, bound for San Francisco. It was cold with the top down, and the stars bristled beyond the mist over the fields and along the dry river beds.

I had seen Madeleine off that afternoon at the Pasadena Station. She was through with Hollywood forever. Afterwards, I drove down to the harbor, where the *Spinney* lay in a stagnant berth. I moved aft and fingered her big iron wheel. I went below, into the cabin partitioned off with plywood and masonite into small compartments. The place was a shambles, with castoff clothing, bottles and cans and oily rags. I flung myself on a stained mattress and lay staring up at the peeling paint. And all the while Madeleine was racing east toward her rendezvous with the bomber man.

It was half past nine when I woke. A dream went skittering off as I swung to my feet. To hell with the ship; she was too much for me right now; I would drive to San Francisco and look up Warwick Tompkins on his schooner *Wander Bird*. I glanced for only a moment at my cabin full of shattered glass and splintered wood before I left.

It is daybreak now and cold. I drive slowly, watching the east grow warm with light, thinking of the last time I saw Tompkins. It was early in June of 1936 when I was mate in the *Yankee* and he was about to sail from Gloucester for San

Francisco by way of Tangier, Rio, Cape Horn, and Talcahuano in Chile. A crowd came down to see him off, but the old-timers shook their heads and mumbled about tackling Cape Horn with an 84-foot schooner that had no power and a handful of amateurs for crew. But Tompkins had gone, and with his wife and two small kids he had battled his way around the Horn, and since that voyage he had been to Hawaii twice and Tahiti once. The only thing wrong was a rumor that he was becoming a radical, but all the same, I envied him his belligerence, his brusqueness, his ability as a writer, and his way of making a go of things even when he was broke. He also had a knack of flouting minor conventions, and once threw a shipboard party in Gloucester harbor with dancing on deck all night. Whoever heard of a thing like that in staid old Gloucester?

Sausalito felt like a sailorman's town. There was a wall of fog beyond the Gate, and San Francisco spread like a blanket across the seaside hills. Here and there ferries paddled in the bay, and on the water front lay the rotting hulks of schooners, barks, and brigs. Hollywood seemed far away.

Tompkins looked almost the same, with the truculent thrust to the jaw, still impelled by a vast impatience. Gwen, his wife, was exactly the same, with her quiet way of smiling and her sensual body and an old bandanna knotted around her hair.

Without a struggle, I surrendered myself to the sea: to the wind sounds and the smells of tar and salt, to the feel of splicing tools and marline, to quiet hours of painting under the lee of the bulwarks and to lying on deck in the sun, watching the birds perched on pilings pinned to the sky.

At night I lay in my bunk with the firelight dancing on swart deckbeams and yellowed panels, with the bole of the mainmast rearing up in the gloom, hearing the tap-tap-tap of a halyard lost in the night.

And yet—even as I paced, I sensed a certain difference. I was haunted by something Warwick had said during dinner in response to my obvious pleasure at finding the ship unchanged: "Oh yes, the old *Bird* is fine no doubt, but one of these days, my boy, you are going to find you can turn your back on the sea with scarcely a backward glance." A sudden sadness struck me as I realized that the rumors I'd heard must be true: "Poor old Tompkins had to go and swallow the Communist line— he's Red as they come these days—too bad—tough on his wife and kids." But a strange thing happened; I found myself in the grip of a new excitement, anxious to discover just what this power was that had taken my friend and dammed the river of his mind in such a way that it no longer ran to the sea.

I sensed that I was about to stumble upon the key to what was wrong in my life, for the older I grew the more convinced I became that I was flawed in some way beyond my understanding.

Simultaneously I was frightened lest this new discovery should destroy my world of the sea. I wanted both worlds at once, the world of ships and the world of social struggle. I was late, too, and I knew it—twenty-five years old, and for all my fighting and searching and voyaging I had yet to come to grips with life. I was in fact still in kindergarten. Why? Was I too scared to face reality? Too stupid perhaps? Well, then, the best thing I could do was listen to Tompkins with an open mind, and to hell with conventional thinking.

One morning we drove to Oakland, where a rusted steamer was loading scrap iron from Japan. Pickets paraded up and down: I.L.W.U. PROTESTS SHIPMENT SCRAP IRON TO JAPAN. The police stood around kicking their heels on the nails. Tompkins knew one of the pickets, who led us where coffee was being served. I felt ignorant and soft, a tourist for the first time in my life. These longshoremen belonged, and I was a phony on the outside looking in. I smoked and kept my eyes on the cobblestones. Tompkins tried to drag me into the conversation, and I began to resent his arrogance. Who in hell was he to tell me what was wrong with the world. He was bitter, that was all, bitter because he had never been able to break even in the good old hard-boiled American world of free competition.

That same evening a group of people assembled in the schooner's cabin, maybe a dozen in all. They were couples mostly, but there was one unattached girl, very pretty behind no make-up, wearing a plain wool dress that only enhanced her figure. Two of the men had fought in Spain with the Abraham Lincoln Battalion. This was the first I had heard about the International Brigades, and I didn't understand exactly who was fighting for what. They kept using words I didn't know—working class, Fascism, solidarity, imperialist, monopolist. It occurred to me that I was in the midst of some very dangerous people, yet they didn't seem dangerous. They seemed different, that's all—more intelligent than the rest, and above all, more concerned.

But the episode was humiliating to me because I was ignorant. I didn't dare join in: I had nothing to say. I couldn't even understand what they were saying and I began dozing off in my corner, though I wasn't tired. I wanted to escape to the deck, where I could pace alone with the bulwarks and pinrails and shrouds that for half my lifetime had held my world together. The clock in the cabin advanced with agonizing slowness, but finally it was almost half past ten and for two solid hours I hadn't said a word. Gwen went into the galley and I thought I was about to be released, when Tompkins said: "Sterling, all these people are landsmen, so why don't you tell them something about your experiences fishing on the Banks and firing in that P & O steamer?" They swung around facing me as I lit a fresh cigarette.

I warmed up after a bit as I began to work with my inventory of tales, and it came to me that I had a new and intriguing perspective. My stories suddenly were more than anecdotes. They had a point. The men I had shipped with suddenly became part of a larger scheme of things. The abstract terms—proletariat, exploitation, and the rest—began to seem less abstract. I thought of men I hadn't been reminded of in years and found myself moved and angered.

My audience seemed moved and angered too. I had shared a part of my life and felt a new kinship with them. If I could only feel this way in front of the cameras, I'd turn into one hell of an actor. Perhaps I could revolt and still belong.

Gwen came aft with some wine. After I finished, they were silent. It occurred to me that I was right about Hollywood and the rest. It wasn't wrong to have dreams and ideals and to want more out of life than a desk in an office and a little house with a mortgage and all the stuff bleated about in the national magazines.

Also—and how attractive this thought—what could be more unusual than the sometime schoonerman who of his own volition tells conventional Hollywood to go to hell and goes back into the world to contribute something to life.

At least, I thought, it was worth a try. I had nothing to lose but a rancid slice of stardom, and, best of all, it was bound to lead me toward Madeleine.

🖢

CHAPTER 60

It is harder sometimes to drop off the ladder than to climb. That morning in Frank Freeman's office, three men with a combined yearly income of well over a million dollars held a meeting. I waited outside thinking of a girl who was just then in Stamford, Connecticut. That morning I had sent her a wire: HAVE ABANDONED THE SHIP DRIVING EAST AT ONCE WILL PHONE FROM BOSTON MUST SEE YOU DO NOTHING RASH STOP LOVE.

The door opened and Bert Allenberg came out. "Look, sweetheart [Bert was my agent], Frank and Henry are both upset. I'm going to talk with you for a bit. Then you talk to Ginsberg by yourself. Then Freeman will see you." He was tall and cadaverous, with a leathery face gone black and hollow underneath the eyes. Something was wrong with his stomach.

The door opened and Ginsberg came out en route to his own office. He was known on the Paramount lot as the hatchet man. He was tough—provided you dealt in dollars—not so tough if you were a dreamer.

"Now look, baby," Bert went on, "you know I think you're nuts for wanting to quit." He checked the hall for strangers. "Let me slip you this one thought. I'm not supposed to let on, but just between the two of us, if you stay Paramount is prepared to give you the lead in *For Whom the Bell Tolls*. Have you read the book?"

"No."

"And, sweetheart, they'll tear up your contract and write you a new one, three pictures a year, thirty thousand dollars a picture. I can't believe it myself, but I happen to know it's true." He flicks a gold lighter; his cuffs are French and his cravat is a marvel of class. One thing you know—meeting Bert—this agency racket pays.

Ginsberg doesn't rise as I take my place in a chair. Through the blinds you can see the little quadrangle where a fountain spurts and goldfish prowl beneath gum-wrapper boats.

"Hayden, I am supposed to convince you not to quit. I'm not going to bother. I haven't the slightest sympathy with you. You are not an actor. You never have been. I doubt you ever could be an actor. You are what we call a Personality.

"We have brought you along until you are what is known as a hot property. You might go a long way in this business. If you would like my opinion, I would say the odds are against it. You have to care in this business, and you don't give a damn. If you walk out on us, you will never work in pictures again. It will be the biggest mistake in your life, and from what I hear you've made your share. Furthermore, you will in all probability be sued by the corporation, and breach of contract suits have a way of haunting a man." He places the tips of his fingers together, takes them apart, then touches them gently. "Does what I have said make sense to you, Hayden?"

"Yes sir."

"Will you change your mind?"

"No sir."

He turns to the work on his desk. "Then I suggest you go talk with your good friend, Mr. Freeman."

This is the part that is rough. He sits peering up through a cloud of cigar smoke, then he leans over to his intercom. "Hold my calls, Sydney." We look at each other, he raises his brows and speaks: "To begin with, Sterling, you place me in an extremely awkward position."

"I know that, sir, and I'm sorry."

"When this thing with the boat came up a few weeks back, I acted on my own initiative because I wanted you to calm down and be happy out here on the coast. I may be boss of this studio, but the Board of Directors and the stockholders don't take it lightly when we present newly discovered actors with eighteen-thousand-dollar boats."

"I understand that too." The boxers pace in their kennel. "Now, Sterling, let's take our time about this. I'm on a diet these days, but say the word and I'll have lunch sent over and we can talk all day if we need to."

"That won't be necessary."

"All right then, tell me what's the matter. Don't beat around the bush. I'm your friends and it won't go beyond this room." He pulls out a drawer and props up his legs.

Round and round I circle. "Well, sir, it's just that I don't feel right as an actor. I wasn't cut out for it. I'm the first to admit I may be fouled up, but with the war going on and all I feel, I have to get out and get out right now."

"Sterling, you're not being open about this. You wanted the

boat so we gave you a boat. We jumped your salary. We starred you in two of our biggest pictures. What more do you want? This war thing is nonsense. Our country isn't in the war yet— if it was, then I'd be the first to understand—"

"Goddamn it, sir, but I can't act and keep my self-respect. It's the only thing I have and I guess I'd better hang on to it."

He brushes the smoke to one side. "Excuse me, you'd better hang on to what?"

"My self-respect. What good is the rest, the money and the schooner and the living, if I don't like to look in the mirror when I'm shaving?"

He swivels around and stares for a time at the sky, nursing the long cigar. When he speaks his voice is gentle. "Sterling, those are fine words, but you know and I know that you're leaving something out. I know what it is and you know I know, and you know I'm fond of you both. Now, I've lived a little longer than you have and maybe I've gone through something like this too. This thing that's eating your heart will pass. It has to. You need to take your time until you calm down a little. Think about it, will you?"

"I don't have to think about it. Madeleine is a big part of my trouble, I admit." I swing around and snap the butt at the hearth. "But I would rather gamble on the thousand to one shot that I'll walk out this door and do whatever it is I have to do. Maybe one day you will make a picture about me, about what I did or tried to do. I don't want to go on imitating men, and that's all there is to it." I wipe my eyes and reach for a cigarette.

"Well," he drawls, "I was going to make you a little proposition, but in view of what you say, I don't suppose it would be much use—would it?"

"No sir."

He sighs and rises. We meet at the door. He puts a hand on my shoulder. "Good luck. We'll take care of the schooner, and if there's anything I can do, let me know."

The door closes. It is quarter to twelve, and I should be on the desert before dark.

🖤

CHAPTER 61

He drove east then, never sleeping more than an hour at a stretch, crumpled up in the back seat with a hammer clutched under his pillowed coat. The day came when he rolled on to T Wharf, and O'Toole looked down in surprise from his loft window. Newspapermen assembled as the retrovert pilgrim detached his California license plates and sent them arching into Boston harbor (splendid gesture and lots of laughs from the crowd).

The reporters are primed. "Say, Sterling, tell us how come you walked out on Hollywood? . . . Sterling, what did Paramount say? Mr. Hayden, is it true you were offered the lead in *For Whom the Bell Tolls*? Now, don't punch me in the nose for askin', but does Madeleine Carroll have anything to do with this, I mean, all this talk in the columns—any truth in that?"

(Just take my time, stare toward the harbor, smile just enough, and then. . . .)

"Aw hell now, you guys understand. Put yourself in my position: you come off the deck of a vessel and they sign you to a contract and they powder you down and doll you up and Christ —I mean, you end up nothing more than a dummy. I couldn't take it, that's all. It's as simple as that."

(You can sense the whisper of admiration that dusts through the little crowd: Geez, this kid's great—a real Joe.)

"Sterling, what are your plans? Will you be going back to sea, Mr. Hayden? I guess Ben Pine would be glad to give you back your berth in the *Thebaud*."

"Well, as a matter of fact, no. I don't know just what I'll do. I've got to run down to New York for a few days [let a whimsical smile spread slowly . . .], and after that? I'm a sonofabitch if I know."

His plan was impressively clear: first he would intervene between her and the man from the Bomber Command. Then he would take a trip into a war zone. Having led an irregular life, he would wage an irregular war—vague intimations of danger, but just this side of bloodshed. Excitement, but no hardship. Good publicity for a cause that was not yet our concern.

They meet just outside Stamford, Connecticut. She wears blue and white, no stockings, low-heeled shoes, and they laugh and draw close as they drive alone in a voluptuous silence.

The car stops. They cross an old stone wall where a brook goes tumbling through a golden field. Beyond the woods lies the blur of Long Island Sound.

His tiredness is suddenly gone, though the last sleep he had was thirty-nine hours ago in Missouri. He clears his throat. "I have a plan. This morning I spoke on the phone with Colonel Donovan. He is sending me to England for three months of Commando and parachute training."

"And then?" She draws her knees up under her chin, facing the west.

"Then I'll come back to the States to help train more civilians until we get involved in the war. And then, we might get married. Maybe we could even keep it a secret, for a little while."

"We might." Her voice is only a whisper.

North Atlantic. November 25, 1941. The stage is set for action, but there is only the westerly gale. The convoy straggles eastwards, forty-seven ships in thirty-foot seas, with an escort of five destroyers left over from World War I. The weather is much too bad for U-boats.

A signal hoist flutters aloft from the Commodore's flagship: "Practice Firing." Alarm bells ring and two thousand men grab mitts and cork floats and rubber vests and lurch toward their posts.

He throws his weight into the hook of the tubular back rest, rams a cartridge home, squints with the face of a born fighter down the cold steel barrel, and then lets go with a blast at a cloud. (If they could see me now, Fred and Bing and Bob, glued to a fifty-caliber anti-aircraft gun, bound for Glasgow, on a secret mission . . .)

He stood one night in a bombed-out railway station, lost in the Glasgow blackout. Through torn steel girders, stars looked down. Little knots of people moved through the station, talking in subdued tones, spreading the news. Pearl Harbor. What, he inquired politely, was the matter with Pearl Harbor? He shook his head in the dark. Sad, he thought, that the British were as susceptible to tabloid headlines as Americans. The Japs bomb Pearl Harbor? Preposterous.

The next day, in London, the embassy people had never heard of him, were not expecting him, had no idea what to do with him. The only man who might help was off in Sussex some-

where, and so they gave him some English money and said to
come back in four or five days.

What the hell was going on? He had sacrificed career, security, and the company of his tentative fiancée to assist in the
war, and nobody gave a damn. If only he had taken the *Spinney*
and run her down deep into the South Seas and hauled some
copra and saved some dough and made himself scarce till all
the shooting was over.

He knew, too, that his burlesque days were numbered, for
now that his country found itself in the war there was bound to
come, sooner or later, an end to the leeway he needed to operate
in. (What I'll have to find is some pretext to detach from the
COI. Then I'll simply fade for the duration. I have no business
being here, to begin with. I would not have been involved at all,
had it not been for Tompkins and his dialectical and historical
materialism, and all that crap about the brotherhood of man.
I'm a windjammer man, a wandering windship man and
nothing more—will be until the day I die . . . The only trouble
is Madeleine—can you imagine Madeleine Carroll married to
the captain of a South Seas trading schooner?)

Alone on the moors stood a great stone house, the training
center for a small group of men from the occupied countries.
It was staffed by recently wounded men from the Argyll and
Sutherland Highlanders and commanded by Colonel Edward
G. Young. He was thirty-six years old, square of shoulder, stiff
of back, with great corded red legs under his kilt, and a fierce
pair of eyes.

"Welcome, Hayden, it is good to see an American."

"Thank you, Colonel."

"You have no military background, I am told."

"No sir."

"Are you by chance trained as an engineer?"

"No sir."

"Just what, Mr. Hayden, is your background?"

"Well, sir, I grew up in small sailing vessels in New England
and I went around the world two or three times under sail and
then three years ago I took command of a small brig and delivered her from Boston to Tahiti and—"

"But what have you been doing recently?"

"Well, sir, this is going to sound kind of strange, but a few
years ago Colonel Donovan suggested I go out to the West Coast
and become an actor."

"Go on."

"I guess it had something to do with my being able to use the acting thing as a cover in case we got in the war."

So they told him to train and he trained—a pale tall figure in British battle dress, minus insignia, wearing American hunting boots and no hat—all wrapped in a Hollywood trench coat. He trained with Dutchmen and Poles and Belgians and French and Danes and Norsemen, all of whom had been in combat. All were fighters, with rank and military bearing and the confidence of men who know their job. Most of the staff had been wounded during an abortive raid on German submarine pens not far from Saint-Nazaire. After the day's work in driving rain, this group would assemble in a dark beamed room, warmed by a small coal fire, for the ration of whiskey—two per man—and to learn the news. First the national anthem, and then the announcer's voice: "Good evening. This is the Home and Forces program of the BBC. Here is the news . . ."

And it was always bleak: H.M.S. *Repulse* and *Prince of Wales* sunk in the South China Sea; Luzon invaded by Japan; Wake Island captured by Japan; the fall of Manila; the *Scharnhorst*, *Gneisenau*, and *Prinz Eugen* escape through the Channel from Brest—and the fall of Singapore . . .

More and more he thought of the warm stone house at Portuguese Bend, above the benign Pacific. He thought of the times they had shared, of the wine and laughter, of the carefree evening strolls—and here he was, hostage to an image of heroism, bogged down in talk of death and destruction and intricate preparations for strangling men and blowing up men and sinking ships and turning townships into crematoriums.

(. . . But so long as I'm free, so long as I'm a civilian, I can always get away. Whatever I do, I've got to remain my own boss, I've got to avoid the military. And wait till I get back home. "Well, the fact is, folks, I've been over in Scotland training with some Commandos from the Argyll and Sutherland Highlanders. That's right. What? No, I was the only American there at the time; and then they sent me down to Ringway Field near Manchester, where I made a dozen or so parachute jumps. What's that? Oh, it's quite a sensation all right. No, you don't get used to it . . .)

His big break came in March when he parachuted for the eleventh time from the belly of a Stirling bomber. But this time he landed in a quarry, breaking his ankle, tearing a cartilage loose in the knee, and injuring the base of his spine. They patched him up, gave him crutches that were much too short, and sent him to Liverpool, where he boarded a fast Norwegian freighter bound for New York City. He smiled to himself as he smelled the river and felt it underneath him and saw the barrage balloons strung out down the battered Mersey.

(Things aren't going so well. I used to pride myself on being a man of action, resourceful, strong, and full of drive . . . but now I'm tending more and more to emerge as a sensitive man. You'd almost think I was a poet or an artist.)

She was only three years old, a diesel vessel that banged and volleyed on its zigzag track west. Her skipper was thirty-two years old, with snow-white hair. It had turned one night when he was torpedoed on the run toward Murmansk with a load of high-octane fuel.

They were in mid-Atlantic when it almost happened again. It was just at dusk, with a fiery sunset above a black horizon and with no sea running. The gong ripped and the siren wailed and the skipper dove for the bridge from his place at the head of the table. The steward came in, drew a cup of coffee, sat down, and lit a cigarette. "Now is the time," he said, "I don't envy those poor engineers."

The acting Commando felt his blood congeal. A stroke of terror stunned him. And all at once he knew that the thing he most feared was true. He was yellow. Look at that steward, perfectly relaxed. Maybe he's scared inside—maybe they're all scared inside. Why not? But he was nothing inside but terror. Yellow.

So they sat that smouldering night, with the vessel heeling from port to starboard and back as the white-haired man hurled her into the west, the gun on the stern blazing, while down in the engine room floors and catwalks danced to the beat of a wide-open diesel that tried to burst from its bed.

They were married in a snow-banked lodge by a frozen lake near Peterborough, New Hampshire. A log fire roared, the toasts were made, and the vows were said.

It was dark when they started the drive toward Connecticut. He was full of pride and she slept with her head in his lap. They stopped at a Catholic Church, where she crossed herself and knelt while he bowed his head and waited. (. . . Oh Lord, I just want to make her happy . . .)

The house in Connecticut was his refuge, far from war, far

from Hollywood. It was set snugly in the lee of a shelving hill, under giant elms, near the head of a salt-water harbor. Here they would make their home when they weren't mixed up in the war. He lay with his leg propped up, watching the fire. Too bad, he thought. If it wasn't for what they would think, I would gladly stay here till the war was finished and gone.

CHAPTER 62

Now, where do I go from here? I'm flawed inside and I know it. But why did it have to be me? Why why why why why? Roosevelt was right: we have nothing to fear but fear. Could it be perhaps that this is a trick of fate to compensate for my being tall and strong and good-looking enough to intrigue every girl I meet? Is this a malignancy grafted into my spine to offset the fact that I'm equally at home in a drawing room or a fo'c'sle? If so—what a hell of a price to pay.

(The problem now is to prevent this fear from showing. The fear itself is nothing compared with the threat of being exposed. The challenge now is to devise some way to dance on the coals of war, to give an illusion of a stalwart man on a constant quest of danger.)

When did this fear set in? Isn't it true that I've been living a lie for years? Wasn't I a fo'c'sle dweller who was not a fo'c'sle dweller? A student who was not a student; a doryman unlike any other doryman; a fireman in effect but not in fact; a kid on the road who never was on the road at all? When is an unemployed victim of the depression not a victim at all? . . . Perhaps when his life is a charade. When is an actor not an actor? When the bulk of his acting is done offstage. But, God in hand, how did it all start?

To hell with how and when. What you must do at once is apply for a lieutenant's commission in the Navy. Because of how it will look, because whatever you do is news these days. Just think what the press will say: Hayden returns from secret mission for "Wild Bill" Donovan of the COI. Seeks naval commission. Requests assignment to motor torpedo boats.

The Navy said no, of course, just as you knew they would—

lieutenancies weren't given to men whose education had stopped halfway through tenth grade. You made a big play out of this because you had already wrangled a job in a test crew that rammed PT boats up and down New York harbor. For three weeks you roared around in the waning winter light, safe behind the skirts of the Statue of Liberty. Your friends agreed it was sad that a man with your sea experience should be offered nothing more than an ensign's commission and were full of admiration when you told the Navy to go to hell with their lousy commission. Spring was in the air that day as you rode back and forth on the Staten Island ferries watching the ships go by. You soaked up the harbor magic and you knew so well that the sea was where you belonged, not laced up in some uniform but stripped to the waist in a world of canvas and wire, and never mind the motorboats choked with valves and pistons, because yours was the world of silence and beauty and freedom as a man. You knew it was time to quit the conventional life. That night you took your wife to a tiny café full of foreign sailors. You celebrated with wine when she lent you the money to buy out Paramount's half of the *Spinney*.

It seems strange when I think of the men she might have married. Hard-driving, prominent men full of self-assurance. Attractive men and worldly men with clothes and dollars and business acumen, with vast houses and plush apartments all over the world.

I was vastly intrigued by the thought of hauling freight in wartime in a big black Gloucester schooner, and got an unlimited draft deferment on the logical grounds that a man might do more good packing cargo under the auspices of the War Shipping Administration than packing a rifle. I flew to Hollywood, bought out the ship, placed her in drydock, flew back to New York, and negotiated a contract to carry ninety-five tons of explosives from Port Everglades in Florida to San Juan. I flew to Nassau and signed up a ten-man Bahamian crew.

The passage from California to Panama took twenty-five days. Captain Tory Forstrom, of the Canal Pilots, had a few kind words of advice. "If I were in your shoes, Hayden, I'd go the rest of the way under sail. If you don't turn that goddam diesel on, the U-boats may not know you're around. I hope you're well insured anyway."

I told him the cost of insurance was prohibitive, and he

shrugged and went over the side. I took his advice and we sailed a slow passage of ten days to Miami, where the Navy declared they would requisition the schooner for their own purposes. We argued this out for a time, but it was no use, so I slipped down the channel one night, slid her across the Gulf Stream, and came to anchor in Nassau's Hurricane Hole. Two days later I sold every piece of mechanical equipment in the vessel for ten thousand dollars cash. The crew quit and I rounded up a new one, paying them a hundred per cent bonus.

Madeleine joined me. We checked into a hotel as man and wife for the first time and the so-called secret was dead. Three weeks later we sailed to Port Everglades, where the explosives were waiting. Now the Coast Guard stepped in. I would need, they said, two watertight steel bulkheads and a specially constructed steel case on deck for the stowage of detonators. This was all the excuse I needed to default on the explosives contract. I had long held the Coast Guard in high esteem, but never as highly as now. My sailing-ship luck still held.

We loaded instead 112 tons of general cargo for Curaçao. An additional fifteen tons of rivets and bolts were carried on deck. We drove hard down the Windward Passage, and all went well until we took a white squall in the lee of Cape Dame Marie at the southern tip of Haiti.

She lay down flat and most of the deckload went by the board. I bellowed at the mate to let go the foresheet, but he remained rigid so I belted him to one side and did what I could myself. The squall passed and she gradually came back to her feet. Not a ropeyarn had carried away, and I blessed the shipwrights and riggers who had hung her together twenty years before.

For nineteen days we flogged into a savage head sea with a small gale blowing. The vessel became strained, and began to work heavily. She worked so much I could slide a pencil beneath the timber at the break of her poop when she hung suspended with a third of her hull free of a roaring sea. Then she would plunge into the trough and break the pencil in half.

It was lonely back aft and for the first time I began to read books of essays and history. Like the burst of a tropic dawn, it came to me that there had to be more in life than messing around with schooners. I remembered some of the things that Tompkins had said and I cursed myself for destroying the books he had given me about socialism and the fight for a better world.

As we neared the South American coast, I discovered some-

thing else. My navigation was off. Day after day, no matter how
I reckoned, nothing came out as it should. Then Joe Williams
the cook came aft. He had been with me all along and I had
promised to help him immigrate to the States.

"Skippah," Joe said, "the mate an' the boys is tryin' to pile
this vessel up. They's changin' your course each time you lies
down an' sleeps."

I acted my part with style. Placing a .45 automatic atop the
afterhouse, I called all hands aft. Mule was mate. He had biceps
as big as my thighs and what Joe reported as "the bigges' damn
cock in His Majesty's Crown Colonee." But none of this apparatus
was doing the Mule any good. He trembled all over. "Mule,
what's wrong?" I asked.

He shook his head. "You've been changing the course," I
said. He found his voice after a bit: "Skippah, it's just that out
here the land's too far away from one another. It's just that
me an' the boys don' like the way you been carryin' sail, that's
all, so we change yo' course a wee bit."

I made a speech and tossed the pistol around the way they do
in Westerns, and all the time I kept staring at the Mule. After
that, my navigation improved.

We had been thirty-two days out when the pontoon bridge
at Willemstad swung open and we were towed through to a pic-
turesque berth by a sea-wall street with crooked houses looking
down. The cargo came out wet, and I found myself engaged in
endless consultation with brokers, agents, insurance adjusters,
and customs inspectors. I took great pains to conceal the fact
that the ship was constantly leaking, but expenses were heavy
and I felt all adrift when it came to calculations, administration,
and details.

The United States Marine Corps maintained a small detach-
ment of men in Curaçao to keep the Shell Oil properties free
from sabotage. Six of these men gathered one night in the
Spinney's aftercabin, all of them broke, bored, and tough. I
opened a case of Haig & Haig pinch, sent Joe ashore for the ice,
handed each man a bottle, and we started in to drink.

It might have been three in the morning when the manager
of the Americano Hotel, where we had ended up, tried to evict
my friends. He was kind to me because he knew I had been in
pictures, but the Marines were stubborn, so he called the police.
I threw the manager into the street and they put me in jail
instead.

At ten in the morning my agents bailed me out. I sold them the schooner outright for fourteen thousand dollars and the Marines saw me on board a plane bound for New York.

It was four in the morning when I joined Madeleine in a room at the Beekman Towers Hotel. We had champagne with breakfast on a tiny terrace above the East River, with high-breasted tugs sweeping downstream and the sun rising over Brooklyn. At nine sharp I picked up the phone directory, got the address of the Marine Corps recruiting station, and within the hour I had enlisted for boot training at Parris Island in South Carolina. My image shone brighter than ever.

The fear of failure is fierce where sex is concerned. Each failure you never forget—like the time of the President's ball in Washington, D.C., to do with the March of Dimes. There were parties everywhere, so the Hollywood delegation was kept on the run that night. Wherever we went, there were girls: gorgeous girls daringly dressed; girls of every conceivable combination of coloration of gown and hair and make-up. I was drinking with care that night so as not to proscribe myself, when a voice from nowhere said: "Hayden, I want you to meet the most beautiful babe in the capital of the United States." Then he whispered loud: "She's fabulous, kid. She belongs to a congressman, but he's out West and he's getting old and she's dying to feel a man between her legs, so you're all set, kid, take it from Jock Dinwoodie." He slapped my back and I turned to meet this sweet nepenthean creature. She was everything he said. More. I was taken aback, she seemed so young, so innocent-eyed and soft. We danced away and before a word was said the ogre within spoke up: *will I be all right this time?*

I drank with infinite caution, striving to attain the precise level of intoxication—as determined through endless trial and error. It was late when we reached my suite. She lay on the couch, kicked off her shoes, and asked: "Sterling, have you been wondering about my legs?"

"As a matter of fact, I have."

She did a pirouette on her back with her head toward me while her legs climbed up on the wall and her skirt fell back revealing legs so flawless they seemed to negate themselves. Her stockings were secured by a spidery webbing of coal-black straps that embraced a small pink mound.

I kissed her upside down. "Not so fast," she laughed. I might have explained myself. Please, doll, I might have said, can't you understand that if only we keep on going I can damn well break this barrier that lurks in my mind just now and maybe once this hurdle is cleared there would be no problem again.

She slipped to her feet, took her purse, and vanished into the bedroom. I belted down my drink and fixed another fast. She reappeared taking some pins from her hair. "Is five minutes too long a time to wait?" Her voice was rather low.

"Oh mercy no." I laughed as the door closed and I went for the bar with the walls of the room all plastered with question marks. Drambuie and Scotch I drank, half and half, and I mocked at the questioning ogre because I was still very much prepared. I kept my clothes on till the last minute, knowing full well what might happen once I started to take them off; knowing, too, that the final test would come when I felt her legs give way ever so gently as I forced them apart with fear.

One more drink and I slipped into the bedroom where she lay staring out with large and luminous eyes. Her things were neatly folded and a towel lay on the floor. I could feel it happening now. I went into the bath and tore off the clothes, all wild with sullen anger. I took an ice-cold shower, toweled off a little, and lay down beside her softly. She shivered wildly—and then subsided. "You shouldn't have taken such a cold shower," she said.

"I know."

"You must be tired."

"I am."

"Or maybe you drank too much."

"It seems that way."

She was gone when I woke up.

South with a Bronx platoon. South in a day coach with vomit-stained cushions, sealed windows, and a pair of toilet bowls caked like the bowl of a pipe. Southward-ho and each of seventy recruits has his pint and his comic books and the baggage rack overhead is jammed with sodden bodies. All my life I can say how I thumbed my nose at the Navy, threw away my ship, and exiled myself to boot camp. Scant solace now.

"You! You big guy there in the middle. Take three steps forward!" The sergeant had a southern drawl and a crisp face pierced by pale blue eyes uncomfortably close together. We stood in a brick-lined quadrangle. A squad of men nearby was doing close-order drill to the lash of the voice of a lieutenant. The sergeant circled me twice, whipping his thighs with his swagger stick. "So this is the big-shot actor from Hollywood. Well, Hayden, let me tell you if you think just because you're married to Madeleine Carroll you're going to get special treatment down here, you got another think coming."

"Yes sir."

"Because, Buster, let me tell you, and this goes for the rest of you slobs, beginning now I want you to know the shit's on good." He blew his nose through his hand, unfolded a handkerchief, wiped the snot from one finger, and sauntered away, leaving us to his corporal.

There was, I soon discovered, only one way out. I had to get commissioned, even if it took pull to do it. Fortunately, two men were selected from each recruit platoon and sent to officers' school in Quantico, Virginia. I passed through boot camp, put in three weeks as a drill instructor, then went on to Quantico, where I joined a class of two hundred and seventy recent college graduates. Even here the discipline galled, but if you did what they said, your life was simple enough. It seemed incredible that any man in his right mind could spend his life in the Service.

More annoying than anything was the fact that I was conspicuous. Americans are good at staring. If your face is familiar or your name has been in the press, you are stared at, pointed at, yelled at, laughed at, and whatever you do well is taken for granted while any mistake is a matter for great attention.

I decided that the best way out of my military bind, once I was commissioned, was a set of orders transferring me to Donovan's COI, by then known as the Office of Strategic Services. I pulled strings and Donovan said he would see what he could do. Eighty per cent of my class were ordered out to the Pacific. Only three of us went to the OSS.

Confusion was rife that summer of 1943 in Temporary Building Q., the OSS headquarters hard by the reflecting pool that separated the Washington Monument and the Lincoln Memorial. Here was where businessmen overnight became majors and colonels under the benign auspices of the A.U.S., the Army of the United States, quite a different thing from its parent, the United States Army. Mixed in with the brass was a minute residue of enlisted men and junior officers able and willing to fight.

All the services were represented, and everyone was working up a scheme. Everything shimmered in secrecy, and it was a rare man who knew what his fellows were doing. Brooks Brothers was the unofficial costume-maker while Abercrombie and Fitch functioned as an uptown Quartermaster Corps, supplying air mattresses and sleeping bags and all the paraphernalia so dear to the heart of small boys and civilians turned semi-guerrillas.

After a series of false starts in the direction of China, I was handed an enlisted man from the Navy who was fluent in Greek, telegraphy, and cipher, and we were dispatched to Cairo to harass the enemy.

To complete my metamorphosis and cut my last tie with Hollywood, Madeleine went to court and obtained legal permission for a change of name. Henceforth I was John Hamilton.

The chiefs of the various OSS headquarters overseas had a spectacular talent for living in style. The Cairo villa looked like a bastard version of the Taj Mahal. The high wall around it was pierced by a tall iron gate; there were broad verandahs of inlaid tile and a profusion of shade trees above vast stretches of lawn. A young platoon of servants glided in endless circles, the punkahs revolved overhead, and through a leafy crevasse you could gaze each dawn on a pair of Egyptian girls as they combed each other's hair.

It came as no surprise that not only were we not expected but the colonel commanding had no idea what to tell us to do. I had placed my cap under my left upper arm as I stepped smartly into his presence and stood at rigid attention. He threw me a warped salute and puzzled over my orders. A secretary entered with tea—which made it quite clear that this was a British Theatre of War.

"Haven't I seen you somewhere before?" he asked.

"I don't know, sir."

"Your face is familiar, did you play football in college?"

"No sir, I never went to college."

"Oh." He rummaged around in some files and emerged in triumph with a formidable sheaf of documents. "I suggest, Lieutenant, that you study these Intelligence reports. Familiarize yourself with the situation in Greece. But I warn you, you will find it a most complex situation."

"Yes sir." The papers were stamped Top Secret. Each morning for ten days I reported in, picked up my sheaf, and sat in a tiny office trying to learn what faction in Greece was doing what to whom. All the reports were British.

The colonel was called to Washington for a top-level conference. Weeks passed. I borrowed a jeep from the Motor Pool and cruised alone down to Alexandria, where I promoted a fast cruising sloop from the Royal Egyptian Yacht Club and had myself some sailing.

The colonel flew back. Nothing happened for ten days, then he called me in and said: "Lieutenant Hamilton, may I ask first just why it is you never return my salute?"

"The Marine Corps doesn't salute bareheaded."

"Oh." He smiled. "What did they tell you back at the Q building you were going to do out here?"

"They said something about my getting together a group of escapees from Greece, fitting out a cargo ketch, and running her up through the Greek Islands."

"The British have that all sewn up."

"I see."

"Well, Hamilton, a report has just come in that there is a man named Tito up in Yugoslavia. They say he's a Communist, but apparently he's in control of quite a large guerrilla organization, so why don't you hop up to Bari, Italy, and locate our Major Huot and see whether you can be of some service."

And with what seemed like a sigh of relief, he gave me a fistful of orders.

CHAPTER 63

I remember the man quite well. He was born one afternoon, at the age of twenty-seven, on the east coast of Italy, where the harbor of Bari was scoured by a raw November norther that whined in from the wastes of the Adriatic. Three years later he died in a stucco motel-apartment next to a liquor store at the base of Laurel Canyon, near Schwab's drugstore in West Hollywood.

Brief as this life span was, it transported him to such heights of exultation as perhaps few men know, because he had, before this, been dead for a long time. So great, in fact, was the shock of his awakening that certain seeds were planted which would lead to his undoing, to his eventual self-betrayal. And he was aware of this at the time.

That his awakening shocked him must pass without question now. We are not prepared for such things because we have been cautioned against them, isolated from them and insulated from discoveries that—as he said—can only be likened to an avalanche thundering down from an Everest of truth.

I shall tell what this man went through in the first—or twenty-eighth—year of his life. After that our paths diverged, slowly, so that I never saw him again.

At birth he stood six foot five in his leather jumping boots and weighed close to two hundred and thirty pounds. A British parachute emblem and a small American flag were neatly stitched to the sleeves of his combat jacket. There were also the conventional military insignia, and a .357 Magnum revolver strapped to his leg. His name was John Hamilton and he was a second lieutenant in the United States Marine Corps (Reserve).

Lieutenant Hamilton was baptized down on the Bari docks, where an air raid was in progress. A mob of Italian stevedores ran madly from three Allied freighters moored in a row behind a long breakwater. Sirens wailed as the Heinkles came in low, and the gun crews from Oslo, Boston, and Limehouse pumped tracers over each other's heads with no effect whatever.

There was hardly time to be scared. What's more, we were trapped on the end of a dock, and eighty partisans from Yugoslavia went right on with what they were doing in spite of the commotion, loading ammunition, blankets, and high-octane gas into a pair of wooden schooners. Their base ship, a small old crippled steamer named *Makarska,* stood nearby.

Boss of this operation was a man named Stipanovitch who threw up a captured machine pistol and blazed away at the bombers. "Bloody fucking buggers!" he roared over and over again in a deep voice that boomed through a broad mustache. Shrapnel went whanging through the air, a building inshore became an inferno, and, as a precaution, the partisans began dumping drums of gas in the harbor.

Hamilton wanted to fade. He had started to run toward the lee of a latrine when it dawned on him he had best make an effort to get off on the right foot. He stopped and lit a cigarette. "Hamil-tone!" boomed Stipanovitch, "give to me please one nice cigarette if you will." The lieutenant's lighter flared and he noted with surprise that his hands were perfectly steady. Good Christ! —he thought—I'm not a coward at that! Stipanovitch was yelling: "Some fucking welcome for you, eh Hamiltone?" He turned to a ten-year-old boy with a shy face and only one leg: "Here boy," throwing him the gun, "cool this bugger off."

Hamilton was stunned to discover that almost overnight he had become an integral part of the human race. Never before had he belonged to anything more than a ship. And here he was, still working with schooners, even living afloat on board the 600-ton steamer *Ljubjana*, but now he was working with men whose spirit made anything he'd seen before sophomoric. He thought of the things that Tompkins had said back in San Francisco, all the socialistic pamphlets and booklets that he had read furtively only to become stricken with guilt and burn the offensive trash in some incinerator. And here were alleged Communists, led by an avowed Communist, Tito, who for years had fought with savage tenacity and skill at a time when fighting the Axis was not popular in some of the better places. These same men had fought without the support of Russia or anyone else; had fought in spite of reprisals, had fought through bitter winters high in the mountains, with little clothing, next to no food, and only the arms they could scrape from the backs of their foes. All this time, the "legitimate" Royal Yugoslav Government was settled down in a command post in Claridge's Hotel in far-off London, issuing communiqués as to the efficacy of their man in the field, Colonel Draja Mikhailovitch, and his "Glorious Fighting Chetniks . . ." One thing was plain: there were two sides to every story; and if the OSS, charged with conducting Intelligence operations for the U.S.A., hadn't even heard of Tito until a few weeks ago—they had better find out what was what with the world.

Three days after Hamilton's arrival, he was put in charge of establishing a new partisan base of operations in the quaint old port of Monopoli some thirty miles south of Bari. He had 400 Yugoslavs—fifty of them girls—and a fleet of fourteen schooners, six ketches, and two brigantines; all of them more or less equipped with auxiliary power. To these ships fell the task of running the German blockade across the Adriatic to the partisan island of Vis off the German-held coast of Dalmatia. Their average cruising speed was seven knots. From the nearest point of the Italian coast to Vis was a distance of eighty miles. By plunging through the Allied minefield late of an afternoon a schooner always had a fighting chance of reaching Vis at dawn—barely in time to be backed into a precipitous cove where she could be hastily camouflaged with pine boughs festooned in her rigging, unloaded the following night, the camouflage repeated, and then driven toward Italy as soon as the weather served. A further and much more hazardous journey, undertaken in small fishing boats, would, if all went well, see the supplies landed on lonely ragged beaches flanked by Nazi garrisons. All that then remained was to pack the matériel by burros and men up and into the Dinaric Alps and from there to the various partisan units.

It was a bold clandestine plan, with the Yugoslavs themselves doing most of the dirty work. But that it came off at all was due in large measure to a relentlessly dedicated group of visionaries attached to the OSS. Majors Huot and Coon were there first, but Captain Hans Tofte and Lieutenant Rob Thompson were the ones who cudgeled a conservative British command into releasing stockpiles of captured Italian equipment to the radical Tito.

As the partisan saga unfolded day by day Hamilton found himself committed in a way he had never known before. Night after night he pounded out long letters to people back in the States, to Tompkins in particular, while out on the docks sweating partisan stevedores sang wild Serbian songs. He had never known such men. There was a ferocity about them, not just in the way they looked but in the way they worked, straining and sweating for hours on end, refusing to pause or accept relief until ordered to do so by the giant Randic, who along with Stipanovitch co-ordinated the loading. He told how, when a sack of flour was split, with no command a man would collect what had been spilled and sew up the bag with care.

The Italian garrisons on the Yugoslav mainland and in the captive islands were guilty of outrageous atrocities, inspired perhaps by their legendary failure to match the men in the mountains. Consequently, the natives of Monopoli gave the Yugoslavs a wide berth. Priests and demobilized soldiers in particular found urgent business always, in alleys or behind locked doors, when a pair of partisans came swinging down a street.

Dorcic was a mild man from the island of Cherso. Before the war he had been an accountant, and now he worked mostly as tally clerk of the loading. "My wife," he said in a soft voice, "and my two daughters, and my little boy, were walking down the street on their way to get some water. They passed the Italian barracks and a soldier on the second floor put down his newspaper, picked up an automatic rifle, and killed them each with a burst. My little boy was all curled up and rolling and a truck came along and the driver swerved to run right over him, but he was dead already I think."

A week before Christmas, Hamilton was asked to borrow a hatch cover from an Italian freighter interned in the port. It was raining and they were loading grenades and ammunition into a sixty-foot ketch. The name of the steamer was *Cherso*. He took four men, one of them Dorcic, and went on board and the mate of course said yes. Down on the maindeck an argument broke out between crew and partisans. Dorcic unbuttoned his battle-dress jacket, scratched his chest, dropped his hand, looked aloft in despair, then drew his pistol and killed two men. And all at once he cried.

January 22, 1944

Dear Warwick:

I've just come back from the other side. One advantage of being an officer, by the way, is you censor your own letters. If the British read some of mine they'd have a fit. I told you in earlier letters how reluctant some of the local British are to really go all out for the Yugoslavs. My eyes are being opened to a lot of things and it comes as one hell of a shock to realize I read the truth about Yugoslavia in the stuff you sent me two years ago. By the way, send me more so I can learn what's going on in the rest of the world.

More and more I understand what you felt when you said: "You will one day be able to turn your back on the sea." I know now that my entire life before this was one endless search for pleasure. Well, maybe it isn't too late to make up for the wasted years.

Some time back a high British general paid us an official visit here. I didn't have time to tip off my friend Stipanovitch and the British arrived all decked out with red bands on their sleeves and caps and there were drivers holding car doors open. It was quite a show. In the middle of this up comes S. from the bowels of a schooner all smeared with dirt. He marches up to the brass, stamps his heels, and throws the clenched-fist salute (this is frowned on by the partisans here, by the way). "General," says my friend, "I must ask you the one question. On the Dalmatian coast we have gunboats made from fishing launches with antitank guns made fast on deck. They go almost as fast as eight

knots, some of them. Here in Italia are five once upon a
time Royal Yugoslav motor torpedo boats with armor plat-
ings and hinges and they go the forty knots. Now why, I
ask it of you, why does your command not turn them loose
to us partisan peoples? Why?"

The general smiled as he touched one toe to a stone. "My
dear chap," he says, "there are such things as politics to
be considered, you know."

Stipanovitch exploded: "And I say fook your politics."
And with that he threw his fist to his forehead, whipped
it down to his flank, and marched off. But the PT boats
are still laid up near here (with Italian crews still on board).

Like I said, I have just returned from the far side of this
miserable body of water. They sent me across with my
sergeant to try and lay out a new supply line away to hell
and gone up across from the city full of canals. It was what
you might call one hell of a hairy trip. The first stage was
simple. Then it came on to blow hard out of the north and
cold. They gave me a forty-five-foot craft cut way down
low with half a dozen machine guns (Italian and Bulgarian
for Christ's sake) and ten of the toughest guys you ever
saw. Top speed was seven knots. Armor plate was two
frameworks of boards filled in with rocks and gravel from
some beach. Well, we did our moving at night. Days we
pulled into little overhanging dents in the coast where
we spread the net and hid.

No Allied aircraft dome near this part of the world, so
the Krauts patrol up and down in little training planes
called "Storchs," with wheels hanging down, and when the
pilot sees you he leans over the side and drops little bombs
by hand. Finally, we got to an island with three letters that
I'd better not name, and I made some arrangements and
had the new supply route all mapped out. But the Germans
launched a drive afterwards and occupied all those islands.
So much for that.

On the way back south the water pump let go. We paddled
and drifted into the mainland, said goodbye to the boat,
and took off on foot toward where some friends were
rumored to be. They were too. (By the way, were you
kidding with that stuff about the F.B.I?) (Why would they
read your mail?) Now listen to this if you will:

We hooked up with about thirty of the toughest bastards

on earth. None of them had had a bath in years. All of them
had been in the thick of the fighting and marching all up
and down Bosnia and Croatia. They would only take one
cigarette at a time, which they passed around in circles.
And there we were. Stuck.

Two days later a scout came tearing in with word a
German gunboat made out of a trawler was weatherbound
down the line. No one said a word. They just loaded up two
sorry-looking horses with machine guns and ammo and we
all took off. The boat was about a hundred and twenty feet
long, with gun platforms all over and naval cadets on guard.
She lay in a cove so small she was tied up aft to some trees.
Still nobody gave any orders. These people know combat like
some of us know schooners—excuse me, *used* to know
schooners—

Well, we fanned out on a bluff full of dwarf pines directly
over the vessel. A kid no more than twelve stayed with the
horses and kept stuffing dead grass in their mouths. This
fat bastard comes out on the bridge in his slippers and
yawns and stretches and the fellow in charge of our group
fired at him—and missed. Hell broke loose, of course.

Now I'm not proud of this, but when I looked down that
Springfield's barrel (the one my Uncle Mont Sterling had
given me) and lined up some guy, I couldn't do as I should.
Instead I raised the level and squeezed. Right next to me
was my sergeant, John Harnicker, just as cool as you please,
which is what you get for being a regular Marine. It was all
over quickly, with not one of us even wounded. Some Kraut
held a towel out a porthole and they sent a boat and it made
me sick to see the crew—mostly just fuzzy-faced kids—
some with their faces half shot off and one holding his eye
in his hand, which he kept trying to put back.

A French surgeon was in our band. He had been fighting
for two years and I assume he was maybe a Communist.
He went to work operating on the wounded. He shared his
cigarette with two Germans and in place of anesthetic they
took the butt of a pistol and gave the patients a crack on
the temple which laid them out for a time.

It was rough but they fired up the Bolinders and steamed
offshore to an island jammed with refugees trying to get to
Vis [censored]. I have never in my life seen anything like
these people. They were packed in the hold like slaves in

the good old days. Old women and old men and about two dozen wounded. It was still rough so we battened down the hatch, and I have never smelled anything like that hold that night.

The wind and the sea were fair, which was a damn good thing. I steered half the night and must admit it felt pretty good but we were racing to get to Vis [censored] before the daybreak patrol, which took the edge off the pleasure.

Obviously we made it. What comes next I don't know. I shouldn't say anything about this, but right now three or four of us are under a sort of informal arrest. Beat this one if you can: after our last trip, the OSS learned that twenty or so American nurses had crash-landed in Albania when the pilot missed Italy en route from North Africa (stay on the ground when you can). Well, when the brass in this outfit heard about that they became all fired up— one man in particular, who had just arrived from the States, where he had been credit manager for a chain of restaurants —Sam Golden—does the name mean anything to you?

He called the four of us in and said he was leading a rescue party to look for the girls and this is how we would do it. I should have said we knew this was coming and had all agreed to abide by the word of our spokesman (a man who for two years fought in Burma with Wingate). The major has it all figured out like we were holding up a bank. And when he gets through, our spokesman speaks up: "Major, we knew this was why you called us in and while we will gladly go into Albania we think the operation should be led by a man with combat experience."

"Meaning you?" asked the credit man.

"Yes sir."

Which is why we aren't working right now. It is rumored they're going to break us up. It was great while it lasted. I'm going to try and get dropped inland over there. Yours, SMRT FACIZMU—SLOBODA NARODU

CHAPTER 64

They worked their way north with the sun. Spring was a long time coming to the wild Croatian mountains strung in a wind-torn line.

Everywhere he went violence hung thick on the land, in the lowlands held by Germans and in desolate valleys where the old people lived. They were too old to fight but not too old to be killed, to be raped, to be ground into pulp by the treads of tanks, to be starved and driven from their homes. Often they were herded down rutted roads into open gondola cars, each coupled in front of a locomotive hauling a troop train in order to thwart guerrillas who otherwise would—and did—plant mines where the troop trains rolled.

These human detectors rolled past fields not planted that season, and were cut loose at the top of each downward grade, rolling for miles, with the gun-quilled trains marking time in their wake. The old women clutched their shawls and the hawk-like menfolk gazed out ahead, their arms closed tight on their women and their eyes cold as the eyes of death.

Once he saw a baby. The column in front of him paused, he didn't know why, in the center of a small town. There were three hundred men in all, picked men who for years had borne the brunt of the fighting.

They shuffled forward slowly and came at last to a crossroads where a knot of peasants stood. He saw one woman, not so young, holding a bundle wrapped in a ragged shawl. Men were clustered all about this woman, men he had seen in action maybe three dozen times. Men who had carried comrades fifteen, twenty, thirty miles, barely ever pausing, up endless stony trails, who thought nothing of infiltrating towns to carve SS throats with long thin knives. These men, burned black, lousy, whispered now, bending tenderly down and touching the shawl with horn-fingered hands, making cooing sounds, the sudden tears unheeded, then turned away, wiping their eyes with greasy sleeves, with a clank of battle gear as they got back into column.

Late one afternoon, they reached the Sava River, and the commissar said: "Tonight, Hamiltone, we sleep in a place with fire."

"Okay," smiled the American, knowing they would be lucky if they slept anywhere for more than two hours at a stretch. This was the village where the peasants kept a boat that would ferry them to the far side of the Sava, which meant there was less than a hundred miles to go.

When they smelled the smoke they split two ways—half left, half right—diving fast for cover. One small patrol went forward and found the smell was of burnt-out hovels, of rain-wet embers mixed with charred flesh and bones.

"Ustachi!" The word passed fast through the brush. Dread word. Worse than Nazi, worse than Fascisti, worse than Chetnik even. "Ustachi," the name of treason, of the Croat Nationalist Terror Organization led by the master traitor Ante Pavelic (long afterwards executed by Tito's government, causing an outcry from certain persons in high places in far-off lands, not excepting Rome).

One babbling old man returned with the patrol, the sole survivor, who told that men on horses were pounding through the valley handing out reprisals to those who aided the partisans. Where scant hours earlier three hundred people lived, now nothing remained but ash, and smoke, and chimneys row on row like tombstones. The old man jabbered in the soft warm rain.

They flung together a raft frapped with vines, and when this was done he stood to one side alone and looked at the river passing broad and black through the land. He threw a stick out wide and watched it drift down toward a bend, bound for the distant Danube and thence through the "Iron Gate" to the sea. And all at once he knew that he was beaten, that he was no selfless radical, no reckless humanitarian. He felt like a traitor as they crossed the river and plunged on into the night.

CHAPTER 65

Hamilton returned from Croatia in a B-25 in early July to find his wife had been transferred to the 61st Station Hospital in Foggia, a bombed-out town ninety miles north of Bari. He rested a week, spent one weekend with her, then made several journeys to the Dalmatian Islands, on one of which he was ambushed and almost captured. In August they ordered him to pick out a suitable Italian fishing craft, convert her to a minor-league blockade runner, and begin running across to the environs of Cape Linguetta, on the Albanian coast, with agents and supplies.

It was apparent to those who knew him that Hamilton had changed. He no longer went looking for trouble. And, to top it off, he came down with jaundice so that he was out of commission occasionally. They gave him a room on the top floor of the big apartment building that housed the OSS headquarters.

We talked one day for a long time, sitting in his room that looked out on a great brawling courtyard surrounded by blocks of apartments, all of them bursting with life.

"How goes it?" I asked.

"All right," he said, getting up and looking at himself in the mirror. He didn't look yellow at all. "But I can't seem to shake this goddam thing, feel lousy the moment I get on my feet." He closed the double doors and lay back in a chair.

A battered copy of *Moby Dick* lay by the side of the bed, along with *Progress and Poverty*, by Henry George, and *Fifty South by Fifty South*, written by his friend Tompkins.

"Now I'm going to tell you something," he said. "I'm not sick so much as scared."

"Bull shit."

"No, it's true. You know the last time I was sick? At Parris Island boot camp the winter of '42, just around Christmas, when I had what they called 'cat fever,' waiting to be shipped out, waiting to go out to the Pacific. And before that, the last time I was sick was when I was nine years old, right after my old man died, when they sent me away from home for the first time. What do you make of that?"

"I don't make anything of it."

"And another thing. A funny thing happened after I saw Madeleine and they sent me over to Hvar—"

"You mean the ambush on Korcula?" I asked.

"No, it was over before I knew it, I'm not even sure what happened." He poured some cognac and went on: "This was different. You remember that medieval castle hangs over the town of Hvar itself? Well, we were down at the Jug headquarters in the ravine—had been for about three days—when these Stukas came in, four in a line, strafing and bombing. The only person killed out of ninety partisans and three hundred villagers was a chap whose name I don't recall. He was about twenty-two and he had come to the island that same night after three years' fighting in Bosnia. They said he was one of the great fighters of the Liberation Movement.

"Guerrillas are buried at night, if they're buried at all. So they waited till it was dark and even had a little band. It was pitch black down along the harbor but you could see the castle on top of the hill—what was left of it. The band struck up the dirge, everyone fell in line, and we shuffled up toward the graveyard. The only ones who weren't there were a girl on the switchboard to Stari Grad and a sentry on top of the castle.

"But Jesus you should have heard that music. I swear that, note for note, it was almost the same tune as the Tahitian farewell song *Maururu a Vau*. It started me thinking as we marched along. All I could think of was getting through the war alive and maybe finding a schooner and going back to the sea. I looked up and the castle became that peak above Papeete they call 'Le Diadème,' and the stars became the stars you see in the tropics, and then the music stopped.

"Well, they laid the corpse by the grave and, one by one, three men stepped forward to address this kid who had been killed. Manola was there, Srecko Manola, the toughest partisan I've ever met. He had fought in Spain with the International Brigades and was tortured in Belgrade, and when he pulled off his cap and boomed out *Druge Nikolai* under those stars it gave me the shivers. People around me were sobbing as he told the dead boy that the things he had done would live for a long time. And I stood there, vowing to keep on fighting. But then the band played that dirge again and I thought back to Marguerite and the schooners . . ." He shook his head and poured till the glass spilled over.

"Well, the band stopped and a squad fired two volleys in the air and a shovel clanged and I looked up and there was the moon rising from behind the castle, with the sentry in silhouette. Right then I felt sick as a sonofabitch." He drained his glass, swung to his feet, and threw the doors wide open.

The noise came wallowing in. Across the court, people were eating and drinking, dogs and cats were fighting. Everything was there, charcoal fires, big beds and little beds, curtains billowing out, and kids raising hell on the roof. He stood for a time, then closed the doors and flung himself on to the bed.

"The next day I went up to the castle and I lay in the sun all day, looking out to sea. I thought of the dead kid and the soft, rich sonsabitching people who wallow in food and heat and make big dough out of wars. And I said to myself: 'Hamilton boy, you better wise up. You better calm down while the calming down's good and just take care you come out of this fucking war in one piece.' "

He drank once more and stood with his back to the courtyard with a week's growth of beard and a nicotine stain on his fingers. "That's about it. I came back here and ever since then I've been sick. Off and on, that is."

After that he took the fishing boat, which he'd renamed *Yankee,* down the coast to the tiny port of Otranto at the outermost tip of the heel of Italy's boot. He had a pilot named Voyeslav Ivosevitch, the big Marine sergeant, Harnicker, eight Yugoslav seamen-gunners, and a cook called "Tony" who had been butler to Gene Tunney.

They shipped him home in November, out of Naples, in a troop transport. His wife stayed behind in Foggia.

CHAPTER 66

Thirty days leave they gave him, thirty solid days—never mind the nights. After all, he was married, and there was his wife doing her bit in bombed-out Foggia. The city did something to him. It was like a grenade when you pulled the pin and threw it away, but he'd stay on his feet this time. There was something down at the Colonel's Shelter in Temporary Q. about sending him out to the Pacific. He'd see about that.

Just now he hurried himself through Grand Central Station toward Track 23 and the commutation train that would take him to where his duty lay. I must be good this time. I shall make a genuine effort to make up for letters not written, birthdays ignored, and Mother's Days damned.

Her new car was waiting under the lights of the Darien depot.

"*Well*, Buzz, how good to see you, my dear."

"You too, Mother." Connecticut seemed like an advertisement

come true, twinkling Christmas lights, sedate old houses, fine new homes. Everything felt incredibly safe. No snow either. He never wanted to see another flake of snow.

She lived in the house that he and his wife had rented. He went into the bedroom, took a bottle out of the grip, glanced at the big bed, then fixed himself a drink.

He came down to find her in front of the fire. Vases were choked with flowers and ivy spun webs in the southern windows. "Now Buzz, stand still and let me look at you." They looked at each other.

Next the ceremonial feeding, the gingerbread tit, the ancient guilt-ridden dependence. She passed him a plate filled with cubes of molasses cake. He took one and polished off his drink. "Now sit down," she said, "and tell me all about it."

"All about what, Mother?"

"About what you did in the war."

"Mother, didn't you get my letters?"

She ruffled like an angry gray penguin. "Hah, I certainly did *not*." He made another drink, rejecting her gingerbread breast. "Oh Buzz, I'm so sorry to see you're still drinking."

The glacier within him was cracking. Chunks of guilt-hate broke adrift, plunged into the sea of his mind and nuzzled around, six parts submerged . . . I've got to get hold of myself. No more booze. Make the effort just this once. Laugh and joke and talk to her.

He looked at the magazines. They were laid out on a table, lined up like a general's decorations. *Good Housekeeping, Ladies Home Companion, Reader's Digest, Better Homes and Gardens, Fortune, Time* and *Life*. She advanced with her next offering, hopeless and undaunted: "I bought this, son, just for you." It was a copy of *Yachting* magazine.

Defeated, he flung himself erect and went for another drink.

"Fasten your seat belts, please," said a voice that brought him awake. He was in a DC-3. His seat belt was fastened. His mouth felt lousy and there was snow down below. Jesus, he thought, what in hell goes on? "Good morning, Lieutenant Hamilton, how do you feel this morning?" This stewardess was male. "Say Jack, where in hell are we?"

"We're coming into Bangor."

"Bangor?"

"That's right, Lieutenant, Bangor Maine."

Good god, he thought, I must have called Linc Colcord.

The town of Searsport hadn't changed. Perhaps the only enemy New England knows is change. Beyond the library windows lay the snow and then the gun-metal bay, white clouds flying above the distant islands.

There was hot buttered rum to spare. We talked of ships for a time. Old ships always, long-gone, sunken, dismasted, and ships that were still alive but withering. Too much ship-talk makes a man grow restless.

It was Linc who changed the subject. "I don't mind telling you, Sterling, you had me worried there for a time with your letters full of this socialistic nonsense."

"There was more to it than that."

"Of course there was. But I know you pretty well. I know you're inclined to be headstrong, inclined to jump in with both feet without thinking things through."

I smiled, looking around at this room so full of the sea: sea books, sea pictures, carved name boards, and charts and pamphlets, and I knew there was more sea here than in all the ships afloat. Maybe that's the way it had always been: romance went with dreams. I found myself thinking of Tompkins out in Sausalito. Things weren't going the way I had expected. Maybe it was the rum. Maybe so long as I kept on getting loaded I'd never have a chance, because the rum unleashed a flood of non-sea thoughts, of desires to join in the common cause and do something about changing the world a little.

It griped me that Colcord had no interest in the partisans, even when I told him stories that were, I thought, a nice blend of maritime adventure and social comment. Like the night I took the converted fishing boat and ran her across to Albania, where thirty Italians were holed up in a deep cave. They had been on the march for over a year, hiding out in the mountains of Greece, trying desperately to make their way to Italy. That was the night an E-boat went by offshore as we lay in the cove. I had agreed to carry the Italians back to Otranto, but I reckoned without my pilot, Ivosevitch. He took a Thompson gun ashore with the rubber boat, and then I heard the firing. He came back on board alone. "We go!" he had cried. All the Italians were dead. I didn't know what to say to this man whose wife had been raped to death.

It is late now and the rum has sole command and Linc is saying: "Well, Sterling, it bothers me that you're still a radical.

And I know what you're thinking too. You're thinking I'm an old fogy who doesn't know what's going on."

"You're not far off."

"Well, let me tell you something: I went through my socialistic period in my late twenties, and it lasted a damn sight longer with me than it will with you. This whole thing is nonsense. You wouldn't last ten days in a totalitarian state. Get through the war and then get yourself a schooner. Go down into the West Indies and set up in a charter business. You'll do well."

"I'm not sure I'd last there either, not any more."

"For God's sakes, why not?"

"Because all my life I've escaped. Now I'd like to take a hand in things."

"Oh balls!" I notice he has two cigarettes going, which makes him drunker than I am. "What we have in this country is *freedom*. What would happen in your Communist world if two men talked like this?" He swings around and, very slowly, draws the edge of a finger across his throat.

I shrug and get to my feet. The clock on the mantel shows midnight, a good time to call the coast. After Linc turns in, I'll put in a call to Tompkins—just to make sure he's there.

Sausalito seemed the fairest place on earth, a kingdom of sunshine with just enough of the sea, held at a good safe distance by hills.

At the outset I was dismayed to find myself lionized. My letters to Tompkins, it seemed, had been circulated among many of his friends. The *Wander Bird* lay in the same old berth, stripped now of canvas and gear, landbound.

Night after night the people gathered. They came from the Bay counties and from as far south as the Big Sur. There was quiet music with supper on deck and later a fire of driftwood in a Franklin stove. Through the big open windows one could see the ferries passing and freighters maneuvering out by the quarantine anchorage.

I stopped drinking and tried to give up smoking. A feeling of change began to envelop me. I saw myself in a different light: the future was taking shape, and it was filled with promise. The only trouble was, when these discussions veered from my personal experience I knew again the old sensation of sweeping ignorance. It was no accident, I realized, that the talk was pretty much confined to the Balkans.

The days passed quickly, and I knew it was time to get back east and do something about my immediate future. But meanwhile a long-range plan developed. "Just think," someone had said, "what would happen if you went back to Hollywood. There's nothing so wrong with being a picture star. You could go around the country in between films. You could talk to kids in schools, not about socialism because you don't know much about it, but about the questions that have been troubling you. You wouldn't be lecturing people, you'd be sharing some of the central problems of your life. And that means their lives, too."

"You see, Hayden," someone else broke in, "you happen to be lucky. People are drawn to you. Tomorrow morning you could borrow some clothes and go to work on the docks, or as a seaman, or as a fisherman. You would, with a ten-day beard, pass as a hobo. And tomorrow night you could be accepted in the Pacific Union Club by the shipowners, go into any Legation in town, or to any dinner party on Nob Hill."

"Also," Warwick said, "you can write and you can talk—once you loosen up. Of course, most people in the United States don't read. In a city like New York, two hundred and fifty thousand people read the *Times* and two million look at the *Mirror*. But you can reach the big audience, too."

"I'm no Cooper or Gable or Flynn. All I've done is a couple of pretty pictures."

"But the war won't last forever. By the way, what comes next, where do you go once your leave is over?" Warwick clasped one knee and looked about at his friends, obviously pleased that this troubled guest from overseas was coming to grips with himself.

"Well," I began, "while I was in Bosnia I ran across a partisan colonel who was a courier between Tito and the Loyalist underground in Spain. He said it was odd that the Americans had no liaison of any sort with these guerrillas while the British had. So when I leave here I'm going to Washington to pull a few strings to get myself sent into Spain." I paused and then looked up.

It was getting late. It had been a good evening, and I felt that all these people were friends, that they were impressed by some of the things I had told them . . . What I had not told them was that the Spanish business, courier and all, wasn't true. But I was rather proud of my lie. It was like a novel, and, besides, the long-term dream was an attractive one. (He would, once the war was over, return to Hollywood, claw his way to the top, and become the only actor out there whose stardom was justified.)

With ten days of leave remaining, he checked into a suite in Washington's Carlton Hotel. It was the nineteenth of January, 1945. His new sense of purpose was strong, and he systematically contacted all his and his wife's friends who might possibly be of service.

A few days later he met with Mr. Wallace, the Vice-President, who did not seem much impressed by the Spanish tapestry he was trying to weave. He needed more facts, and more documentation. One morning he picked up the phone and put in a long-distance call to the foreign editor of the *Daily Worker* in New York: "May I speak with Mr. North, please."

"Who is calling?" said the voice on the other end.

"Captain John Hamilton of the Marine Corps."

"Would you repeat that, please."

"This is Captain John Hamilton of the Marine Corps. I have just returned from a year with the Yugoslav partisans and I would like to speak with Mr. North."

There was a considerable span of silence. Mr. North was not in the office, so Hamilton spoke with an assistant. He presented his credentials, using prominent Yugoslav names and those of some men he had known on the Coast.

Several days later two men met for lunch in the Golden Eagle Café on West Twelfth Street in Manhattan, just off Fifth Avenue. One was a Marine and the other Mr. V. J. Jerome. The officer did ninety per cent of the talking, explaining his interest in the Spanish underground—his underground, trying to elicit some information that might buttress his case. Jerome was totally noncommittal. The captain might as well have been a banker from Boothbay, Maine.

Two nights later the captain dined at the White House with Mrs. Franklin D. Roosevelt and a man named Creekmore Fath, who worked for Mr. Wallace. Not until the dinner was nearly over did he get to tell his story. He felt acutely uncomfortable, but having come this far, he couldn't back out. Mrs. Roosevelt had no suggestions.

They shipped him out on the second of February. He was bound for Paris and thence to Germany to join an OSS unit attached to the Intelligence section of the United States First Army.

There was one consolation; his wife had been transferred to France, where she was assigned to a hospital train somewhere between Dijon and Paris. And there was the promise held by the future.

CHAPTER 67

By the time he reached Paris all of his gall was gone. They endorsed his orders and shunted him up toward Belgium, where the First Army lay coiled in the Ardennes Forest, licking its wounds, counting its dead, grateful to God and armor that the Battle of the Bulge was past.

The jeep was driven by a man who was far from home. "Captain," he said, "if you don't object to the question, haven't I seen you before?"

"Not that I can recall," said the officer. It was cold, colder by far than Maine. Maybe, he thought, when I get near combat my circulation slows down. "Captain, if you don't object to the question, is that there a German soldier suit you have on?"

"I'm a Marine."

The driver whistled. "A United States Marine? Man, you must be lost or something."

Colonel B. A. Dixon was the G-2 of the First Army. We met late one night in his office-trailer outside the Belgian town of Spa. Three or four of his staff were ranged around on the floor. A bottle of cognac stood on a table, and the place was wreathed in smoke. The colonel glanced at my orders. "I don't mean to be impertinent, but what in hell is a Marine captain doing up here tonight?"

"Well, sir, I—"

"Ah ah—" He raised one hand. "Don't tell me. You're OSS—ten thousand dollars says you're one of Donovan's beagles. Right?"

I said he was right.

"Well, if you're looking for Hitler, he's not here."

Everybody laughed, and they gave me a shot of the liquor.
The colonel seemed relaxed. "Gentlemen, I am going to tell you
about the OSS. The OSS is the most fantastic damned organization in all of our armed forces. Its people do incredible things.
They seduce German spies; they parachute into Sicily one day
and two days later they're dancing on the St. Regis roof. They
dynamite aqueducts, urinate in Luftwaffe gas tanks, and play
games with I.G. Farben and Krupp, but—" he paused and threw
up his hands, "ninety per cent of this has not a goddamned
thing to do with the war."

When the laughter died down, he turned to one of his men.
"Stone, when you leave here, why don't you escort this gentleman up to the OSS house on the hill. And Hamilton, when you
get tired being mysterious, come back and we'll put you to work."

For three and a half years I had managed to sidestep the war.
War in the sense it is known only to the man in the line who
fights—with no real knowledge of why it has to be, no com-
mitment beyond his conditioned response to military discipline
and love of country. That and the lack of any practical alternative.

The horror of war was finally clear as it swallowed men
whole, rejected their identities, dulled their senses, lashed them
with terror, then spewed them into this raid or that patrol, any
time of the day or night.

Now I could benefit by my Yugoslav adventure (to give it
its proper name) for the social and political orientation it gave
me. It seemed only natural that men should understand why they
were fighting just as they were made to understand how to
handle weapons. The average citizen hated military service,
not so much because of the dislocation of his life and the
sacrifice it involved, but simply because suddenly he was booted
about, ordered around, and slammed up into the line because
"they" said so.

I recalled the partisan procedure, which saw to it that every
combat unit, from the squad on up, had its political commissar,
who shared command and who made sure that before twenty
men with a rusted rifle apiece attacked an armored column, they
knew what they were fighting and why. The average G.I. had
more ignorance to overcome than any other fighting man
on earth. That he was able to was a monumental achievement.

Me? I was different. I hung back where the food was hot and the birds still lived in the trees, and I slept at night in a room. (The distance from the front to army headquarters cannot be measured in miles. The two are light-years apart.)

In response to Dixon's suggestion, I went to work with the political Intelligence section of his headquarters. The officer in charge was Major Shep Stone, who assigned to me six technical sergeants who spoke perfect German, and ordered us to forage around in the wake of the combat men in quest of anti-Nazis—genuine anti-Nazis.

Naturally, as the gas-green carpet of the Wehrmacht was peeled back bit by bit there came squirming into the light millions of anti-Nazis. It was tough, they said, waving their handkerchiefs and wringing their hands with joy, to have lived under Hitler. But, only the night before, they had heated the water that would quickly yield this democratic douche.

The real anti-Nazis were dead, or in exile, or in Belsen, Auschwitz, Buchenwald. Names, we thought at the time, that would teach us all a lesson we'd never forget.

There must have been anti-Nazis along the road from Cologne to Marburg where our forward progress stopped. I'm sure there were. We simply couldn't find them—except for a handful of Communists involved with the labor movement in big industrial centers like Düsseldorf and Essen.

We were in Marburg when President Roosevelt died. Sam Knoll, one of the sergeants, came in with the news. He cried while he read the dispatch. I thought of Greenwich and the coupon country around Brookline, Sewickley, and all the Bel Airs and Hamptons. I thought of a club car called "The Assassination Special . . ." "There will," I said to Sam, "be a high old time tonight in some circles."

In June/July, the OSS ordered me to "proceed to 53 ports as designated, in Germany, Denmark and Norway, and make a photographic survey of bomb damage, port facilities, and so forth." Why?—I had asked—Are we getting ready for the third world war? But the colonel had no sense of humor.

I had a small team of men and we scoured Germany from Wilhemshaven to Lubeck and then passed lightly over the other two countries. I had a German Ford with a box on the back big enough to hold a bicycle, sleeping bags, and other gear. It was big enough, too, to accommodate a fair-haired girl who needed to be smuggled through Sweden—from Oslo to Copenhagen. She never did say just why she needed smuggling.

With the war in Europe over, I saw Madeleine briefly in September. She had taken an apartment in Paris and spoke longingly of remaining in Europe for several years. And we knew, without knowing why, without much discussion, that the marriage had dissolved. All that remained was the need to petition a court to recognize this fact.

We agreed I would get the divorce in Reno. That was my only certainty. Afterwards there was only fatigue and an ocean languor. I found myself thinking of a big steel schooner forlorn and neglected near the head of the Schleswig Fjord.

The day we said goodbye I had driven slowly down toward the Ile St. Louis with a truck full of rations. It was three months since we had seen one another.

Oddly enough, I didn't feel sad. When you can't love properly, you can't be properly sad. I brushed this thought to one side. Very well, I would drop off the rations and go. And keep on going.

The rations stood in the hall. I was breathing hard. Our eyes remained averted. "Thank you," she said.

"Oh, that's quite all right"—one hand on the door.

"Would you," she asked, "before you leave—have just one glass of sherry?"

"Well, yes—thank you." Our eyes met. The living room was cool, and beyond the balcony was Notre Dame. A barge was passing upstream, with a woman who bustled about, taking in her laundry. Smoke curled from the copper stovepipe, the windows were full of flowers, and a man stood with his back to the sun, puffing on his pipe. I wondered what it was like— having a home and a job.

We drank . . . The first time I tasted sherry was at the big house in Portuguese Bend.

After a few sips and a few inconsequent words, there was a knock. Madeleine shrugged and I watched her move down the hall, then I belted myself from the bottle.

The visitor, a man, asked for Hamilton. It was Captain Georges Dekaris, the French surgeon I had first met on the coast of Dalmatia when we captured the German gunboat. He had heard I was in Paris, and had been on my trail for a week.

This was the excuse I needed, the crutch that would take me away.

"My wife," I explained, "is busy. I was just leaving. We will dine together, non?"

He was slightly befuddled by this, and his eyebrows arched. "*Mais oui.*" He kissed her hand goodbye. I did the same and we went.

BOOK V

ABYSMAL VOYAGE

CHAPTER 68

Grass, like a moss-green beard, clung to the links of the *Wanderer*'s anchor chain. It was July and the Bastille Day celebration drew swarms of tourists down on the lazy island. Four months had gone by since he stood to the wheel of his ship and swung her across the lagoon. What had he done with his time? One story had been written, dispatched, and rejected. False starts had been made on the book with the title (tentative, of course) *The Abysmal Voyage*. After the false starts, a handful of chapters in rough draft—maybe sixty pages in all—fragments really, no part of an organized plan. Like the idea of joining up with the Spanish underground.

So the days dribbled by, and his mind, like a radar screen, described endless circles scanning an empty horizon. With a careless eye half-closed, he sometimes looked to his purse. And when his money was gone, what next? He hadn't the faintest idea.

Always he wandered about the island, searching for distraction. A waterfall here, a village there, or an islet slung in a stream. He found himself drawn to a long low stretch of land extending for about a mile from the foot of the mountains, wooded with coconut palms, and crossed by a river which, emerging from the Tuauru Valley, emptied gently into the sea, not far from Venus Point.

East of the lighthouse, perhaps two hundred yards away, on a rolling sand dune abundantly shaded by palms, lay a small thatched hut. Two men lived here, and two girls. All were painters. One of the men was from Marseilles, the other from Corsica. The Frenchman had lived there for nine years. They had no clothes to speak of, no car of course, not even a bicycle. A well provided water; the trees provided milk; and the reef provided almost all their food.

And I sat there sometimes, watching them work, sharing their bad red wine, smoking, thinking, wondering what the source of their simplicity was. These were men who lived as I dreamed of living. They did not protest against the state of the world (and in this I felt superior)—they simply retired from it, seeming quite at peace with themselves. I felt like a charlatan. I was just as much of an outcast here as I'd been in Beverly Hills. And I thought of the words of Turnley Walker: ". . . the bleakness was always a part of you . . . you were an exile here as well . . ." One afternoon the Frenchman, Jean Masson, said: "Our peace will not last much longer. The big planes now come. The Fête of the Bastille is a tourist carnival. And I have heard it said this week that next year Hollywood will come to Tahiti to film once again the story of the mutiny on the *Bounty*. Soon I think I must move." He paused, surveyed his canvas, and sipped his wine.

"Go where?" I asked.

"I do not know. MoORéa is building hotels. Tautira is building hotels. Perhaps I will go to the Marquesas or Tuamotu or to Mangareva." He raised his brows, dragged on his cigarette, and picked up his brushes.

Later that afternoon I was cycling slowly toward Papeete, lost in thought, when I suddenly remembered another scene on another beach in another world.

. . . It is 1955, or '56, or maybe '54. The beach is Laguna, fifty billboard-lined miles south of Los Angeles. We're making a feature picture, cheap and fast, out of sex and violent action, improvising as we go to make up for a script (co-written by the director) with shopworn scenes, bad dialogue, and weak characterization. They call it *The Come On*.

It is late afternoon. Sixty people hover about the camera, which stands with its legs in the sand, under an umbrella. Parked close by is a shiny aluminum dressing room shared by Russell Birdwell (a famed Hollywood press agent, recently turned director), and the female star of the picture, Miss Anne Baxter (the two just now are friends). My trailer (an older model) stands alone on top of the hill, two hundred yards from the beach, in the middle of a housing development.

To the south, in the distance, one can see a vertical headland known as Dana Point. If you narrow your eyes, there on the clifftop, through a century of history, you can also see the man named Richard Henry Dana hard at work scaling dried hides toward the beach below. A whaleboat rides in the surf, and riding offshore is the brig *Pilgrim,* loading the cargo that will take her to Boston and, thanks to Dana, into immortality.

"All righty, boys and girls, we're ready to go. Call Miss Baxter, please. Call Mr. Birdwell. We're going to try it again." The assistant director has spoken. "Mr. Hayden . . ." He cups his hands: "Mr. Hayden! Places, please!"

Miss Baxter appears in a one-piece bathing suit, all white, except around the edges, where the make-up has worn off. I'm supposed to be forty per cent beachcomber, five per cent commercial fisherman, five per cent gunfighter, and fifty per cent lover. According to the script, Miss Baxter is a thrush who sings in a Mexican night club and drives men mad with lust. We've been having a hairy time with a robbery and a cache of gold— or maybe that was a picture I did before. In this scene we've slipped the cops, stripped down about as far as the censors allow, for a little hanky-panky on the beach.

"Stand by," snaps the Bird from his folding chair. I toss my shirt to Sid, the wardrobe man, who has a big cigar and a big belly, even bigger than mine. I wonder about my words—once we're snuggled down in the sand—they don't come. The hell with it, they will in a minute. Miss Baxter always knows her words, maybe because she has money invested in the show.

"All-l-l right. Go!" Hand in hand we frolic along the beach, smiling, smiling. She tosses her head and ruffles her hair, and she walks on tiptoes to make her ankles look smaller. I'm thinking about my lines. As we come abreast of the camera, I say: "Let me look at you." We pause and she looks, which brings her face to face with the lens. We sashay on, the camera following after, going over to our pleasant niche in the sand marked by a preplanted coconut (courtesy of Hollywood Marine Rentals).

I flop in the sand and cradle my tits in my arms. She takes her time. Down first to her knees, like a camel about to be mounted. She subsides, and raising one knee, arches her back. (When I'm working in "quickies," my eyes do double-duty: half the time I look where I please.)

Flat on her back she goes, automatically adjusting her legs to the best camera angle. Some of the men in the crew saunter innocently sideways toward the place where the view is best. The Bird has his eye on these, they'll pick up their checks tonight. She tickles my arm and I smile, wondering who speaks first. She does, and when she stops I start, rattling out words that make the dialogue director frown and scratch his head. The hell with it, I'm close enough, and besides it's getting late and they're running out of light. So long as I don't lose myself altogether, they'll let the scene run on.

We're out of words and I'm wondering whether it's me. Archie the First Assistant kneels in my line of vision and gives his fingers a silent snap, as though he were rolling dice. Aha, now is the time for the kiss. I bend to my work, wondering how the Bird feels . . . It lasts a long time, and gives me a chance to rehearse the rest of the scene.

"Laura!!" A voice rings down the beach. Here we go. I shield her with my body and manfully turn toward the setting sun, and there stands a woeful sight, a wounded character actor. He clutches a prop-shop .45 and it's all he can do to walk. I palm my plastic capsule, bloated with chocolate syrup, a little more carefully. He advances remorselessly, and I keep my chest thrown out while I get ready to jump him. I begin to count to ten. He's a little late, I'm going to reach ten before he gets to his palm tree—the poor bastard has to die hanging on to that palm tree . . . Screw it, I'll go to twelve.

And now like a hero I lunge, the gun goes off, I clap the capsule to my chest and fall backwards, taking pains not to kick sand in the face of Miss Baxter. I try to rise to protect her, but mine is a horrible wound and I fall back. My syrup looks pretty good. I gasp and heave, my eyes fixed on the upper rim of the lens shade (once, years ago, I crossed my eyes in a scene like this, and the producer never forgave me).

The end is near, and with lips compressed, I turn toward the character actor who's about to die. No rush though; the gun droops, then the head (all good actors die slowly). He keeps clutching his tree.

"Christ!" shouts the Bird. "Hurry up and die!" And the actor goes out like a light. Now, I think, we're almost home. If I can heft this thrush up into my arms, we'll make it.

"Father!" she cries. Then she faints. I look around in despair. The sun is kissing the horizon (if I were a navigator tonight, I would get me an amplitude). I pick her up and stagger off down the beach, toward the sun. It's time for a drink.

"All righty, boys and girls." Archie is all smiles, homeward bound. "That's a wrap! We're moving into the studio for the rest of the picture—thank God—tomorrow morning. Nine sharp: Stage 16: Scene 145: the seduction scene in the graveyard. Nighty night, now."

Later, music drifts from the shiny trailer. Men are hard at work, dragging the palms, bottoms first, across the beach toward a truck. Pronged antennas guard the brow of the hill. I climb to my dressing room and turn to look at the sea, where, only a blur in the distance, I see the brig *Pilgrim*, standing offshore for the night.

CHAPTER 69

Reno, that day in '46, lay ill-concealed under an icing of snow. I drove up from the eastern slopes full of resolve and moved my things into a rooming house next to the public library. "Oh yes, Mister, things is nice and quiet here. Yes, Mister, you can set up all night if you please, ain't nobody else on this floor— least not at nights they ain't. No sir, Mister, I don't know whether folks from out of town can take out books from the library—ain't ever been asked *that* question." She gave me a queer look as I dusted off my books and ranged them on the mantel—Nietzsche and Marx and Whitman; Lenin and Rousseau and Veblen; and H. G. Wells and Dos Passos and Tom Paine—Voltaire and Debs and Dickens.

These next six weeks would amount to a prison sentence. But haven't most great men done valuable work in prison? I would make the most of this time, letting it serve as a springboard to the task that lay ahead. I would keep such hours as the partisans kept in their war against Fascism. From sunset to sunrise—work. From dawn till midday—rest. From noon till dusk I would take long walks in the fields or in the nearby mountains.

I had given up smoking and drinking on the day, two weeks before, that I signed the new deal with Paramount. Quite some deal it was: fifteen hundred dollars a week the first year, two thousand a week the next—guaranteed four months off each year from June through September—time for a lecture tour . . . "Hey Sterlin', so you came back, eh? Thought you were through with pictures."

"Yeah, boys, I'm back all right."

"Why Sterlin', what made you change your mind?"

"Well now, boys, I'll tell you. I'm a little concerned with the way the world is going. It occurs to me I might be of some use in the fight that lies ahead—"

"S'cuse me, Sterlin', what's this fight we're due for?"

"What I'm talking about is the fight against Fascism—the chance we all have to be of some service instead of—"

"Jumping Jesus, boys, what's got into this guy? Sterlin' now, what's with you?"

Only ten days of my new regime passed before I found myself in a sprawling ranch house with cowhide chairs, cowhide lampshades, with longhorns pegged to the walls and spiked to the fieldstone fireplace and spread on the belt buckles of a genial host who said he was "Lonesome Jack."

"Come out an' stay at my joint, Hayden," Jack had said in a bar. "I got a dude of a place with five bedrooms, six baths, a coupla thousand acres, twelve quarter horses, and no friends I can call my own."

A Filipino houseboy was serving drinks in great wide glasses embossed with Longhorn heads. A blonde bunny-girl stood on the raised hearth with her pelvis nicely silhouetted against the fire. "Ooh," she giggled, "it's so nice and snuggly here." Jack came in wearing a cowboy outfit. "Jack," said his blonde, "you are just too cute for words." Jack had eighty-seven cowboy suits, complete with matching boots and gloves, and changed costumes at least five times a day.

My girl seemed out of place. We sat on a cowhide couch holding hands for comfort. We had met in a snowstorm at nine thousand feet where I was trying to learn to ski. She had a kindly hesitant face and an almost flawless figure. She neither smoked nor drank; she sipped her whiskey and cigarettes. Her heart and lungs were pure. It was some consolation to me that, even though I had reneged on my firm resolve, at least I had picked a girl who was pure.

So pure that she left at an early hour. Jack had passed out on one of his cowhide couches. The blonde was feeling no pain as she warmed his hand between her legs and ran her finger-mouse up his pants on a zigzag course to go "Gootchee gootchee gootchee" under his chin.

Giving the blonde a wide berth, I slipped out the back door, bundled up in my sheepskin coat, cracked a bottle of aquavit, and sat in a barber chair set out on a boulder square in the middle of the tumbling Truckee River.

The night was alive with stars. They crumpled and blazed as I tucked myself in the chair, swiveled facing west, lit my thirtieth smoke of the day, and peered into the future. I was coming adrift inside. Already I regretted returning to Holly-wood. The aquavit rippled down and the icy river roared. A motor gunned and the blonde zoomed off in one of Jack's Cadillacs.

Everything was going or gone: marriage, war, my militant future going. A big boy full of busted resolves and shattered resolutions. A bureau drawer full of odds and ends, letters from Tompkins, letters from Mother, letters from Colcord, and letters from comrades in distant Yugoslavia: an honorable discharge (what else?) and a citation from Tito's government and a Silver Star.

Was there another man on earth with a Silver Star who didn't know why he had it? Maybe it was for "Quitting with Valor": quitting the COI; quitting a naval commission; quitting the *Spinney;* quitting the ranks of enlisted men; quitting the Marine Corps and switching to the OSS, then switching from OSS–Bari to OSS–First Army . . . Quitting the sea and the films and the ranks of the men who fight for principles; then walking from Madeleine's arms into the cold embrace of Paramount. And what would I do when they wound me up and pointed me into the cameras? Would the nervousness still crawl?

What did I care for labor? For racial discrimination? For civil liberties and the war between the classes? Oh, I cared in my own fashion. I cared just enough to embrace these things as props, flailing away night after night at semi-drunken parties.

Something was terribly wrong. How much longer could I run? I bowed down and sluiced my face with water, killed the bottle and lofted it into the night. Then I cranked the chair back and lay looking up at the stars. And I understood why it is that some men pray: for all the good it does.

❧

CHAPTER 70

A black warm fragrant room. My watch shows five forty-five. I stare up, trying to remember, but everything is vague. No hard edges.

Where in hell am I? The bed feels unfamiliar. My head hurts a little. Moist warm hair is splayed on a dim face beside me. I ease myself erect and toward a crack of light. Steady now. The door gives way, creaking. My clothes lie flung around in a mess of empty glasses, choked-up ash trays, and red lace underthings. A bird in a cage looks on. I dress fast. One wall is covered with photos, all of the same girl: tall—well built—with long black hair. My keys and wallet are safe. I look at the phone—no number. I look at a magazine and find her name, address—at least I'm in West Hollywood. Exit softly and search for the pickup truck. It is parked two blocks away, far from the curb. There is a ticket beneath the windshield wiper, made out to John Hamilton.

It is early in June and my home is a dressing room at Paramount Pictures, 5451 Marathon Street, Hollywood 46. I have $13,000 in the Melrose branch of the Bank of America. I call myself a "progressive." I am one of Paramount's stars. I drive south until I see the ocean lying green offshore, swollen under the mustard sky. A signboard says: SLOW DOWN   ENTERING NEWPORT BEACH.

I am not so sleepy now, but my mouth feels caked, and my eyes too. Today I shall go on the wagon again. I think of that dough in the bank, sitting there, doing no one any good. So invest it, buy a boat. Why not? You're in bad shape. You need a stabilizer, not dames, pills, or booze. You need a ship for a home.

And so all the morning I prowl the bay. Thousands of fancy boats live here, big and little.

Then I come to a tall schooner I know very well: *Puritan*.

My first ship. Here she lies a captive, swinging idly to moorings fore and aft in front of a sumptuous dwelling all done out with anchors carved on shutters, a flagpole and a pinrail set with flowers.

I go to a nearby phone and call my agent, collect. His voice has a furry edge: "Hiya, Sweetie, where the hell you been? . . . Oh? Well, what are you doing down there? . . . No no no, that's okay. Nothing doing yet. Relax, Baby, they're paying the money, aren't they? . . . Tell you what you do; come in at three this afternoon. We'll have us a little talk. Okay, Baby? Right."

A little farther on there is a big white sign: "Newport Harbor Yacht Dock," and I prowl up and down, appraising each hull. A schooner stands out from the rest. She hasn't been used in years; her varnish and paint are shot; her rigging is tattered and gray. Whoever owns this ship doesn't deserve her. I squat and size up the lines of her hull, go on board and sense the way she feels, then I lie on deck and gauge the sweep of sheer and rails and spars. I guess her dimensions to be 65 on deck, 49 on the water, 16 feet of beam, with a draft of eight foot six. She is worth—to me this morning—fifteen thousand dollars, the price of a cheap tract house. Her name is *Wetona*—we'll take care of that.

Now I sit in a broker's office: "She's a damn fine boat," he says.

"I know that. What will it take to buy her?"

"Well, he's been asking eighteen five. Only last week he turned down eighteen, cash."

"Offer him thirteen five."

"What about the survey? You'll want a surveyor, won't you?"

"Give me a hammer and an ice pick and I'll make my own survey."

Two hours later I bought her, for fourteen thousand, cash. From this moment on, things were bound to improve.

It is here that the deals are made. This is an agency—an Artists' Manager's office. It looks like a bank out front, or maybe a mortuary, with a red brick façade. A dozen doors lead discreetly off from a lavish reception room. Well-knit secretaries glide to and fro, and two switchboard girls plug and unplug their flashing lights.

The nearer the front, the bigger the office suite, and the smaller and sharper the man. It is three by the hands of the temple clock: "Mr. Allenberg has been detained at Fox, Mr. Hayden, so won't you make yourself at home and he'll be along just as fast as he can." Thank you, ma'm. I sink in a leather chair and riffle magazines and papers: *Daily Variety, Weekly Variety, Hollywood Reporter, Fame, Box-Office Digest, Wall Street Journal,* a copy of *Fortune.*

The clock shows half past three: "Mr. Allenberg is so sorry, Mr. Hayden, but he had to see Mr. Mannix at MGM. Do you mind waiting? He won't be long, I'm sure. Would you care for a cup of coffee?" No ma'm, thank you just the same.

. . . And the funny part of it is, I don't know why I'm here. Three months in town and no work yet, but the money rolls in . . . I take out a pen and sketch the schooner's layout below deck. I fiddle around with names. What will it be this time? *Outward Bound? Tropic Bird? Quest? Columbia?* Or how about *Horizon? Vagrant? Downeaster* . . . I circle the name *Quest.*

I saunter out into the reception room. Four, by the temple clock. Everyone is busy. Handsome, polished sub-agents move in and out servicing the stars, servicing the studios. Sometimes they service the fading box-office queens as well.

A woman comes through the door from the Story Department. No longer a girl, but graced with that certain look. She is cinched up tight beneath a beige wool suit, a trench coat slung over her arm. We know each other well. We met here one day, the day her first story was turned down. I rise as she crosses to me and says: "When you get tired of reading that nonsense, let's go have some coffee."

I cross to the desk and say: "When the boss comes in, tell him I had to leave. Tell him I had to go see Zanuck."

I have to admire this girl. She is bright. Not like the ones I date. Her husband is even brighter . . . a writer? or does he teach some place? If I had one ounce of sense I'd find a girl like this. But the trouble with the intellectual girls I meet is that they're married or just sexually diminished. For three months I've been leading two separate lives: one devoted to politics; one devoted, let's face it, to sex. A bad blend. The first week I was back in town I joined the American Veteran's Committee and the Hollywood Independent Citizens' Committee for the Arts, Sciences and Professions. Fair enough. But it hasn't worked out quite right. Everyone else seems to know one another. They know parliamentary procedure; and how to organize fund-raising drives and membership drives and co-ordinating committees.

They know about the Constitution and the Bill of Rights and who their representatives are. They know all about what went on in Spain, in Greece and Yugoslavia (hell, they know more about Yugoslavia than I do). While they speak of Teheran and Yalta and Bretton Woods, all I can do is drink three to their one and try to look intelligent.

"Sterling, let me ask you something."

"Shoot."

"When are you going to get off this merry-go-round you're on and really commit yourself?"

"That's a good question. I don't know."

"That's no surprise. You are screwed up."

I get to my feet. "Sure I am. But we live in a complex world. I know I'm confused but damn it—"

"No. You're not. You're not as confused as you think." She looks me straight in the eye. "Do you know what I think?"

"What?"

"I think you're scared."

"Scared? Of what, for Christ's sake?"

"Of giving yourself. You're a fair talker once you get started, but you're always on the outside."

"Well, when are you going to stop talking and do something?"

"Such as?"

"Join the Party."

"Well?" We stare at each other. There's the faintest of smiles on her mouth. Whatever I do, I can't and won't stop now. "Any time," I say.

"Now?"

"Sure. Why not?"

She fumbles around in her purse. I feel like you feel when you dive from the foremasthead fifty feet into the sea on a bet. "You know," she is saying, "you're all right at that. I didn't think you had the guts." I write my name on a small white card. "I'll send this along to the proper place," she is saying, "and we'll see if they accept you."

Accept *me?*—I am thinking—what a hell of a strange idea.

It was dark outside as I drove to the studio, picked up my things, and swung south toward Newport Beach. I kept thinking: You've made a big mistake. You're not ready. You joined because you were scared, just like parachuting, just like hauling trawl from the bow of a dory in the wintertime. Like riding freights; quitting pictures; quitting the COI; quitting the *Spinney*. You've done it again.

Maybe so, I thought as I slid back the hatch and hove my things in a bunk. But I wonder whether there has ever before been a man who bought a schooner and joined the Communist Party all on the same day?

I smiled in spite of myself as I poured from a tall green bottle.

CHAPTER 71

I went to my first meeting one warm June night in Los Angeles. It is eight o'clock, and maybe a dozen people are gathered. They share two things: employment in the film industry, and a strong conviction that Marxism, judiciously applied, can help make a better world.

The meeting is called to order by a tall white-haired man with a kindly face and the hands of a working stiff. One girl is pregnant. Two others are busy with knitting. Most smoke, but no drinks are served. The wanderer arranges himself in what looks like a quiet corner. He fidgets and smokes, but seems to pay strict attention to everything that is said.

This is a three-hour meeting. From eight until nine the discussion concerns the Hollywood of those behind the scenes, the Hollywood of wages and hours, of labor-management strife. Everyone joins the discussion—except for the wanderer, but if the others notice, they are too polite to show it . . . Give him time.

From nine to ten is the dialectical hour, devoted to intensive study of Marxist-Leninist principles. The words are strange ones: "surplus value," "proletariat," "bourgeoisie," and "deviationism." Why, hell, the only deviation he is familiar with has to do with a compass. His lack of knowledge appalls him. This is not what he had in mind, and not what he came to hear. This is dull and dry and incredibly obtuse. He yawns through his nose; his eyes grow small. The room becomes diffused and distant. The voices drone and the hands of his watch stand still. Once or twice his cigarette slips through his fingers, leaving a scar on the floor.

The final hour is best, taking in the whole world. Everything he hears is new—that Chiang Kai-shek is Fascist; that Hitler was something more than simply a rabble-rouser; that already certain fabled industrialists are laying the groundwork for the next great war. Still he remains aloof; perhaps he is only at home these days with nonpolitical people, who know as little as he does.

Tonight he is scheduled, once the meeting ends, to talk with a man named "John," an important person in the Party apparatus. They are to meet alone, at the foot of the hill, in a place called "The Grotto."

We sit in a booth in a dark and quiet corner. The man across from me has an angular face with deep seams, and no eyebrows. He orders coffee black while I—not without guilt—ask for a shot of Scotch. He reminds me at once of Srecko Manola, the partisan colonel who had been in the International Brigades and had, so they said, endured more torture in a Belgrade prison than any of his comrades.

I sense two things: this man is the genuine article, not a hothouse revolutionary; and he sees through me as I see through myself sometimes. He wastes no time in chatter: "Hayden, tell me why you joined the Party."

"Well now, I joined, that is, I wanted to join because, well it seems to me the people in the Party not only know what's going on in the world but they have the guts to determine a course of action, and furthermore they're able and willing to implement this action with— Well, I know that in Yugoslavia, for example, before the war it was a lot like it is here; there were plenty of ruthless bastards up on top of the heap, and there were a number of intellectuals in the middle; but when the going got rough and it was time to be counted, it was the Communists who stood up and fought."

"What were they fighting for?" It seems as though he can't get the thoughts out fast enough.

"They were fighting for a way of life in which the interests of the people would take precedence over everything else, including of course the interests of the privileged few."

"Hayden, have you any sort of trade-union background?"

"No. The first union I ever belonged to was the Screen Actors Guild."

"Some union," he says, with a smile that isn't too reassuring.

"But I thought you went to sea for a long time. How come you never belonged to a union?"

"Because I went in sailing vessels. They never were organized."

"You fished. You fished out of Boston. What about the Atlantic Fisherman's Union?"

"I never belonged."

"Why?"

"All the Gloucester vessels were non-union. I guess I just went where the unions weren't."

"Were you ever a scab?" He smokes with the butt in his mouth to the bitter end.

"No, I was never a scab."

"Suppose the studios found out you were in the Party. What then?"

"Hell, they'd throw me out."

"You have a contract, don't you?"

"Sure. But I'm told contracts are pretty loose affairs, when it comes to something like this."

"Doesn't this bother you? Suppose somebody in your group turned stoolie?"

"To hell with it. I'd go back to sea."

"Suppose you were called before the Tenney Committee and asked the big question: 'Are you now or have you ever been?' What would you do?"

"Well. Well—I don't know. I'd have to think about it."

He fires a glance at his watch. Ash falls on his sleeve. "Why do you suppose I wanted to talk with you this way?"

"I've no idea."

He rakes a match on his shoe. "Well, don't worry about it." He flips a quarter onto the table, settles a hat low on his head, and says: "I'll leave first. Some nights there are people in this town with nothing better to do than follow me." He rises. "And this is one of those nights."

I watch him go. He is very tall. He moves slowly, which seems to require an effort. I call for another drink, this time double.

Friday: Newport Beach.

The schooner *Quest* lies moored in a deluxe basin with her nose to a row of trailers, patios attached, part of an oceanside haven for the retired. It is three in the afternoon and I am scraping varnish aft. Flynn comes sauntering down the dock wearing a white windbreaker, a beat-up yachting cap, and a shapely young girl done out in a brand new yachting outfit on his arm. He carries a camera case slung from his shoulder. Although we have not met, I recognize him. They pause and I ask them aboard.

"Hayden," he says, "I've been hearing about you for years. Maybe some afternoon you'll come out on the *Zaca* and give me a sailing lesson."

"I've heard a bit about you too. Matter of fact, I first heard about you out in Port Moresby, New Guinea, from a guy named MacKenzie who had a recruiting schooner. He said you owed him money."

"Oh yeah, I know who you mean." He laughs. "He's a bloody liar. The truth of the matter is, I had a—shall we say 'social disease' at the time. After I left, it seems his wife came down with it."

We go below. "Oh," he says, "let me introduce my companion—" He checks himself and turns to the girl. "I'm terribly sorry, darling, but what's your name again?"

"Judy, Judy Johnson." Her voice is very thin.

He opens the camera case and extracts a thermos flask. "Judy and I just met, you see. Until yesterday noon Judy was a carhop in an El Segundo drive-in." He pours a drink the color of junket. "Judy has aspirations. Something to do with acting." He holds the drink in surprisingly small hands. "I shall do what I can to help her. Cheers."

We talked for several hours, making our supper on vodka and Scotch. The girl had nothing to say. She had one drink, then kicked off her booties, crawled in a bunk, and slept.

We talked of ships. He knew places and people—but not ships. I found this reassuring. I maneuvered the talk to the war. To the Adriatic, the Jug schooners, the boats that ran the blockade, to the nights on the Illyrian coast. It made a heady brew. A certain wistfulness was evident in the empty set of his face, and I gathered, since he offered no counter-talk, that his war had been passed at Warner's. I broke out the album of pictures replete with hand-built gunboats; with mangled men; with women in battle dress wearing grenades for jewelry. He listened well, drinking remorselessly, but with no apparent effect.

I thought of the night before. Why was I tongue-tied in the company of progressives, yet eloquent when faced with a man like Flynn? I went so far as to think that even he might be made to discover that there was more to life than dames and stardom and all the jazz that went with his way of life.

The carhop stirred. Without looking, he unzipped her slacks and hid his hand. She sighed and spread her legs. "Where's your girl, old chap?" His voice was a little thick.

I told him I was in between girls—more or less.

His face flared. "Now here's what we'll do, old chap. I'll take Judy out to the *Zaca*, then what say the two of us take a little drive down to Laguna Beach, to a spot called the Coast Inn. Nothing but dames down there."

He roused the girl and they left. I guessed he wouldn't come back. An hour passed and a chap named Jim came by, a yacht broker in the midst of a divorce. We had a drink and I mentioned the Coast Inn.

"Let's go," he said. And we went.

The night was hot. Laguna was overlaid with that neon-mission look so dear to the heart of the neo-Californian. The bar hugged one leg of a drab hotel, and was filled with noisy people and a loud jukebox that bubbled. The table we found was twice the size of a phone book. I looked around the room and saw a good-looking girl smoking and staring at me.

She wasn't pretty but her coolness set her off from the rest of the room. I wondered about her body. I began to work my way across the room when she rose swiftly, came straight toward me, then veered off toward the hotel lobby. Two or three guys whistled as she left. I beckoned to Jim and we went outside. At first I thought she was gone, but she and her friend were standing and talking in front of a parking lot. We exchanged names and after a while drove back toward the ship.

Capitalism could rest in peace this night.

CHAPTER 72

Santa Barbara, California. May 1947. The green eye flashes on top of the breakwater's pylon. The town lies in tiers of lighted streets piled on soft and rolling foothills. Offshore one lone sea buoy groans as the surge goes by.

Ten months we've been together. I have peace I've never known before. Since the first of the year we've lived like this, with our backs to the world, here in the harbor. No parties no politics no meetings, just work on the ship all day and read and dream at night. The feel and smell of the sea, and the cries of the birds. What more could any man want?

. . . You live like vegetables. What happened to all your dreams? What went wrong with your new convictions?

We're doing all right. I've stopped drinking—pretty much. We'll honeymoon in New England. I'll save my dough and in less than a year we'll buy a proper vessel and walk out on Hollywood.

. . . Again? Tell me, do you love this girl?

She's all there is. I don't have anything else.

. . . How long do you think it will last?

I don't know.

. . . Tell me something else. Why did you quit the Party?

Because I'd rather be wrong on my own than be right on somebody else's say-so.

. . . Nobody was dictating to you. Maybe they led you, but mostly they just shared.

Also I was scared, just a little.

. . . Then you're glad you quit when you did?

Not exactly. It's late. I'm turning in.

. . . Have a nice marriage.

The church, bleak, poorly proportioned, swells with canned organ music. Family and friends are gathered. Flowers are banked. The organ rests, vows are made, and tears are shed. Best wishes all around, and a jolt from the father's flask.

Everyone waves as the tie is slacked and the long haul east begins. Commence honeymooning.

Cape Ann, Massachusetts. June 1947. Down a winding road comes a loose black Chrysler sedan to run through a wood, then curve once more, with Gloucester dead ahead. Good old Gloucester, now in her dotage, gone frilly and dainty out around her foreshore where the summer homes face the sea.

The man searches in vain for vessels that used to be, for men whom he used to know, and for a childhood now lost.

His wife sits apart, pressed to the groin of the door. They speak in monotones, their manner veiled and hostile. Since Nevada there has been nothing but battle.

"Yankee Clipper Inn," the hand-weathered sign peeps from a nest of roses. The place is cozy, and the manager gushes: "So nice to have you with us, Mr. and Mrs. Hayden. Mr. O'Toole said you wanted a room with a view of the sea, right this way please. Mr. O'Toole says they are expecting you not later than half past six."

Double beds. The tariff is twenty a night, and the sea horizon is barren. We unpack as though we were mother and son, stuck in the same room.

She clears her throat and speaks in a voice that is scarcely audible: "Call your friend, Sterling. Tell him we're not coming."

"The hell you say."

"I said: 'Call your friend and tell him we're not coming to dinner.'"

"Betty look, what in hell do you want?"

"I want a husband, that's what I want. I want a man for a husband. Understand? A man. Not someone who is so insecure he has to show old movies to his friends of a dame dancing the hula—some broad he laid in Tahiti."

"Honey look, for the last time; that was eight damn years ago. She was a mighty fine girl. Larry knew her too. They're good pictures. He's never seen them—"

"At least there's somebody hasn't seen them."

"Honey, I promised. He asked me to bring them. He's gone and rented a projector and a screen and what on earth—"

She looks up: "I said no. N-O. You want to go there for dinner? Fine. You want to get drunk with your friend? Fine. But *no* movies."

"Okay okay." I stretch out flat with a pillow over my head.

O'Toole throws open the door. His face hasn't changed but his belly is so big it makes his arms seem small. "Hey hey hey!" he roars. His wife, Ida, comes up with the new baby. She is all smiles. You can smell the dinner cooking. A small boy with a large head scoots from sight as we enter. "Larry, you little clown, come here and say how-do-you-do," bellows the proud father. The back door slams.

I hand O'Toole a package that clinks. "What's this?" he asks, with his wide-eyed grin.

"Aquavit," I say, "aquavit and beer." The room is small and a fire keeps throwing sparks. O'Toole looks at my wife. "So this is the new bride? Oh, what a little darlin'." He slams me on the arm. He gives the door a kick, rustles a cigarette, prods the fire, and bowls on through the kitchen. From a nearby room comes the outraged wail of the baby. Larry returns, cupping his hands and roaring: "Never have kids. Do any damn thing at all, but DON'T HAVE KIDS!"

We are left to ourselves for a moment. I feel her watching me; it doesn't feel the way it did that night in the Coast Inn bar. An expensive new projector sits on the table. O'Toole comes back with a tray full of drinks. Suddenly he pauses. "The film? Where in hell's the film?"

"It's out in the car," I say.

A few hours later I'm watching the scene unfold in front of my mind. Try as I may, I can't be sure whether this is a dream or a memory of what actually happened there in the cottage.

Everything is just a bit fuzzy, and the room blazes with light. Ida sits in a corner chair, rocking gently, a plain and kindly person, sprung by an Irish artist from the clutch of the telephone office. Across from her is my new wife, showing no warmth and sipping her drink slowly.

O'Toole dances on center stage, his shirttails out and his face bright with laughter and booze. He bellows out an island song in his bastard jargon: "E fare-ute Papio, E fare-ute Papio. E fa, nave nave, E fare-ute Oh!!" He loses his balance, lurching sideways, spilling the top off his drink.

I work at the damned projector, fumbling my film through sprockety teeth and recalcitrant gates. I'm drunk but not this drunk, and when I feel her eyes upon me, I shiver.

"Kill the lights," I say.

"Kill the lights!" cries Larry, lunging at switches, dropping his cigarette. He comes to my wife, bends down, and plants a kiss on her forehead: "Hiyah, Mommy, having a good time?"

I flip the toggle switch, the machine makes grating sounds, and the beaded screen looms like a moon close-up. But then suddenly a ship appears on a broad and polished sea. She rolls, her sails bellied gently against a cloudless sky. In the silence of the room, she seems like an echo, like something that never was. O'Toole drinks up. I watch his face, his mouth half open. He frowns, sighs, and shakes his head: "Old dying Jaysus, what a wonderful thing to see."

The spars rise overhead, swaying in easy rhythm. O'Toole appears at the brassbound wheel, stripped to the waist and

smiling. Someone bangs on the bell—the watches change . . .
Hansen is seen, rippling with muscle, cross-legged atop the
capstan, playing his flute, with his beard all combed and blond
in brilliant sunshine.

An island appears ahead, soaring skyward. Birds dart and
wheel, circling the mastheads. The brig is coasting the shore as
spume tears from the reef to veil the near lagoon . . .

Ida returns, having taken a look at the baby. I slip out to
the kitchen and fill my glass till it slops—knowing what lies
ahead.

Then the drums begin, and a palm leans back. Now the drum-
beat quickens, and a girl places a flower in her hair. The flower
gives way to youthful shoulders and breasts, and the screen is
filled by a sensuous body clad in a skirt of grass that ripples
and tosses from side to side and around and around with lean
thighs showing through.

O'Toole keeps shaking his head. I hear a noise somewhere, a
soft thud—my wife has left. I don't budge.

The rest seems none too clear: there are shots of canoes
under sail and more dancing, and then the screen goes white.

"That's it," I say. O'Toole is cursing the world. His wife says
good night and goes. He gets to his feet and looks at me in
dismay: "Where in hell's your wife?"

"Gone. She's tired. We've been doing a lot of driving."

He starts to speak, shrugs, and I pack up the film and leave.

The Cape lies silent, grazed by a waning moon. Why did I do
it, I wonder? But I have to smile whenever I think of those
pictures. Nothing too bad can happen so long as the ships last
and the sea doesn't disappear. If the marriage founders, I can
dump the *Quest* for twenty thousand or so—fly to the Baltic, or
the Mediterranean or England, pick up a vessel and go back to
sea.

I am folding my coat when she speaks: "Sterling, I want
you to drive me to Boston in the morning, I'm flying back to the
coast."

"Very well."

"And mark my words: I'll get even with you if it's the last
thing I do."

"Have it your own way."

I can hear the Atlantic pounding.

CHAPTER 73

Outside Papeete a ways, maybe seventeen kilometers as the Broom Road goes, just south of the Punaruu Valley, lives a remarkable Chilean named Carlos García Palacios. The *Wanderer* had not been long in port before we met, not by accident, but because I, wanting someone to talk with, had cycled out to his home.

He came to the door that day, a smallish man in his late or middle sixties, balding, with mellow eyes, a stubble of beard, and a most discerning smile. "Oh," he said straightaway. "It is the captain of the big American schooner. I knew we would meet one day."

"I've heard a great deal about you," I replied.

"And I the same." He shuffled across his verandah and we seated ourselves facing the nearby road. A bus went by, filled with goats, children, beer, pigs, and maybe two dozen Tahitians. You could hear a guitar above the laughter and the noise of the engine.

"In fact," he went on, "I have observed you from time to time working with your typewriter. It is true you are making a book?"

"Not really. I would like to write a book but all I can write is letters."

He regarded me, the stub of a cigarette stuck to his lower lip. His teeth were nothing but stumps, dark and rotting.

"People here on Tahiti, they cannot understand you. Some say you are bitter and rude, others that you are charming. A few think you are Communist." He laughs gently. "I said to my vahine: 'They cannot all be right.' So tell me, Captain, what kind of a man you are?"

I sat back, laughing. "A Communist with a schooner, quite some combination."

A striking island girl came strutting across the lawn, her *pareu* swinging from side to side. She chewed at the stem of a hibiscus, and wore a man's straw hat at a rakish angle.

"Agnes," he said, "say hello to the captain of the big American yacht." I winced at the word as I rose.

"M'sieu." She said, extending a limp hand shyly.

"Agnes," he said, "is my vahine. We have been together now

for almost five years. Perhaps you are wondering what an old ghost of a man has done to deserve such a girl?"

I was wondering precisely that.

"I must confess," he went on, "I cannot provide the answer. Unless it is because I do not ask indiscreet questions. Also because I stay here. You see, Captain, I have searched for many years for the perfect place to die. This I think is it." He crossed his legs and rubbed at one calf with his palm.

The girl picked up a kitten and pressed it between her breasts. The kitten closed its eyes. She drifted away, kicking at pebbles and sticks. Another girl brought tea.

"I believe," he was saying, "you are acquainted with my dear friend Gres, the painter."

"I am. He asked me to sit for him a week or two ago."

"I know. And how did you like your portrait?"

"Well, it was different from what I expected."

He passed me a cup and continued: "I think I understand. You see, I have seen the picture. Do you know what Gres said? He said to me: 'The man Hayden has a very unusual face. It shows great strength, and also great fear, at the same time.' Perhaps that is why you did not like your picture."

After we had talked for several hours, he said at last: "You are not a happy man."

"Of course not."

"Why do you say it like that?"

"Why? It's simple. How can a man be happy in the world we live in? There's too much wrong with it."

"Has it not been that way always?"

"Perhaps, but, Carlos goddamn it, the pressures are greater these days. We know too much. Here we have this world all loused up, and we're hell bent on lousing up some poor damn planet a billion miles away."

"And for all of this sickness you blame capitalism."

"No, not all, but one hell of a high per cent. So do you—from what you were saying earlier."

"I did not quite say that. What I said was, the abuses and the excesses of capitalism are wrong, not capitalism itself."

"And I maintain the abuses and excesses are inherent in the system. A century ago it worked. Not any more. Maybe it does for some, maybe it does for you and for me and those who are lucky, or bright, or resourceful enough to take care of themselves, but not for most."

"Yet you are not a Communist?"

"What's a Communist? I'm not a member of the Party. I'm not under the discipline or the influence of the Party, not that I know of. What's more, I never was, even when I was a member. You, I think, can understand such a statement as that."

"Yes."

"Damned few people do. Take this island. Let's assume that tomorrow Tahiti was cut off from the world: no planes, ships, tourists, drunks, preachers, paratroopers—nothing. No contact whatsoever with the rest of the world—indefinitely. Then you know what I'd believe in? You know what I'd fight for? A scientifically balanced society in which the needs of the people were balanced and met by law. A society in which the means of production were shared and shared equally by every person here, with no exploitation of any person or class of persons. Now, does that make me a Communist?"

He chuckled, massaging his bony legs. "My friend, I am very much afraid there are many, including some of your close friends, who would think exactly that."

"They have a lot to learn."

"Sterling, earlier tonight I was thinking how much I would give to be in your shoes. But now I am not so sure. You see, I too was a socialist once, not a Communist."

"What's the difference?"

"A Communist is a man who believes totalitarian methods are justified in the achievement of the socialist objective. Will that do?"

"Yes, that's close enough."

"I was thinking how fine it would be to be young again. But I had forgotten the unrest. Youth means unrest, which makes you very young, just as it makes me very old."

"I am restless and unhappy. I know what's wrong, damned good and well; I know what I'm against, but I can't settle what I'm for. And that's why I'm always asking questions."

My voice trailed off, and he chuckled, massaging his wasted leg. A dog barked, and a damp wind came down from the hills.

"I will tell you something," he said. "You must write your book. It is very important. You must let nothing interfere. It might be a turning point for you."

"No, I passed my turning point, believe it or not, ten years ago. Ten years ago I caught up with myself. I'm speaking of something called psychoanalysis."

His face changed. Slowly he peeled the butt from his lip, looked at it, and threw it out on the grass. "Why would you indulge yourself in a thing like that?"

"Read the book," I said.

Instead of riding back, I walked, pushing the bike, smelling the fragrance of the evening smoke, hearing the thunder off in the west. I felt a little ashamed to have talked so frankly to this man I barely knew.

I thought of the time I had come—or tried to come—to a showdown with myself.

CHAPTER 74

The time and the place are not important, nor are the other things. The list of people, events, successes and failures, jobs tackled and not tackled, is always incomplete. None of these things matters anyway.

I lived in a downward spiraling, diminishing, darkening world. I lived on a ship that was no ship, with a wife who was no wife (no fault of hers).

I lived in the past and in dreams. The future didn't exist, and the present I couldn't control. I liked to think that nothing mattered—prestige, service, status as an actor, all such things were dead.

The incredible part was, this was happening to me. I had known of such things, of people rendered impotent, unable to manage their lives. But they were different. They were *they*, not *me*. They were the odd-balls.

But I had been the golden boy, capturing the imagination of the crowd, born to the sea. I had been the man who didn't care, who thumbed his nose at all the proper things beloved of proper persons.

But now the past was dying. I had raked its coals till all that remained was ash. My stories were all told out. No new friends came, and only sleep was pleasing.

I worked some. I was "starred" in a picture late in 1946—something to do with flying. I did nothing in 1947—for which Paramount paid me seventy thousand dollars. I made two films in 1948. Both were abortions—conceived and dead in less than three weeks. From June 1946 to June 1949 I worked 75 days— out of 1,095. The rest of the time I did nothing. Through all these days, my wife's devotion was single-minded and exclusive. Our dependence on each other excluded the rest of the world. We ate each other up.

A son was born in August of 1948. We named him Christian Winslow Hayden after a mutineer and a painter who hid on the coast of Maine.

Eleven months later, our second son was born, Dana Morgan Hayden, named after an author and a buccaneer (or maybe a whaleship—I never decided which). And the marriage got more complicated—our exclusive little society had had its walls breached.

I drank a good deal, but drew the line at real benders. Apparently the same force that prevented me from giving myself to life also blunted the self-destructive process. I could drink till I passed out. But, always, four hours later I'd roll out, plunge or shower, then bundle up and read till dawn, when I ran or walked or cycled or rowed for hours. Then I'd settle back and drift through the daylight hours like a ghost, with never a drink till dusk.

There were times now and then when the circle was broken. At such times something within me stirred—not much—just enough to accomplish a change of scene or a change of the boat that passed for our home. While still on the honeymoon, the *Quest* was sold for seventeen thousand dollars. I turned around and bought a schooner in Maine for half this price, then shipped her out west, where I polished her with twenty thousand dollars until she shone like a ship in a bottle. When she was still undergoing repairs and we needed a place to live, I bought the big schooner *Gracie S.* which hung like a derelict in inner Los Angeles harbor. Then she was sold and her place taken by a forty-five-foot Norwegian ketch, and there we were, anchored off the parched red flank of the San Pedro hills, living on the bottle-ship, with the ketch as something to sail. I gave the ketch my favorite name at the time: *Outward Bound.* She was my mistress, though she was old and tired, and only her name held promise. We made a proper pair.

Relief, when it came, came fast: I decided not to throw myself into the struggle of life, but to throw my mother into it. It was summer, more or less. Thor Heyerdahl had come to town in the course of a lecture tour. I called him and offered a quiet weekend of rest as our guest on board the schooner. He came down the dock that day, a spare and pallid figure, with his lips compressed and his hair severely combed, dressed in a double-breasted suit and lugging a small valise along with a carton of film.

For a day and a half we puttered around. I let him do most of the talking, and did not conceal my admiration for the entire Kon-Tiki experience. The scientific aspect meant little or nothing to me. I was impressed by this man who could conjure up a scheme, then ram it to completion through all kinds of difficulties. I wondered at the intangibles that make one man calm and determined, and another man apparently similar so profoundly irresolute.

My mother was living nearby, and it happened that on this particular Sunday afternoon she came to visit.

"Mother," I said, "I would like to introduce Mr. Thor Heyerdahl."

One step back she took. "Oh. Oh my heavens. Not *the* Thor Heyerdahl."

The raft man bowed from the waist.

"Oh," she was breathless. "Mr. Heyerdahl, do you know that last year some of the girls and I drove through a snowstorm to hear you lecture at Hartford?"

He said he did not know that. "Just wait till I write and tell Susie about this." She turned to me. "Now, Buzzie, why don't you do something like that?"

"To tell you the honest truth, Mother, if they had asked my opinion I would have said that goddamn raft could never make it."

"Well," she ruffled her arms, "I must say, Buzzie, it would be a good deal better than sitting here the way you have been doing."

That night I decided my mother needed help. Perhaps if she talked with a psychiatrist she might learn to leave me alone, to free me. I sat alone on the dock, smoking, my wife below in the bottle-ship sewing. My mistress, *Outward Bound,* lay along-side, moored firmly fore and aft.

CHAPTER 75

You know your turn has come and you get to your feet with a sigh as the double doors open. You grunt a good morning and strip off your coat and bury yourself on the couch.

Three months ago you came to see this man about your mother: "Doc," you said, sitting up of course, loaded with poise, "I'm a grown man. My problem is very simple. I have a mother who loves me very much. She loves me so much she follows wherever I go. I'd like you to help her, make her understand that she has to get off my back."

For more than an hour you talked and then he said in his quiet and ruminative way: "Mr. Hayden, I have talked with your mother, as you know. She has, I agree, certain peculiar characteristics, just as all of us do. She might benefit by therapy, but on the other hand she is not a young woman. She has no desire to alter her way of life. But I'm just wondering, Mr. Hayden, about you. From what I have learned in our chat this morning, it occurs to me that you might well benefit by some intensive work yourself."

Me? Is there something wrong with me? It's true what they say about headshrinkers: every damn one of them thinks everyone else is nuts. I smoke for a time in silence. Nothing else has worked: not the running, searching, drinking, screwing; not the battling, and the dreaming; not the escapism or the Communism or the nihilistic thinking. I nod my head: "Yes. I know that. Maybe I've known it for a long time."

"Think it over, why don't you?" His voice holds no emotion.

"I don't have to think it over."

This is an unsung voyage. No headlines this time, no farewells, no girls on the sidelines waving. Prone on a leather couch in a squared and silent cabin, with nothing to steer by but the clouded compass rose of something called "the analytic procedure," whatever in hell that is.

All of which is fine, so far as theory goes. But you soon discover that this is a new kind of voyage. For months on end you flounder. With a brave flourish you severed your ties with the land and you plunged, only to find yourself more lost than ever before.

To your dismay the analyst seems maliciously detached. You thought he would give you a hand when things got rough. Some laugh. The joke is all on you—at twenty-five bucks an hour. Five hundred a month you pay for the honor of lying flat and talking to a blank screen.

Now and then he speaks in a lusterless fashion: "You must make an effort, Mr. Hayden, not to allow the day to day problems of your life to come betweeen you and your thoughts of the past . . . Just say whatever comes into your mind . . ."

Of course, you don't, and the silent thoughts go like this: Fuck you, Doc. If you were a good analyst, you'd be working with prisoners or in Harlem instead of here in Beverly Hills. How about that? Why don't you go downtown and analyze away the prejudice and poverty? Jerk. My wife and I are battling more and I thought analysis might make the marriage get better; instead it gets worse.

Through the wall comes the steady growl of traffic. I gouge at my eyes.

Silence. And now the voice behind me: "Out loud, please, Mr. Hayden." All right, I'll beat this bastard at his own game.

I speak in a fine harsh tone: "All right. You want what comes into my mind, I'll give you what comes into my mind: I'm in plenty of trouble, Doc; haven't worked in a hell of a long time. So far as this town's concerned, I might as well be dead. Paramount fired me. Everyone knows that. I'm spending fifteen hundred bucks a month just to keep on living. Nothing coming in, and there's five thousand left in the bank. These aren't the right thoughts, are they? I ought to be talking about crawling between the baby sitter's legs, but I can't because yesterday something exciting happened.

"My agent called and said that John Huston over at MGM is starting a film called *Asphalt Jungle*. He's interested in me for the lead role. Goddamit, I've got to land this part. If I do, I'm all set. I know you're allergic to answering questions but this one's important. I'll tell you why: Let's say I get a chance to make a test for this part. Tests are rough, the worst thing about the whole racket. I always tense up in front of the camera. I don't want to, but I do. Now for the next few days why can't I just sit up and talk to you man to man and maybe you can explain this fear to me?" Silence. He doesn't even rustle.

"Don't you understand, Doc, I've got to get this part. Once I get it I can relax and pick the parts I want and we can get

down to work. For Christ's sake, don't you want to help me and
get rid of me and go on to somebody else?"

I wonder if he's asleep. Maybe he's reading a magazine or
counting up his bank balance.

"Doc, it's like this. You don't need talent to star in a motion
picture. All you need is some intelligence *and* the ability to work
freely in front of the lens. Why do I always freeze? Shit! I went
through the war. I jumped out of bombers. I played kick-the-can
with E-boats when all we had was a lousy forty-foot dragger
with six machine guns and a top speed of six knots. Yet whenever I get a close-up in a nice warm studio I curl up and die.
Why? Doc, if you don't mind. . . ."

He clears his throat. "I'm afraid our time is up for today."
Now he rustles about and rises. He's dressed in a seersucker
shirt with a stupid bow tie, built like a quarterback, tidy little
mustache, neat little eyes, fine little tweedy fellow. Reminds me
of my stepfather, except that he isn't broke . . . He opens the
double doors and stands there like a dummy.

I tuck in my shirt and tighten my belt. "Same time tomorrow?"
"Same time tomorrow." Articulate sonofabitch.

⚓

CHAPTER 76

The executive offices of MGM are housed in the Thalberg building, a white and sepulchral affair. Leo the Lion looks down
from his throne on the water tower, and studio cops at the
nearby gate keep out the tourists, unemployed actors, and Red
writers whose minds are laden with bombs. I pace in the shade
of a billboard, waiting for my new agent. I spot him a block
away. Take away his car—a customized Cadillac with a special
canvas hardtop—and what do you guess is left? Harold with his
tri-buckled shoes, his crotch-length ties, and the cuff links as
big as his wrist.

"Hiya, baby, now look, baby, this is the break of your life.
Now do me a favor, sweetie, and just this once show some
enthusiasm, will ya, huh? I'm going in with you, see? Then I'm
doing a fast fade and you and Huston can get to know each
other and—"

"We know each other. We flew to Washington two years ago

when he was on the Committee for the First Amendment, pro-
testing the Un-American Activities Committee's investigations."

"Then we're in. Now, like I said, I'll do this fast fade, and after
you're through, call me in Schary's office. Got it?"

"Sure, Harold, sure."

When you're greeted by John Huston, you know what it's
like to be met. You step into a big corner office full of people
and smoke. His feet are on his desk. The moment he sees you, he
swings to his feet and cleaves the room with his eyes on you
alone. You suddenly sense that simply by coming here today
you have relieved this rangy man of some immense burden.
You are the one man alive he wanted to see at 2 p.m. sharp.
He waves one arm and the room is instantly cleared.

He buzzes his secretary: "Hold *all* my calls, my dear. If Mr.
Mayer calls, tell him I've gone to Santa Anita." He cocks his
feet on the desk. "Well now, Sterling, how in hell are you?"

"Pretty well, John, pretty well."

"May I tell you something? I've admired you for a long time.
They don't know what to make of a guy like you in this business.
Maybe we'll change all that."

Only seldom do you find a face like Huston's in an office. It's
one that belongs on the road, in a boxcar doorway, in a mine,
or in a Left Bank garret.

"Now, Sterling, I want you to do this part. The studio does
not. They want a top name star. They say you mean nothing
when it comes to box-office draw—I told them there aren't five
names in this town mean a damn thing at the box office. Fortunately, they're not making this picture. I am . . . Now let me
tell you about Dix Handley.

"Dix is a loner who hails from a Southern farm. Dix is you
and me and every other man who can't fit into the groove. Some
of us are lucky, but Dix has never been. He is angry and doesn't
know how to control it. So he does the only thing a man with
his limitations can do—he becomes a hood . . ." His voice tapers
off and his eyes are almost closed. With a jerk he gets to his
feet and paces around the room. "Now there's one thing I can't
control. We will have to make a test. Tests stink. The bagmen
up front don't know about things like this. We'll give you the
book and the script and the test scene. Soak it up. That's all I
have to say. Except don't worry."

We shake hands: "I'll do the best I can."

* * * * *

As always, I am well ahead of time as I park west and south of the sepulcher, facing the sea of course. I tell the cop at the gate my name and he runs a chubby trigger finger up and down a list. He shakes his head and dials the local security police. "Go on in," he says, disappointed.

No nervousness as yet. Good sign. Too good to last. Don't think about it. Chorus girls pass in black mesh stockings with busily bouncing breasts. Don't look back. Never look back, not when you're happily married . . . How come, I wonder, no nervousness today. All good actors are nervous just a little. Maybe I'm not an actor.

The stage is huge and dark. The cop inside the door looks me up and down like I'm here to repossess the furniture. The set is a small one bathed in a pool of light, and the crew all speak in whispers. I can't locate Huston. A tall dark handsome actor, the one they're testing in front of me, rises from a cot and throws himself at the scene. Maybe he said to his analyst yesterday: "Look, Doc, I'm testing for Huston tomorrow . . ." I swore this morning I would turn over a new leaf, do the impossible deed— stop smoking and make the test all at the same time, which is why I brought along a fresh pack. I take one and inhale so deep my head shrivels.

They cut and I hear my name. I step on the butt, take several deep breaths, and advance toward no-man's-land. Huston intercepts me, throws an arm around my shoulder, and walks me around the stage. His voice is urgent but I'm thinking about the scene. When we stop we're next to the camera and there are introductions all around.

A girl named Jean Hagen sits on a high stool. She is a redhead with a glorious smile, pretty but not too pretty, fresh from Broadway, and set to play in the picture. "A consummate actress" was the way Huston phrased it.

"Kid," he says, "play it the way it feels best. Lie down, sit up, walk around, do any damn thing you please. Wherever you go, we'll follow. Take your time. Let me know when you're ready." He drops in a canvas chair and starts to read a book. The girl smokes, not looking at me just yet. It is absolutely silent.

Have I got the words, I wonder. Just like old times. I mess around with my shirt, trying hard to concentrate. I sit on the edge of the cot and clutch at the cage of my ribs. A minute passes, maybe more. Huston has closed the book. Our eyes meet and I nod.

I hear the single word, "Action," and freeze. I feel like I just woke up. A million dollars wouldn't buy from me the gist of the scene. I look bewildered to Jean. "The dream," she says, "you said you would tell me the dream." Her face is warm.

Then slowly my joints unlock, I shiver a little, and for the first time I begin to act. I'll tell her my dream because she is my girl and I want her to be proud. I tell about the time when I was a kid breaking the horse that belonged to my old man—the horse they said couldn't be broke. I stayed with that damn horse, and found that Pa had been watching me. He bragged about me to the men, and walking back to the house he held my arm.

My eyes go back to Jean. She is proud. I've been banging around a long time and nobody's ever been proud of me since that time on the farm. Now I've got to tell her the rest, about how times got tough and Pa lost the farm. He died a year later. Then I hit the road. I swore I'd come back some day and get back our farm. I grabbed a rattler and started west.

Now it all comes out, about the flophouses and drinking and the first stick-up I pulled—because I was broke and cold and wanted to get back home. That's all, just lie in the grass. I came close once or twice, but they caught up with me and I went to prison instead.

I want to go on, but all I can do is sit on the edge of the bed. I know there's more I have to tell her. I try to speak but the pain won't let me. I rock back and forth, and something inside feels like it's tipping over. My eyes begin to back up, but this is a sound stage and guys like me don't cry in the middle of the morning.

When I look to her this time, I can see the smile is there, but her eyes are shining in a different way, which is all that matters, so I just let go and I feel the goddam tears rushing down all hot and the next thing I know they cut the arcs and the work lights come up softly.

I grab my coat and start to leave. I should thank everybody, but all I want is to get the hell outside.

Huston overtakes me, but I can't look up yet. But I can hear what he says: "The next time somebody says you can't act, tell them to call Huston."

Harold Hardtop phones: "Hiya, sweetie, how's things, what's cookin' down in boat department?"

"Not much, Harold."

"Okay, baby, now hold on to your hat 'cause I just got back from MGM and, sweetie, we're all set. We got the part!"

"Well, what do you know about that."

"I know it's the break we been prayin' for, baby. Now, sweetie, listen to ol' Harold when he gives you a little advice."

"Go on."

"Now, don't think I'm stickin' my nose into your personal affairs, but you know what come close to lousin' up this whole damn deal?"

"No, what?"

"The fact that you kids live down on that boat. The boys running the studios figure any guy lives fifty miles away on a boat don't care one hell of a lot about his career."

"I see."

"So why don't you take a tip from your ol' buddy here and get your ass uptown here along with the rest of the slaves?"

"I'll give it a little thought."

"Yeah. Yeah you do that. So long, baby. Give the wife my love."

FOR SALE: One model schooner home . . . in lieu of which was leased (furnished)—at $750 a month—a modest mansion with a kidney-shaped swimming pool and a knotty-pine den: with a three-car garage, deep freeze, two refrigerators, dishwasher, clothes washer, clothes drier, and perhaps twenty thousand dollars worth of additional hardware and furnishings— plus a blue-chip address.

On quiet nights you could hear the neighbors clipping coupons up and down the line. Alan Ladd lived two blocks away in a three hundred and fifty thousand dollar home. Bob Crosby lived nearby in a three hundred thousand dollar home. You could tell it was the fall of the year because the air was full of World Series chatter. And all around town the major studios were bursting with optimism because for once they agreed on something: television would never last, was just a fad. The American people weren't about to exchange nights at the movies for a womb with a view . . . So said the experts.

We shot the final scene of the picture first, in Lexington, Kentucky, where the loner named Dix Handley died one afternoon, in the prime of life, of wounds received during the holdup of a jewelry store. He came barreling down the wrong side of the road in a stolen car, broke from the arms of his mistress,

scaled a fence, then staggered through a blue-green sea of grass
to pitch forward dead—ninety yards from his daddy's old farm.

On the way back to California my wife and I dropped off at
Chicago, where I exchanged one week's salary for a bottle-green
Cadillac. As we drove west, the thought ran through my mind
. . . I guess I've swallowed the anchor. One sliver of hope remained. When the film was done, I would launch myself on a
long voyage, in something called "analysis," "deep analysis"
. . . whatever that meant.

CHAPTER 77

The couch and pillow are warm. Who went before, I wonder?
Maybe a homo, maybe a nympho, maybe the Doc himself, catch-
ing a little snooze.

"Doc, I had a dream last night, but I don't know what it
was . . . Maybe I should get divorced. Just kind of a dummy
affair. Then maybe I could come here with the marriage shunted
to one side and we could really accomplish something.

". . . Doc, there was a girl in *Asphalt Jungle* named Marilyn
Monroe, brand-new girl. Huston thought she was great, everyone
thought she was great—except my wife, who thought she was
nothing. I wanted to talk to Monroe, but I didn't dare. Never
even went near her, barely dared look at her when she was going
the other way. Now why in hell is that? I tell you, Doc, jealousy
is the worst thing in the world. I may be all screwed up, but
jealous is something I'm not . . . One day I took Jean Hagen to
lunch in the Metro commissary. Jean is happily married. Her
husband and I are friends—and yet my wife blew up . . . Doc,
I'm trapped. There's nothing in this world I want so much as to
come in here and work constructively, but my mind is choked
with everyday problems like this. This marriage is shot all to
hell, and yet I can't let go. Another baby due in September . . .
Jesus, me with three kids.

"All right now, Doc, let's come to grips with something. I've
got the toughest decision to make that has ever hung over my
head. I'm in the Marine Corps Reserve. Since the war in Korea
started, I've felt this thing closing down around me. Suppose they
call me up and we come to the loyalty part: 'Are you now or

have you ever been a member of the Communist Party?' What do I do then? If I say no, I perjure myself. If I say yes, and the word gets around, then I'm dead.

"Every studio in town has black lists. Some of them have half a dozen lists. Funny damn thing: I thought after the Huston picture I'd be in some demand, but I've had not one offer since I left Metro five months ago. I had a talk yesterday afternoon with my lawyer about how to protect myself. He thinks we should write a letter to J. Edgar Hoover asking if there isn't some way I can admit having been in the Party without screwing my whole life up."

"That seems reasonable."

"I'm not so sure. The F.B.I. isn't going to let me off the hook without my implicating people who never did anything wrong— except belong to the Party."

"Didn't your attorney suggest the F.B.I. would probably treat this information confidentially?"

"Yes, he did; but from what I've heard about the Bureau and its ties with the Un-American Activities Committee, I sure as hell doubt it."

"Maybe you should try another attorney."

"I can't afford it. And besides, Martin Gang is a powerhouse in this business; maybe some day I'll need him . . . I'm a genius for getting into untenable positions. The man who is a hard-core Communist has it all laid out: he goes before a committee if he has to and tells them to screw themselves. The man who was never in the party has it easy. All he has to do is say: 'No, I am not now and I never was a member'—unless he is one of those rare persons who, having nothing whatsoever to conceal, nevertheless elect to stand on their constitutional rights, thus safeguarding the rights of others. But the ex-Communist? He's had it.

"You know, I don't know why I got out of the Party any more than I know why I joined. I could say a lot of things about those people I knew in the Party—and you know something? It would all be good. I never heard anything that was subversive.

"I'd like to take a two-page spread in the *Hollywood Reporter* and in *Variety* and I'd let go the goddamnedest blast, let people know who the real subversives are. I wrote this out last night: 'You loudmouthed self-styled patriots in this business had better wake up. I was in the Party for six months. I know a bit about what goes on. You think those people are trying to subvert your precious Hollywood? They're not. They happen to believe in planned social order. They look up to Russia as the leader of the world socialist movement . . . Now, you people allegedly believe in free competition. You want the world to follow in our footsteps, so you invest billions of bucks all over hell and gone trying to influence people. Yet when the socialist world does this you scream "foul" ' . . . That's what I'd like to say."

"Why not do it then?"

"Because I haven't got the guts, that's why. Maybe because I'm a parlor pink. Because I want to remain employable in this town long enough to finish this fucking analysis. Because when it comes time for the divorce I'd like to be able to see my children, and the courts downtown are full of judges who would look askance at a divorced man who was an ex-Communist to boot. That's why! How many reasons do you want, sitting there on your throne."

What's left of the hour is passed in total silence . . .

It is miserably hot outside. Time for lunch. Nothing to do but wait till they release the Metro picture and I am a hot property. It is mid-May now. The film comes out next January—eight months more to wait.

I drive toward the sea; toward a place in Malibu where a stretch of empty beach leads to a nest of caves. The sea looks oily and green. I crawl in a cave and sleep.

May 23, 1950

Mr. Martin Gang
Gang, Kopp & Tyre
6400 Sunset Blvd.
Hollywood, California

Dear Mr. Gang:

This department is sensitive to the problem outlined in your letter of May 16, 1950.

You are advised herewith that no machinery exists whereby a former member of the Communist Party of the United States can, as you phrase it, be cleared.

I would suggest that, in view of the problem outlined, you, on behalf of your client Mr. Sterling Hayden, contact the Chief of the Bureau at the Federal Building in Los Angeles.

A copy of this letter is forwarded herewith to Mr. ——. Upon contacting him, it can be arranged for your client to appear and make available to this office whatever information is at his disposal.

> Very truly yours,
> J. Edgar Hoover
> Director
> Federal Bureau of Investigation

CHAPTER 78

"Good morning, Doc."

"Mr. Hayden." He closes the doors. He looks sleepy, or maybe hung over. The leather couch is cool.

"Doc, I'll make it fast this morning because we're due downtown at nine-thirty sharp. I didn't drink last night and so I woke up around four this morning all slept out—no dreams either. Well, I went for a walk down on the beach.

"There weren't any stars, and it was pitch black when I parked out by Malibu. I started to walk northwest, into a damp wind. For some reason I was scared. No, scared isn't the right word—I was terrified. But I kept on going and my eyes adjusted so I just could make out the beach and the shapes of the driftwood.

"Sometimes I stopped, stepped to the edge of the surf, and stared seaward with the wind about six points off my starboard bow. Felt like I was back on a ship again. It's funny that a man can be alone at sea a thousand miles from land, on a pitch-black night, and not be afraid. On land you never know who in hell might be around . . .

"I walked some more, and then all of a sudden I made out this huge figure bearing down on me. He had a kind of parka hood that was turned up and he came on fast. I always walk with a stick I keep in the car. This guy had a stick too. I couldn't see it but I could hear it hitting the sand. I had all I could do to keep from taking my stick and slashing away at this man. Instead I dove to one side and lay there, hoping he hadn't seen me, and he went right on past, never hesitating.

"Once more I went on walking, but I could feel this bastard behind me. I kept looking back. Then I started to run, and I knew he was running behind me. I wheeled around and flailed away in great wild empty circles. There was nothing there. I broke and ran toward the highway and headed back toward the car.

"A police car cruised by. When it passed me, it slowed down, and for some reason I dove toward the ditch, scrambled through a barbed-wire fence, and hid in the brush. When I came to my wagon I checked the back seat to make sure no one was hiding there; I locked all the doors and headed back into town. Now, what do you make of that?"

". . . No, you won't talk. You want to know what I make of it . . . Well, I don't make a goddamned thing of it, to tell you the truth. I don't even know whether that figure was real or not."

"You don't?"

"If I had to make a guess, I'd have to say it was not . . . Maybe this afternoon after I'm through informing, I'll go back and check on the footprints."

I close my eyes. Nothing comes into focus . . . All I see is what looks like a big bed with black blankets . . . It heaves and falls and looks like the sea on a dark night with no wind . . . It looks like a couple making love underneath the blankets . . . This isn't a dream at all: I'm making the whole thing up.

I feel like a bear led on a chain by the lawyer. The lawyer drives his car. It is a big car. The lawyer is my shepherd—I hope.

We veer to the right up the Vine Street ramp and onto the Hollywood Freeway. He cranes his neck, sees his chance, stomps on the gas, and edges into a lefthand lane.

"Martin," I falter, "I still don't feel right about—"

"Sterling, now listen to me. We've been over this thing time and time again. You make entirely too much out of it. The time to have felt this way was before we wrote the letter."

"Yes, I guess you're right."

"You know I'm right. You made the mistake. Nobody told you to join the Party. You're not telling the F.B.I. anything they don't already know.

"That isn't the point."

"I know, it's rough. But mark my words, you'll feel better after its over."

The elevator flows to a gentle stop. I hear the doors roll shut

behind me. Now he can let me off my chain. I won't run away.
I won't leap out the window. I'll be a nice friendly actor sits in
a nice bright room smokes like a city dump and spills his guts all
over the floor.

The chief of the Bureau comes on smooth. His office is done
up in seals and flags and pictures of Mr. Hoover (signed) and
other heads of state. His voice has rounded corners: "Mr. Gang,
of course I have no way of knowing what it is your client
wishes to say this morning. But I would like to avail myself of
this opportunity to congratulate you both on the decision you
have made. If it is of any value to you, Mr. Hayden, I might also
say that you are not alone in your predicament."

The lawyer is busy smiling. It isn't every day that an attorney
has a chance like this to take care of his client and the National
Interest all at once. "Do you mind," he asks, "if I place a call to
my office?"

"Please do, Mr. Gang." The host selects a phone. Business as
usual. This gives me an opening. "Sir, I have one request: While
I'm obviously willing to disclose certain things about myself, I
would like to ask if we might let it go at that. What I mean is
that I do not want to disclose the names of other persons who
might be in some way involved."

"Mr. Hayden, it is not the function of this Bureau to approve
or disapprove. You have indicated a desire to assist the Bureau
in its investigative work and I leave to you what you say or do
not say. However, I would also suggest that if you are going
to co-operate with the Bureau, you do so to the fullest extent of
your ability."

The attorney comes off the phone. The decks are well cleared
now. The chief of the Bureau says: "Now I am going to call in
one of my assistants who is a specialist in the Hollywood scene.
He is much more expert than I. You may, Mr. Hayden, give this
gentleman any information at your disposal." He leans on a
silent button.

It is not so cool here now. A man comes through the door. He
is gray and calm and friendly. The chief leaves. This is my last
chance. I wish I could rise, yawn once, and politely say: "Gentlemen, thank you just the same." I think of the Bosnian, Srecko
Manola, who racked up four straight years of torture. His fingers
were broken across table edges—and rebroken while still un-
healed. They clamped his testicles in vices, and yet he came out

alive and fought again, without having compromised himself, let alone others.

Gang sounds the pitch pipe, and I come chiming in: "Well, I uh don't quite know how to begin. I uh—" The calm gray man is poised. He holds a yellow pencil, not my favorite color. "Feel free, Mr. Hayden," he is saying, "to begin wherever you choose. Why not go from the beginning and say anything you please."

Christ, everybody wants to know what's going on in my mind. And none of them gives a damn. The only ones who had no axe to grind are the ones I'm about to brand.

I talk for more than an hour. If I'm telling him anything he doesn't know, this doesn't come through on his face. I dodge whenever I can: "No sir, I never did know their last names . . . No sir, the actors and actresses I met were never identified as belonging to the Party. So far as I was concerned, they were simply persons deeply interested in the carpenters' strike, in the fight of the CSU against the IATSE . . . The study group that I joined was composed of back-lot workers one hundred per cent . . . No sir, I am not familiar with that name . . . Yes sir, I have heard that name . . . That is correct. Yes sir. No sir."

Now he is walking with us toward the elevators. It seems we walk past endless ranks of green steel filing cabinets. My contribution this morning has been an invaluable one. I am free to call him any time should further thoughts arise. And he may call on me from time to time in the hope I may supply some missing connections.

My chain hangs heavy now. He locks his car door. I lock mine. After all, you never know. Maybe we're being tailed. Maybe one of the people I just fingered—the pregnant wife or one of the girls with the knitting—will come tooling up in her red Cadillac convertible and rub us out.

"There now," says my shepherd, "that wasn't too bad, was it?"

I don't have much to say. The car stops at Hollywood and Vine, and I take my chain and clank off down the street.

It is eventide, on the day of the great Confession. The house this patriot leases looks down on UCLA. A splendid house it is, set off by two acres of grass. It is owned by a former child movie star long since matured, and happily married three times over, and domiciled in Texas.

The house could stand some repairs, but all around are the faded remnants of her glorious childhood stardom: bars on downstairs bedroom windows; built-in soda fountain upstairs in the second den; a sliding mystery panel that leads to a wall-eyed safe.

Things have changed, of course, over the passing years. The property has been subdivided, what with taxes and all. Where her private bowling alley and pony stable and poolhouse once were, a separate dwelling now stands, behind a chain-link fence.

All is not lost, however. Behind huge electric gates (no longer operative) lies a run-down fairyland where once Miss Cinderella would while away the joyous golden hours with less than Cinderella-like playmates. Here still stands her kingdom, with its toadstool-shaped games room complete with kitchenette. Here, too, is a miniature enchanted forest full of miniature boulders imported, and small reflecting pools, and a little waterfall that once did flood an honest and truly brook—in response to a hundred and ten volt pump. Here, too, still stands what's left of a small stone boy with clipped stone wings who is manfully trying—as small boys will—to pee in a clogged-up pool; his bladder, however, has rusted, and also his pekker is chipped.

This evening I walk alone outside the house, putting a little distance between me and my bottle of rum, which stands on a wrought-iron table. René, my next-door neighbor, is throwing a poolside party with lots of girls. René sells skis and barbells and his nights are full of music.

My children sleep in a room with the iron-barred windows of Hollywood. The baby is kicking up a storm tonight. The rum burns down my throat. What was it the analyst said? "You know, Mr. Hayden, that there are times when alcohol, properly handled, can bring relief."

Yes, Doc. But there are times when it doesn't work, no matter how much you drink. There are times when you can't even come up with a buzz, let alone get drunk and forget.

"Sterling?" Her voice comes out of the night. "When are you coming to bed?"

"Just as soon as I kill this bottle, that's when I'm coming to bed."

She drifts back into the house. "Sweetie," I might as well have said, "I'm sorry. It's no use. We never had a marriage. The man who is coming to bed once this bottle is killed isn't the man you married. That guy is dead, because today he finally sold out all the way."

CHAPTER 79

I slam the door behind me. Now see this ill-starred pair, analyst and patient: "Sonofabitch, Doc, I'm not sure I can take much more of this. I don't ask for any miracles, but I would like to get just a little relief. Things aren't getting better, they're getting worse. Sixteen months now I've been coming in here five damn days each week. Sixteen months is a long time when a man is out of work and his marriage is nothing more than an endless fight.

"Last night I made a list of the men I know, of what they are getting from life. To survive, a man has to get his kicks some way, in his personal or his professional life. He can get along with one or the other, and damn few men have both. Every last man I know has either one or the other. But not me. I'm all fouled up on both fronts.

"I'll make no bones about it, I'm thinking of quitting analysis. When a man's bogged down, when the thing he is trying to do isn't working out, then he has to damn good and well change his way of living. If you would only hold out some hope to me, then it might be different.

"I'll say this, too, that if it hadn't been for you I wouldn't have turned into a stoolie for J. Edgar Hoover. I don't think you have the foggiest notion of the contempt I have had for myself since the day I did that thing . . . Fuck it! And fuck you too.

". . . You know what I did yesterday? I quit taking those acting lessons. You know why? Because I found myself at three in the afternoon sitting in Kreitzer's basement, working out on a character called Liliom. There I stood, leaning against an imaginary Viennese lamppost, smoking a real cigarette. An imaginary girl came strolling through the park and sat down on a park bench. To attract her attention I had to ditch the cigarette, pull myself together, and do a nifty little dance round and round in circles . . . Can you picture it? There I was, tripping about like a queer with a burr in his pants, and after a bit I slid down beside her on the bench and we played a little scene. Finally, I had to lean down and pick a white flower and hold it under our noses, give her a horny look and whisper: 'White acacias—drifting down—ahh—h—'

"Doc, I hear you chuckle. Don't, there's more. In comes another one of Kreitzer's students, a long-legged, frigid Miss America type, and we go to work on a scene from a Western. I was Will the pioneer, and me and Becky was heading West to start a new life together. Well, I sat there, perched on a chair on top of a table, and I clucked to the horses and we went rattling West. All of a sudden Kreitzer goes: 'Sthing! Sthing! Sthing!' Arrows hitting the wagon. So Becky and I bail out and I hide her behind the wheels, and I take my Winchester, which is really Kreitzer's yardstick, and I plunge into the mesquite. I lie there breathing hard, the Indians all around, and all the time Kreitzer is watching my eyes to see if I feel the scene. Then he gives me the cue and I grab my yardstick and take careful aim and go: 'Bang! Bang Bang! Bang Bang Bang!'

"I tell you, I felt like a frigging clown. So I sat up and broke the scene and I busted that yardstick over my knee, fired the splinters into a corner, got to my feet, grabbed my coat, and said to the maestro: 'Look, friend, I'm thirty-five years old. I am not the most balanced man in the world, but this is simply carrying things too far.' I stalked out the door and that was the end of that. Miss America was still sitting between the wheels in her little white shorts with her tiny fish mouth.

"So, you know what I have left? I have my hour each day with you . . . That's all . . . Oh, this afternoon I'm supposed to meet my agent, some kind of a long-range deal that will make me a wealthy man. He won't say what it is. Very mysterious. Just like in here. The older I get, the more mysterious everything becomes . . .

"Doc, any comment about what I was saying before? No. You wouldn't dream of such a thing." Silence.

I wrench myself into consciousness. He stands by the door, with his Hitler mustache—a stubborn wartlike fellow. "I'm sorry —I must have dozed off."

"Till tomorrow, then, Mr. Hayden."

"Same time?" I ask.

He nods, smoking but not inhaling.

RKO-Pathé looks like a New England resort hotel that has been on a binge long enough to beat its way from east to west until at last it found itself in Culver City.

My agent is late as always. He draws me aside and we perch on the arm of the steps: "Sorry I'm late."

"You are like hell," I snap. He shoots me a troubled glance. "You upset or something, Sterling?"

"Maybe. Tell me what goes on."

"Sterling, look: would you have any objections to it if I leveled with you?"

"Go ahead."

He looks at his nails. Whatever he needs, it is isn't a manicure. "This headshrinker routine, you still involved?"

"Jess, you run your life. You shack up with a different broad each night. You complain about your home life. And I'll take care of myself, okay?"

"Sorry. All right now, look: it hurts me to say this but, kid, we got plenty of troubles. I work my tail off trying to get you work. I come close. Each week maybe three times I come close . . . Nothing." He throws up his hands. "I don't get it. I honestly don't get it."

"Why not? I get it. I don't blame these people. Why should they hire me? They know I don't give a damn for the business. They know I've only turned in one good performance so far— and that in a John Huston picture. Maybe I'm too pink for some, and too rude for others. How much more would you like, by way of explanation?"

He seems relieved as he says: "Good. I'm delighted to hear you say that. Because it leads right up to the thing that brings us here this afternoon. Now, this guy you're about to meet is a very dear friend of mine. I gave him my word of honor I wouldn't let on to you who he is or what it is he wants. He also happens to be just about the wealthiest man in the business. What's more, he is as honest as they come, maybe more. Now, I want you to promise Jess here that you won't blow up. Just listen to what it is he has to say. It's a deal, okay?"

"Sure it is."

Like warpath Indians we advance down the empty corridor to a sign that reads: Lessor Production Enterprises. We enter. The girl at the desk is pert and cute. We are, it seems, more than welcome this afternoon. She leads the way with Jess following closely. It is all he can manage to keep his hands at his side. He turns and winks at me.

We enter a paneled office, and a small figure rises from behind a massive desk: "Sol, shake hands with Sterling Hayden." He emerges from behind his barricade and we shake hands. Jess laughs sharply. "Okay Sol, I got him here, the rest I leave to you."

Jess leaves, but Sol seems in no hurry to come to the point.
"Sterling," he says, "I have admired you for a long time
now. You are an unusual man. You hold this town at arm's
length. You fight off prominence. I do too. Hollywood has laughed
at my pictures for a good many years, and yet, there are very
few men in this business I couldn't buy and sell a hundred times
each day—like that!" He snaps two pudgy fingers.

My eyes go round the room. On a far wall is a photograph of
a world-champion swimmer poised atop a cliff. His hair is long.

"Sterling, you don't know yet why you are here, do you?"

"No, not exactly, but I'm beginning to have an idea."

"Why?" he asks.

"You tell me," I say, smiling to be polite.

"Very well, I will. You are a man, from what I am told, who is
concerned about the world. You would like to make it a better
place. Isn't that so, perhaps?"

I nod, watching him and waiting, tilted back in my chair.

"So would I. Throughout much of my life I have devoted
myself to bringing pleasure and happiness to hundreds of millions of people. I have been lucky. When one of our pictures is
premièred in India or in Africa, it is an extremely important
occurrence. Here in the U.S.A. my pictures don't open like that,
but I don't mind—not the least little bit."

On another wall stands a winsome girl dressed in a buckskin
smock. A curly-haired boy with a monkey on his shoulder is holding her hand.

"Sterling, you're a bright man, you know what I'm leading
up to."

"I have a pretty good idea."

"You know, Sterling, I can walk down any street in this
world and stop any person I meet, and when I say the word
'Tarzan' they will understand me. They will smile. From just
that simple word they derive a certain pleasure—"

I can't believe it yet.

"To come to my point: shortly we'll need a new Tarzan. This
is not such a simple problem as some folks seem to think. We
here all feel a deep responsibility to the hundreds of millions
spread out across the world who are fans of the man called
Tarzan."

My face must have changed, for he raises one hand and says:
"No, please, let me finish. Maybe you don't realize that Tarzan
represents the free man who stands alone against the forces
of evil. He is against the machine. He is against exploitation.

He stands for all the things that you, Sterling, would like to stand for. That is why I wanted to talk to you. That is why I am going to ask you not to give me your reaction until you have gone home and thought about it and maybe talked it over some with Jess here."

"Well—sure, why not."

"Fine. Now I have given your agent some papers that show the kind of business we do all over the world. You will be amazed when you study these figures. Show them to your investment counselors, think of what they mean, and then let's sit down and talk some more."

I find myself on the verge of several wisecracks. Something holds me back. He has his way of thinking, and I have mine—whatever it is these days . . .

I rise and go for the door. "Oh," his voice catches me, "there is one more thing, since you are already here. I would like to call in my associates and let them take a good look at you. Perhaps you could strip to the waist."

"Not today," I say. "Thanks just the same."

I bolt to the open air. The thing that galls is the thought that they might be right . . . Maybe if I were stripped of all my pretenses, this would be my natural level.

I remember a remark my stepfather once made. I see him picking his chin with his back to the boiler there in Emma's kitchen: "You are going to grow up to have a forty-six-inch chest and a size-three hat."

I crank all the windows down as a cop comes past on his three-wheel traffic cart. He chalks my left rear tire. Our eyes meet. "Ugh," I say, "you copper—me Tarzan." He shakes his head a little. I pound my chest three times, cough hard, and flick the ignition switch.

CHAPTER 80

The little First Lutheran Church of Santa Monica stands on its quiet corner. On a normal day this is a church like any other, modest and calm, flanked by orderly rows of modest homes set back from placid streets. This, however, is not a normal day. It is nine o'clock in the morning, April 11, 1951. The church has been hired for the day by the motion-picture company shooting a film tentatively titled *Skid Road.* Starred are Viveca Lindfors, Thomas Mitchell, and Sterling Hayden.

ACTION. The cameras whir, a long shot (silent). Here comes the smiling congregation made up of docile extras, dressed in their Sunday best. Fresh-scrubbed extra-children throw covetous eyes toward heaven. Extra-ushers simper and the flock vanishes inside the church. CUT.

ACTION. Full shot. Interior of church (silent). Up the aisles come the two hundred extras, models of decorum. (Note: this is as close to heaven as an extra is apt to get, sitting indoors all day on cushioned pews; warm but not too warm, dry—save for a beer or a snort sneaked in between the shooting.) They arrange themselves with dignity, chins high, eyes burning with a holy light worth all of their extra's pay. CUT.

Bodies and faces sag, the light in the eyes grows dim. The children skeedoodle fast to the school set up in an empty bus. Down with the pious posture, and up fast with the morning headlines.

HAYDEN CONFESSES ALL—HAYDEN EX-RED— HAYDEN BARES COMMIE PAST—HAYDEN WASHES OUT RED TAINT—EXPOSES CONSPIRACY

"Stand by please," says the assistant director, and the papers vanish rustling. All eyes are eagerly focused on a door to one side of the pulpit. Feelings of virtue mount—somebody else is in trouble.

ACTION. Long shot (silent), over the congregation, then moving in fast to focus on the door just to the left of the pulpit. An expert rushes down the aisle, and checks focus. The hidden cue-light blinks, and the door opens slowly on the Lutheran minister, dressed in black. He closes the door, pauses, then steps ponderously up to his pulpit. The camera dollies up fast, to rest with its one masked eye peering at the man with the troubled face.

Sweat starts from his brow, swells, and runs dripping down his face and into his collar. The smile he is trying on does not fit this morning. His chest heaves. What is wrong with this shaky preacher fellow? His arms go up and his eyes go out. "My friends—" he whispers hoarsely. And behind the camera his faithful extra-flock looks up to him in wonder. Not all, however. Some are reading now and he sees their headlined papers. Sweat trickles into his eyes, rolls down under his shirt, and is dammed by his belt. His eyes show vacant spaces . . . CUT.

In the beginning came the subpoena, salmon-colored, mortgage-sized, folded thrice, slipped by the man with the U.S. Marshal's badge into the hand of the preacher in the studio commissary.

"Geez, Mr. Hayden, only the other night me an' the missus was saying: 'Now, that Hayden's a real nice manly actor—' Always admired you, Sterl; never did think I'd ever be serving *you* with no subpoena . . . Here, I'll slip it to you quiet like; then I guess if I was you I'd sure go call my lawyer."

The preacher folds himself into a green pay station. He dials too fast, wrong number, then again. "Martin? Martin, this is Hayden. I just got subpoenaed."

"Who by, your wife?"

"No, the [sshh—look around—cuddle the ear of the phone] by the Committee [shh-h-h-] by the House Committee on Un-American Activities."

"Well, is that so?" (Help me, Martin, help me.) "All right, we'll have to move fast. I'll contact Wheeler, their Hollywood investigator. Meet me tonight—my office—eight o'clock sharp . . . And, by the way—better bring your wife—and also you might wear that rosette that goes with the Silver Star."

"Yes, Martin." (Oh, thank God for Martin Gang—thank God I went to the F.B.I.—Martin knows what to do.

The handsome-looking couple enters the elevator, along with two burly bull-faced gents that look like football coaches. The clock shows eight sharp.

The lady exits first, her tall husband next, respectable in tweed, but with the sweaty hands of anxiety clutching at his bowels.

Their lawyer is waiting for them, and begins to josh with the head coach, who says: "We even shared the elevator with your client, but figured we wouldn't say boo till he was represented by counsel." The sub-coach is silent.

Counsel's ploy: "Well, gentlemen, my client is very upset.

I will tell you right now that he went to the F.B.I. last year—
after the start of the Korean War. We said what we knew at that
time, and we hoped that would be the end of it."

Head coach's gambit: "Now look here, folks, I'm sorry about
this. I know how it is, but, Martin, my hands are tied. The
Committee is, as you know, a duly constituted investigative
body charged with protecting the security of these United States."

"Is there," counsel intervenes, "any chance that my client
could testify behind closed doors? We have an obligation to this
man and to his young wife here and to their children. There's a
fine career at stake, gentlemen. My client is, as you know, a
war hero with several combat medals. I'm sure that such a man
might act foolishly or impulsively at times, but surely not sub-
versively."

"Now, just one minute here, you're acting as though the Committee's activities are punitive. This is untrue. The investigative
function of the legislative branch of the government is the very
backbone of the democratic process. It is dedicated to the preservation of the cherished ideals of all of us. Therefore, it seems
to me that it is a man's duty and privilege to tell the whole truth
before this duly constituted body. . . ."

The meeting lasted a long time.

The studio stages its own kind of hearing in its executive
office building. The room is packed with eight or ten executives.
The top-dollar lawyer enters again with his putty preacher-actor
client. The room is heavy with smoke and tension. One of the
top bagmen, fresh in from New York City, bold in his dollar
manner, says: "Anything new?"

"Nothing," says the lawyer. "The schedule stands. The
testimony will begin at the end of next week, maybe before."
Groans.

The man from New York is angry. "Hayden, I must be frank
with you. This entire venture has been placed in serious
jeopardy. We have made a substantial investment in the film,
and it's too late to shelve the project. Already the publication of
the subpoena story has had its effects. The pressure groups are
outraged. My colleagues and I placed great faith in you, in spite
of your discouraging career in recent years. We gambled,
gambled half a million dollars on you. Now what are we to do?"

The putty man shakes his head in silence.

The lawyer's voice rises: "It just may be that we'll have to

testify sooner, before the end of production. It might be
dangerous to wait too long, with public hostility and all."

Local exec wailing: "But my God, Martin, he's in every single
shot from now till the end of the picture. If we stop shooting
now, we're dead. Jesus, imagine the losses. You've got to get the
Committee to hold off. Otherwise it'll be a disaster. And this
had to be my first production."

The New York man is silent for a while, then speaks: "Gentlemen, I have confidence in Hayden. Look for God's sake at his
war record. This boy is no Red. He's our boy. He's no radical
dedicated to force and violence. Right, Sterlin'? True or false, I
ask it?"

Putty voice mumbles: "I think it will be all right."

The New York man sums up: "Sterlin'—one word of advice.
Go straight, tell the truth. Ask yourself: 'What will my children
think?' Always make them proud of you."

Exit puttybones.

Analytic hour number 300, plus. Seven a.m. sharp (making
room for acting). The putty man enters fast, flings off his coat,
and sits down. "No couch crap this morning, sorry."

The analyst sighs, his smile flickers and fades. "What is wrong
this morning?"

"Doc, I can't go through with it. Since the subpoena two weeks
back I've tried and tried to convince myself. They know I was
a Party member—they don't want information, they want to put
on a show, and I'm the star. They've already agreed to go over
the questions with me in advance. It's a rigged show: radio and
TV and the papers. I'm damned no matter what I do. Co-operate
and I'm a stool pigeon. Shut my mouth and I'm a pariah."

"I suggest, Mr. Hayden"—the analyst's sober voice—"that
you try and relax—just lie down . . . Now then, may I remind
you there's really not much difference, so far as you yourself are
concerned, between talking to the F.B.I. in private and taking
the stand in Washington. You have already informed, after all.
You have excellent counsel, you know, and the chances are
that the public will—in time perhaps—regard you as an ex-
emplary man, who once made a mistake."

"But I don't have to. I can sit in that hearing room and
answer the sixty-four-dollar question. I can say: Yes I was in.
I was in the CPUSA for six months in '46. Period. Don't ask me
to name any names, gentlemen, because if you do I'll tell you
to go to hell and that is that."

"Of course, you can. Why don't you?"
I have no more to say.

Suspense . . . Suspended now in the trackless void of a brilliant starlit night, with the tubular hull hurtling east at twenty thousand feet above an unseen land. Unseen, that is, except for snug and lonesome lights of mountain ranches and barren crossroads towns. Except, too, for darts of orange flame from oil-well exhausts gnawed by the teeth of a westerly windstream as it scours at the endless prairie.

One man alone. One man at bay this night, his back braced in mute consignment to what lies ahead, standing his watch wide-eyed and alone—in spite of the wife by his side with whom he is holding hands. All over this hurtling cavern are others who read and talk and laugh out loud, or smoke and play at cards, or sleep. He feels now the way you always feel when you've lost control, when your vessel runs wild in the grip of a thundering gale, when you pitch from a plane with your life strapped on your back in silken folds.

Halfway across the country tomorrow becomes today, and he knows that today must be the most desperate day of his life. This is a date he will never forget: April 10, 1951. He turns his watch ahead to Eastern Standard Time. Nine more hours and he'll enter his nation's capital with his tail between his legs . . . He folds his arms. He sighs out loud—and for no good reason sleeps.

It is driving rain as the big plane sets down. A knot of news hounds is huddled under an arch. The man and his wife lean on the wind and hustle along amid snapping flashbulbs. His lawyer is waiting and so is the man named Wheeler who came East some days ago to arrange the details of the performance. They enter a limousine. The anxious attorney in the jump seat swings to face his client. He shuffles papers, his rain-cured hat set at a cocky angle: "See these? Don't ask me how we got them, but they're ten pages of notes on an F.B.I. report of a trip you made years ago, still in uniform, to see friends in San Francisco. You were followed there and back. Recall the trip?"

"Yes."

"And do you recall writing a letter from Italy to your friend Tompkins in which you said, quote: 'Warwick, I tell you, a small platoon of these partisans could capture Parris Island armed with nothing but yo-yos.'?"

"Yes, come to think of it, I do."

"Did you pay a visit to the printing plant of the *People's World* and write on a bulletin board: 'Smrt Facizmu—Sloboda Narodu,' which means 'Death to Fascism—Freedom to the People'?

"And did you have lunch in a San Francisco hotel with . . ."

"Look, Martin, why go through all this crap? I don't have to be reminded of what I did. I've told the truth all along and I'll tell the truth today. They're not going to trip me up. I may be yellow, but I'm not a liar too."

Wheeler objects: "Why do you keep on saying you're yellow?"

"Because I am, that's why. Can you think of a better reason?"

Out of the wet we come and into the spotlights. "Please, boys, please," say the lawyer and producer. The hallways are jammed. An usher leads us through. We come to a cloakroom. "Five minutes to spare," says Wheeler, quite pleased with his world this morning. I wash my face and hands, tuck in my shirt, and check on the cigarette supply. I feel empty and taut like a drum.

Then up a flight of marble stairs to an empty hallway and a pair of giant doors. Wheeler knocks and one great door swings in.

Three hundred people crowd the hearing room. Standing room only. Through a fog I see up on the stage eight or nine men ranged behind a concave counter. One wall is solid with cameras.

I am shown to a chair at a little table with a microphone. I shift around, trying to clear my mind, trying to arrange my legs beneath the yellow table. Yellow is big this season. Directly before me a man lies flat on his back shooting into my face with a camera labeled CBS–TV.

The curtain rises and the chairman raps for order with his Legion gavel. Those who flank him look tired or bored. He mutters something about a quorum, and reels off the names of his colleagues: Potter, Scherer, Moulder, Walter . . . I miss the other names.

I am sworn to tell the truth. A man named Tavenner will be the moderator—we met in the cloakroom briefly. The Chair refers to him as "counsel." My lawyer remains discreetly offstage, along with my wife, who is being displayed like a service flag draped in a front window. I check my costume, which has been selected carefully. The suit is brownish tweed, cut to suggest the outdoorsman—with a trace of the poet thrown in. The collar is buttoned down around a loose-knit tie. Socks are black and shoes are cordovan, and in the left lapel rests a tiny fleck of combat ribbon.

Counsel studies his script, collaborated on by Gang, Wheeler, and Hayden. It is a good script, runs to forty pages, and tells a lively tale. Up on the dais it is being studied with circumspection, out of camera range.

Counsel is all smiles. And why not? He is accustomed to facing non-collaborators who sit in the witness chair and chew him up and down. He is used to facing men and women who refuse to dance to his tune. Today the Fifth Amendment will not trouble him.

Now counsel sounds his pitch pipe and I begin to sing. Once I begin, what follows seems almost anticlimactic.

Strange. In almost all countries a man who collaborates with those who would punish freedoms arouses the hatred of his countymen. And yet today, in the United States of America, the way to loyalty is this—down the muddy informer's trail. Very strange indeed.

I am well prepared. Few stoolies have played this hall who were better prepared than I. I have nine pages of neat notes typed out on filing cards. And on the tenth page is an index of dates, names, places, and an itemized list of donations to seditious causes dedicated to the liquidation of segregation and racial prejudice and other minor hatreds.

I drone on, and up on the stage the muckrakers grow restless. Wood the Chairman dozes, and at last I am nearing the promised Land of Loyal Ones, and now the time comes for the payoff.

Congressman Moulder clears his throat. "I just want to say to you, Mr. Hayden, that after listening to your testimony today —and this is for the record—I personally find you to be an intensely loyal and patriotic American citizen."

Oh, thank you, sir, so much. Hey! You execs back out on the coast! Your boy came through. It is okay. You will not lose your dollars. . . . Do you hear me? Is it okay—for me to come back to work tomorrow???

Congressman Walter speaks: "I will add something to what Mr. Moulder just said: I agree. I think that by his courageous and forthright testimony today this witness has set an example that thousands of others might follow. Do you feel that is so, Mr. Hayden?"

"Oh yes sir. I would like to say one more thing. I urge upon everyone who might find himself in my position to come forward and get this thing off his chest. It is a big burden, believe me." Eyes go down in abject modesty.

"I know that is so, Mr. Hayden."

Other voices mumble jingoistic drivel . . . And above this crowded room like a mirage stands a group of people who once were friends of mine. They look at me with grave and saddened faces. No one says a word. I think of Larry Parks, who not ten days ago sat in this very chair and by pleading with the Committee—by begging them not to make him crawl in the mud—consigned himself to oblivion. Well, I hadn't made that mistake. Not by a goddamned sight. I was a real daddy longlegs of a worm when it came to crawling.

Stoolies should never be tall. When you are, they can pick you out as you shuffle down the long marbled hallways. Voices keep calling: Congratulations, Hayden—That took guts, Hayden, to do what you just did—Don't worry, Sterlin', your career won't suffer none—

"Hear 'em, hear 'em?" laughs Gang. "Mark my words, boy, you are going to emerge from this thing bigger than ever before. I wouldn't be at all surprised if you became a kind of a hero overnight. Wait till they hear about your testimony out on the Coast tonight . . . Why, you're going to end up smelling like a rose."

Westward bound late in the evening. A change of planes in Chicago, time for coffee and to buy the papers.

HAYDEN WENT TO PARTY!—ACTOR HAYDEN RED— HAYDEN COMMIE BUT WENT STRAIGHT AFTER SEVEN MONTHS

April 10, 1951 (AP). Big dashing ex-Marine Captain Sterling Hayden today admitted to the House Committee on Un-American Activities . . .

Westward bound again, not too tired to read all the reviews, searching for signs of how the public will react.

I am about to turn off the light when a small news item stops me. Top of an inside page.

HAYDEN PAL DIES

Boston (UP). Lawrence J. "Larry" O'Toole, 42, artist, sailor and adventurer died today . . . On the same day that his best friend and fellow-adventurer-actor Sterling Hayden figured in the news by testifying before the . . . O'Toole

once helped Hayden sail a square-rigger from Gloucester to
Tahiti . . . O'Toole was known to sailing men and artists
all over the world.

Quickly I cut off the light. His face appears clearly. I see him
that cold fall day where he carved at a figurehead with the
wind rattling the loft windows down on T Wharf . . . I see him
laughing all through the November hurricane . . . I see him
sketching as we cross the Equator, in his sheepskin coat because
of the Humboldt current . . . And, most vivid of all, I see again
the night—our last at sea together—with the brig eighty-seven
days out of Gloucester and Tahiti under the lee . . .

I hope you went out fast—before you heard the news of what
your old shipmate was up to.

Tomorrow becomes today. It is the eleventh of April, 1951.
Perhaps the bells should toll in the little Lutheran Church of
Santa Monica.

CHAPTER 81

Skid Road was completed and in less than ten days I was cast in
another picture. You're a fine citizen, you are, just bursting with
patriotism. And to prove it to you, baby, we'll put you to work
slapping leather and manhandling women and swaggering in
through those swinging saloon doors flinty-eyed and brave. We'll
turn you loose with a costume cutlass and let you fight for the
honor of our starlet girls with the eager loins.

I swung like a goon from role to role—*Denver and Rio Grande;
Kansas Pacific; Golden Hawk; Take Me to Town; Hellgate; Cry
Baby; Flat Top; The Star; Renegade Canyon; Fighter Attack;
Delay at Fort Bess; Arrow in the Dust* . . . They were all made
back to back in an effort to cash in fast on my new status as a
sanitary culture hero.

These were the dismal years of the black list. These were
the years of excommunication, when thirty or forty hostile-
witness writers were sent into exile, only to find that producers
were willing to—very discreetly, of course—buy more than a
hundred scripts underneath the table.

Not often does a man find himself eulogized for having behaved in a manner that he himself despises. I subscribed to a press-clipping service. They sent me two thousand clips from papers east and west, large and small, and from dozens of magazines. Most had nothing but praise for my one-shot stoolie show. Only a handful—led by *The New York Times*—denounced this abrogation of constitutional freedoms whereby the stoolie could gain status in a land of frightened people.

CHAPTER 82

At least the steady work meant that the analysis could continue, though now under the auspices of a new man. This is not such a friendly doctor, this heavy-headed, caustic fellow with thick horn-rims and a heavy accent.

He is what might be called a flenser, a stripper of blubber. He is not disposed to the silent school of treatment. Listen to how he speaks now, very slowly: "Mister Hayden, it has been three years almost since you entered analysis with a colleague of mine. Some weeks ago you resumed treatment with me after a— shall we say—hiatus of some six or seven months. And already you complain of a lack of progress. You are convinced that your marriage is doomed. You have passed through the initial stages of legal divorce. Yet now you speak at length of reconciliation. You justify this by expressing concern for your children."

"Yes."

"Five times you have become separated from Mrs. Hayden. Each time you reconcile. And with each reconciliation the situation between you becomes more intolerable. Can you not accept the reality of the divorce? Later you can modify your arrangement and re-enter your children's lives."

"I'm concerned with what will happen to the children. They won't have a chance. She'll get hooked up with some guy as fouled up as I was when we met."

"But what chance do they have now, in a home full of hatred? I think you are talking nonsense."

Silence, then once more the incisive voice: "Just tell me your thoughts, please."

"I was wondering just why I'm so damned obsessed with this question of custody. Thousands of men with kids go through what I'm involved in. They make up their minds even though they're sick at the thought of being cut off from their kids."

"I believe if we knew the answer to that question you would need no further treatment."

"You know, it's a peculiar thing: I used to think if I could only work freely as an actor, then I'd at least have half a life. Then I'd have enough perspective to get through analysis and maybe have some decent chance of happiness. But I just keep going in circles because of this custody thing."

"I would like to ask you a question. Your wife was deprived of the custody of a daughter by a former marriage—that is correct, is it not?"

"It is."

"Has it ever occurred to you to confirm this?"

"No, it never entered my head."

"You profess to be in anguish over custody matters and you never thought to determine the facts of the case."

What was left of the hour flew past.

🌾

CHAPTER 83

They call it custody. The word cries out wrath, bitterness, frustration, hatred. A curious word to apply to the kingdom of children.

You and your lawyer together, a junior partner, a heavy-jowled man inclined toward overweight, mild of voice and manner, yet bright and ambitious. You're on your way downtown to the Hall of Records. The traffic is snarled as you crawl by the Interchange. His voice sounds sad: "Sterling, I have an idea what we find down here today will not make attractive reading. And whatever we find I think you're all wrong. I think you are consumed with this custody business. The divorce as it stands is all you have any right to expect now. Let it stand. Take your final decree next summer, then give her enough rope, and she'll do the rest herself. And suppose you did somehow win custody. How would you manage the kids?"

"That's my worry."

"I'm your friend as well as your lawyer. I have two kids of my own and I don't mind telling you it's all we can do, my wife and I together, to keep things under control."

We enter a run-down building and go to a floor so crammed with high green files the floor is lost in darkness. The man on the desk seems tired as he looks at the slip of paper and vanishes down a tunnel. He returns empty-handed: "Sorry, gents. Not here. Must be in Pasadena." The lawyer never quits: "If you don't mind, I'll take a look for myself."

"Go ahead," says the tired one, "just you. Your client got to wait out here."

We sit at a long scarred table. He reads first, then passes me the papers. For nearly an hour we read in silence. Now and then he points out a salient word or phrase. A window is open, the city noises and the heat come funneling in. It is not a pleasant time, but now I know I'll fight. My chances don't seem so bad any more.

A month goes slowly past and one evening I enter the lawyer's building just in time to say good night to the clipped, neat secretaries.

"How are you, Mick?" I ask.

"Tired. That's how I am." He slumps in a swivel chair behind a desk piled high with blue-bound documents. "Well," he says, "what's troubling you tonight?"

"Mick, my mind is made up. You told me to take my time. I have, and now I'm going to get custody of my kids. If you won't help me, then I'll find a lawyer who will."

"Sterling, if you were as single-minded about your career, you'd be the biggest name in town."

"Okay. You tell me that my chances are poor. You tell me that there are judges in town who think the worst mother is preferable to the best father when it comes to custody of young kids."

He squints through a cloud of smoke: "I've heard them say it myself."

"I understand that the only chance I have involves hiring a team of detectives—and you don't know any good detectives— and then over a period of at least five months we build up a record of sustained neglect of the children. This is an air-tight affair that is documented and that the detectives can attest to in court.

"Furthermore, you say that women in this position are adept at knowing when they're under surveillance. This, combined with the fact that I'm paying her plenty of money for a good maid and a squad of baby sitters, makes what I'm trying to do damn near impossible.

"And to cap the whole thing off, it is the standard operating procedure in cases like this to clinch the deal by busting into the house and getting photographic documentation." I subside into a chair. He takes a pill and kindles his long cigar: "You should be a lawyer. You summed it up pretty well—except for one or two little things."

"Such as?"

"Such as the fact that you are already saddled with an interlocutory decree of divorce. The property settlement is in effect. All of this works in her favor—gives her plenty of latitude to go on with her life."

"Okay then. I'll reconcile and stick around for a couple of months. That will dismiss the present divorce. Then we'll start all over from scratch."

He frowns. "You're prepared to do a thing like that?"

"You're goddam right I am."

"Very well. There is a little matter of money. You didn't touch on that. You owe this firm several thousand dollars already. You are living right up to the hilt. Detectives don't come cheap. What's more, they're apt to blow the whole deal sky high. Surveillance might run as high as twelve, maybe fifteen thousand dollars, maybe a hell of a lot more."

"Okay, I'll get it."

"How?"

"How? For Christ's sake, I'll earn it, how else? I'll keep on making these crap pictures. I'll make crap television. I'll do anything that has to be done."

"And you realize that every crappy picture that you make takes you further away from the possibility of better parts?"

I wave my hands to dismiss this.

"All right." He gets to his feet, circles the room twice, and comes to rest on a couch of ersatz leather. "The most important part of the deal is this. Custody is never settled. Matters of custody aren't like normal litigation. Don't ever forget I said that. We're going ahead because you won't listen to reason. You aren't the smartest client I have, but you just might be the most stubborn.

"Suppose you do win custody. Suppose you do find a proper house and a proper substitute mother and you live the life of a celibate." He pauses long enough to smile. "Then all a wife has to do after a suitable period of time is come back into court and claim what's known as 'a change of circumstance.' All of which will be at your expense, her lawyers, your lawyers, court costs—the works. And if she's lucky enough to hit the right judge at the right time and she sits on the stand looking sweet and contrite, then she'll regain custody. And if she doesn't, she'll come back again—and again and again. And sooner or later she'll fall into the hands of a ruthless attorney who, quite apart from the merits of the case, will pick up the ball and run for the sake of space in the papers—and a tidy fee, of course."

"Go on."

"That's all." He squints and smiles. "You still want to go ahead?"

"Absolutely."

"Let's see now, what is the date today?"

"January 26."

"I have to go East on business. I'll be gone ten days or so. When I come back, I'll make some inquiries and we'll see what we can do. And while I'm gone, you might look around and try to come up with a detective who isn't a jerk."

"I'll do that."

We both rise. He pats his belly. "By the way, you look good these days. How do you keep in shape?"

"Simple. I can't sleep much, so I walk. Every morning from four till seven, I walk nine miles. It's tough in this town—trying to walk—the cops see you and think you're nuts or a prowler or maybe a peeping Tom."

"Give me a ring some morning. We'll go for a walk together."

"I'll do that too, after we get the kids."

Almost a year later, a white Ford station wagon winds up a long canyon to a house in a row of houses. A man is driving. Four children come down to the car, each one carrying a little bag, each one clinging to a toy or tousled woolen animal. The car descends the canyon now, and the man at the wheel has tears in his eyes as he drives to a tiny cliffside house with a slantwise view of the sea.

Then another trip, and now the rack on top of the car is loaded with family hardware, all of it new. Crib, playpen, jump

seats with beads by the tray. More cases and cartons are unloaded, the key is left in the mailbox, and the car drives east
through the city to a white apartment house where one final stop
is made. A tall German woman comes out and settles herself up
front:

"Hilda," I say, "these are my kids. Kids, this is Hilda. She is
going to look after you because you will live with Daddy now."

"This is Christian," I go on, "and that is Dana and that of
course is Gretchen and Matthew is asleep there under the
blanket."

"Kids, we're not going back to that little house on the hill.
We're going out to the desert to a ranch for a week and then
we'll move into a big old house with a pool, on the other side
of those hills, next to Turnley and Flora and—"

"Daddy," Christian says, "do we still go to the same school?"

"Nope, you'll go to a brand-new school."

"Daddy?" Dana's face is hostile. "When do we get to go back
to Mommy again?"

"We'll talk about that later. Not for a long time."

Hilda sits in silence. Somehow she doesn't seem like a mother.
We climb up a freeway ramp. Thanksgiving is Thursday next,
and I don't know, really, driving east why I feel such an ache
inside.

BOOK VI

COLD STAR
BLAZING

CHAPTER 84

— TELEGRAMME —

HAYDEN SCHOONER WANDERER PAPEETE TAHITI
TRYING GET YOU LEAD AS STRONGLY DEDICATED CAPTAIN OF
SINKING OCEAN LINER POWERFUL DOCUMENTARY TYPE PICTURE
METRO ENTIRELY ON ILE DE FRANCE LOCATION OSAKA JAPAN
STOP SIX WEEKS FORTY THOUSAND TRY FIFTY CABLE COLLECT IF
INTERESTED PLEASE

— TELEGRAMME —

ACTOR STERLING HAYDEN   YACHT WANDERER   TAHITI   PAPEETE

HAVE GREAT GUEST STAR ROLE FOR HOUR LONG TELEVISION DRAMA
BASED ON JESUIT PRIEST WHO SINGLEHANDEDLY FORESTALLED
SIOUX MASSACRE STOP CAN YOU FLY BACK FIVE THOUSAND ONE
WEEK REHEARSE ONE WEEK SHOOT ROUND TRIP TRANSPORT PAID
FEEL EXCELLENT CHANCE BOOST FINE CAREER STOP CABLE PLEASE
COLLECT STOP REGARDS

— TELEGRAMME —

PLEASE TELL HAYDEN THAT SNOWSHOE THOMPSON TELEVISION
SERIES TOP AUSPICES TOP SPONSOR TOP NETWORK TALENT OFFERS
HIM BEST CHANCE MUCH MONEY PLUS SHARE OWNERSHIP PER-
PETUITY PLUS CREATIVE PARTICIPATION STOP WILL BE MADE
AWAY FROM HOLLYWOOD STOP GUARANTEE THIS IS TOP ACTION
DRAMA PIONEER PERIOD STOP SAY HELLO IN ANY CASE

— TELEGRAMME —

STRONG POSSIBILITY EXCELLENT ROLE FINE PICTURE STARTS
MIDDLE OCTOBER SIXTY THOUSAND FOR TEN WEEKS WORK CABLE
PLEASE SOME REPLY NO ANSWER MY LAST FIVE CABLES STOP
CABLE GRIPPO COLLECT

— TELEGRAMME —

HAYDEN   SCHOONER WANDERER   A QUAI   PAPEETE   TAHITI

WOULD YOU CONSIDER LEAD FRENCH PRODUCTION SCREENPLAY
FROM CONRAD NOVEL TWO MONTHS LOCATION GREECE STOP
DO YOU SPEAK ANY FRENCH STOP CABLE REPLY SOONEST

— TELEGRAMME —

THOUGHT HAD TWO MOVIES BUT WARNER BROTHERS STUPIDITY
ABOUT YOUR RELIABILITY KILLED SAME STOP HAVE OTHER STRONG
LEADS BUT MUST GUARANTEE PRODUCE BODY STOP WOULD YOU
PLAY LEAD IN HEMINGWAYS THE KILLERS CBS NOVEMBER FIRST
REHEARSAL SHOWDATE NINETEENTH LIVE NETWORK FROM NEW
YORK TEN THOUSAND PLUS TRANSPORTATION ROUND TRIP NO
COMMISSION AS FEEL URGENT REPEAT URGENT YOU APPEAR THIS
SHOW OR CAREER MUST SUFFER BADLY REPLY AT ONCE STOP
URGENT SIGNED

CHAPTER 85

1959 was fading fast and so was this odyssey of mine that I had
begun back in January. One result was a feeling of relief—after
running away comes the time to run back home. Another feeling
was of sadness, of conclusion. Nothing lasts, save anxiety.

And what had it all proved, the headlines, the laughter, the thousands of dollars poured out, the letters of congratulation, the soft winds and the harsh words, the squalls and the gales and the calms . . . what did they all add up to?

Nothing tangible, certainly nothing I could show on a statement of profit and loss. And yet I felt that something was coming to life inside. Even as the voyage was about to end, I sensed that its momentum might endure.

I knew what I had to do, take the vessel back up to San Francisco, sell her, put the children in school, brazen it out with the creditors, and write a book. Perhaps (so I rationalized) I was expecting too much of myself, a man grown soft in the service of the easy dollar, when I thought to languish in the South Seas in 1959 with a polyglot crew of flaccid young men and women who were, in blunt terms, seeking some relief from an ultra-civilized world.

But before turning back I felt the need for a final tilt with adventure. And so that first week in September found the *Wanderer*, late one afternoon, threading the pass off Papeete bound for the island of Mehetia with nine or ten men on board. The Africas had all flown out to the States, so the Hayden children moved aft. Two Tahitian girls shared the work in the galley. We would be gone ten days or so, and the kids would see a genuine desert island, lush and beautiful, that island I had first seen from the masthead of the *Yankee* bound around the world, twenty-two years ago.

Headlong she goes into the teeth of an easterly gale, with the night hung low. Four bells in the graveyard watch, with blankets of spray rattling down the length of the deck. On through the night she lunges, with the kitchenware clanging and the mainsail reefed.

Dawn, when it comes, is only a glimmer above the eastern horizon. With the sea this rough, it will take us two days just to come up with the island, and once there, it will be too rough to land. Why not swing her off and go snoring in for a sheltered roadstead near the eastern tip of Tahiti? I alter the course, the sheets go surging out, and she flies fast with the wind well aft of the beam, rolling and burying her rail. Tahiti bursts from the wrack, I check off the miles, and the landmarks rise . . . a headland here, and a gorge there, and once a shower of waterfalls.

Tautira rises beyond the bows, veiled in falling rain. Skirting

the hook of the reef, the vessel slips through the pass, the sea
subsides, and we gain our haven.

Christian's voice comes aft from the jibboom's end: "Hey pop,
look, a river! Hey pop, will you row us in?"

"Row yourselves in," says father.

The boy sniffs the wind and watches the ruffles race offshore.
The sails come buckling down. I feel contrite. What good is a
father if he can't take the trouble to row up unknown rivers in
far-off lands?

Taking the big binoculars, I squint inshore and mutter: "Say
now, boys, this is a pretty goddam good river. This is the first
one we've come across powerful enough to burst through the
beach and into the sea . . ."

Over the side they tumble, three boys, one girl; and I ship
the oars as the boat is shoved free of the schooner. I bend my
back to the work, the oars whip and the tholepins clunk as I
up the beat learned long ago on the Banks of Newfoundland.

I drive the whaleboat hard across the tongue of a sandbar of
silt and leaves and shells. The current bores out, but inch by
inch we gain, the children chanting and rocking in time to a
Grand Banks tune.

The sweat starts, the forearms burn, and the outraged disc
low in the back flashes tiny slivers of pain. In on the land, near-
naked kids go chasing around and around and nets are slung
from overhanging boughs and big pirogues lie in rows on the
grass.

The pass to the river is forced and the boat bursts free into a
black and oval pond fringed with deep-grass meadows and
the roots of ironwood trees. A rutted road leads by, bound toward the quiet village. The vessel's topmasts fade from view
below the dunes. "Good for you, Daddy"—Matt is speaking—
"thought you were going to poop out back there." Not a chance,
my boy, not with this boatload of critics.

Then there is a spellbinding passage of time while I push
the oars in gentle short jolts that send the boat backwards
through a carpet of lily pads with white and purple blossoms.
Two wide-eyed pilots are draped in the bows, announcing each
new enchantment: "Over there, look quick! A cow with a bird
on his head . . . Go on, that's not a cow, that's a bull . . . Who
says? . . . I say . . . How do you know, wise guy? . . . Because
he has balls, that's how I know, wise guy."

Far up ahead in the valley twin rainbows span one plunging
crevasse, fighting hard for a proper foothold till a cloud swallows

them both. A soft warm rain begins to come down. "Port, Pop, port—quick—I mean starboard. Aw, which is it anyway, when you're going backwards like this?"

And the rain comes suddenly hard and the goosebumps grow as we swing around bends, ground on bars, and shove free until Dana calls: "Look, Pop—right in there—a perfect little shelter underneath those trees." The prow parts some reeds and we slide in under a webbing of branches so entwined that no rain comes leaking down. Fish glide beneath our black transparent floor. Gretchen and Matt sit before me huddled together for warmth, shivering in unison, and I strip off my shirt, wring it out, and button it over their shoulders. Christian says under his breath: "The Wind in the Willows."

A fine tableau, the family enshrouded in oceanic silence, almost hidden from sight on a bronze-black river road. Here just now, for better or worse, is a family, five people solitary, marking time until they return to a world of chaos.

Yet, who will mother and care for these kids? And who will mother the father—a man all adrift in the tropics? You can swagger around with no visible means of support, but how do you make a family into a family without a woman around?

The squall stands out to sea. What minutes ago was mild warm rain is now no more than mist. Now the sunlight streams and the banks of the river steam. We leave our hide-out and I pole the whaleboat upstream. A towrope leads ahead where the kids churn and chant like peasants. Laugh and splash and roll in the river and roll in the sand and make your rafts of twigs and lie in the sunlight dreaming. You're homeward bound, and you'll never come back. And if you do, it won't be the same.

That night back on the schooner I pace the empty deck. After a time the need to detach is so strong that I go below and into the sleeping bag stuff wine, writing paper, tobacco, matches, and a packet of letters and photographs.

On deck again, I light a lantern, jump into the whaleboat, shove free, and row toward the unseen beach where the surf is asleep by the sand. I drag the boat up high, turn it bottom up, and, kindling a fire in its lee, I build my sleeping place.

I take my time with the wine, which glows red in the firelight.

I think of the girl back in the States. It's more than a year since we have been together. You're not the same man she used to know, lying in the lee of a whaleboat by a smoking driftwood fire, with the mountains backed up to the stars. Perhaps I should write her. Perhaps if she knew she would be waiting when I came home.

I put more wood on the fire. The tear of the riding light winks from behind the forestay. I kill what's left of the bottle and reach for the pad of paper.

CHAPTER 86

The dream was a vivid one. You are sailing fast on the port tack bound in through a slot in the land. Scores of welcoming craft much smaller than yours surround you as you go. You stand to the wheel in the clear light of an autumn day and the Golden Gate bridge soars above the trucks of your spars. The breeze from the hills falls on your ship as you heft your crotch and spit in your hands and work at the wheel, past Lime Point, past Alcatraz with its one tall chimney stuffed with a snake of smoke.

Through big binoculars you stare toward Sausalito to the wharf where a crowd has gathered. Taking your time, you search for the girl named Lorna, knowing she must be there. What does she wear this windy November day: the clinging gray-wool dress trimmed out in black, or the blue or the green or the black? Just let her be there, that's all.

Past Hurricane Gulch you fly with your rail caressing the bay. You take a cigarette, ignoring the morning's resolutions—no time to abstain just now.

A burst of wind comes down. The schooner reels, recovers, closes fast with the shore. Close enough! You chop one arm in command and the gang in the bows let sheets and halyards go by the run as you claw at the wheel, watching her swing up, biting the wind, as the jibs come running down. She glides toward the wharf, peering out with hawsepipe eyes while over your head the mainsail thunders its salt-bleached folds. You see her now. She waves, one hand clutching her throat. Your own throat tightens in response. The ship is checked and snubbed to the dock (precisely where the voyage began, ten months ago). Ignoring the crowd, you swing to the dock, and step toward Lorna fast.

No use. The dream is gone and you stare instead at the pale

blue ribs of your dory roof. The remains of the driftwood fire rest in their scooped-out pit. Two empty wine bottles project from the sand. Beyond the surf the *Wanderer*'s topmasts rise crimson out of the shadow. Under your body lies crumpled writing paper. You smooth its folds and stare at a drunken scrawl: "Dear Lorna: This is the letter I promised never to write—"

You turn through the pages quickly, then, touching a match to one corner, you toss it into the pit, where it flares, crisps, and blackens. Ashes, like the past.

But remember the first time you saw her, on that seamy sound stage where you were slumped in a canvas chair awaiting your turn to act—an admiral (of all the comical goddam things) in command of a blowed-in-the-glass task force.

She stepped out of nowhere into a shaft of light and into your life as well. Exquisite. Fumbling for a smoke, you rose to your feet quickly. Men hovered around her—one unseen clown whistled. You leaned on a stepladder looking at her, knowing that this was the start of something. Never mind that she seemed too young (or you too old).

That was late in October. Six weeks passed. My children came to live with me. And one day I called her, and she said: "I was hoping you would call." Everything seemed right at last, the New Year fast approaching, the right girl at last, the new house and the spanking-new custody agreement.

There was a rich new satisfaction, seeing her seated each night across the big round table where spoon-level faces beamed. From the book-lined living room came the crackling of logs and the primitive incense of smoke. The soft meetings of eyes, the touch of a shoulder, grazing a thigh in passing. Sometimes the children giggled in embarrassment and happiness—and so did we.

All through 1955 the flame burned, swelling, guttering sometimes under a gust of discord, yet springing up afterwards always. Then, near the end of the year, it was solemnly agreed that before the new year was out the marriage would be celebrated. She flew back East to be with her family for Christmas.

Engaged, engaged to be married—again. Oh yes, oh yes oh—long ago, faraway, gone. Bleak Christmas! And now the gifts, the holly, the wreaths, the tinsel, all mixed with ersatz snow at fifty-nine cents a can (shake well before using). The rebel despaired, threw customs and folkways and Yuletide carols out the front door, and late one night made a long-distance telephone call.

"Operator—Merry Christmas to you, too—I'd like to speak with Mr. Edison Kennel in Seattle, please. . . . Hello, Ed? Hayden. Yeah, same to you, Ed. Now tell me something. How much will you take for the schooner? Twenty? All right—will you take ten thousand cash and hold a mortgage on the balance? Right! We have a deal. See you next week."

1956 was the year of the big schooner resurrected once more. The year too of disengagement, and night after night the bottle of whiskey. The final disaster came one day in Seattle, late in spring, when the bore of rage and frustration smashed whatever was left of her love and hope.

Turnley Walker saw her to the airport that morning. We met in the car later. His face was swollen with anger. I sat numb behind the wheel. "Sterling, you and I are dear friends. I love you. But where in the hell is your heart? I don't give a damn about your childhood and your analysis. You're sick. This girl loves you. She was willing to marry you. She has endured God knows what abuse over the years from you and your wild ideas. And you snatched four little kids away from their mother, claiming she was unstable. Unstable, for Christ's sake . . ."

Long ago, faraway, gone. 1957 saw the death of the dream we shared, saw us out of touch, out of sight, out of reach, though we tried—once or twice—to salvage the wreck. But the flame was cold to the touch—was sealed—like a nerve in a tooth that is dying or dead.

The schooner seems all but deserted. Palms rustle. Surf creams in on the sand. A pirogue glides by. I break camp. With an oar for a shovel I scatter the ashes, then row to the ship. We swing the boat on deck, set the big lower sails, grapple the anchor home, and swing her off for Papeete.

CHAPTER 87

Sprawled in the shade and across from Papeete's sea wall lies the large whitewashed store known throughout the South Seas as "Etablissements Donalds, Ltd." For six months I have used their bookkeepers to watch my stock of money. My cash reserve lies in its small white pouch lost in a safe the size of a small garage.

This morning I enter briskly, account book in hand.

The half-caste clerk in the counting room sees me enter the door; he leaps from his desk, draws from the hip, and shouts "Bang. Bang-bang" as he crouches low, firing at a travel poster. I manage a sickly smile. "Oh ho!" he grins. "Veree good thzees cow-boy. Veree tough thzees hombre cowboy capitaine." His fellow clerks giggle.

I nod toward the safe. *"Le sac, s'il vous plaît."* His brows go up and down. He shakes his head, making sucking sounds. "If you do not mind, Capitaine, please you must speak now with the manageur."

I rap on the frame of the big office door. Come in, says Monsieur le Directeur, and as I enter the smell of disaster curls up like steam from his desk. He is bland of face and polite, never more so than now. *"Bonjour, Capitaine,"* he says, searching through his papers, and finally extracting a balance sheet. His eyes run down the figures. He clears his throat and leans toward me just a little. "Capitaine, I am sorry to ask this, but could we have perhaps one thousand dollars—just on account, if you please?"

"Could you what? According to your statement, I have still on deposit the sum of two thousand three hundred dollars. Therefore I do not see—"

"Oh no," his smile is very bland. "You are mistaken, Capitaine. That is a correct amount, but it is debit, not credit."

He rises and shows me the paper. It is all in longhand French, beautifully engrossed. I know he is right, of course—what book-keeper has ever been wrong? "Very well, M'sieu; it will take a day or two. I must cable my bank."

"But of course," he says, checking my smile with his.

I step outside. Something is wrong, I'm not the man I was ten minutes ago. Suddenly it's cold and I shiver. Where to turn, what to do?

This is no place to be broke. It's bad enough back home, but along this water front I've been a man to be reckoned with, the hard-boiled bastard who thumbed his nose at the law, the father-superior minus the wife, who could raise kids all by himself, the proprietor of the largest, best known "yacht" in this part of the world. Busted. And here I thought I had just cash enough on hand to lay in sea stores, pay my dues to the vultures, button up my crew, and sail with maybe ten bucks left over.

The Law of the Jungle says that the social climate of a given place must vary in direct proportion to the strength of the purse in the pants, or the values inherent in Letters of Credit and drafts on far-flung banks, resting, secure and insured, between brass-edged billfold leaves.

Moments ago I lolled in a tropical clime. Now this zone I inhabit is polar. What I thought was a cloud trapped in a mountain valley turns out to be a glacier. Penguins with spears stand on the barrier reef. Moorea Land lies bleak and forbidding, its cruel crags swept bare by endless icy gales . . . Store fronts no longer beckon with laughing eyes: they leer instead with gold-laid teeth filed sharp—stained with a marginal juice.

Affluent strangers passing are now become my betters. Bare-chested sailors, whores and retread vahines, drifters and drunks —these are my colleagues now; just as they were in that dread depression time of long ago, down on the docks and under the Els of many a seaport town.

A giant Matson cruise ship rides white and sterile above the customs shed. Liverish trippers in loud cruise wear pass by with stateside twangings. They sweat and peer through foggy glasses in search of the friendly cruise director. You would swear to God they were helpless. Not so! They carry their brains, their brawn, and their beauty all folded neatly away in padded billfolds. They are the ones who are strong. I am the one who is weak.

— TELEGRAMME —

RDI—RUDIN—GANGOT—HOLLYWOOD—CALIFORNIA—USA

PLEASE EXPLAIN YATES REPUBLIC AXIS I ADMIT AND REGRET INABILITY COMPLETE SIX TV FILMS PURSUANT TO CONTRACT BEST PROSPECT MUTUAL PROFIT LIES MY COMPLETION ONE FEATURE DOCUMENTARY FILM TO IMPLEMENT SAME MUST HAVE BALANCE DUE OTHERWISE WILL RETURN AND SELL OR ENCUMBER SHIP STOP FILM TO FEATURE HAYDEN PLUS SCHOONER MOVING THROUGH OCEANIA CONCEPT EMPHASIS ON ROMANCE BEAUTY IN ESCAPIST SENSE MAKING POINT LIFE MORE CIVILIZED HERE THAN HOMELAND A LA SWISS FAMILY ROBINSON ALSO LEGIT BURIED

TREASURE SEQUENCE IF SIX OR EIGHT THOUSAND NOT FORTH-
COMING SOLE ALTERNATIVE IS SELL OR HOCK LIGHTS GENERATOR
FILM URGENT REGARDS HAYDEN

— TELEGRAMME —

ERNEST K GANN—PEBBLE BEACH—CALIFORNIA—USA

REQUIRE TEN THOUSAND BANK OF INDOCHINA PAPEETE ENABLE
ME CLEAR DEBTS CLEAR PORT RETURN USA FINISH BOOK STOP
STUDIOS WITHHOLDING BALANCE DUE ME CHARGING BREACH CON-
TRACT WILL REPAY WHEN ABLE CONTINGENT SALE OF VESSEL
PLUS POSSIBLE ADVANCE ON BOOK REGARDS HAYDEN

— TELEGRAMME —

LOU FISHER—340 BROADWAY—NEW YORK—NEW YORK

THIS CABLE PREDICATED YOUR OFFER CASH AID THAT NIGHT
BEACH PARTY MATAVAI BAY REQUIRE TEN THOUSAND HOLD FORT
COMPLETE BOOK PLUS FILM REPAY WHEN ABLE MAY RETURN
NEW ENGLAND LATE 1960 BANK INDOCHINA PAPEETE REGARDS
HAYDEN

— TELEGRAMME —

GRANT COOPER—3910 OAKWOOD—LOS ANGELES—CALIF—USA

SERIOUS FINANCIAL BIND HERE NOW DUE CRISSCROSS BOOKKEEP-
ING CAN YOU ARRANGE MORTGAGE VESSEL IN ABSENTIA SHIP NOW
FREE AND CLEAR ALSO UNINSURED ALSO UNABLE HAUL DRYDOCK
FOR INSURANCE SURVEY DUE WAITING LIST STOP SOLE ALTERNA-
TIVE RELUCTANTLY REQUEST YOU ATTEMPT BORROW ONE THOU-
SAND EACH FROM EX FRIENDS JACK WEBB JOHN FRANKENHEIMER
FRANK LLOYD MARTIN MANULIS TEAM HARRIS KUBRICK ARCHI-
TECT PEREIRA COMPOSER DAVID ROSE ANDRE KOSTELANETZ
MAYBE HERB CAEN CHRONICLE BARNABY CONRAD MATADOR CON-
TRACTOR POMEROY FRISCO URGENT AM PREPARED PASS HAT
SAUSALITO URGENT HAYDEN

Life on the ship goes on, but at a faster tempo now. From
the cave of her lazarette comes a prepaid flow of cordage and
wire and chain as we work on the *Wanderer* to get her ready

for the long voyage home. But her tanks are almost empty; the shelves of her galley, the deep-set fo'c'sle bins, are mostly empty too. Plenty of beans remain, and hash, and powdered eggs and half-bad potatoes.

There's plenty of beef on the hoof in the brand-new crew. Not a college man in the lot. Call the roll: Mate, Peter Campbell, 25, from the North of Ireland. Licensed British shipmaster, the veteran of three years as mate of a steamship trading north from Melbourne to Shanghai. A quiet, friendly sort not given to small talk, and a consummate navigator. Stone broke.

Engineer: Alfonso Jaramillo, 27, from Valdivia, Chile. Trained as a naval architect, he built a 40-foot fishing smack, powered with a cast-off Chevrolet engine, slipped out of port one night, and sailed from Chile to Tahiti in 99 days, navigating with a schoolboy's atlas. Sober and kind to the children. Stone broke.

Seaman: Reinhold Posselt, 23, German. He worked his way from Hamburg to Papeete, by way of Australia and Singapore, as harvest hand, miner, longshoreman, busboy. By trade an electrician. Stone broke.

Seaman: Bert Gunzel, 22, German. A friend of Posselt's, he is a dogged worker—nothing is too dull or dirty for him to do it well.

Seaman: Grant Cooper, Jr., 17, fugitive from Los Angeles. Tall, strong, broad in the shoulders, and awkward sometimes. A fine worker and blessed with a sense of awe. Not really broke at all.

Cook: Viritua Poia, 26, Tahitian. Built like a welterweight, with tattooed chest and arms. He speaks no English, and smokes in his bunk. Good with the kids, having four of his own and a young wife. No Tahitian is ever broke where there are other islanders.

Six men on deck all told, a minimal crew considering the five-thousand-mile thrash to weather that faces them now in a 98-foot schooner without winches. Four kids, of course, with no woman or other child on board, no doctor or nurse or teacher. This is how it is, the old-time way of the windship—provided the bills are paid.

— TELEGRAMME —

HAYDEN—WANDERER—PAPEETE—TAHITI—SEPT 16, 1959

COOPER SAYS TELL YOU NO MORTGAGE POSSIBLE RUDIN SAYS
TELL YOU ABSOLUTELY NO FURTHER MONIES WILL BE ADVANCED
BY CFI CORPORATION DUE YOUR BREACH OF CONTRACT HOLD
STEADY ISHMAEL SIGNED WALKER

— TELEGRAMME —

REGRET NO SUCH FUNDS AVAILABLE AFTER BUILDING BOAT DEN-
MARK AM HIGHLY RECOMMENDING YOUR NEED TO PUBLISHERS
NEW YORK IN HOPES THEY WILL OBLIGE STOP COULD SEND FEW
HUNDRED IF URGENT FOR SURVIVAL REGARDS GANN

— TELEGRAMME —

REGARDING YOUR PROPOSED LIST CONTRACTS RE LOAN I STRONGLY
ADVISE AGAINST SUCH PROCEDURE THIS TIME AM MAILING PRI-
VATE PROPOSAL PERSONAL LOAN TIDE YOU OVER UPON ARRIVAL
FRISCO TELL SON HELLO REGARDS GRANT B COOPER

— TELEGRAMME —

URGENT STOP ALL ALIENS YOUR CREW MUST HAVE US PASSPORTS
OR PERMANENT VISAS LAW IMPELS ALIENS DEPARTURE WITHIN
29 DAYS ARRIVAL STOP FAILURE COMPLY SUBJECTS YOU SUB-
STANTIAL FINE STOP ARREST STOP DEPORTATION OF ALIENS PLUS
VESSEL SEIZED UNTIL FINE PAID SUGGEST YOU PROCEED NEAREST
US CONSUL FIJI OR PAGO PAGO STOP DISCUSSED THIS GREAT
LENGTH IMMIGRATION LOS ANGELES THEY COULD DO NOTHING
STOP INSIST FOREGOING ABSOLUTELY ESSENTIAL DUE YOUR
TICKLISH DILEMMA WITH LAW AS OF MOMENT STOP G B COOPER

— TELEGRAMME —

IN REPLY YOUR CABLE YES I WILL SEE YOU CALIFORNIA GLADLY
BUT BEYOND THAT CAN PROMISE NOTHING LOVE LORNA

🙚

CHAPTER 88

Like it or not, when they strike up the deficit waltz you get to
your feet and you dance and you dance till the music stops.
You dance and you sway and you stomp with your feet while
in a circle all around sit friends and foes and strangers, intent
on making a careful audit of you and your waltz technique. Not
for their children's lives would they be in your shoes this dance
nor step forth and be your partner.

So what do you do? You laugh as you sway and with watery
deficit eyes you go round and round, calling and bowing and
hoping that somewhere lost in the crowd is the person willing
to share this waltz with you.

Not everyone declines. Not a man you have known for years
who lives on a hill with a lovely wife and fine kids not far from
the bay where the *Bounty* once anchored.

"Nick"—spading the grass with a toe—"I hate like hell to
ask you, but as a matter of fact, due to a little miscalculation
on my part, it so happens I'm broke, and I was wondering, Nick,
if you could see your way to loaning me a thousand bucks—till
I get back to the States, that is, and get back in harness again?"
Now up with the eyes firmly and look square into his. Now he
looks down, but not for long, as he says: "Sure. I'll bring it
down to the ship this afternoon."

God bless you, boy, I think as I fire up the small French car
and roll back into Papeete, where I see the man named Mullins
walking down the street. He has been here less than a week,
in from Hawaii to see about building a new hotel near One
Tree Hill. There's a rumor that he's wealthy: ranches, cattle,
and cane. Even so, his is the face of a man who, if you ran
across him on a bridge back home, you would swear was about
to leap over the rail. "Hayden," he snaps, "I hear tell you're in
trouble these days."

"You hear what?"

"Come on, kid, you can level with Archie here. I've been broke
all over the world."

"Well, as a matter of fact, it's true. Screwed up my books."

"How much dough do you need?"

"To be perfectly frank, Archie, I need two thousand bucks."

"Sure that's enough?"

"Christ yes."

He takes out a gold-edged billfold, extracts a check, and makes it out for two thousand dollars, drawn on a New York bank.

"Archie, I don't know what to say—"

"Forget it, kid, pay me back when you can." His voice is gruff. We order drinks and up-end fast, for he is on his way to the airport. I drive him out and we have another drink at the bar. I buy him a lei—three leis, each one different, the best in the house.

I roar back into town and saunter into Donalds, Ltd., just before closing time. The half-caste cowboy is off on an errand somewhere. Three minutes later I exit, account squared and seven hundred bucks worth of credit.

But, with the dollar dance, you hate like hell to stop. Why not, while I'm at it, sell all my film, all my lighting equipment, along with the generator? The whole package cost me five thousand five hundred dollars. It has never been used, of course. A sharp dollar merchant now, I will let it go for eighteen hundred dollars, and the news is passed through town.

"But," says a fellow swindler, "it is not worth so much mo-nee, thze feelm she is old, thze lights have been in the air of the open sea, thzere is, how you call it—rust?—on thze generateur . . ."

We agree on his price. "Now, Capitaine, thzere is a matter of currency control, also of customs import duty—I must deduct thzis from the price, non?"

Non.

— TELEGRAMME —

HAYDEN—SCHOONER WANDERER—PAPEETE—FRENCH OCEANIA

ARRIVED HONOLULU TO FIND ALL BANK ACCOUNTS BLOCKED BY DIVORCE ACTION SORRY STOP LUCK ARCHIE MULLINS

Far out from Papeete, near the confluence of the districts of Punaauia and Paea, lived a jolly old exile worth several million dollars. We had only one thing in common, a violent dislike for Los Angeles. He had an unattractive house, several vahines, a Chrysler with fins, and two idle plantations. He was not popular; in fact, he was so unpopular that he kept a chief of the district on a retainer. The chief sat with him and talked and drank, and every morning got dressed up in a sweatsuit and jogged up and down the Broom Road, beyond the place Gauguin lived. We talked for five hours one morning and when it was over he loaned me one thousand dollars, at six per cent interest, payable before the end of the year.

Three days remain until Sunday, the fourth of October—my scheduled date of departure. Carlos Palacios drives up and we sit in his car and talk. "My friend," he is saying, "why this terrible rush? You need not leave, as you said. You must take your time. Always you are on edge; always you do things in haste. Why?"

"Carlos, I don't know. It's always been this way. It is the only way I can seem to get things done. You see, I've cabled that I'll be in San Francisco on the fifteenth of November, and I intend to be there then if I have to carry that damn schooner on my back."

A taxi pulls up, and three men in sweat-soaked linen suits scale the gangplank fast. We have no idea who they are. I roll up my sleeves and follow.

"Aha, Mr. Sterling Hayden." The one who speaks is tense. "I recognize your face, you are the very popular actor in my homeland, Italia. I am a producer of cinema from Rome. My name is Sergio Spina; these men are my director and cameraman. We are here to film a document picture of these islands, but we are troubled because our film and our lights are not yet arrived and we must begin work at once . . ."

Within the hour the deal is closed for two thousand dollars. They will pay the customs import duty, and to hell with the currency control. Only the sea remains to be outfought now.

If only the land were governed by a force as clean and as fair as that of the Law of Storms.

CHAPTER 89

With the sun still in the palm tree tops, the ship warps out into the stream. The pawls of her windlass clank as the links come inching in. Four men heave up and down, two to each crude iron bar, one in the bilge to stow the chain, and another over the side, treading water and scowling, wire brush in hand, scraping slime and muck from each link of the ninety fathoms coming up from the still lagoon.

The German boys work like demons, grunting and cursing, and the sweat has a whiskey smell this morning. When the anchor breaches the surface we clap tackles to it, sway it all the way aft, and lash it under the wheelbox. Eight hundred pounds it weighs—better this weight back aft than up in the bows, when you're bound on an uphill slog to windward for close to five thousand miles.

The diesel fires up and I swing the vessel in one big clockwise circle, then lay her into the dock. We top off the water tanks and the casks on deck are flushed and filled. Then the whaleboat is flooded and the kids have their final bath.

A crowd is beginning to gather, all dressed in their Sunday best, with great leathery brown toes peering through vented white Sunday sneakers. It will be high noon in less than an hour, this October 4, 1959, and Papeete sleeps in the sun. The barometer is steady enough and it is calm in the lee of the land, but the horizon offshore is jagged. I keep one eye on the crowd, alert for the telltale sign of some creditor overlooked. So far so good. (This is why I sail on Sundays.)

Suddenly I see a boy maybe ten years old who works as a runner for one of the Chinese markets. "*Garçon! Ici, s'il vous plaît.*" I reach in the plastic wallet and send him racing off with a slip of paper that says: "Ten cartons of cigarettes, if you please—any brand with a filter." Some day I shall write a story, the title is all picked out: *I Chose Cancer.* A further glance in the wallet reveals a cash balance this moment of just better than forty dollars.

I jump down on the quay and walk off far enough to gauge the trim of the ship. Church bells come and go. Now I squat down close to her bows where the concave waterline rides eight inches higher than it does in normal trim. I run a hand down the planks of the hull. If I knew myself as well as I know this vessel, I'd be of some use to the world. I search the crowd for Agnes and Carlos, then stroll toward the center of town.

Side by side they stand: brewery to starboard, cathedral to port; both happily busy this morning; not on speaking terms but both spawned by the need men have for escape, five francs

a hymn or thirty francs a bottle. Palms stand motionless with
clasped fronds bowed. The strains of a hymn float through open
windows. The brewery-bottling plant gives off a cheerful song
of its own. And down the street is a Chinese coffinmaker hard
at work in singlet and slippers, with his radio raging off in a
corner.

Agnes and Carlos park in the shade of a shed. She wears a
favorite *pareu,* and her eyes are lost in the shadow of a big
straw hat with red blossoms in the band.

I lean on the door. Agnes is slumped down low, one foot
braced high on the dash and her skirt caught up toward her
groin. She looks up slowly, her eyes dim, and she slips from
the car to walk by herself, hands clasped behind her back,
kicking at pebbles and dust.

"Here," he sighs, "I brought you something, not much, just a
little souvenir." He hands me a photograph: in it she stands
by his desk wearing a mischievous smile. The curve of one
breast brushes his cheek as he looks up from his typewriter.
Across the picture is written: "Many men come to Tahiti looking for something that does not exist. You came looking for life,
I think. Perhaps you did not find it but you found what must
come first—yourself. Affectionately."

I clasp his hand, force myself up from the car, and start off
toward Agnes, who leans on a bollard, chucking stones into the
harbor. She sees me coming, skips away, then comes running
back to dust my cheeks with her lips.

Poia stands with his kids in his arms and his wife hanging
onto his belt. They all cry unashamed while the rest of my crew
stand stolid and stiff nearby, each with his girl, not deigning
to show emotion. The kids are waving and laughing as I clear
the rail and head for my office aft.

I spring her free of the dock, open up till we're in mid-lagoon,
then one by one we give her the sails while Dana steers down
channel. I fling one arm in farewell. The horn erupts three times,
and the gang starts coiling down.

Beyond the pass she begins to feel the sea. A phalanx of
squalls marks time on the eastern horizon, waiting for night-
fall, like hoodlums, waiting to rough us up.

Off Venus Point the line of the wind comes down, dragging
the sea like a giant rustling harrow. A riffle at first runs past,
cooling the body and putting the canvas to sleep. Then it grows
till the cordage creaks, the masts cant well to the westward,

and the sea moan rises and erases the thunder of the surf. I start some sheet and the boys take up on the tackles. I work with the wheel till she steadies down with her eyes on the distant arch of a squall. A drift of spray envelops the whole maindeck, and when she feels in the groove I steal a look at the compass: north by east it is—and maybe a half to the east . . .

Tahiti seems swept to the southward. A lei is draped from a cleat. I run the petals under my nose, step to the leeward side of the wheel, and hurl the lei in the wake. Vale! Tahiti.

CHAPTER 90

Nine days of squalls and tedious uphill work carried the *Wanderer* to an equatorial realm where, in Longitude 140 West, she loafed along on the shining pewter dome of an all but windless world. The bare-chested helmsmen had little to do but hand her a spoke sometimes, cooling calloused feet in a nearby bucket of water.

It was late in the afternoon when I emerged from below and found myself transfixed by a scene of such quiet glory that it was all I could do to equate this isolate kingdom with the brawling lands beyond. The watch was at work patching the blownout jib. Bert looked up from his sewing. "If it was always like this," he sighed, "I even wouldn't mind the Cape Horn."

The southeast trade was mild, and a long low gentle ground swell hove in from across the Line, ten or twelve miles ahead. The spars of the ghosting vessel stood straight up and down as she ascended an oncoming swell, paused for a moment as though surveying her realm, then glided silently into a leaden valley surrounded by soft smooth hills that stole her horizon away. Here she rested on the floor of the valley, and then, inclining the plane of her keel, she slipped through the lowland pastures and lifted like a cloud to the crest of the next gray hill.

I made my way to the masthead with the sails asleep in the wind. The eastern horizon was barren of trade-wind cloud, but off to the west and beyond lay a twilight world of crimson and gold and green, with the swollen sun about to plunge into the sea. Night came fast, as it always does in the tropics. The moon came over the hill, bathing the sea and the ship as she slowly plowed northward.

With supper out of the way, I told the crew to turn in. I lashed the vessel's helm and let her take care of herself. We showed no lights, for this was the loneliest road in the world, now that the windships were gone. The cabins were dark as I paced by the hour, smoking, dreaming, and thinking. I tramped the deck with care, mindful of the kids who were sleeping just under my feet. I thought with remorse that throughout this voyage I hadn't given them much of my time.

But, then, perhaps it was all to the good. Maybe it counteracted my overprotectiveness since I'd had their custody. At least they had now seen their father at work—not the big daddy-bear who had dominated their lives back in Sherman Oaks. What a curious time that was. What a pathetic creature a man can be whose childhood needs were not met. If ever a man was obsessed with the challenge of fatherhood, I was that man.

I knew this man well . . . They were starting life anew, he and his four small children (somehow they never mentioned the mother who was absent). This was his chance and he knew it—his long-awaited chance to show what he could do as a parent. His opportunity to fashion with love and dollars an idyllic environment in which his kids could forget what had gone before; in which, furthermore, they could revel for the first time in the delights of the all-American way, family-style, of course.

First, they had had to have a house. Not any house would do; it had to be spacious and easy and yet part of a bustling suburb where mommies and daddies and kiddies all clung to the skirts of an active community life. So the house he leased was big and old and looked like New England. It had an acre of grass and plenty of trees and shrubs, and sat back from a quiet corner away from traffic. There was a porticoed patio with a red brick barbecue pit and a swimming pool in a big back yard. Next to this pool was a tidy little guest house where he installed a tottering proxy-mother whom he had just had flown out from New York.

Dollars were very important. Without dollars, it would seem, an all-American daddy would have a mighty rough time trying to bring up his kids. (But, then, without lots of dollars no man ever gets custody in the first place.) The rent was $500 a month, the gardener took $35 more, and the man who took care of the pool $50. The cook got $225 and the nurse the same. None of which fazed him at all. He had his kids, and nothing else mattered.

His bedroom was also his office (he had it in mind to write). It was situated across a hall from the room of his two youngest children. The older boys had an upstairs suite with ducks on the bathroom walls and banners over the beds. There was an intercom that was piped downstairs to his bedroom. He could hear them breathe or turn over during the night.

No sooner were they settled in than neighboring housewives came calling, early in the morning after their husbands had gone to work, offering their services and bits of advice. He enjoyed their visits and they lingered over coffee laid out in the big dining room. Some came almost daily, one in particular, a former actress who had long blond pigtails and a way of crossing her legs.

But coffeetime over, he invaded the community, warring for his children. He interviewed teachers, joined the PTA (and was promptly appointed to the Fathers' Committee), enrolled the boys in the Little League, put his daughter in ballet school and gave her piano lessons. He even joined the local Democratic Club.

He was a pillar of the town, and none of the neighbors suspected that a large share of his devotion stemmed from his need to "create a proper father image" (to use his lawyer's phrase) that could, should the need arise, be presented to the judge in the Domestic Relations Court. He even went so far as to log all his family's activities. Let them go to a birthday party down the block—and he entered this into his book. Let fifteen kids come over for an evening game of back-yard baseball— and not only did he record the fact but he photographed it as well.

Each time Christmas rolled around he really went into high gear. He festooned the house with endless strings of lights, with snow from cans, with sprigs of balsam and spruce bought from a local merchant (and squirted with fireproofing juice). The first winter they carved this idyll, he built a nine-foot snowman out of plaster and wire mesh, with a ten-gallon hat, a wicked grin, an incense-burning pipe, and a bottle of bourbon in the crook of his arm.

The second Christmas found a genuine gondola displayed in the front yard, filled with dummy toys and a Santa Claus gondolier. But the crowning display was one year's Grand Banks fishing dory hoisted atop the ridgepole of the house. In it were four little mannekins dressed up like the Hayden children. The one on the bow was Christian, a tall slim lad with his cap jammed over his eyes and holding a real harpoon that he aimed at the butt of Santa Claus perched on the nearby chimney. So many people came to look that a special cop had to come each night to keep the traffic moving. And when they gave him second prize in the neighborhood competition he knew that, whatever might lie ahead, his ex-wife didn't have a chance of regaining custody.

As time went by, some mommies came by for drinks, usually if they happened to be at loose ends, or their hubbies were out of town. They were full of admiration: "You know, Sterl'n, the thing that beats me is the wonderful way you care for these children of yours."

"Oh, it's nothing really!"—Daddy-bear leaning back, an appreciative eye on some cleavage—"You see, Ruthie, I came might damn close to losing these children—"

"I know—"

"And I'm a lucky bastard, too, because being in the picture business gives me plenty of time to devote to them. It isn't like the life most fathers lead. I can work for a month or so, then knock off for a few weeks and devote myself to the children . . . Most men can't do that."

"That's true, I guess. But I wish just once in a while Joe would come home and talk to our kids. All he does is take off his tie, roll up his sleeves, grab the paper and a highball, and sit there lost to the world. Maybe, Sterl'n, you'd talk to Joe sometime."

"Maybe." Daddy-bear gets to his feet and pours.

"Of course, we'd have to wait awhile"—Mommy slides low in her chair, crossing her legs as she goes—"You see, Joe's in Suez now, bidding on a contract to build a harbor or something. Won't be back for a month." (A long sigh) "Gad, but it's peaceful here."

What enabled him more than anything else to keep up his massive pretense was his closeness with a remarkable family who lived on the hill nearby, the Turnley Walkers. When he had been casting about for a neighborhood in which to display his parenthood, he quickly realized that he needed them nearby to help with his children. Flora Walker was a fiery ex-chorus girl turned dedicated homemaker and militant community spirit. In addition to caring for a polio-ridden husband and two children, she was on half a dozen committees and ran a sort of out-patient psychiatric clinic for their friends. It was her sponsorship more than anything else that made him acceptable to the community from the outset. And if he had to leave town for a month to work on a film, the Walkers moved into his model home at the foot of the hill, to spare his own children any further dislocation.

The two families grew even closer, and celebrated holidays, birthday parties, and assorted functions jointly.

And that was their life, pretty much. His children all did well in school. Gretchen's nightmares vanished in the course of the second year. His income climbed steadily until, toward the end of this homesteading venture, he was earning around $160,000 a year.

But then at night, when the dishes were washed and the children tucked into bed and the domesticity was cleared away, he often took a drink or two, climbed into the station wagon, and drove through the night to another part of town. There he parked, crept through a certain breezeway, threaded an outpost of garbage cans, rapped a signal on the patio door, and was soon bedded down away from the hostile world, in the arms of a pigtailed mommy.

Then, toward morning, he retraced his steps, re-entered his own wickiup, and after a blast from the shower, slipped into bed . . . barely in time to rumple his pillows before the squawk-box by his side erupted with "Daddy?"—whoosh whoosh breath on the intercom microphone—"Daddy? Good morning, Daddy. Are you awake yet?"

"And good morning to you, War Eagle."

"Daddy, do we get to see mommy this weekend?"

"Yes, boy, this is your weekend with mommy."

"Daddy, can we come downstairs and get into bed with you?"

"Hell yes, son, come ahead."

And so the day began. Tough, but then he always was an early riser.

The night was quickly passed. The sun came over the hill. I slipped the beckets from the wheel, doused the binnacle light, and steered by the feel of my realm. North by east she went. Some faces appeared in the frame of the nearby hatch, warm soft sleepy faces, small brown hands clutching towels and tooth-brushes. "Good morning, Daddy—you been there all night?"

"No—not really." I had to laugh—thinking.

CHAPTER 91

No artist will paint this scene . . . A windless night and soft, with a lightship chained to a leaden sea 'neath a mass of lumi-nous cloud . . . The sea that never sleeps all but sleeping now where it heaves in from around the world, a dark and desolate prairie, nothing abroad on its surface save three ships con-verged, and, at the edge of its plunging slope, the far-flung blink of the light on the Southeast Farallone.

The schooner ghosts in from the west, and all unchallenged passes the anchored lightship, and, hauling her wind, rounds to not far from the pilot boat *California*. The eastern sky glows with the lights of San Francisco. The lightship's welcoming beacon stabs the night at fifteen-second intervals, and from the main ship channel nearby comes the clang of a gong and the groan of a whistle buoy.

Pilot boats never sleep, and from the *California* comes a hail of recognition. It sends over a small boat, and over the rail climbs the burly form of a pilot wearing a soft felt hat. "Koshkin," he says. "Hayden," I say, and we shake hands. He gives my shoulder a rap. "Well, Hayden, you made it right on the nose. Here, I brought you the morning *Chronicle*. Herb Caen says in his column you'd be home on the fifteenth—damned if you didn't make it with two hours to spare. Good passage?"

"Best passage I ever had. We pushed her a bit now and then, blew out both jibs half a dozen times, used up all our oil. Out-side of that, nothing." I slam my hands together.

He paces the deck for a bit, scouring the ship and her gear, then he claps one hand on a shroud. "This is a great old vessel. Wish I'd been with you."

We drop below, and Poia comes aft with coffee. The pilot

hands me a packet of letters. "Good news. Talked with your lawyer this week. He's lending you fifteen thousand dollars for a mortgage on the ship."

"My God." I open a letter and find a check signed Grant B. Cooper. Some capitalists aren't so bad.

Koshkin stands and peers at the kids. "How did they take the trip?"

"Took it just fine. Never used so much as an aspirin or a Band Aid—all forty-one days up from Papeete."

He drains his coffee and starts toward the hatch. "Oh, your lawyer said something else. Whatever you do, don't go to your berth in Sausalito yet. You've got some immigration problems, I gather, so you'll have to anchor in quarantine and wait for clearance."

I expected as much, but it always seems the same, the contrast between the scene envisioned and the event. "There's one little problem: like I said, we're out of fuel. Don't have enough to steam more than four or five miles."

"No problem. I'll send you as much as you want."

"Oh, thirty gallons?"

"I'll send fifty."

He drops into his boat and waves as she dances off: "If that judge gives you a bad time, give the Pilots a ring. We'll send down a delegation."

The boat comes back with the fuel and I'm handed a cardboard box. A note is stuck in the top: "This is for those kids." Fresh bread, fresh milk and butter, two cartons of ice cream, and a small well-frosted cake.

I waken the kids with a shout: "Roust! We're having a celebration; ice cream, cake, the works."

Sleepy faces rise, hands rubbing eyes. "Aw, Daddy, you and your silly jokes—" Then they see the cabin table, and a shout goes up. "Yipes!" All come tumbling out.

Then the exhaust begins to bark, and we swing past the *California* with our horns splitting the night. I settle her down with her bows on the Golden Gate. The loom of the city grows and the lights on the land come clear: Point Bonito, Mile Rock, Point Diablo, one by one. Then all at once the city itself bursts free with dazzling hillside lights and the amber span of the massive bridge marks the end of the long sea road.

Cooper steers and the crew and kids stand hushed by the fo'c'sle hatch, awed by the sudden burst of life. The ebb flows hard as we steer toward Alcatraz, its high walls bright with light.

We veer toward the city now, to skirt long fingered piers. Gunzel and Posselt gaze at the city. "Look, Reinhold," Bert's voice is hoarse. "The Bank of *America!*"

We come to the quarantine anchorage. "Let go," I say, and the kedge slips over the rail. "Give her forty fathom to the water's edge." My voice is drowned in the rumble of trucks from the truss of the Oakland Bridge.

Six bells chime out. Six bells of a Graveyard Watch, November 15, 1959. Four thousand four hundred and fifty miles she has put under her keel since she breasted the pass at Papeete . . . Average speed, 4.47 knots.

Not later than six that morning a fine new Coast Guard craft comes smartly alongside with the official boarding party. Meticulous men, immaculate in blues and whites and browns, full of easy banter, ready to josh with the kids and do what they could to modify certain regulations. But the aliens are confined to the ship, pending my efforts to clear them. We haul down the yellow flag.

Now a glossy cruiser comes strutting across the bay with Spike and Russ Nyborg shouting and waving, along with Al Cristofani and Walter Anderson, the shipyard men who had done so much for the ship. They are followed almost at once by two boatloads of reporters and newsreel men. Again the old routine: question and answer time, the crew ignored, and the kids backed up to the rails with the flashbulbs making them blink. At last they leave. We tidy up below, scrub down on deck, and the lines are coiled with care. We pick up the kedge and rumble across toward the berth in Sausalito.

Welcoming craft appear to run like a pack of sleek white hounds nipping the flanks of the vessel. There is no wind at all this morning, in sharp contrast to the dream I had by a driftwood fire beneath an upturned whaleboat. Everything feels diminished, particularly since Spike's words: "The Walkers couldn't make it. They want you to leave the kids with them while you get things squared away."

I throttle down and we glide past the smiling water front. The sun pours down and the cars on the causeway dart toward parking places. People leap out to wave and fumble with cameras. Up in the warm green hills the people stand on porches peering through telescopes instead of at Sunday papers.

Our old mooring basin lies half in the clutch of a new marina. No swinging room remains and its entrance is only a slot. A self-styled wharfinger shouts: "You'll have to anchor, Hayden, and wait for slack water. Too much current now, see?" He dumps a crate in the water.

Spike leans on the rail, eyes on me. "Spike, we'll back the bastard in."

"What else?" He hocks and spits toward an outboard shaped like a hot rod.

This is the last go-round, one final show-off. I bend to a match, roll up my sleeves, open the throttle, and ram the wheel hard over. Now idle down, reverse and rev up, idle and jam her ahead—three times in fast succession. She carves a ponderous arc. When the time is right, I back down hard, and she pounds in now, full in the face of some pilings. The ebb sets her sideways swiftly.

A clown near the end of the bulkhead, dressed in a yachtsman's suit, starts jumping up and down: "Go ahead!" he screams. "Go ahead, you're going to smash the dock!"

I cup my hands and answer, no louder than necessary: "For Christ's sake, why don't you shut up." He subsides, clutching his skipper's hat.

She pounds in, stern first, threading the eye of the slot. In an offhand manner Spike slips a line down onto the neck of a passing piling. "Fourteen inches," he says, "fourteen inches to spare." Posselt whips some turns on the capstan.

"Check her," I say.

"Check her," he grunts, corded shoulders rippling. Two bowlines snake ashore. The ebbing current seems bent on fouling things up. "Surge," I say, "surge just a touch as she goes."

The wet line stiffens and stretches with water wrung from its strands. She hangs fire now, and notch by notch I haul the throttle back. Reverse gear growls and the diesel whines and the whole ship trembles as she springs herself, inch by inch, across the grain of the current.

Spike chews fast, his arms akimbo. I open her up some more. He boots the line. It rings like steel. "Ishmael," he says, "if that bastard parts, you're going to back straight through the post office clean up to the cell block and knock Red out of bed."

Luck and the springline hold. With mud from the bottom churning, she claws her way into the berth just one ship-length ahead of the place where the voyage began. I ring down with a

vengeance: "Finished with engines!" The long haul home is
done. The coffinmaker rests—this final nail driven into the
casket containing his past.

𝔐

CHAPTER 92

You feel like a man, strong as a gale fresh from the sea, tearing
through the countryside, kicking up dust in your wake. You race
through city streets, rattling the window panes, slamming doors,
charging through traffic. Everywhere, day and night, the sun
shines and people turn around as you go breezing through. You
look in their faces and the swing-hipped girls smile back and
the cabbies laugh when they speak of the voyage.

There are always the exceptions, of course, and the lawyers
downstate set up the tune and cry, so you pack up papers and
children and gear and dump the lot in a top-down Volkswagen
bought with mortgage money. It's held in your lawyer's name
because the bill collectors are hot on your trail. But they'll have
to stand in line. You'll pay when you can and the ones who
needle you most are the ones you'll pay off last. You drive till
you almost doze, then pull off the road and stretch out in a
field. The kids throw schooner sticks in an irrigation ditch which
plods along while you sleep like a log in the clover. A trooper
pulls up to give you a ticket because it's dangerous for kids to
be playing by the sluggish ditch—and only last week some poor
kid drowned not a mile away. You get to your feet and the
trooper looks up from his knee and a smile replaces a frown as
he speaks of his dream to go to Tahiti, and the kids all grieve
as he tears up the ticket.

You know you are nearing Los Angeles when a sign pro-
claims GENE AUTRY'S MOTION PICTURE RANCH, and
memories rise of ersatz cowboys, phony sheriffs, and bewildered
girls milling about on mock wooden sidewalks that run past
mock stores while ulcered producers crack the whip on caged
directors in chukker boots and baseball caps who are trying to
breathe some life into barren scripts. Then the winding descent
into the San Fernando Valley swarming with housing tracts,
supermarkets, bowling alleys, and used-car lots—swarming and

all but awash in a welter of neon and chrome and concrete pierced with glass. The smog burns and the cars go belching past and I slow down so the kids can look at the old house, and I shake my head in silence, wondering how I managed to live here as long as I did.

The Walkers' house stands on a hillside facing north, detached from the battle of progress. Some gifts are exchanged and the tired kids are soon lost deep in the folds of sleeping bags that bring to these suburban rooms the far-off scent of timber and oil and tar.

Turnley comes to the point: "Let me tell you about Lorna. She is going to be married early in December in Europe. He's a hell of a fine guy, looks something like you."

The sound of his voice rolls in my mind like distant summer thunder ("Run, Buzzy, run like a good boy quickly and close the windows"). My voice comes evenly out: "I was afraid of something like that."

He clears his throat and his eyes are averted now as he sloshes his drink around: "The strangest part of it is that she met him through me—five or six months ago—right here in this room, as a matter of fact."

I get to my feet, feeling suddenly tired and old, freshen my drink and kill it, say good night and head for the door. He calls me back and says: "She asked me to tell you that she'd like very much to see you here some evening and talk for a time."

I nod my head and leave.

One night later that week, I drive up to the Walkers' for dinner, and I sit toying with my food for the better part of an hour. Then a car door slams outside, and I can hear her voice in the kitchen. Turnley and I move to the living room, where we make conversation until the kitchen door opens and she comes in, followed by Flora with after-dinner coffee.

She looks like I knew she would, like the girl by my side each night in the long watches all up and down the sea road we never knew together. Her coffee cup is trembling.

The Walkers leave together. I put a log on the fire and turn off a light or two.

We talk for more than an hour, drinking Drambuie and Scotch half and half, just as we once had on special occasions. Whenever I look toward her eyes I feel her slipping from me. She explains the cablegram, saying she wanted to see me one last time to be certain that the move she was making was right.

The flame dies and when it is gone the words that follow seem burned out too. She smiles through tears, and I bank the fire, turn off the lights, and follow her through the door.

In the low fog that now clings to the hillside, we part without a word. She gets in her car, and I climb in mine, and we ghost down the winding road. At the foot of the hill she turns to the left and I wait till her lights are swallowed in the fog, not fifty feet from the house where we met. I cross the intersection and blindly drive toward nowhere.

The rest of the year is spent in a welter of legal gymnastics. You go into court and you sit in impotence through hours of wrangling and clinching and dodging. During a recess you fly up north to search for a house you can lease. Please be patient. You see, I can't sign anything because I've got to get the court's okay to move my kids from Los Angeles. Yes, I know it sounds preposterous, but that's how it is. And I tell you if they keep me there, you're going to see the damnedest display of footwork. There isn't a man alive could force me to stay in that place.

You went back to court eight days before Christmas to decide who should have the kids over the holidays. After the first of the year, another court and another judge will settle the question of whether the voyage was in contempt of court. You're one of a bitter pair seated at opposite ends of an arc, four lawyers ranged between you. Never before have you felt such blinding hatred.

All rise, please now, till the Honorable Judge is seated. This court is now in session. You look in the face of the man empowered to tweak your tail or pat your back or slug you. The legal minds now tangle, men best trained to settle disputes such as one next door, Bandini Fertilizer *vs.* the City of Los Angeles. The gag is removed at last, and you try to explain to the judge your conviction that an unfit parent does not become fit simply because it is Christmas time. The judge breaks in with a warning about your speech, and makes it plain he has the right to rule that neither parent shall have the children over the holidays. Yes, your honor, I'm very sorry, I didn't mean to get carried away.

Now the plaintiff speaks and the tears begin, and now you

feel nothing so much as sadness and a puzzled admiration that she has survived in spite of herself. A ten-minute recess is spent outside in hushed consultations while the reporters try to find out what is happening. Back in the courtroom you are told that after the first of the year you may move to San Francisco and try to write your book or whatever it is. Thank you, sir. You may also pack up your children's things quick because they aren't going to spend the holidays with you in the neighborhood where they've lived for five years. They're going to be with their mother for twelve days, not in her house, because she doesn't have a house, but in the home of her sister, who is a stable member of a stable community. She will pick them up two hours from now at five sharp and return them at five on New Year's Day and—Goddamnit, sir, excuse me, I've got to see my children Christmas Day. He hadn't thought of this. Yes, father, you may see your children for five or six hours Christmas Day. This court is now adjourned.

Then on the seventh day of January 1960, at ten o'clock in the morning, in Department 34 of the Superior Court of the County of Los Angeles, Judge Emil F. Gumpert presiding, you wait to hear another verdict. You feel good about this one— things are going well—you're all set up in a home just across from Sausalito, overlooking the bay, and the kids are beginning to settle down in their new school. Maybe the judge will even give you five days in jail and one hell of an ending for the book. After all, what you did was right for yourself—and whatever that is has to be right for the children too.

You look at the witness box where yesterday, sworn to tell the truth, you hitched up your sleeves, shoved the microphone out of your way, and said that, given the choice between throwing yourself into contempt of court or contempt of life, you did what you had to do. You had meant no disrespect to the court but the truth of the matter is that you'd do it again if you had to.

Judge Gumpert enters the room. The one regret I had through-out the voyage is that some of its repercussions would have to fall on this particular man. One day I'll tell him so to his face, though maybe he knows it already.

The judge is about to rule when counsel for the defense rises once more with some wretched motion to disqualify this court. The judge's face and temper are sharply drawn this morning. His patience is almost gone as he turns to one side, wiping his glasses, then looks to the ceiling and swings back, saying: "The objection is overruled." He takes up a piece of paper, adjusts his glasses and reads: ". . . Since the time of his divorce some five years ago . . . this man has been almost continually harassed by a mass of repetitious and unsuccessful court proceedings which have drawn heavily on his time, his finances, and— where his children were involved—upon his emotional resources . . . Custody was awarded to the father after nineteen days of testimony behind closed doors, during which forty-three persons testified and more than a hundred exhibits were received in evidence . . . the voyage, Hayden has admitted, was a willful defiance of the law that tends to impede the administration of justice . . . Despite this, in a true effort to do justice, every situation must be considered on its merits . . . For years he has labored to shield the children and give them a normal childhood . . . His act was regrettable and foolish, but this court accepts his sworn statement that he meant no disrespect to the court . . . It is the ruling of this court that Hayden be sentenced to a fine of five hundred dollars and serve five days in jail . . . The sentence is suspended."

With as piercing a look as you've ever known, his eyes leave yours and he steps down from the bench.

My small gray car rides like a chip in the wake of a rouge-red Jaguar roadster piloted by one of the most prominent actors of the studio. The guard on the gate waves him through, smiling and touching his visor. The top of my car is up and the guard doesn't know me until he looks at my pass. Then his face opens up like a tulip: "Well well well. Welcome home, Sterl'n. How was the trip on the yacht?" Welcome home, my ass. I drive on in, park, and sit for a while.

Along comes a man of the West, tall in his gorgeous cowboy boots. His eyes have a steely glint as he saunters along, playing quick-draw with himself and lapping an ice-cream cone. I think of the guards on the gate, frozen not far from a time clock, positioned precisely as when I saw them a year ago. I glance at my watch, and leave the car for the studio office building.

The big shots give me the big hello. They're all lined up in a row, not one not two but five of them, just aching to hear exactly how I intend to repay them forty-nine thousand five-hundred and eighteen dollars and thirty-six cents (plus interest).

For more than an hour we talk. It ends as I knew it would: they are not in the least impressed by my decision to leave

Hollywood, by the book I have outlined in some detail, nor by my request that they simply relax for Christ's sake and not belabor me with lawsuits to recover money that doesn't exist and bloody well won't exist until I dredge up a book, nor even when I say with a smile that there might be a law to force me to report for work but there's no law that can make a man act.

They give me the small goodbye. I tell them I'll see them in court. I turn in my pass at the gate, and a block from the work-house I pull to the side of the road, throw back the top, fire my coat in a heap, roll up my sleeves, and head for the Golden Gate.

CHAPTER 93

The bridge that night lay lost overhead in the grip of a southerly gale, and the rain came slashways down, with the man at the wheel of the car straining his eyes at times to pierce the sea-ward abyss. No wilder the night than the thoughts that slashed through a mind made up to sever the cord that bound him still to his ship—a ship that had been his friend.

He drove very slowly down the winding hillside road where it led to the lights of a water-front village charged with warmth for a man by himself alone. He drove through drenched deserted streets, and the smell of the land was strong, and across from the No Name Bar he turned from the street and parked.

Out a long wet dock he went, where yawls and ketches rode with the wind in their toothpick rigs whistling a landlocked tune. Under a naked lamp he paused by the *Wander Bird,* and looking down at her jut-jawed derelict hull he caught, through the veil of rain and time, some shadows thrown by his youth. He shifted his canvas bag and kept on walking to where the dock gave way to a tier of chained logs awash in the slop of the storm, and his city shoes were soaked by the time he came in the lee of the big old pilot schooner.

It was half past nine by the galley clock when he said to the engineer: "Alfonso, I'm about to sell this vessel to a wealthy sport from Texas. I'd like a little time alone. Come back around midnight."

He brewed some tea and threw his remaining possessions into

the white seabag. Then, slitting the cap on a bottle of aquavit, he poured a proper blend and sat on a fo'c'sle bench. He heard the moan in the rigging as he looked at the beams and the kness and the massive bole of the foremast. He drained his mug and poured. His narrowed eyes now filled with a pageant of fo'c'sle faces, faces of sailormen swept from the seas by Time. He looked in the coffin-sized bunks quarried deep in the hull and heard the laughter of children.

He drained his mug and he poured. Then he moved slowly aft and ducking the breaktimber came to a cabin that once contained five hundred cherished volumes: All gone now. Gone with the bulkhead clock. Gone with paired bronze bells stripped from the deck. Gone with a lot of things.

He lay for a time in his bunk with the lamp turned low while one hand caressed a hackmatack knee studded with tree-nails and driftbolts made of bronze. He lay looking up at the conical eye of a prism and it seemed that he heard again the wild old offshore song with the water racing aft just beyond his reach, while the ship went thundering downwind, lee rail buried.

He wakes when the watchman returns. And rolls out. And, cradling the aquavit, goes on deck to stand for a time by the helm. Across the bay, through the wrack of the storm, the city lies hunched with her back to the alien sea. A slug from the bottle now as he stands to the wheel of a ship gone out of his life. The wind roars down, raking the spars, lashing the sea-worn hull. The rain tastes cold like snow not mixed with salt.

He stands by the wheel for most of a helmsman's hour, entranced at times by the dim-lit compass rose. Then he palms the emptied bottle and hurls it into the bay. Grabbing his bag, he slips over the bulwarks and down to the heaving logs where, under the tall ship's lee, he turns and stares at the legend:

WANDERER   SAN FRANCISCO

With his back to the wind he plows up the dock and reaching the land turns left. He corners the squat brown bank, crosses the Bridgeway Road, turns right past The Tides bookstore, and steps from the storm to the warmth of the No Name Bar.

He buys a drink and turns to a ship lost in the night and drinks to a life that was.

He turns to stare at a face in the back-bar mirror: a vague face with bleak and querulous eyes. The eyes lock and he drinks to himself alone. Vale! Wanderer.

A NOTE ON THE TYPE

THE TEXT of this book was set on the Linotype in a new face called PRIMER, designed by *Rudolph Ruzicka,* earlier responsible for the design of Fairfield and Fairfield Medium, Linotype faces whose virtues have for some time now been accorded wide recognition. The complete range of sizes of Primer was first made available in 1954, although the pilot size of 12 point was ready as early as 1951. The design of the face makes general reference to Linotype Century (long a serviceable type, totally lacking in manner or frills of any kind) but brilliantly corrects the characterless quality of that face.

Composed, printed, and bound by
The Haddon Craftsmen, Inc., Scranton, Pa.
Typography and binding design by
VINCENT TORRE

A NOTE ABOUT THE AUTHOR

STERLING HAYDEN was born in Montclair, New Jersey, and received his elementary education in the public schools there. After residence in a number of towns up and down the Atlantic seaboard, and after a short term in a tutoring school in Maine, he ran away to sea (1933)—and to a life of self-education. For seven years he followed the sea, eventually receiving master's papers in sail. In 1940 he gave up the sea for motion pictures, but left film work a year later to serve in World War II. Until he left the United States in 1959 on the voyage described in this book, he was active in films and television. Mr. Hayden lives in the San Francisco Bay area with his wife and seven children.

August 1963